Politics and People

The Ordeal of Self-Government in America

POLITICS AND PEOPLE

The Ordeal of Self-Government in America

ADVISORY EDITOR
Leon Stein

EDITORIAL BOARD
James MacGregor Burns
William E. Leuchtenburg

BEHIND THE SCENES
IN
WASHINGTON

James D. McCabe

(Edward Winslow Martin, pseud.)

ARNO PRESS

A New York Times Company

New York — 1974

Reprint Edition 1974 by Arno Press Inc.

Reprinted from a copy in The University
of Illinois Library

POLITICS AND PEOPLE: The Ordeal
of Self-Government in America
ISBN for complete set: 0-405-05850-0
See last pages of this volume for titles.

Manufactured in the United States of America

Library of Congress Cataloging in Publication Data

McCabe, James Dabney, 1842-1883.
  Behind the scenes in Washington.

  (Politics and people: the ordeal of self-government
in America)
  Reprint of the 1873 ed. published by Continental Pub.
Co., New York.
  1. Washington, D. C.--Public life. 2. United States
--Politics and government--1865-1883. 3. Washington,
D. C.--Description. 4. Credit Mobilier of America.
I. Title. II. Series.
F198.M12 1974   320.9'73'082   73-19158
ISBN 0-405-05880-2

BEHIND THE SCENES
IN
WASHINGTON

P. Dep.t.   Capitol.   Market.   Long Bridge.
   Patentoffice.   Washington Monument.
Postoffice.   Navy Yard.   Arsenal.   Engraved by Rommel & Foster.
   City Hall.   Smithsonean.   Treasury Dep.t
         Willard's Hotel.   White House

BIRDS EYE VIEW OF WASHINGTON, D.C.

BEHIND THE SCENES

IN

WASHINGTON.

BEING

A COMPLETE AND GRAPHIC ACCOUNT OF THE

CREDIT MOBILIER INVESTIGATION,

THE CONGRESSIONAL RINGS, POLITICAL INTRIGUES, WORKINGS OF THE LOBBIES, ETC. GIVING THE SECRET HISTORY OF OUR NATIONAL GOVERNMENT, IN ALL ITS VARIOUS BRANCHES, AND SHOWING HOW THE PUBLIC MONEY IS SQUANDERED, HOW VOTES ARE OBTAINED, ETC.,

WITH SKETCHES OF THE LEADING

SENATORS, CONGRESSMEN, GOVERNMENT OFFICIALS, ETC.,

AND AN ACCURATE DESCRIPTION OF THE

SPLENDID PUBLIC BUILDINGS

OF THE

FEDERAL CAPITAL.

BY

EDWARD WINSLOW MARTIN,
AUTHOR OF "SECRETS OF THE GREAT CITY," ETC., ETC.

Issued by subscription only, and not for sale in the book stores. Residents of any State desiring a copy should address the Publishers, and an Agent will call upon them. See page 519.

PUBLISHED BY
THE CONTINENTAL PUBLISHING COMPANY,
AND
NATIONAL PUBLISHING CO.

Entered according to Act of Congress, in the year 1873, by

J. D. McCABE, Jr.,

In the Office of the Librarian of Congress, at Washington, D. C

PREFACE.

THE City of Washington, the Capital of the Republic, is the most interesting place in the Union to the American people. It is not only the seat of Government, but it is the centre from which radiate the varied influences which affect every citizen of the Republic, from the millionaire to the man dependent on his daily earnings. The vast interests of the country, as represented by the various branches of the National Government, all centre here, and must prosper or suffer according to the fidelity and ability with which those who are placed here by the people to watch over and direct them, execute their trust.

The capitalist, whose funds are invested in the bonds and securities of the United States, keeps an anxious eye upon Washington, and scrutinizes the conduct and utterances of the officials in charge of the Treasury with a vigilance hard to describe in words. The very mention of the name of the

National Capital brings up to his mind a vision of the grand edifice in which lie treasured up the resources in which he has so deep an interest. The working classes of the country, business men, and all who are dependent upon their earnings, watch with anxious eagerness the acts of those who are charged with the control of the currency in which those earnings are received, and of which the appreciation or depreciation must affect them powerfully for weal or woe. The finances of a nation being its life blood, the National Treasury has, not inaptly, been styled the "Heart of the Nation," since from it ebbs and flows the monetary stream which keeps the body politic in health. For this reason, if no other, Washington would be the point of supreme interest to the Nation.

But the Capital has other claims upon the interest of the country. It is the seat of the Law-making Power, the point at which the will of the people has its highest and final expression. Here are made the laws which promote or mar the country's prosperity; here are gathered the men in whose hands the people have placed the execution of their will as expressed at the polls, and it is the habit of the Nation to watch with the deepest concern the action of its Legislators, to mark how far this expression of its wishes is complied with or evaded. Too often the "Senators and Representatives in Congress assembled" forget that they are the servants of the People, and assume to be their masters; but the People are not so forgetful, and watch their course with a jealous eye.

PREFACE. 7

Washington is also the centre of the vast Civil Service of the Republic, the headquarters of the army of the sixty-thousand office-holders who conduct the public business in the various portions of the Union, the point to which are directed in their final results all the operations of this complicated and important system. If the workings of the great "Governmental Machine" at the Capital are wrong, every minor portion, in the remotest part of the country, must suffer. If impure men control affairs at this point, no part of the civil service can escape the effect of their crimes.

Of late the whole land has been ringing with the most startling and appalling reports of corruption at Washington, and these reports have involved the reputations of the most prominent public men in the land, men whose names have hitherto been without the shadow of a stain. The press of the country has rung with accusations and denunciations, which have been repeated so persistently, and enlarged upon so constantly, that the people have commenced to wonder if there is anything like legislative or executive honesty left in the Government. On all sides there is a very earnest desire to get at the truth of these things, to obtain an insight into the facts, so that men may judge for themselves whether they are falsehoods or melancholy realities. All have an interest in these questions, and all have an earnest desire to know more of the practical workings of affairs at Washington than can be obtained from the crowded columns of a newspaper.

The present volume is offered to the public with the hope of supplying this want. It is the aim of the Author to make it a faithful picture of life at the Capital; to show the workings of the General Government as they go on from day to day; and, by presenting a plain and unvarnished statement of facts, to enable the reader to understand for himself how much truth and how much falsehood there is in the reports with which the land has been rife for so long a time past.

The accounts of the *Crédit Mobilier* Scandal, the Lobby, and other peculiar features of the Capital, are given without bias. A simple statement of facts is made, and the intelligent reader will judge of them for himself. It is believed that the legitimate curiosity of the people concerning these things will find ample means of satisfaction in these portions of the work.

Washington is a point of great interest and attraction to the American people, for still another reason. It contains a number of the finest "sights" to be witnessed in the New World. Whatever we may accomplish in the future in architecture and the arts, there can be no doubt that Washington now possesses attractions superior to those of any other American City. Here is the great Capitol, the most majestic and beautiful edifice on the Continent, which affords so much pleasure to the lover of the beautiful, and which, in itself, requires days for the proper examination of its attractions; its beautiful halls, its marble corridors, its galleries of statuary and paintings, its magnificent frescoes and art treasures in bronze and marble. Here are gathered the stately and imposing edifices of the Patent-Office, and the Departments of State, the Treasury, and the Post-Office, each in itself a worthy object of pride to the whole country.

It is the wish of every citizen of the Republic to visit Washington, and to enjoy the pleasure which a personal examination of the "treasures of the Nation" affords. Thousands every year avail themselves of the opportunity of doing so. During the session of Congress the city is full of sight-seers, who come from all parts of the country, and during the long recess, even in the hottest and most uncomfortable months of the year, they come thronging into the city to see the glories of which they have heard so much. Thousands have never enjoyed this pleasure, and must defer it to a still distant day; but there is no American who does not cherish the hope of seeing Washington before he dies. To all such—those who have seen the city, and those who have not—this work is offered as a means of pleasure and instruction.

The former can enjoy once more the delights of a visit to the "Seat of Government," and live over again in memory the pleasures they once experienced; and the latter, by the comforts of their own firesides, can, it is hoped and believed, obtain a more intimate knowledge of the Federal

City from the pages of this work, than they could by a mere visit to Washington during the session of Congress, or for some such limited period. It is hoped that those who contemplate visiting Washington will find this work useful, by enabling them to know how to economize their time, and by pointing out to them those things most worth seeing, and those which had better be avoided.

E. W. M.

March 1st, 1873.

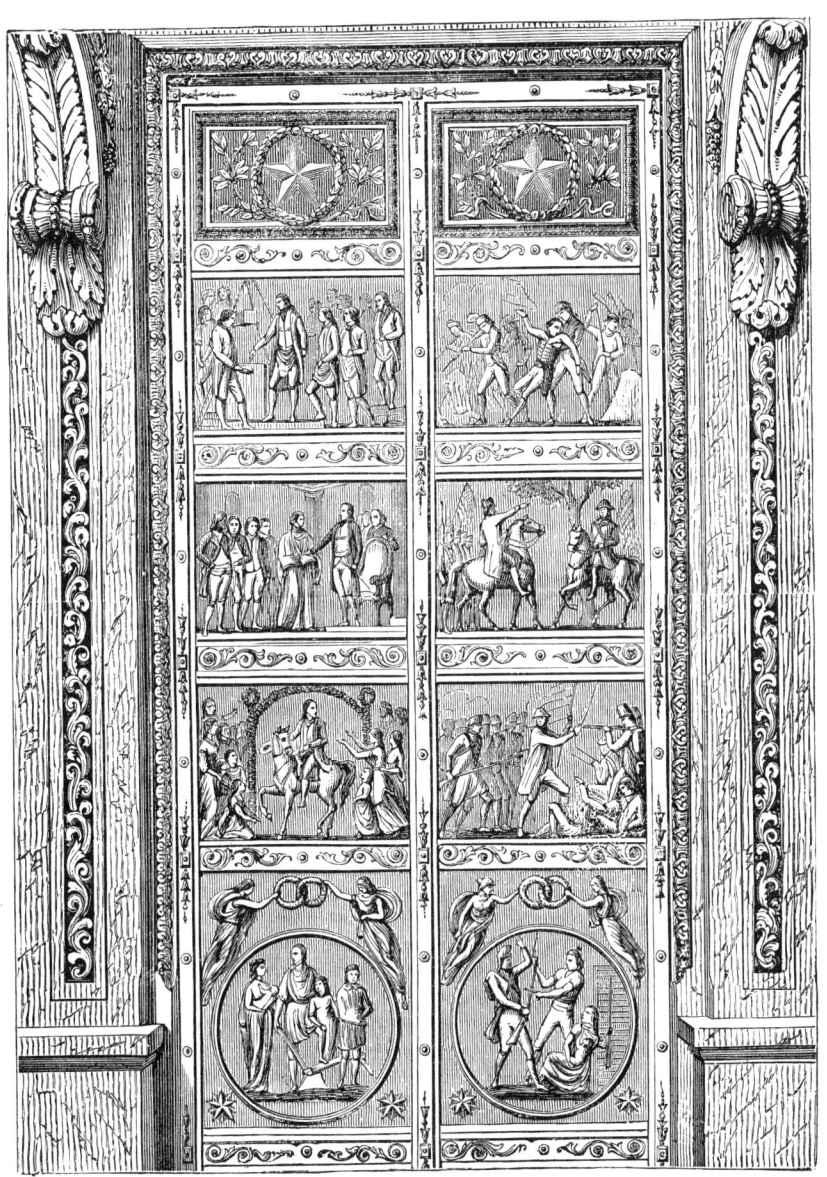

THE BRONZE DOOR IN THE SENATE WING OF THE CAPITOL.

CONTENTS.

CHAPTER I.

HOW WASHINGTON CAME TO BE THE CAPITAL.

Reasons for selecting Washington—History of the Location of the Capital at Washington—The insult to Congress—First Propositions—Disputes as to Location—Quarrel between the States—Offers of Maryland and Virginia—The Compromise—The Capital located on the banks of the Potomac—The Act of Congress incorporating the District—Proclamation of President Washington—The District named in honor of Columbus.. 23

CHAPTER II.

THE FEDERAL CITY.

The Federal City definitely located—It is named after George Washington—Prediction of Thomas Lee, Esq.—The Boundaries of Washington City defined—Sale of the Land—The City laid off by Major Ellicott—The original plan—Real estate speculations—How Washington became a City—The Primitive Capital—Slow growth of the City—The War of 1812-15—The Battle of Bladensburg—Capture of Washington by the British—The Public Buildings burned by the British Army—The return of the Government—A blessing in disguise—Rapid growth of the City—Opening of the Baltimore Railway—The First Telegraph—The Routine of Washington life—The Rebellion—Changes in the City—Washington during the Civil War—Effects of the War................................... 34

CHAPTER III.

THE WASHINGTON OF TO-DAY.

Location of the City—Topographical features—General Plan of the City—Arrangement of the Avenues and Streets—Pennsylvania Avenue—Its History—Its Attractions—General Aspect of the City—Private Residences—Residences of Notable Persons—The Corcoran Mansion—Lafayette Square—Its History and its Inhabitants—The Decatur Mansion—Mr. Colfax's Residence—The Old Club House, and its Reminiscences—Mrs. Madison's Home—The Story of her "Polisher"—General Sherman's Residence—The Washington Aqueduct—A magnificent Work—How Water is brought into the City—The Parks and Squares—Statues and Monuments—Railway Connections with the Union—The Long Bridge—The City Hall—The Churches—The Hotels—Hotel life in Washington—The "National Hotel Mystery"—The Markets—The Schools and Colleges of Washington—Benevolent and Charitable Institutions—The Soldiers' Home—The Cemeteries—Congressional Cemetery—Monuments and Inscriptions—The United States Arsenal—The Old Penitentiary—Scene of the trial of the Assassination Conspirators—The Old Capitol—The National Armory—The Government of the Territory of the District of Columbia............ 49

CHAPTER IV.

THE NEW CAPITOL.

Prominence of the Capitol—Its History—The first Edifice—It is burned by the British—The Capitol of 1825—Plans for extending the Capitol—Laying of the Corner Stone of the New Capitol—Daniel Webster's great Speech—Completion of the Work—Description of the present building—External Ornaments and Statuary—Crawford's famous Group—The Cost of the Capitol—The North Portico—The Bronze Doors—Description of the North Wing—Its Paintings and Statuary—The President's Room—Washington's First Cabinet—The Marble Room—The Marble Stairs—The New Senate Chamber—The South Wing—The Old Hall of Representatives—A Beautiful Chamber—The National Gallery of Statuary—The Bronze Doors of the House Wing—A Grand Work of Art—The Story of Columbus in Bronze—The New South Wing—The Speaker's Room—Leutze's Great Painting—"Westward Ho!"—

CONTENTS

The New House of Representatives—A Magnificent Sight—The Mysteries of the Basement—The Committee Rooms—The "Heating and Ventilating Apparatus"—The Dangers of the House of Representatives—The Central Building—The Crypt—The Mailing Rooms—The Central Portico—The Rotunda—Its Statues and Paintings—A Beautiful Picture—The Great Dome—Ascent of the Dome—Brumidi's Frescoes—View from the Dome—The Dome illuminated—The Capitol Grounds—Crawford's Grand Statue of Freedom—Greenough's "Washington"—The Superintendent of Public Buildings—The Capitol Police...... 80

CHAPTER V.

THE SENATE OF THE UNITED STATES.

Organization of the Legislative Branch of the Government—The Senate—Its Organization—Its Character—How Senators are chosen—Contrast between the old time Senators and those of to-day—The Senate in Session—Scene in the Chamber—Conduct of Senators—Untimely Applause—Pen and Ink Sketches of Senators—Vice-President Colfax—Senator Hamlin—Senator Patterson, of New Hampshire—Charles Sumner—Sketch of his Career—Henry Wilson—A self-made Man—The new Vice-President—Senator Sprague—The "handsome Senator Conkling"—Simon Cameron—A Veteran—"Parson Brownlow"—John Sherman, of Ohio—The Western Statesman—Senator Morton—Senator Trumbull—"Fighting Johnnie Logan"—A brilliant record—Senator Harlan—Senator Blair—A good Story—Carl Schurz—His romantic history—A daring Adventure—Senator Pomeroy—"Old Subsidy"—A crushing Downfall—Scene in the Kansas Legislature—Indignant Virtue—Pomeroy's Defence—Senator Caldwell—How they make Senators in Kansas—The Commercial Value of a Legislature—Report of the Committee of the United States Senate—"A Novice in Politics."...... 143

CHAPTER VI.

THE HOUSE OF REPRESENTATIVES.

Organization of the House—Apportionment of Members—The House in Session—A Characteristic Scene—Rivalries—Partisan Outbreaks in the House—Mr. Toombs's idea of Free Speech—A very

CONTENTS.

"Personal" Explanation—A Free Fight in the House—Disgraceful Scenes—Party Discipline—Recollections of "Old Thad"—Party Leaders—How to keep an Obnoxious Member out—Speech Making—A happy Expedient—Congressional Salaries—A Glance at the "Perquisites"—Abolition of the Franking Privilege—A Triumph of Public Opinion—Pen and Ink Portraits—Mr. Speaker Blaine—Ben Butler—A Scotchman's Opinion of Butler—A Good Story—N. P. Banks—Horace Maynard—General Garfield—W. D. Kelley—The Champion of Pig Iron—James Brooks—Fernando Wood—Oakes Ames—The Chief Engineer of the Crédit Mobilier. 189

CHAPTER VII.

A GLANCE AT THE LOBBY.

Natural history of the Lobby—"Deluded Souls"—Why shrewd Men and Women go to Washington—The growing Demand for Legislative Aid—The course of Monopolies—How Congress plunders the National Treasury—Popular Demand for a Cessation of Subsidies—The true View of the Case—Congressional Breaches of Trust—How the Lobby is worked—Arrival of the Lobbyist in Washington—His Mode of Procedure—A Public Man's Foes are his own Household—A mild Form of Lobbying—Laxity of Public Sentiment upon the subject—Reckless Charges—Difficulty of Proof—The popular Suspicion—The Women of the Lobby—A startling History—Division of the Women of the Lobby—The Women of the Hotels—How they conduct their Operations—Sad State of Affairs—Scene in the Hotel Dining Room—The "Beautiful Woman's Private Table"—Who are caught by it—Susceptible Officials—A Spectacle of Roman Virtue—How to snare a Congressman—The office hunting Women—Humbugging a Secretary—A little Morning Call at the Department—The great Man fooled—Managing the Senate—How to secure a Confirmation—The Widows who have Claims—How to make a small Claim cover a large one—Preserving Appearances—The Story of Mrs. Billpusher—Cheap Hospitality—Who pays for it.......................... 215

CHAPTER VIII.

THE CRÉDIT MOBILIER.

History of the Crédit Mobilier—Its connection with the Pacific Railway—The Oakes Ames Contract—Liberality of the Government towards the Road—A sharp Transaction—Bleeding the Government

—Congressional Aid—The kind of Aid needed—" We want more Friends in Congress "—Ames undertakes to manage Congress—" Satan in Paradise "—How Ames let his Congressional friends into a " Good Thing "—History of the Purchase of the Stock—The Crédit Mobilier cheats the Government again—Estimate of the Profits of the Crédit Mobilier—Where the Money came from—How to win Friends in Congress—Quarrel between McComb and Ames—Letting the Cat out of the Bag—Charges against Congressmen—Indignant denials of the Crédit Mobilier Congressmen—" We never owned any Stock "—Fatal Mistake of the Congressmen—A Lie out somewhere—Meeting of Congress—Demand for an Investigation—The real Issue—Report of the Committee—A pitiful Affair—Congressmen convicted of Falsehood—The Innocents in Congress—Detailed Statement of the Facts in the Case of each Congressman—The two Victims—A Congressional Committee Trying to humbug the People—The Truth of the Matter—The Crédit Mobilier Senators—The Facts in each Case—The Evils of a bad Memory—Oakes Ames's Note-book—Senator Patterson's Documents—The Case of Mr. Colfax—Detailed Statement of it—Terrible Chain of Circumstantial Evidence—The Vice-President's Dilemma...... 248

CHAPTER IX.
THE DEPARTMENTS.

Organization and History of the State Department—The New Building The Secretary of State—Duties of the various Bureaux of the Department—The Treasury of the United States—A noble Edifice—The Secretary of the Treasury—Detailed Statements of the various sub-divisions of the Treasury—Martin Renehan—The War Department—Its Organization—The United States Army—Army Headquarters—The Navy Department—Organization of the Bureaux—Department of the Interior—Its Organization—The Patent Bureau —The Patent-office Building—The Museum—An interesting Collection—The Washington Relics—The Declaration of Independence —The Model-room—Triumphs of American Ingenuity—The Post-office Department—The General Post-office Building—History and detailed Description of the Department—The Dead-letter office—The Bureau of Agriculture—Its Prospects and Promises. 302

CHAPTER X.
THE PRESIDENT OF THE UNITED STATES.

Statement of the Duties and Privileges of the President—How he is chosen—The Inauguration—Reminiscences of the Inaugurations in

CONTENTS.

Washington—An interregnum in the Government—Inauguration of Abraham Lincoln—What it costs the President to live—Economy in the White House—A poorly-paid Official—The President's Title—His Visitors—His Enemies—Difficulties of his Position—The Cabinet—The White House—Description of it—Internal Arrangements—The East Room—The State Apartments—The Private Apartments—The Etiquette of the White House—" Who's who " in Washington—Rules for social Intercourse among Officials—The President's Levees—The Scene in the East Room—The Comicalities of a Levee—The New Year Receptions—A brilliant Scene—The State Dinners—How they are conducted and what they cost—That "wonderful Steward"—Description of a State Dinner—The Sorrows of the White House—Who have died there—The daily Life of the President—How President Grant fills up the twenty-four Hours—A busy Life—General Grant at Home with his Family—Social Evenings at the White House—An independent President.................................. 352

CHAPTER XI.

THE SMITHSONIAN INSTITUTION.

History of the Bequest of James Smithson—The Plan for diffusing Knowledge among Men—Organization of the Smithsonian Institution—The Building—The Museum—Description of the Collection... 397

CHAPTER XII.

THE UNITED STATES OBSERVATORY.

Location of the Observatory—The Work performed here—The Chronometer Room—The Equatorial—The Transit Instrument—The great Astronomical Clock—A Scientific Curiosity 408

CHAPTER XIII.

MAKING MONEY.

The Currency of old Times—How paper Money came to be used—The art of Engraving—How the Treasury Notes are prepared—Precautions against Counterfeiting—The Bureau of Engraving and Printing—Description of the Processes of making and issuing Treasury Notes—Precautions against the improper use of the Plates—Description of the Paper used—Printing the Notes—The Work of the Bureau—A "System of Checks and Balances" 413

CHAPTER XIV.

JUSTICE.

The Judiciary Branch of the Government—The Supreme Court of the United States—Who comprise it—Its Jurisdiction and Powers—The "Old Senate Chamber"—Description of it—The "most Interesting Room in the Capitol"—Reminiscences of the old Days of the Senate—The Supreme Court in Session—The Opening of the Court—The Chief Justice of the United States—An enviable Position—A Roll of great Men—The former Chief Justices—Chief Justice Chase—Reputation of Judge Chase—Well won and worthily worn Honors—The Attorney General of the United States.................. 431

CHAPTER XV.

THE NAVY YARD.

History and Description of the Navy Yard—A Model Establishment—The Grounds—The Officers' Quarters—The Machine Shops—Excellence of the Work done here—The Iron-Foundry—The Ordnance Department and its Work—The Pyrotechnical Laboratory—The Ship Houses 443

CHAPTER XVI.

COUNTERFEITING.

Efforts to Prevent Counterfeiting—How the work of Counterfeiting is carried on—Description of the Process—Making Counterfeit Money—Who are the Counterfeiters—The Treasury Plates in the hands of Counterfeiters—Where the Work is done—How the Counterfeit Bills are circulated—Who are the Customers for Counterfeit Money—An infamous Business—The Profits of the Business—Its Dangers—How Counterfeiters are Detected and Captured—The Penalty for Counterfeiting... 447

CHAPTER XVII.

THE PUBLIC SERVANTS.

Number of Office-Holders in the United States—Immense patronage of the Government—The Number of Officials in Washington—How

Offices are given—Who procure them—The rush for Office—Mr. Lincoln's Opinion of Office-Seekers—Offices given as a Reward for Political Services—The Government Employés in Washington—Their Life and Peculiarities—How Offices are taken away—Demoralizing Tendencies of Official Life—An Independent Official and an Indignant Cabinet-Minister—A Roland for an Oliver—Daily Life at the Departments—A Tread-Mill Existence—Facts about Salaries—Blackmailing the Government Clerks—How Political Contributions are made—An infamous System—The Penalty of a Refusal—A Satisfied Ambition—Advice to Office Seekers—Anecdote of Judge Chase—The Female Clerks—Account of the Women employed in the Departments—Who they are—Their Lives and Duties—Injustice to them by the Government 454

CHAPTER XVIII.

THE ARMY MEDICAL MUSEUM.

Ford's Theatre—Scene of the Assassination of President Lincoln—The Medical Museum of the U. S. Army—Value of the Museum—The Officers in Charge—Objects of the Institution—The Collection—The Library—Curious Objects to be seen here—The Craniological Cabinet—The Japanese Manikin—The Microscopic Department—Wilkes Booth's Skull—General Sickles's Leg—The "Treasures of the Nation" 479

CHAPTER XIX.

THE LIBRARY OF CONGRESS.

The new Halls of the Library of Congress—A Model Library—Description of the Arrangments for storing the Books—History of the Library—The first Purchases—Vandalism of the British—Mr. Jefferson's Library—Growth of the Collection—The great Fire—Destruction of a Part of the Library—The new Collection—Mr. Spofford appointed Librarian—What he has done for the Library—The Collection increased—Purchase of Peter Force's Library—The new Copyright Law—Rules of the Library—Description of the Collection—An Object of National Pride—The Law Library—The most complete Collection in the World—Description of the Law Library 487

CHAPTER XX.

WASHINGTON NIGHT LIFE.

Monotony of Washington Life—The Search for Excitement—Gambling in Washington—The "Hells"—Dangers of such Places to Strangers—The First Class Houses—The "Congressional Faro Bank"—Description of the Establishment—Precautions against Intruders—A magnificent Establishment—A Palace of Vice—The Proprietor—The Suppers—The Game—How it is Played—Who are the Players—A Distinguished Company—The great Men of the Land—Where the People's Money goes—Picture of the Group around the Table—Food for patriotic Reflections—The Theatres—Their Business and Frequenters—The Canterburies 499

CHAPTER XXI.

OLD PROBABILITIES.

The Signal Service of the United States Army—"Old Probabilities" on Duty—The Signal Service in War—The Peace Establishment—How Candidates are admitted—The School at Fort Whipple—Practical Instruction—The Duties of the Service—Organization and practical Workings—The Signal Stations—Watching the Weather—Sending in Reports—Work of the Washington Office—Making up the Synopsis—The Probabilities—Excellence of the System—Tracking a Storm 511

THE BRONZE DOOR IN THE HOUSE WING OF THE CAPITOL.

FRONT VIEW OF THE CAPITOL.

BEHIND THE SCENES

IN

WASHINGTON.

CHAPTER I.

HOW WASHINGTON CAME TO BE THE CAPITAL.

Reasons for selecting Washington—History of the location of the Capital at Washington—The insult to Congress—First propositions—Disputes as to the location—Quarrel between the States—Offers of Maryland and Virginia—The Compromise—The Capital located on the banks of the Potomac—The Act of Congress incorporating the District—Proclamation of President Washington—The District named in honor of Columbus.

It puzzles many good people to understand the reason of the selection of Washington City as the Capital of the Nation. There were so many sites, so many thriving towns and fine cities offered to the choice of the wise Fathers of the Republic, which presented superior advantages and attractions to the one actually chosen, that some persons find it difficult to comprehend why they were passed by, and a wilderness selected as the "heart of the nation." The truth is that Washington City, like most of the "features" of our Governmental system, is the result of a compromise. Its story is both instructive and interesting.

The long agony was over. The War of the Revolution had ended in the triumph of the American cause, and the new Republic had taken its place among the nations of the world. It was the youngest and weakest of all the members of the great family, and its future was shrouded in doubt. The seven years war had greatly exhausted it, its treasury was empty, and its credit was not worth mentioning. Its currency had become so much depreciated that even its own citizens counted their treasury notes by the bushel. Freedom and independence had indeed been won, but a still greater task demanded the energies of the men who had carried the country through the Revolution—the laying of the foundations of the Republic in a manner which should assure the permanence of the edifice to be erected upon them. First of all, the credit of the Republic was to be improved. Money was the prime necessity for carrying on the Government, and it was very scarce; so scarce indeed, that the army which had won the independence of America, could not be paid the beggarly wages due it. It required all the influence Washington possessed to induce the troops to disband peacefully, without their pay, and in spite of his exertions several outbreaks did occur to the annoyance of the Government. One of these was the cause of one of the most important of all the acts of the Federal Congress at this period.

During the war the Government of the Confederation had led a sort of vagabond existence, moving from place to place at the approach of the Royal army. The close of the war found the Federal Congress sitting at Annapolis, in Maryland. From this place it passed to Philadelphia, thence to Trenton, New Jersey, and, finally, the seat of Government was removed to New York. It was during the continuance of the sessions at Philadelphia that the incident to which we have alluded, occurred.

In June, 1783, a band of mutinous soldiers broke into the hall in which Congress was in session, and in a grossly insulting manner demanded of that body the back pay due them for their services during the war, which amounted to a considerable sum. The soldiers were with difficulty expelled from the hall, and the Representatives turned to the consideration of the affront to which they had been subjected, and which they felt deeply. Some of the members had, previous to this, been of the opinion that it would be better to locate the seat of the General Government at some place removed from the corrupting influences of a large city, and this affair did much to bring the entire body to an acceptance of their views. The question was earnestly discussed in private, and was at length formally introduced into Congress by Elbridge Gerry, of Connecticut, in a resolution authorizing the building of a Federal City on the banks of the Delaware or the Potomac, provided a good location and the requisite amount of land could be obtained on either of those rivers. On the 7th of October, 1783, Mr. Gerry's resolution was adopted, with an amendment making provision for buildings on both the rivers named. On the

26th of April, 1784, the resolution was repealed, it being impossible to carry it out in that form. In October, 1784, Congress met at Trenton, New Jersey, and one of its earliest acts was the appointment of three commissioners with authority to lay out a district between two and three miles square, for a Federal City, the said district to be located on the banks of the Delaware. Nothing was done by the commissioners, and the next January Congress met in New York, when efforts were made to locate the district on the Potomac, but without success.

In September, 1787, the Constitution of the United States was adopted, which provides that Congress shall have power "to exercise exclusive legislation, in all cases, whatsoever, over such district (not exceeding ten miles square) as may by cession of particular States and the acceptance of Congress, become the seat of Government of the United States."

This clause of the Constitution fixed definitely the size of the Federal district, and was the first real step toward its acquisition. Efforts were at once made to fix the location with equal exactness. The State of Maryland, thinking it an advantage to have the Capital of the nation within its limits, made the first offer. On the 23rd of December, 1788, the Legislature of that State tendered to Congress "any district (not exceeding ten miles square), which Congress may fix upon and accept for the seat of Government of the United States." The offer was discussed at a considerable length in Congress in 1789.

It was admitted by all parties that the district ought

THE UNITED STATES TREASURY.

to be located in a section of the country which should be easy of access from all parts of the Union, and that it ought to be as central as should be consistent with the wealth and population of the section chosen. The North and the South—for the sectional division of the country had appeared even at that early day—each desired to secure the location of the new city within its own limits. The former insisted that the Capital should be built on the banks of the Susquehanna, while the South declared in favor of a site on the Delaware or Potomac. New York, Philadelphia, Germantown, Havre de Grace, Wright's Ferry, Baltimore, and Conococheague (now Washington City), each had its partisans. The South Carolina delegates bitterly opposed the selection of Philadelphia, because Philadelphia was a Quaker City, and the Quakers were hostile to negro slavery. Some of the delegates opposed the selection of a large city on the ground that undue influence would be brought to bear upon the Government; while others ridiculed the idea of building a city of palaces in the backwoods, and cited the example of the European States whose capitals were their largest cities. The controversy grew warm and bitter, and came near resulting in a serious misunderstanding between the States. On the 5th of September, 1789, the House of Representatives adopted a resolution declaring that, "The permanent seat of Government of the United States ought to be at some convenient place on the banks of the Susquehanna, in the State of Pennsylvania." This resolution gave great offence to the Southern members, and even Mr. Madison went so far as to declare that, had such an action on the part of Congress been foreseen, Virginia would not have ratified the Constitution. The matter was made worse by the immediate passage of a bill by the House for the purpose of carrying the resolution into effect. The vote stood thirty-one to nineteen. The Senate amended the bill by inserting Germantown, Pennsylvania, instead of the location on the Susquehanna, which amendment was accepted by the House. The House further amended the Act by providing that the laws of Pennsylvania should continue in force in the new district until Congress should order otherwise. The Senate decided to postpone the consideration of this amendment until the next session, and the matter went over. Germantown was thus actually chosen as the Federal City, and it needed only the consent of the Senate to the last mentioned amendment to make the transaction complete.

Thus far none of the States but Maryland had taken any official action in this matter. The South was very greatly excited over the course of Congress, some of the Northern States were dissatisfied with the selection, and it was felt that the danger to the harmony of the new Confederation was very serious.

On the 3rd of December, 1789, the General Assembly of Virginia passed an Act ceding to Congress a district on the banks of the Potomac. The coöperation of Maryland was asked in inducing Congress to accept the grant, and a sum not exceeding $120,000, was pledged by Virginia for the erection of the necessary public buildings, on condition that Maryland, on her part.

would contribute a sum not less than two-fifths of that amount for the same purpose. Maryland at once agreed to the request of Virginia, and pledged herself for her share of the money. Other States now made offers of territory to Congress, but no immediate action upon the subject was taken by that body.

The great question which at that time occupied the attention of the country, was the funding of the public debt. Congress was divided upon the subject. An amendment had been presented to the House, but had been rejected, providing that the General Government should assume the State debts to the amount of twenty-one millions of dollars. This question had become very closely interwoven with that of selecting a Federal district. The Northern members were in favor of the assumption, but were opposed to the location of the district in the South, and the Southern members, while divided upon the financial question, were unanimously in favor of accepting the offers of Virginia and Maryland.

Jefferson was at this time Secretary of State, and Hamilton Secretary of the Treasury. Both were anxious to avert the danger which the vexed questions threatened, and after discussing the matter confidentially, they came to the conclusion that a compromise was the only possible settlement. Hamilton urged that the Southern members should consent to the assumption of the State debts by the Government, and declared that he felt sure, if they would do this, the Northern members would consent to locate the Capital on the banks of the Potomac. It was agreed that Jefferson should ask the Southern members who were hostile to the financial scheme, to dine with him the next day, and that he should lay the matter before them, and endeavor by such arguments as he was master of, to win their consent to the proposed compromise. The dinner was given, the plan proposed by Hamilton was discussed, and a sufficient number of votes pledged for the assumption bill. Hamilton, on his part, undertook to win over the Northern members to the Capital scheme, and succeeded. The assumption bill became a law, and Congress, in the following Act, definitely accepted the offer of Virginia and Maryland.

"AN ACT for establishing the temporary and permanent seat of the Government of the United States.

"SEC. I. *Be it enacted, by the Senate and House of Representatives of the United States of America in Congress assembled,* That a district of territory, not exceeding ten miles square, to be located as hereafter directed, on the river Potomac, at some space between the mouths of the Eastern Branch and Conococheague, be, and the same is hereby, accepted for the permanent seat of the Government of the United States. *Provided, nevertheless,* That the operation of the laws of the State within such district shall not be affected by this acceptance until the time fixed for the removal of the Government thereto, and until Congress shall otherwise by law provide.

"SEC. II. *And be it further enacted,* That the President of the United States be authorized to appoint, and by supplying vacancies happening from refusals to act, or other causes, to keep in appointment as long as may be necessary, three Commissioners, who, or any two of whom, shall, under the direction of the President, survey, and by proper metes and bounds define and limit a district of territory, under the limitations above mentioned; and the district so defined, limited and located, shall be deemed the district accepted by this Act for the permanent seat of the Government of the United States.

"SEC. III. *And be it enacted*, That the said Commissioners, or any two of them, shall have power to purchase or accept such quantity of land on the eastern side of the said river, within the said district, as the President shall deem proper for the use of the United States: and, according to such plans as the President shall approve, the said Commissioners, or any two of them, shall, prior to the first Monday in December, in the year One thousand eight hundred, provide suitable buildings for the accomodation of Congress, and of the President, and for the public offices of the Government of the United States.

"SEC. IV. *And be it enacted*, That, for defraying the expense of such purchases and buildings, the President of the United States be authorized and requested to accept grants of money.

"SEC. V. *And be it enacted*, That, prior to the first Monday in December next, all officers attached to the seat of Government of the United States, shall be removed to, and, until the first Monday in December, in the year One thousand eight hundred, shall remain at the city of Philadelphia, in the State of Pennsylvania.

at which place the session of Congress next ensuing the present shall be held.

"Sec. VI. *And be it enacted,* That, on the said first Monday in December, in the year One thousand eight hundred, the seat of Government of the United States shall, by virtue of this Act, be transferred to the district and place aforesaid. And all the offices attached to the seat of Government shall accordingly be removed thereto by their respective holders, and shall, after the said day, cease to be exercised elsewhere; and that the necessary expense of such removal shall be defrayed out of the duties on imposts and tonnage, of which a sufficient sum is hereby appropriated.

"Approved, July 16, 1790.

GEORGE WASHINGTON,
President of the United States."

On the 19th of December, 1791, the Legislature of Maryland passed the following Act ratifying and confirming the cession of the District of Columbia.

"*Be it enacted by the General Assembly of Maryland,* That all that part of the said territory, called Columbia, which lies within the limits of this State, shall be, and the same is hereby acknowledged to be, forever ceded and relinquished to the Congress and Government of the United States, in full and absolute right and exclusive jurisdiction; as well of soil as of persons residing or to reside thereon, pursuant to the tenor and effect of the eighth Section of the first Article of the Constitution of Government of the United States: *Provided,* That nothing herein contained shall be so construed to vest in the United States any right of property in the soil, as to affect the rights of individuals therein, otherwise than as the same shall or may be transferred by such individuals to the United States : *And provided, also,* That the jurisdiction of the laws of this State over the persons and property of individuals residing within the limits of the cession aforesaid shall not cease or determine until Congress shall by law provide for the government thereof, under their jurisdiction, in manner provided by the Article of the Constitution before recited."

On the 3rd of March, 1791, Congress adopted an amendment repealing so much of the Act already given as required the district to be located *above* the Eastern Branch, and authorizing the President to include as much of the Eastern Branch and the land below, above the mouth of Hunting Creek, as should be deemed desirable. By this same amendment, the town of Alexandria was made a part of the District of Columbia, and it was provided that none of the public buildings should be located on the Virginia side of the Potomac. President Washington thereupon issued the following proclamation fixing the boundaries of the District:

"*Whereas,* By a proclamation, bearing date the 14th of January of this present year, and in pursuance of certain Acts of the States of Maryland and Virginia, and of the Congress of the United States, therein mentioned, certain lines of experiment were directed to be run in the neighborhood of Georgetown, in Maryland, for the purpose of determining the location of a part of the territory of ten miles square, for the permanent seat of the Government of the United States; and a certain part was directed to be located within the said lines of experiment, on both sides of the Potomac, and above the limits of the Eastern Branch, prescribed by the said Act of Congress.

"And Congress, by an amendatory Act, passed on the 3d day of this present month of March, have given further authority to the President of the United States to make any part of the said territory, below the said limit, and above the mouth of Hunting Creek, a part of the said District, so as to include a convenient part of the Eastern Branch; of the lands lying on the lower side thereof, and also the town of Alexandria;

"Now, therefore, for the purpose of amending and completing the location of the whole of the said territory of ten miles square, in conformity with the said amendatory Act of Congress, I do hereby declare and make known that the whole of the said territory shall be located and included within the four lines following, that is to say,—

"Beginning at Jones' Point, being the upper cape of Hunting Creek, in Virginia, and at an angle in the outset of forty-five degrees of west of north, and running in a direct line ten miles, for the first line; then beginning again at the same Jones' Point, and running another direct line at a right angle with the first, across the Potomac, ten miles, for the second line; then from the terminations of the said first and second lines, running two other direct lines of ten miles each, the one crossing the Eastern Branch aforesaid, and the other the Potomac, and meeting each other in a point.

THE NEW DEPARTMENT OF STATE.

"And I do accordingly direct the Commissioners named under the authority of the said first mentioned Act of Congress to proceed forthwith to have the said lines run, and by proper metes and bounds defined and limited, and thereof to make due report under their hands and seals; and the territory so to be located, defined, and limited, shall be the whole territory accepted by the said Act of Congress as the District for the permanent seat of the Government of the United States.

"In testimony whereof, I have caused the seal of the United States to be affixed to these presents, and signed the same with my hand. Done at Georgetown aforesaid, the 30th day of March, in the year of our Lord 1791, and of the Independence of the United States, the fifteenth. GEORGE WASHINGTON."

The District was laid out, in conformity with the instructions of the President, by three Commissioners, appointed under the Act of Congress, in January, 1791. They were Thomas Johnson, David Stuart, and Daniel Carroll. On the 15th of April, 1791, they superintended the laying of the corner stone of the District, at Jones' Point, near Alexandria. This act was performed with the ceremonies prescribed by the Masonic ritual. The District was called Columbia, in honor of the great discoverer of the Continent. The District remained unchanged until the year 1844, when Congress retroceded to the State of Virginia that portion lying south of the Potomac, including the town of Alexandria.

CHAPTER II.

THE FEDERAL CITY.

The Federal City definitely located—It is named after George Washington—Prediction of Thomas Lee, Esq.—The boundaries of Washington City defined—Sale of the land—The City laid off by Major Ellicott—The original plan—Real estate speculations—How Washington became a city—The Primitive Capital—Slow growth of the city—The War of 1812-15—The Battle of Bladensburg—Capture of Washington by the British—The Public Buildings burned by the British Army—The return of the Government—A blessing in disguise—Rapid growth of the City—Opening of the Baltimore Railway—The First Telegraph—The Routine of Washington life—The Rebellion—Changes in the City—Washington during the Civil War—Effects of the War.

HAVING thus acquired a Federal District, and having definitely located its boundaries, the next step was to lay off the new city which was to be the Capital of the nation. This task was entrusted to Major L'Enfant, a distinguished engineer, who was informed by the Commissioners that the new city would bear the name of "Washington."

Long before the Revolution, Thomas Lee, the grandson of the distinguished founder of the Virginian family of that name, declared that the Colonies would one day become independent of the mother country, and that the seat of Government, under the new order of affairs, would be located near the falls of the Potomac—a remarkable prediction, which was literally fulfilled. Impressed with this belief he acquired large estates in

Virginia near the head of tidewater on the Potomac. Washington, when a poor surveyor, was struck with the advantages of the location for a similar purpose, and when President, expressed himself warmly in favor of its selection. His wishes are believed to have had great weight in determining the final action of Congress.

The boundaries of the city are thus stated by the Legislature of Maryland:

"The President of the United States directed a city to be laid out, comprehending all the lands beginning on the east side of Rock Creek, at a stone standing in the middle of the road leading from Georgetown to Bladensburg; thence along the middle of said road, to a stone standing on the east side of the reedy branch of Goose Creek; thence south-easterly, making an angle of sixty-one degrees and twenty minutes with the meridian, to a stone standing in the road leading from Bladensburg to the Eastern Branch Ferry; then south to a stone eighty poles north of the east and west line, already drawn from the mouth of Goose Creek to the Eastern Branch; then east parallel to the said east and west line, to the Eastern Branch; then with the waters of the Eastern Branch, Potomac River, and Rock Creek, to the beginning—which has since been called the City of Washington."

The land on which the city now stands belonged to Daniel Carroll, Notley Young, David Burns, and Samuel Davidson. These gentlemen deeded the land embraced within the limits specified above, to Thomas Beall and John Mackall Grant, trustees, who conveyed the same to the Commissioners and their successors in office, for the United States, forever. The following are the terms of the sale as mentioned by General Washington in a letter to the Secretary of State, dated March 31st, 1791:

"The terms entered into by me, on the part of the United States, with the landholders of Georgetown and Carrollsburgh, are, that all the land from Rock Creek, along the river to the Eastern Branch, and so upwards to or above the Ferry, including a breadth of about a mile and a half, the whole containing from three to five thousand acres, is ceded to the public, on condition that, when they shall be surveyed and laid off as a city (which Major L'Enfant is now directed to do), the present proprietors shall retain every other lot; and for such part of the land as may be taken for public use, for squares, walks, etc., they shall be allowed at the rate of twenty-five dollars per acre,—the public having the right to reserve such parts of the wood on the land as may be thought necessary to be preserved for ornament. The landholders to have the use and profit of the grounds until the city is laid off into lots, and sale is made of those lots, which, by this agreement, become public property. Nothing is to be allowed for the ground which may become streets and alleys."

The task of laying off the city was confided to Major L'Enfant, who began his labors under the supervision of the President. He proved stubborn and hard to manage, however, and Washington removed him, and appointed Mr. Andrew Ellicott in his stead.

Mr. Ellicott at once proceeded to lay off the plan of the city. After drawing a meridional line, by astronomical observation, through the site selected for the

Capitol, he designed two sets of streets crossing each other at right angles. Those running north and south he distinguished by means of numbers; those running east and west by means of letters, taking the Capitol as a starting point. Avenues were then run boldly across the city, at various distances from each other. Connecting the most prominent points. They were named after the States.

Congress amended the original plan of the city by including in it a series of magnificent improvements, not one of which has ever been carried out, with the exception of the equestrian statue of Washington.

When the plan was completed, an Act was passed, allowing aliens to hold lots in the city; and copies of the plan were sent to Europe. Extensive investments were made by foreign capitalists, but they did not prove renumerative. It was believed that the best quarter of the city would be the immediate neighborhood of the Capitol, and the principal investments were made in that section; but the result proved the neighborhood of the President's house the most attractive, and the Capitol Hill lots entailed serious losses upon their purchasers.

Meanwhile the work of creating a city had been begun. The law authorizing the removal of the Government to Washington City, required that the public buildings should be ready for occupancy before the first Monday in December, in the year 1800. The task before the Commissioners was not a slight one. The new buildings had to be erected in what was almost a forest. President Washington exerted himself to have the work finished by the appointed time, but he labored under many disadvantages in his efforts, not the least of which was a lack of funds. The money advanced by Virginia and Maryland was insufficient, and was soon exhausted, and though Congress authorized loans for the purpose of completing the work, money was scarce and hard to obtain. Washington made a personal application to the Legislature of Maryland for a loan of $150,000, and that body on the 22d of December, 1796, granted a loan of $100,000, on condition of the individual responsibility of the Commissioners. The money was procured on these terms, and the work pushed forward with such energy that on the 15th of June, 1800, the Commissioners reported the buildings ready for the use of the Government, though much remained to do before they were completed. The public offices were at once removed from Philadelphia to Washington City, and on the 3d of November of that year, Congress assembled in the Capitol.

It was but a miserable, straggling village, this Capital of the Republic, in the days of its infancy. It had all the inconveniences and annoyances of a new settlement, and was utterly destitute of the comforts and pleasures of Philadelphia. Those who had opposed its selection ridiculed it unmercifully as "The city of magnificent distances." They did not even do it the poor justice it was entitled to. Yet there were some who had faith in the destiny of the new city, and who could look beyond the present and enjoy the promise of the future. The Honorable John Cotton Smith, of Connecticut, thus describes the appearance of Washington City, at the meeting of Congress in November, 1800:

"Our approach to the city was accompanied with sensations not easily described. One wing of the Capitol only had been erected, which, with the President's house, a mile distant from it, both constructed with white sandstone, were shining objects in dismal contrast with the scene around them. Instead of recognizing the avenues and streets portrayed on the plan, not one was visible, unless we except a road with two buildings on each side of it, called the New Jersey Avenue. The Pennsylvania Avenue, leading, as laid down on paper, from the Capitol to the Presidential mansion, was then nearly the whole distance a deep morass covered with alder bushes, which were cut through the width of the intended avenue during the then ensuing winter. Between the President's house and Georgetown a block of houses had been erected, which then bore, and may still bear, the name of the *six buildings.* There were also two other blocks, consisting of two or three dwelling-houses, in different directions, and now and then an insulated wooden habitation,—the intervening spaces, and indeed the surface of the city generally, being covered with shrub oak bushes on the higher grounds, and on the marshy soil either trees or some sort of shrubbery. Nor was the desolate aspect of the place a little augmented by a number of unfinished edifices at Greenleaf's Point, and on an eminence a short distance from it, commenced by an individual whose name they bore, but the state of whose funds compelled him to abandon them, not only unfinished, but in a ruinous condition. There appeared to be but two really comfortable habitations in all respects within the bounds of the city, one of which belonged to Dudley Carroll, Esq.; and the other to Notley Young, who were the former proprietors of a large portion of the land appropriated to the city, but who reserved for their own accommodation ground sufficient for gardens and other useful appurtenances. The roads in every direction were muddy and unimproved. A side-walk was attempted in one instance by a covering formed of the chips of the stones which had been hewn for the Capitol. It extended but a little way, and was of little value; for in dry weather the sharp fragments cut our shoes, and in wet weather covered them with white mortar. In short, it was a 'new settlement!' The houses, with two or three exceptions, had been very recently erected, and the operation greatly hurried in view of the approaching transfer of the national government. A laudable desire was manifested by what few citizens and residents there were, to render our condition as pleasant as circumstances would permit. One of the blocks of buildings already mentioned was situated on the east side of what was intended for the Capitol Square, and being chiefly occupied by an extensive and well kept hotel, accommodated a goodly number of the Members. Our little party took lodgings with a Mr. Peacock, in one of the houses on New Jersey Avenue, with the addition of Senators Tracy, of Connecticut, and Chipman and Paine, of Vermont; and Representatives Thomas, of Maryland, and Dana, Edmond, and Griswold, of Connecticut. Speaker Sedgewick was allowed one room to himself—the rest of us in pairs. To my excellent frierd Davenport and myself was

THE PATENT-OFFICE.

allowed a spacious and decently furnished apartment with separate beds on the lower floor. Our diet was various but always substantial, and we were attended by active and faithful servants. A large portion of the Southern Members took lodgings at Georgetown, which, though of a superior order, were three miles distant from the Capitol, and of course rendered the daily employment of hackney coaches indispensable.

"Notwithstanding the unfavorable aspect which Washington presented on our arrival, I cannot sufficiently express my admiration of its local position. From the Capitol you have a distinct view of its fine, undulating surface, situated at the confluence of the Potomac and its Eastern Branch, the wide expanse of that majestic river to the bend at Mount Vernon, the cities of Alexandria and Georgetown, and the cultivated fields and blue hills of Maryland and Virginia on either side of the river, the whole constituting a prospect of surpassing beauty and grandeur. The city has also the inestimable advantage of delightful water, in many instances flowing from copious springs, and always attainable by digging to a moderate depth; to which may be added the singular fact that such is the due admixture of loam and clay in the soil of a great portion of the city that a house may be built of brick made of the earth dug from the cellar; hence it was not unusual to see the remains of a brick kiln near the newly erected dwelling house or other edifice. In short, when we consider not only these advantages, but what, in a national point of view, is of superior importance, 'he location on a fine, navigable river, accessible to the whole maritime frontier of the United States, and yet easily rendered defensible against foreign invasion,—and that, by the facilities of internal navigation and railways, it may be approached by the population of the Western States, and indeed of the whole nation, with less inconvenience than any other conceivable situation,—we must acknowledge that its selection by Washington as the permanent seat of the Federal Government affords a striking exhibition of the discernment, wisdom, and forecast which characterized that illustrious man. Under this impression, whenever, during the six years of my connection with Congress, the question of removing the seat of Government to some other place was agitated—and the proposition was frequently made—I stood almost alone as a Northern man in giving my vote in the negative."

The faith of the Connecticut Statesman was not misplaced. The wretched little village has grown into a fair city, whose splendors are the pride of the nation. From any point the city shows well; but it is perhaps from the grounds of the old Arlington estate, on the Virginia side of the Potomac, that Washington appears most regal. Across the river the city glitters and sparkles in the clear sunlight. At the river's verge is the huge unfinished monument to Washington, with the Treasury Department and the White House rising in stately grandeur behind it. Still farther away is the solid square of the Patent Office, seemingly a vast block of marble from this distance; and back of all, and high over all, on its lofty eminence looms up the great Capitol, its glorious dome seeming to reach the clouds.

The defects of the city cannot be seen, distance truly lends enchantment to the view, and the Federal City makes almost as noble a picture as does Paris to the gazer standing on the hill at Saint Cloud.

Washington was incorporated as a city by an Act of Congress dated May 3rd, 1802. It grew very slowly. It had been expected that the location of the Government at this place would induce settlers to flock to it, but those who entertained such expectations simply cherished foolish hopes. The city, as we have said, was partly a forest and partly a swamp. The few dwelling houses that had been erected were small and inconvenient, and, besides this, very few persons believed that it would ever be the permanent Capital of the Union. It was confidently expected that Congress would soon transfer the seat of Government to some more desirable spot, and few were willing to risk a removal thither while this uncertainty existed.

The city continued to struggle along until the second war with England. That struggle inflicted a severe disaster upon it, which in the end, however, proved a blessing in disguise. In August, 1814, a British fleet under Admiral Cochrane, with three thousand troops under Major General Ross, arrived in the Chesapeake from Bermuda, and joined the squadron already there under Admiral Cockburn.

On the 20th of August, twenty sail, under command of Admiral Cockburn, entered the Patuxent River, and anchored off Benedict, where a force of four thousand British regulars, under Lord Ross, was landed, for the purpose of marching upon Washington. The next day the little army set out, without cavalry or artillery, and on the 24th reached Bladensburg, about three miles from Washington. Here the British encountered a force of eight thousand Americans, under General Winder. With the exception of about four hundred marines and sailors under Commodore Barney, the American force was composed entirely of raw militia, who made scarcely any resistance. The militia were soon put to flight, but Barney made a gallant fight with his little band. He was incapable of resisting such heavy odds, however. His position was turned by the enemy, and he was obliged to give the order to retreat. He was wounded and taken prisoner, and the road to the Capital was gained by the enemy.

General Ross at once marched his army into Washington, which he found deserted by the Government. The archives and such valuable property as could be removed had been secreted, but the public buildings, with their contents, were left at the mercy of the enemy. The Navy Yard and the vessels lying in it were fired by the Americans before withdrawing. The British army marched directly to the Capitol, which, by order of Admiral Cockburn, was immediately set on fire. This done, the enemy marched to the other end of Pennsylvania Avenue, and fired the Treasury Department and the President's mansion. The Long Bridge was also burned, and communication with Virginia severed. The next day, the 25th, the building occupied by the War and Navy Departments was burned, as were also a number of private houses. A fearful tempest swept over the city during the night, causing great destruction of life and property. The British, fearing an attack from the Americans, withdrew from the city on the night of the 25th, and embarked in their fleet which had ascended the Potomac to Alexandria.

The Government came back to Washington after the departure of the enemy, to find a ruined city, and it was generally believed that the barbarous action of the British had definitely settled the question of removal in the affirmative. "When Congress next assembled, the subject of rebuilding these edifices came before that body, and the question as to the removal of the legislature was necessarily discussed. An effort was made for the removal of the seat of Government. The national feeling, however, coöperated with other considerations to influence the decision; it was voted not to remove, and the requisite amount was enthusiastically voted to efface the memorials of British triumph. From this time, the corporation of the city seemed to be animated with a new soul, and individuals, relieved from the fear of change, risked all they had in real estate. Landed property rose in value, and hope, energy, and active business took the place of despair, listlessness, and wasting and repining indolence. New streets were opened, dwelling houses and stores were then erected. The trade came to the city, the boarders left Georgetown, and came to Washington, and a new face was put on everything in the city. Churches were built, institutions of learning arose, and large, if not ample provision was made for other necessary improvements on the face of nature. This work has been going on ever since the close of the War (of 1812-15); but it must be pleasant to the citizens of Washington to reflect, when all things are taken into consideration, that they are not indebted to the Government, in equity, for one dollar for all their grants and favors; but that, in truth, the Government is indebted to the city for more than a million of dollars, putting a fair value on the property now owned within the city, which cost them nothing. Blessings are said to come in clusters, for as soon as the city began to flourish it became healthy. The low grounds were drained."

The rapid growth of the Union produced a corresponding expansion in the labors of the different departments, and the Capital grew in importance and in size. Towards the close of the year 1834, the railroad connecting it with Baltimore was completed, and the city was thus brought into rapid communication with the North. The completion of the magnetic telegraph, in 1844, also gave an impetus to its growth, which, until the Civil War, was steady and unflagging, rather than rapid. Previous to the Rebellion it was rather a retired place. During the Session of Congress it was busy and gay, but in the long recesses it seemed to be asleep. In the summer it was insufferably dull, hot, and dusty. Every body lived in the expectation and hope of the coming winter and the meeting of Congress, which were sure to bring crowds of strangers with them. As the month of December approached the city began to fill up, hotels and boarding houses lost their deserted aspect, and the proprietors' grum faces began to smile again. The Departments commenced to show signs of life and activity. Clerks and officials who had dozed away the summer months, assumed energetic and important airs, and every body in any way connected with the Government, appeared to undergo a marvellous transformation. The winter was gay and lively, but when the "Honorable Members" of the two Houses took their flight, the old dulness came back and settled over everything.

With the Rebellion came a remarkable change in the city. It was no longer simply the Capital of the Nation, it was also a great military post. The plains around it were crowded with camps, sheds, trains, etc., and the host of Government Officials filled every available building in the city. The streets were full of soldiers, and regiments were constantly marching through the city. Long lines of red earth works bristled on the Virginia heights and on the hills back of the city, and from over the river the distant boom of the cannon could be heard at almost any time. In less than a year the population had increased from 61,400 to nearly a quarter of a million, which was its average size during the War.

All sorts of people came to Washington during the War, changing the character as well as the appearance of the city. Whatever had been the state of its morals previous to the great struggle, there can be no doubt that they were at a very low ebb during the Rebellion. Honesty, both private and official, was thrown aside, and corruption reigned supreme. Intrigues and immoralities of all kinds became the order of the day, and these crimes were unjustly laid to the charge of the

Washingtonians proper. The truth is, that the genuine residents of the city held themselves aloof from the strangers who inundated the place. They were powerless to resist the tide of excess which had so changed the character of their old home, and so protested against the orgies of the new comers by taking no part in them.

At the close of the Rebellion, the army was disbanded, and the Government was brought back to a peace footing. There was at once an exodus from Washington of those who had lived off the public plunder during the four years of the War. The city had been benefited in many ways by the presence of the army, and the vast crowd of civilians during that period. It had grown to a considerable extent, both in size and in its permanent population. New interests had been developed, and its trade had received an impetus which marked the beginning of better days. The increasing demands of the Government had already brought, and continued to bring many skilled workmen, and people of various pursuits, large numbers of whom came to settle there permanently; so that the War left the city far more prosperous and thriving than it had found it. Since the close of the War its growth has been rapid. In 1850 the population was 40,101; in 1860, it was 61,400; and in 1870, 109,204.

THE WHITE HOUSE.

CHAPTER III.

THE WASHINGTON OF TO DAY.

Location of the City—Topographical features—General plan of the City—Arrangement of the Avenues and Streets—Pennsylvania Avenue—Its history—Its attractions—General aspect of the City—Private residences—Residences of notable persons—The Corcoran Mansion—Lafayette Square—Its history and its inhabitants—The Decatur Mansion—Mr. Colfax's residence—The old Club-House and its reminiscences—Mrs. Madison's home—The story of her "Polisher"—General Sherman's residence—The Washington Aqueduct—A magnificent work—How water is brought into the City—The Parks and Squares—Statues and Monuments—Railway connections with the Union—The Long Bridge—The City Hall—The Churches—The Hotels—Hotel life in Washington—The "National Hotel Mystery"—The Markets—The Schools and Colleges of Washington—Benevolent and Charitable Institutions—The Soldier's Home—The Cemeteries—Congressional Cemetery—Monuments and Inscriptions—The U. S. Arsenal—The old Penitentiary—Scene of the trial of the Assassination Conspirators—The old Capitol—The National Armory—The Government of the Territory of the District of Columbia.

WASHINGTON City is situated on the left bank of the Potomac River, between that stream and a tributary called the Eastern Branch, a few miles below the head of tidewater. It is 295 miles from the Ocean; 226 miles southwest of New York; 432 miles southwest of Boston; 544 miles northeast of Charleston; 1203 miles northeast of New Orleans; 497 miles east of Cincinnati; 763 miles southeast of Chicago; 856 miles east of St. Louis; and 2400 miles, in an airline, east of San Francisco. The Capitol, which is nearly the centre of the city, is located in 38° 52′ 20″, North Latitude, and in 77° 0′ 15″ Longitude West from Greenwich. The Potomac is navigable for ships of the largest size to Greenleaf's Point. The British fleet anchored here in 1814; and the frigate Minnesota, one of the largest vessels of her class, was built at the Navy Yard some years ago, and carried down the stream after being equipped. The situation of the city is advantageous in many respects. Its front is washed by the Potomac, on the eastern side is the Eastern Branch, and on the west a stream called Rock Creek, which separates it from Georgetown.

"The general altitude of the city plot is forty feet above the river, but this is diversified by irregular elevations, which serve to give variety and commanding sites for public buildings. The plot is slightly amphitheatrical, the President's house, on the west, standing on one of the sides, and the Capitol on the other, while the space between verges towards a point near the river. The President's house and the Capitol stand centrally with regard to the whole, though situated at a distance of a mile and a half from each other, the former forty-four feet above the Potomac, and the latter seventy-two feet. The summit of the hill on which the Capitol stands is the commencement of a plain stretching east, while that to the north of the President's house tends to the westward."

Washington is laid off in a peculiar manner. According to the original plan, the Capitol was designed to be the centre of the city, and the starting point of the whole system of streets. This plan has been adhered to in the main, though in some respects it has been altered. The streets running east and west are designated by letters. They are divided into two classes or sets—those north of the Capitol and those south of it. Thus, the first street north of the Capitol is A Street North, and the first street south of it, A Street South; the next is B Street North or South, and so on. The streets running north and south are numbered. Thus the street immediately east of the Capitol is First Street East, and that immediately west of it, First Street West, and so on. These distinctions of North, South, East, and West, are very important, as forgetfulness of them is sure to plunge a stranger into hopeless bewilderment as to localities. The streets are laid off at regular distances from each other, but for convenience, other thoroughfares, not laid down in the original plan, have been cut through some of the blocks. These are called "Half Streets," as they occur between and are parallel with the numbered streets. Thus, Four-and-a-half Street is between Fourth and Fifth streets, and runs parallel with them.

The Avenues run diagonally across the city, cutting the streets at acute angles. New Jersey, Pennsylvania, Maryland and Delaware Avenues intersect each other at the Capitol, or rather radiate from that point. Pennsylvania, New York, Vermont and Connecticut Avenues intersect at the President's house. These avenues are from 130 to 160 feet in width. They are fine streets, and when all are completed and are lined with buildings, will give to Washington a system of public thoroughfares unsurpassed by those of any city in the world. There are about twenty-two avenues in the city. The streets number about one hundred, and are from seventy to one hundred feet in width. The circumference of Washington is fourteen miles. Within these limits are over two hundred miles of streets and about seventy miles of avenues. The paving and grading of the streets and avenues have been done almost entirely at the cost of the city. The General Government has been prompt to claim every privilege accorded to it by the original plan, but has done very little for the city.

The principal thoroughfare is Pennsylvania Avenue, a noble street, one hundred and sixty feet in width. It traverses the entire length of the city, from Rock Creek, which separates Georgetown from Washington, to the Eastern Branch. It was originally a swampy thicket. The bushes were cut away to the desired width soon after the laying out of the city, but very few persons cared to settle in the swamp. Through the exertions of President Jefferson, the avenue was subsequently planted with four rows of Lombardy poplars—one on each side and two in the middle— with the hope of making it equal to the famous *Unter den Linden*, in Berlin. The poplars did not thrive, however, and when the avenue was paved, in 1832 and 1833, by order of Congress they were cut down. The street is now well paved and lighted. It is handsomely built up, and contains many buildings which would do credit to any city. The principal hotels and stores are situated in this avenue, which always presents a busy and enlivening appearance. The public processions and other festivities take place here, the broad avenue affording ample room for such displays. The distance from the Capitol to the President's house is one mile and a half. The best point of view is from the grounds of the Treasury Building. Standing on the steps of the Treasury and looking down the avenue, one sees a broad, noble street stretching away until it enters the thick green shade of the trees in the Capitol Square, and above these trees rises the glorious Capitol, flashing and glittering in the sunlight.

Washington is in the main a well built city, and is improving in this respect every year. The Government buildings are, of course, superior to any thing in the country. Some of the business edifices would do credit to New York, and there are many private residences that will compare in elegance and beauty with any in the land. The increase in the prosperity of the city, and the constant expansion of the Governmental machinery have attracted much wealth to Washington, and persons of means and culture are constantly seeking it as a place of permanent abode. The handsomest quarter of the city is the west end, in the vicinity of the White House. Many of the residences are the property of the Senators and Representatives from the various States, who maintain permanent establishments here. The majority of the houses are built of brick. Some of them are stuccoed or painted in imitation of brown stone or marble, but the greater portion retain the natural color of the brick which is a bright cheerful red, due to the fine quality of the clay from which it is made, and which is found within the city limits. Brownstone, the lighter colored stones, and even marble are making their appearance in the better quarters. The Baltimore style is generally followed in the construction, and the houses built within the past ten years will compare favorably with those of any American city.

The residence of Mr. W. W. Corcoran, one of the leading bankers of the Capital, is perhaps the most complete and elegant private establishment in Washington. It stands on H Street, opposite Lafayette Square, in the midst of extensive grounds which are enclosed with a brick wall. It was built by Mr. Swann, the father of Ex-Governor Swann, of Maryland, who resided in it for awhile. It has had a number of distinguished occupants, among whom were General Gratiof, Mr. Packingham, the British Minister, Daniel Webster, and Count Montholon, one of the recent French Ministers. The house is built of brick, with brownstone trimmings, and consists of a central building with a low wing on each side. The interior is filled with rare and costly furniture and works of art, and is a sight worth seeing by the lovers of the beautiful. The grounds lie back of the house, and are beautifully laid off. They are filled with the choicest flowers, and are ornamented with fountains, statuary, conservatories and picturesque summer houses.

On Lafayette Square are some of the most noted houses in Washington, noted for their history and not for their magnificence. At the northwest corner of the square is a double house built of brick, three stories in height, fronting on the square, and extending back on H Street. In the earlier days of Washington it was a dwelling house. It is now used as a Government office. The gallant Stephen Decatur had his home here. He was a great favorite in Washington as elsewhere, and there are many old residents who still speak of him with moistened eyes. The story of his quarrel with Barron is well known, as is also the fatal ending of that quarrel. On the evening before the duel Mrs. Decatur gave a party at this house, which was largely attended. The Commodore was present, and received his guests with the cordial hospitality characteristic of him. Mrs. Decatur was unusually gay, having no idea of the sorrow that the morning was to bring to her. Decatur was calm and smiling, and remained in the drawing-room until the last guest had departed. The next morning, he rose early, and proceeded with his friends to Bladensburg, whence in a few hours he was brought back to his home to die. He had been mortally wounded in a duel with Captain Barron.

At the southwest corner of the square, on Sixteen-and-a-half Street, is a plain stuccoed house, known as No 7 Lafayette Square. It is painted white, and the windows are shaded with green blinds. A semicircular stairway leads up from the street to the entrance, and the building looks simple and modest in the midst of its elegant neighbors. Tradition says that Mr. Monroe once lived in it, and that it has sheltered several of the Vice-Presidents. It is quite an old house. Levi Woodbury, when Secretary of the Treasury, and afterwards of the Navy, lived here. He was the father of Mrs.

Montgomery Blair. Mr. Southard of Georgia, and Mr. Stockton, a purser in the Navy, also occupied it. A year or two before the Civil War, it was the residence of Daniel E. Sickles, Member of Congress from New York. The trees in Lafayette Square were young then, and the guilty wife could easily see the signals of her lover from the Club House opposite. It was just across the enclosure, at the foot of those noble old trees which shade Fifteen-and-a-half Street, at its junction with Pennsylvania Avenue, that the blood of Key was shed to heal the wounded honor of Sickles. For several years the house has been occupied by Vice-President Colfax.

Near the middle of the square, on Fifteen-and-a-half Street, or Madison Place, as it is called, is a large, but plain, red brick building, three stories in height. It was built and occupied for some time by Commodore Rodgers of the Navy. After his death it was a fashionable boarding house, and subsequently became the Washington Club House. Key was carried here after he was shot by Sickles. Upon the accession of Mr. Seward to the Secretaryship of State, he made it his residence, and lived here during his term of office. It was here that the cowardly attack was made upon him as he lay helpless on the night of the assassination of President Lincoln.

On the northeastern corner of the square is the house in which the widow of President Madison resided from the time of her husband's death until her own, which occurred about twenty years ago. She is well remembered in Washington, and was deservedly popular.

THE BUREAU OF AGRICULTURE.

During her life it was always the custom to call on her on New Year's Day, immediately after calling on the President. Politics had no place in her drawing room, and political foes were good friends under her roof. In her earlier years Mrs. Madison was exceedingly fond of gayety, and being a very handsome woman, she was very popular with the gentlemen of her acqaintance. She was always remarkable for the elegance and dignity of her manners, and made one of the most charming mistresses the White House ever possessed.

Mr. Gobright in his "Recollections of Men and Things at Washington," tells the following story of her, which will bear repeating. In the year 1816, the President held one of the most brilliant levees ever witnessed in the Executive Mansion. Mrs. Madison was the centre of attraction. "Mrs. Madison," says the chronicler, "like Mr. Clay, was very fond of snuff. The lady offered him a pinch from her splendid box, which the gentleman accepted with the grace for which he was distinguished. Mrs. Madison put her hand into her pocket, and pulling out a bandanna handkerchief, said, 'Mr. Clay, this is for rough work,' at the same time applying it to the proper place; 'and this,' producing a fine lace handkerchief from another pocket, 'is my polisher.' She suited the action to the word, removing from her nose the remaining grains of snuff."

At the corner of H Street and Vermont Avenue is the Arlington Hotel, one of the fashionable boarding houses of the city, and very popular with the "Powers that Be." Senator Sumner, and other celebrities reside in the neighborhood.

On I Street, near New Jersey Avenue, is a row of three large double houses of red brick with free stone trimmings. They constitute the famous "Douglas Row," so called in consequence of having been erected by the late Senator Stephen A. Douglas. His residence was the central mansion, and in his day it was one of the most charming homes in the city, made doubly attractive by the presence of his beautiful wife, one of the most queenly of American women, and as lovely in character as in person. Ex-Mayor Wallach occupies the house at the corner of New Jersey Avenue, and that at the other end of the row is the residence of General W. T. Sherman, commanding the armies of the United States. It was purchased by a number of prominent citizens just after the close of the War, and presented to General Grant. Upon his election to the Presidency, it was purchased and given to General Sherman.

It is located in a handsome part of the city, and upon high ground, which affords an abundance of fresh air. There is a large yard at the side, tastefully laid off, and the street is broad and well paved and graded. In front, the gigantic Capitol looms up grand and white in the distance, and far beyond it the blue waters of the Potomac glitter in the sunlight.

The streets are lighted with gas, and are traversed by lines of street railways which connect the various portions of the city. Some of these roads are good, but others are wretched affairs, and a decided improvement might be made in the whole system.

The city is supplied with fresh water from the Potomac. It is brought from the Great Falls of the Potomac, above Washington, by means of an Aqueduct, which is one of the finest works in the world. This aqueduct is a conduit of masonry, circular in form, with an interior diameter of nine feet. It is built of brick, and is lined with hydraulic cement.

At the Great Falls a massive stone dam is built across the Potomac, by which a sufficient head of water is always obtained for the purposes of the aqueduct. At the Maryland side of the Falls is a structure of cutstone, which guards the head of the aqueduct from ice, freshets and driftwood. It contains also the gates by which the flow of the water through the aqueduct is regulated. The aqueduct passes under the bed of the Chesapeake and Ohio Canal, and is carried for several miles through a rugged country abounding in picturesque scenery. Brooks and creeks are crossed by means of small bridges, and the hills are pierced by tunnels, which are models of engineering skill. The aqueduct itself lies for the greater part of the way underground, but its course may be traced by the embankment which covers it, and which looks like the bed of a railway from which the rails have been removed. At the Mountain Spring Brook, the aqueduct emerges from a long tunnel, and crosses the brook by a graceful elliptical arch of masonry of seventy-five feet span. About one mile and an eighth byond this is the famous Cabin John Bridge, a stupendous arch of granite, spanning a ravine at a single leap of 220 feet. The top of the bridge is 101 feet from the bed of the ravine. This magnificent work is the largest arch of masonry in the world.

From Cabin John Bridge the aqueduct passes on to the Receiving Reservoir, about two miles from Georgetown, entering it through a tunnel 800 feet long cut through the solid rock. The gate houses here and at the Distributing Reservoir are built of massive masonry, in the most substantial manner. The Receiving Reservoir is an immense lake created among the hills by a strong dam sixty-five feet high, and several hundred feet long. From this the water is carried two miles farther to the Distributing Reservoir on Lee's Hill in Georgetown. This structure is nearly a mile long and a quarter of a mile in width. From this point the water is conveyed to Georgetown and Washington in iron pipes, the fall being about 145 feet. The aqueduct and the reservoirs were begun in November 1853, and on the 3d of January 1859, water was brought into Washington for the first time. The work was performed by the U. S. Engineer Corps, at a cost of nearly four millions of dollars. The supply of water is ample for a much larger city than Washington. The capacity of the aqueduct being 67,596,400 gallons of water every twenty-four hours.

When the original plan of Washington was drawn up, the Government reserved a number of sites for parks and public grounds. Some of these have been laid off, but others exist only on the maps. The principal of those in existence are the *Capitol Park, The Mall*, or square in front of the President's house, Lafayette Square, immediately opposite, and the circles and triangles at the intersection of the various avenues.

Lafayette Square is a small enclosure on the east side

of Pennsylvania Avenue, immediately opposite the President's mansion. It is tastefully laid off, and is ornamented with fountains, shrubbery, and flowers. In the centre stands the equestrian Statue of General Andrew Jackson, erected by the Government to the memory of the hero of New Orleans. It is of bronze, and is made of the cannon captured by General Jackson in his battles with the British during the second war with England. The general is represented in the exact military costume worn by him, with cocked hat in hand, in the act of saluting his troops. The charger is poised upon his hind feet, with no other stay than the balance of gravity, and the bolts pinning the feet to the pedestal. The figure of Jackson is eight feet in height, and that of the horse in proportion. The statue rests upon a pedestal of white marble, at the base of which are planted four brass six-pounder guns taken by Jackson from the English at New Orleans. The cost of the statue, including the iron railing, was $28,500. The work was executed by Clark Mills.

At the junction of Pennsylvania and New Hampshire Avenues, and 23rd Street West and K Street North, there is a large circle formed by the intersection of those thoroughfares. In the centre is an equestrian statue of Washington, also by Clark Mills. It is of bronze, is colossal in size, and is mounted on a handsome pedestal, on the sides of which are reliefs illustrating some of the prominent scenes in the life of Washington. Washington is represented as he appeared at the battle of Princeton, where he forced his horse directly in the face of the British battery, after endeavoring several times to rally his troops. The terror stricken animal recoils from the storm of balls which plough the earth about him, but the rider is calm and undismayed.

Washington is connected with the Northern States by two lines of railway. One of these is known as the Washington Branch of the Baltimore and Ohio Railway, and the other is the Baltimore and Potomac Railway, nominally an independent road, but in reality a branch of the Pennsylvania Central. The Baltimore and Ohio Depot is in New Jersey Avenue, near the Capitol. At this present writing the Baltimore and Potomac Road is without a permanent depot.

Communication with the south is maintained by railway and steamboat. The Orange and Alexandria Railway enters the city from Virginia, crossing the Potomac by the Long Bridge. It furnishes direct communication with Richmond and Lynchburg, Va., and all points in the south and southwest. A line of first class steamers connects Washington with Aquia Creek, in Virginia, some fifty miles down the Potomac. From this point there is railway communication with all parts of the south.

The Long Bridge connects the city with the Virginia shore. It is a little more than a mile in length, and is provided with a draw at the point where it crosses the channel of the river, by means of which vessels can ascend the Potomac to Georgetown. During the Civil War this bridge was of great importance to the Government forces, and was strongly fortified. Remains of the old earthworks are still to be seen at the heads of the bridge.

Apart from the Government buildings, the only prominent public building is the City Hall. It is situated in Judiciary Square, and faces the intersection of D Street North and Louisiana and Indiana Avenues, on the south, and is bounded on the north by H Street, on the east by Fourth Street West, and on the west by Fifth Street West. It was begun in 1820, and was completed in 1850. It is situated in one of the handsomest parts of the city, but is an awkward, ugly building, built of brick and stuccoed in imitation of marble. At a distance it presents an imposing appearance, but upon coming closer one finds it a pitiful affair. It has a frontage of about two hundred feet, but is very shallow. It is the headquarters of the local Government, and is also used by some of the District and Municipal Courts.

Immediately in front of the City Hall is a handsome pillar of white marble on which stands a statue of Abraham Lincoln, cut out of the same material. The height of the pillar is thirty-five feet. The statue is life-size. It was erected by the voluntary contributions of the citizens of Washington, and with the pillar cost $7000. It is the work of Mr. Lot Flannery, of Washington City, formerly a lieutenant in the United States army.

Prominent among the noted buildings are the Churches. Many of these are large and handsome; but the majority have no architectural pretensions. There are five Baptist churches; six Roman Catholic; seven Episcopal; two " Friends' Meeting Houses;" one Jews' Synagogue; three Lutheran churches; eleven Methodist Episcopal; two Methodist Protestant; one New Jerusalem; seven Presbyterian; one Reformed German; one Unitarian; two colored Baptist; one colored Presbyterian; and seven colored Methodist churches in the city, making a total of fifty-seven religious edifices completed and in use. Others are in course of erection. The largest, and one of the handsomest, is the Metropolitan Methodist Church, a new structure.

Trinity Church (Episcopal), at the corner of Third Street West and C Street North, is perhaps the wealthiest and most fashionable, and by many is regarded as the most beautiful church edifice in the city. St. John's (Episcopal) is a plain little building just opposite the White House. It is noted as having been the place of worship frequented by a large number of the Presidents, and the scene of many fashionable weddings.

The Hotels are large, and are managed upon the plan common to all large cities. Their rates of board are high, and in the winter the rush of visitors to the city is so great that they are well filled with guests. They claim to be equal to any in the land, but the truth is that they are among the most indifferent establishments in America. They are not always clean, and they lack the air of comfort peculiar to the hotels of the north and west. With every advantage in the way of well supplied markets, the table they set is usually poor, and the attendance is indifferent.

Hotel life in Washington has not many charms, but it has two attractions which those who pursue it enjoy —excitement and variety. Many of the higher officials

THE GENERAL POST OFFICE.

and members of Congress board at the hotels. The "clerks" are not able to afford such magnificence, and they content themselves with lounging about the public rooms during their hours of leisure. At the breakfast table of any of the principal houses you may see a goodly row of legislative faces, some of which do not show over well for the work of the past night. The conversation is generally political. Nobody thinks or talks of anything else but politics here.

During the greater part of the day the hotels have a silent, deserted air, but early in the morning, and after the close of the daily sessions of Congress and the labors of the Departments, they fill up rapidly. The halls, sitting rooms and gentlemen's parlors are crowded to excess, with a noisy boisterous crowd, all talking at the same time, and producing a very Babel of sounds. The air is hazy with tobacco smoke, and the floors are slippery with tobacco juice. Governors, Senators, Members of the House, clerks, contractors, lobbyists, members of the various Rings, citizens, strangers to the city, and loafers are mingled in true democratic confusion, and the only peaceful man in the place is the inevitable card writer, who is working steadily and silently at his little table by the light of his St. Germain lamp.

Up stairs the scene is different, but as animated. The parlors and halls on the first floor are brilliantly lighted. Richly dressed and frequently beautiful women, some the wives and daughters of the men below, and others whose exact status is uncertain, hold their court here. All are here for the season only, and the long evenings when there are no receptions or parties on hand, hang heavily upon them. They resort to a thousand and one ways to dissipate the blues, for there is no prospect of their being able to draw their husbands or fathers out of the smoke beclouded halls below. Sometimes an impromptu hop is gotten up, and sometimes the proprietors of the hotel offer to their guests a formal entertainment of this kind. The fair dames are adroit politicians, and never neglect an opportunity to advance the cause of the particular member to whose fortunes they are attached. They catch the infection as soon as they reach the Capital, and the disease lasts till they leave it.

The principal Hotels are located on Pennsylvania Avenue. The largest lies nearest to the Capitol, and is called the *National Hotel*. This is a famous rendezvous of politicians, and has played a prominent part in the political history of the country. In 1857 it came near being the scene of a deplorable tragedy. Mr. Buchanan, the President-elect, had reached Washington for the purpose of entering upon the duties of the Executive office, and had taken lodgings at the National. He was suddenly stricken with a serious sickness, which the physicians were unable to account for. The rumor at once went out that he had been poisoned by his political opponents. A number of the guests of the house were also seized with the same disease, and efforts were made to discover the cause of the mysterious malady. "It was believed," says Mr. Gobright, "by some persons that the sickness resulted from decayed kitchen refuse in the sewer connected with the hotel. Accordingly the proprietors at once set to work to remove the unhealthy deposits; and since that time there has been no return of the 'National Hotel disease.'" Several persons died, and others were a long time recovering from the effects of the attack. The *Metropolitan Hotel*, formerly known as *Brown's*, is the handsomest of all the public houses. It is built of white marble, and presents a fine appearance. *Willard's Hotel*, at the corner of Pennsylvania Avenue and Fourteenth Street, is next to the National in size. It extends from the avenue back to F Street, and occupies about one half of the entire block. It is a popular house, and is as well conducted as any in the city. These are the principal houses. There are about a score of others in various parts of the city, all of which enjoy a fair share of patronage during the winter season.

The Markets are ordinary and unattractive structures, but they are among the best in the country with respect to their contents. The season is earlier than that of the markets of the most of our large cities, and the citizens of the Capital have here an opportunity of obtaining the first and best fruits of the ground. The meats come from the highlands of Virginia and Maryland, and are of a superior quality. Venison, wild turkeys, ortolan, reed birds, and canvas-back ducks are to be found here in profusion in their season, and in perfection. The shad and other fish and the oysters of the Potomac are noted for their excellence.

The Schools of Washington are as yet in their infancy. There are five large "public schools," which correspond to the "high schools" of other cities, and a number of primary schools, with schools for colored children. The system is similar to that of the other large cities of the country, but is still susceptible of great expansion and reform. The people have of late years given to their public schools more care and attention than was their habit in former times, and there is every reason to believe that they will soon be placed upon a basis which will enable them to meet the wants of all classes of the community.

There are many private schools in the city, some of which are excellent; also several male and female boarding schools.

Among the higher institutions of learning are Columbia College, the National Medical College, and Gonzaga College (under the control of the Roman Catholic Church), all of which are deservedly ranked among the best schools in the country. Columbia College is situated on Fourteenth Street, near the northern boundary of the city. It was incorporated in 1821, and has sent forth some of the brightest names that have ever graced the annals of American law, theology, and science. The National Medical College, though mentioned as a separate institution, is really the Medical School of Columbia College. The Howard University is a flourishing institution for the instruction of colored people.

The Benevolent and Charitable Institutions of the city are numerous and are well conducted. Some of them are provided with large and handsome buildings. The *Alms House*, which serves also as a work house for the confinement of petty offenders, is situated on a slight hill to the east of the Capitol. The *Columbian Institution for the Deaf, Dumb, and Blind,* is located in the northeastern part of the city, near the Government Printing Office. It is in a beautiful suburban district known as Kendall Green. The buildings are mediæval Gothic in style, and are very picturesque and attractive. They are among the first objects seen as one enters the city by rail from Baltimore. The course taught is thorough and systematic, and the pupils are fitted here for positions which will enable them to earn their own support after leaving the institution. A writer in a recent number of *Scribner's Magazine* thus speaks of the first graduating class, which left the institution in 1869 : " Some of the students became paid correspondents of newspapers ; others translated publications from the French and German ; one invented and received a patent for an improvement in the microscope ; one was tendered a situation as editor upon an influential semi-weekly newspaper ; and during the vacations nearly all became valued assistants in various directions. . . . . The graduates of that class, with one exception, were called to high positions as instructors ; the excepted one entered the service of the Patent Office, where he has since risen to the post of Assistant Examiner, having won that rank in a competitive examination with seventeen aspirants. The members of the class of 1870 have been summoned to similar fields of labor in the different States. One of the graduates of the latter class is now a valued teacher in a Canadian institution. Another, after ably filling a position in the Census Bureau for a period of three months, accepted the situation of instructor of the most advanced class in one of the State Institutions—a duty which has never before devolved upon any mute or semi-mute."

The Hospital for the Insane of the Army and Navy and District of Columbia stands on a commanding hill, on the left bank of the Potomac, near its junction with the Eastern Branch. The grounds surrounding the asylum are beautifully laid off, and command a fine view of the city. The asylum is an immense structure, with a frontage of 711 feet. It is built in the Collegiate style of Gothic architecture, and is divided into sections, receding on either hand from the centre building and from each other, thus giving corridors in each section for the admission of light. "The centre building is enriched by buttresses on the corners, and a magnificent oriel window ornaments the main tower; the windows are furnished with hood mouldings of cast iron, the whole is surrounded by embattled parapets, and presents a façade of great richness, notwithstanding extreme simplicity of detail. The material of the building is of brick on a foundation of gneiss." The interior is admirably arranged for the proper accommodation and treatment of the patients. The hospital is controlled by a Board of Visitors, who are appointed by the President of the United States, and who serve without compensation. The superintendent is appointed by the Secretary of the Interior.

The *Military Asylum* occupies a high plateau about three miles to the north of the Capitol. The location is exceedingly beautiful, and is admirably adapted to its uses. The view of the river, the city, and the neighboring hills is the finest to be obtained from any point near Washington. The asylum is built in the Norman style of architecture, of rough-dressed Eastchester marble. The central building alone is completed, but when the wings are added it will have a frontage of 593 feet. The central tower is eighty-two feet high. The establishment is designed as a permant home for such veteran and invalid soldiers of the United States army as may be admitted in accordance with the rules laid down for the government of the asylum.

The *City Infirmary* is the principal hospital for the treatment of ordinary sickness. It is situated immediately to the north of the City Hall. It is well conducted, and is under the charge of a corps of competent physicians, assisted by the Sisters of Mercy as nurses.

The " Louise Home " is a noble institution, built and endowed by Mr. W. W. Corcoran, and named in memory of his dead wife. It is a home for elderly ladies of good social position, and is a model establishment worthy of imitation in other sections of the country.

The Cemeteries are the Oak Hill, Glenwood, and the Congressional Cemeteries. The first is the most beautiful, and is the gift to the shareholders of Mr. W. W. Corcoran, whose family vault forms the most conspicuous and elegant ornament of the grounds. The cemetery is situated on the heights of Georgetown, upon the western slope of the banks of Rock Creek, and abounds in picturesque and attractive scenes.

The Congressional Cemetery lies on the hills over

looking the Eastern Branch of the Potomac, and was for a long time the principal burying place of the city. It covers an area of twenty acres, and is the property of one of the Episcopal churches of the city, by which it is kept in order.

It is called the "Congressional Cemetery," because when a Member of Congress dies during his term of office, his memory is perpetuated by the erection of a plain cenotaph in these grounds. There are at present about one hundred and fifty of these memorial stones in the cemetery, one for each member who has died during his official term since the Capital was located at Washington.

There is also a vault for the reception of the remains of public men dying in the city. They are placed here until they can be removed to their last resting places. It is a very plain structure, and is situated near the centre of the grounds. The bodies of President Taylor and Senator Calhoun were deposited in this vault for a few days after their decease.

There are a number of interesting monuments to be seen in this cemetery. Among them are those erected to the memory of William Wirt, Major General Macomb, General Scott's immediate predecessor in the command of the army, General Gibson, General Archibald Henderson, Commodore Isaac Chauncey, and Abel P. Uphur, of Virginia, formerly Secretary of State. Among the inscriptions on some of the tombs, are the following:

"Sacred' to the memory of PHILIP PENDLETON BARBOUR, associate-justice of the Supreme Court of the Uni-

THE PRESIDENT LEAVING THE WHITE HOUSE,
TO BE INAUGURATED

ted States, who was born in Orange County, Virginia, on the 25th of May, 1783, intermarried with Frances Todd Johnson, on the 4th of October, 1804, and died at Washington city on the 24th of February 1841."

"This monument is erected by order of his majesty Frederick William III., King of Prussia, to the memory of his resident minister in the United States, the Chevalier FREDERICK GREHUM, who departed this life on the 1st of December, 1823, in the 53rd year of his age."

"Sacred to the memory of Gen. JACOB BROWN. He was born in Bucks Co., Pennsylvania, on the 9th of May 1775, and died at the city of Washington, commanding general of the army, on the 24th of February, 1828.

"Let him who e'er in after days
Shall view this monument of praise,
For honor heave the patriot sigh,
And for his country learn to die."

"JOSEPH LOVELL, late surgeon-general of the army of the United States, born in Boston, Massachusetts, Dec. 22, 1788; died in the city of Washington, October 17, 1836."

"PUSH-MA-TA-HA, a Choctaw chief lies here. This monument to his memory is erected by his brother chiefs, who were associated with him in a delegation from their nation, in the year 1824, to the general government of the United States. He died in Washington, on the 24th of December, 1824, of the croup, in the 60th year of his age. Push-ma-ta-ha was a warrior of great distinction. He was wise in council, eloquent in an extraordinary degree, and on all occasions, and under all circumstances, *the white man's friend.* Among his last words were the following: ' *When I am gone let the big guns be fired over me.*' "

" Here lie the remains of TOBIAS LEAR. He was early distinguished as the private secretary and familiar friend of the illustrious Washington; and after having served his country with dignity, zeal and fidelity, in many honorable stations, died accountant of the War Department, 11th October, 1816, aged 54. His desolate *widow* and mourning *son* have erected this monument, to mark the place of his abode in the city of silence."

" The tomb of ELBRIDGE GERRY, Vice-President of the United States, who died suddenly in this city, on his way to the Capitol as president of the Senate, November 23d, 1814, aged 70; thus fulfilling his own memorable injunction, ' it is the duty of every citizen, though he may have but one day to live, to devote that day to the good of his country.'"

" To the memory of GEORGE CLINTON. He was born in the State of New York, on the 26th July, 1739, and died at the city of Washington on the 20th of April, 1811, in the 73d year of his age. He was a soldier and statesman of the revolution. Eminent in council, distinguished in war, he filled with unexampled usefulness, purity, and ability among many other high offices, those of governor of his native state, and Vice President of the United States. While he lived, his virtue, wisdom and valor, were the pride, the ornament, and security of his country, and when he died, he left an illustrious example of a well spent life, worthy of all imitation."

The *United States Arsenal* is located on Greenleaf's Point, at the extreme southern end of the City, at the mouth of the Eastern branch of the Potomac. It commands a fine view of Washington, Georgetown, the Potomac River, Alexandria, and the Virginia shore, and as the channels of both rivers lie close to the eastern bank, possesses every facility for shipping and receiving military stores.

The buildings and grounds are extensive, the establishment constituting one of the principal arsenals of construction in the United States. The workshops are large, and are provided with improved machinery of all kinds for manufacturing ordnance stores and equipments, large quantities of which are prepared and kept here for distribution among the various posts of the army. The Model Office contains an interesting collection of models or patterns of the various weapons used in our own service, and in the European armies. The *Gun-lot* contains an array of heavy ordnance and balls for the armaments of forts and land batteries: and in front of the old Arsenal Square are many trophies won from the enemies of the Republic in battle.

Until within a few years past, the Arsenal grounds contained another large building known as the **Old Penitentiary**. It has been demolished, and its site is now occupied by the Officers' quarters. It was in this building that the trials of the persons charged with conspiring for the assassination of President Lincoln took place; and in the prison yard, which was formerly enclosed with a high brick wall, Mrs. Surratt, Atzeroth, Harold, and Payne, were hanged, on the 9th of July, 1865, for complicity in the murder of President Lincoln, and for the attempt upon the life of Secretary Seward. These dark and terrible memories will long make the spot an object of interest to the curious—an interest which will probably increase rather than diminish with the lapse of time.

Another building, famous during the War, has since been remodelled, and has been so much changed that its longest occupant would not know it. It stood immediately opposite the northeast angle of the Capitol Park, and was known as the *Old Capitol*. It then constituted a single building, now it has been changed into a row of private dwellings, with handsome mansard roofs. It was erected about the year 1812, and a few years later passed into the hands of the Government. The Capitol having been destroyed by the British during their occupation of the city in August, 1814, Congress was without a place of meeting. That body immediately transferred its sessions to this edifice, and remained in occupancy of it until the completion of the Capitol in 1825. Hence its name—the Old Capitol. After its abandonment by Congress it was used for various purposes, and finally became a boarding house. John C. Calhoun lived here for some time, and died here in 1850. During the War it was used as a prison for the detention and punishment of State and military prisoners.

It was a dingy, red-brick edifice of the old English style, and very much like one of the primitive Quaker buildings still to be seen in the city of Philadelphia. It had a gloomy and forbidding appearance, and was in truth as uncomfortable a prison as the country contained. The effect of a confinement there must have been very depressing, and I do not wonder that its former inmates still shudder at the remembrance of it.

The National Armory lies between the Capitol and the Smithsonian Institute. The central building alone has been completed. It is designed as an armory for the Volunteers of the District of Columbia, and as a depository of national trophies, relics, flags, etc.

The government of Washington City is merged in that of the District of Columbia. Early in the year 1871, the two Houses of Congress passed a bill, which received the signature of the President, on the 21st of February, making great changes in the affairs of the District. By this law the District has been given the management of its own affairs. It has been organized as a Territory, with a government, consisting of a Governor and a General Assembly. The Governor is appointed by the President of the United States by and with the advice and consent of the Senate. He holds office for four years, and until his successor shall be appointed and have qualified. He must be a citizen of the District for at least twelve months previous to his appointment, and have the qualifications of a voter. His duties and powers are similar to those of the Governor of a Territory of the United States. The Assembly consists of a Council and a House of Delegates. The Council is composed of eleven members, of whom two are residents of the city of Georgetown, two residents of the District outside of Washington and Georgetown, and seven residents of the city of Washington. They are appointed by the President of the United States, by and with the advice and consent of the Senate. They must have the qualification of voters to be eligible to their office. They hold office for two years, five and six going out on alternate years. The House of Delegates consists of twenty-two members, two from each of the eleven Districts into which the District of Columbia is divided. They are elected by the people, and must have the qualifications prescribed for members of the Council.

The right of suffrage is conferred upon all male citizens of the United States above the age of twenty-one years, who have resided in the District for a period of twelve months previous to an election, except persons of unsound mind and those convicted of infamous crimes. The Assembly has no power to limit or abridge the right of suffrage.

The Government must confine itself entirely to the affairs of the District of Columbia. The inhabitants of the District do not vote for the President or Vice-President of the United States. They send one Delegate to Congress, who is entitled to the rights and privileges in that body that are enjoyed by the Delegates from the several Territories of the United States to the House of Representatives. He is by virtue of his position a member of the House Committee on the District of Columbia.

All the Acts of the Legislative Assembly are subject at all times to repeal or modification by the Congress of the United States, which body retains its powers of legislation over the District as formerly.

By this law the charters formerly held by the cities of Washington and Georgetown are repealed, and all offices of those corporations abolished. The cities are brought directly under the control of the District Government, which succeeds to the possession of the municipal property. The cities retain their names and boundaries, but no longer exist as separate corporations, the government of both being confided to the authorities of the District. The Governor of the District of Columbia is virtually Mayor of Washington.

CHAPTER IV.

THE NEW CAPITOL.

Prominence of the Capitol—Its History—The first Edifice—It is burned by the British—The Capitol of 1825—Plans for extending the Capitol—Laying of the Corner Stone of the New Capitol—Daniel Webster's great speech—Completion of the work—Description of the present Building—External Ornaments and Statuary—Crawford's famous group—The cost of the Capitol—The North Portico—The Bronze Doors—Description of the North Wing—Its Paintings and Statuary—The President's Room—The Marble Room—Washington's First Cabinet—The Marble Stairs—The new Senate Chamber—The South Wing—The Old Hall of Representatives—A beautiful Chamber—The National Gallery of Statuary—The Bronze Doors of the House Wing—A grand work of Art—The story of Columbus in Bronze—The New South Wing—The Speaker's Room—Lentze's great painting—"Westward Ho!"—The new House of Representatives—A magnificent sight—The mysteries of the Basement—The Committee Rooms—The "Heating and Ventilating Apparatus"—The dangers of the House of Representatives—The Central Building—The Crypt—The Mailing Rooms—The Central Portico—The Rotunda—The Statues and Paintings—A beautiful picture—The great Dome—Ascent of the Dome—Brumidi's frescoes—View from the Dome—The Dome Illuminated—The Capitol Grounds—Crawford's grand Statue of Freedom—Greenough's "Washington"—The Superintendent of Public Buildings—The Capitol Police.

FROM whichever direction the city is viewed, the great dome of the Capitol is the first object that meets the eye of the gazer. The building itself also looms up grandly from any point of view, and forms the most conspicuous feature in any view of the city. The site is admirable, and was selected by Washington himself. The building stands on the western brow of a com-

ARRIVAL OF THE PRESIDENT AT THE CAPITOL.

manding hill and towers high above the city. The front of the Capitol faces the east, and the rear overlooks the large and more important portion of the city. The exact position of the edifice was determined by astronomical observations. It stands in Latitude 38° 52' 20" North, and in Longitude 77° 0' 15" West from Greenwich.

The present building is the growth of years. The designer of the first Capitol had no conception in his mind of the grand edifice of to-day. Frequent changes and improvements have been made from time to time in the original plan, and these have not always been made to harmonize with the work already done, but, with all its defects, the Capitol is the grandest and most beautiful building in the New World, and one of the finest and most imposing on the globe. The old building forms the central portion of the present edifice, and, with the exception of the dome, was designed by Dr. William Thornton. The plan was approved by President Washington, and the work was immediately begun. The corner-stone was laid on the 18th of September 1793, by George Washington, and the ceremony was performed in accordance with the Masonic Ritual. Among the articles deposited in the corner-stone was a silver plate bearing this inscription:

"This Southeast Corner-stone of the Capitol of the United States of America, in the City of Washington, was laid on the 18th day of September, 1793, in the thirteenth year of American Independence, in the first year of the second term of the Presidency of George Washington, whose virtues in the civil administration of his country have been as conspicuous and beneficial, as his military valor and prudence have been useful in establishing her liberties, and in the year of Masonry 5793, by the President of the United States, in concert with the Grand Lodge of Maryland, several lodges under its jurisdiction, and Lodge No. 22 from Alexandria, Virginia.

"Thomas Johnson, David Stuart, and Daniel Carroll, Commissioners; Joseph Clark, R. W. G. M. P. T.; James Hoban and Stephen Hallet, Architects; Collin Williamson, M. Mason."

The law of Congress locating the seat of Government at Washington, required the Commissioners to complete the public buildings by December 1800, so that the Session of Congress of that year might be opened in the Capitol. The Commissioners lost no time, and, considering their difficulties and embarrassments, accomplished wonders. By the summer of 1800 they had the north wing ready for the use of the Senate. The walls of the south wing were carried up to a height of twenty feet above the basement and roofed over for the temporary accommodation of the House of Representatives. This wing was popularly styled "The Oven," and was used in this condition until 1804, when the House removed to the hall of the Library of Congress, which was situated in the western end of the Senate wing. Mr. Benjamin H. Latrobe, one of the most accomplished engineers of his day, having been placed in charge of the work, caused the temporary roof to be removed, and completed the south wing. In the winter of 1808, the work being sufficiently advanced, the

House returned to its old quarters. "The old Senate Chamber was of but temporary construction, the columns and entablature being of wood stuccoed, and the capitals of plaster. The staircases were also of wood. On the 19th of September, 1808, the centre of the vault of the old room, of the Supreme Court was removed, when the arch gave way, carrying with it the floor of the Senate Chamber, and killing John Lenthall, clerk of the works. It was the opinion of Mr. Latrobe that this accident was occasioned by striking the centre of the arch too early. The damage to the building was immediately repaired." It was the design of the architect to replace the Senate Chamber with a handsomer and permanent hall.

The House, or south wing, was completed in 1811, the work having been greatly delayed by the Embargo during the years 1808 and 1809. This wing was more substantial and much handsomer than that occupied by the Senate. "The Hall of Representatives was semicircular, with a vaulted wooden ceiling; the entablature was supported by twenty fluted Corinthian columns of sandstone; the frieze over the Speaker's chair was ornamented by a figure of the American eagle, carved in sandstone, by Signor Franzoni; the opposite frieze was also decorated with figures by the same artist, representing Agriculture, Commerce, Art, and Science. Behind the chair of the Speaker sat a figure of Liberty, with the eagle by her side, her right hand presenting the Constitution on a scroll, and the liberty cap in her left, her feet resting upon a reversed crown and other symbols of monarchy and bondage."

The two wings were as yet the only portions of the Capitol constructed. They were built of sandstone taken from an island in Aquia Creek, in Virginia. The foundations of the central building had not yet been begun, and the two halls of Congress were connected by a covered wooden gallery.

The War of 1812-15 put an end for the time to the work on the Capitol, and in 1814, the British set fire to the two wings and burned them, leaving nothing standing but the walls, which, fortunately were uninjured. Upon the return of the Government to the city after the withdrawal of the British, Congress ordered the rebuilding of the destroyed wings of the Capitol and the completion of the entire edifice. Mr. Latrobe was again entrusted with the work, which was begun in the spring of 1815. During the winter of 1814-15, Congress sat in the Post Office building. On the 8th of December, 1815, the two Houses passed an Act leasing a building situated on the east side of the Capitol Park. It was immediately occupied by the Senate and House, and was used for their accommodation until the completion of the Capitol. From this circumstance the building became known as "The Old Capitol." During the Civil War it was used as a prison, and around it cluster some of the darkest and most terrible memories of the great struggle.

Mr. Latrobe resigned the superintendence of the Capitol in December, 1817, and was succeeded by Mr. Charles Bulfinch. Under the supervision of this gentleman the work went on rapidly, and the foundations of the central building were laid on the 24th of March.

1818 Mr. Latrobe's plans were discarded by the new engineer, and the edifice was completed in accordance with the original design of Dr. Thornton. The entire building was finished in 1825.

The Capitol of 1825 was the most imposing edifice in the country, and was regarded by the people of that day as a marvel of beauty and grandeur. It forms the central portion of the present edifice, and is vastly inferior in design and workmanship to the magnificent wings which have been added to the old building. The cost of the Capitol of 1825 was nearly three millions of dollars. The building was constructed of a white freestone. It was in the form of a cross, with a spacious rotunda in the centre and two wings devoted to the use of the two Houses of Congress. It covered an acre and a half of ground.

As the Republic increased in size and population, the two Houses of Congress grew in proportion, and at length the portions of the Capitol devoted to their use became too small to accommodate them with comfort. It became necessary to enlarge the building, and accordingly, on the 30th of September, 1850, an Act was passed making provision for the enlargement and extension of the Capitol according to such plan as the President of the United States should approve. Mr. Fillmore, who occupied the Executive Chair at the time, chose from the many designs submitted to him, the plan of Mr. Thomas U. Walter, Architect, and on the 10th of June, 1851, appointed that gentleman to superintend the work.

On the 4th of July, 1851, the corner stone of the extension was laid by President Fillmore. Mr. Gobright, in his "Recollections of Men and Things at Washington," thus speaks of the occasion:

"On the 4th of July, 1851, the extensive grounds of the Capitol were filled to their utmost capacity. The ladies were there in great force, enlivening and adding gayety to the occasion, together with military companies and civil associations. The President of the United States, Heads of Departments, foreign Ministers, Governors of States, and other distinguished personages, were seated upon a platform on the left partico, at the east front. Several bands of music played during the intervals of the proceedings. The scene was brillant and interesting. It was the seventy-sixth Anniversary of the Nation's independence, and the assembling was to lay the corner stone of the Capitol extension.

"The Grand Master of the order of Masons, Major B. B. French, attended to his part of the programme, and President Fillmore laid the stone, after the manner of that fraternity.

"Mr. Webster was the orator. He said the principles of our Government may be thus briefly stated:— First, the recognition of popular representation; second, the popular voice, as expressed by the majority, becomes law; and third, the law governs all the people, and is recognized as the rule of Government. He had caused to be deposited in the corner stone a statement written in his own hand, as follows:

"'On the morning of the first day of the seventy-sixth year of the Independence of the United States of

America, in the City of Washington, being the 4th day of July, 1851, this stone, designed as the corner-stone of the extension of the Capitol, according to a plan approved by the President, in pursuance of an Act of Congress, was laid by

"'MILLARD FILLMORE,

"'PRESIDENT OF THE UNITED STATES,

assisted by the Grand Master of the Masonic Lodges, in the presence of many members of Congress, of officers of the Executive and Judiciary Departments, National, State, and District, of officers of the Army and Navy, the Corporate authorities of this and neighboring cities, many associations, civil and military and masonic, officers of the Smithsonian Institution and National Institute, professors of colleges and teachers of schools of the District, with their students and pupils, and a vast concourse of people from places near and remote, including a few surviving gentlemen who witnessed the laying of the corner-stone of the Capitol by President Washington, on the eighteenth day of September, seventeen hundred and ninety-three.

"'If, therefore, it shall be the will of God that this structure shall fall from its base, that its foundation be upturned, and this deposit brought to the eyes of men, be it then known, that, on this day, the Union of the United States of America stands firm; that their Constitution still exists unimpaired, and with all its original usefulness and glory, growing every day stronger and stronger in the affections of the great body of the

American people, and attracting more and more the admiration of the world. And all here assembled, whether belonging to public life or to private life, with hearts devoutly thankful to Almighty God for the preservation of the liberty and happiness of the country, unite in sincere and fervent prayers that this deposit, and the walls and arches, the domes and towers, the columns and entablatures now to be erected over it, may endure forever.

"'God save the United States of America.

"'DANIEL WEBSTER,

"'*Secretary of State of the United States.*'

"He referred to the fact of Washington's laying the corner-stone of the Capitol, as forming a chain in the bond of Union, and invoked the spirit of the illustrious dead in behalf of the present and the future. The new wings about to be added to the Capitol, stretching, as they did, North and South, he regarded as an additional cord in binding the States in Union. He would say now, relative to the Capitol, as he had said on another occasion—referring to his speech on the laying of the corner-stone of the Bunker Hill Monument: 'Let it rise—let it rise—let it rise until it shall meet the sun in its coming.' He thought if the immortal Washington could rise and stand forth there that day, he would rejoice in the feelings which existed and ask the blessing of Heaven upon our future union and prosperity. 'Father immortal!' he exclaimed, 'though dead, we shall feel thy influence now and here.'

"The oration was one of Mr. Webster's best efforts,

THE PRESIDENT PASSING THROUGH THE ROTUNDA TO TAKE THE OATH OF OFFICE.

although it was not delivered under favorable circumstances of health. He exhibited considerable physical weakness, and had to resort to stimulants to sustain himself.

"There were present three persons who attended the laying of the corner-stone of the Capitol by Washington, fifty-eight years before the present ceremonies, namely: George Washington Parke Custis, Z. Walker, of Maryland, and Lewis Machen, a clerk in the office of the Senate of the United States."

The work on the extension was pushed forward as rapidly as possible. By the early part of the session of 1858–59, the new halls were sufficiently prepared for the reception of the Senate and House of Representatives, and were taken possession of by those bodies. They were made even more memorable than the old halls by the exciting scenes which preceded the outbreak of the Rebellion, and by those events of the great struggle in which Congress figured. The work of completing the extension went on with scarcely any intermission during the War. In the early days of the conflict the dome, then unfinished, was the best place of observation in the city. From its lofty height one could see the city with its busy, bustling throngs of civilians and soldiers, looking like an immense human hive. Long, dark lines of troops were constantly moving to and fro, and the open country beyond the limit of the buildings was white with the encampments of the great army assembling for the defence of the Capital. Earthworks were springing up, as if by magic, on every hand. The Potomac was full of steamers coming and going, laden with military supplies. Armed vessels swung lazily at anchor in the broad stream below the city, or huddled about the mouth of the Eastern Branch. The hills on the Virginia side were lined with red looking earthworks, over which you could see bristling rows of cannon, stretching away until they were lost in the dense green of the woods, or became indistinct in the distance. With a good glass, you could see at one time, the faint outline of the Southern position beyond Alexandria, and at times you could catch the dull thud of the guns at work on the distant lines. Still, in the midst of all the excitement attending these things, in the face of the danger which actually threatened the Federal City, the work on the Capitol went on. The great dome became huger and more massive, climbing nearer to the skies every day; and at last all was done, and then the great Statue of Freedom was lifted to its lofty position on the summit of the dome, and was greeted with thunders of artillery from all the defences of Washington.

"The extension consists of two wings, placed at the north and south ends of the former building, at a distance of 44 feet from it, with connecting corridors 56 feet 8 inches wide, inclusive of their outside colonnades. Each wing is 142 feet 8 inches in front, on the east, by 238 feet 10 inches in depth, exclusive of the porticoes and steps. The porticoes fronting the east have each 22 monolithic fluted columns, and extend the entire width of the front, having central projections of 10 feet 4 inches, forming double porticoes in the centre, the width of the gable. There is also a portico of ten columns on the west end of each wing, 105 feet 8 inches wide, projecting 10 feet 6 inches, and like the porticoes on the north side of the North Wing and south side of the South Wing, with a width of 121 feet 4 inches. The centre building is 352 feet 4 inches long, and 121 feet 6 inches deep, with a portico 160 feet wide, of 24 columns, with a double façade on the east, and a projection of 83 feet on the west, embracing a recessed portico of ten coupled columns. The entire length of the Capitol is 751 feet 4 inches, and the greatest depth, including porticoes and steps, is 324 feet. The ground actually covered by the building, exclusive of the court-yards, is 153,112 square feet, or 652 feet over three and a half acres.

"The material of which the extension is built, is a white marble, slightly variegated with blue, and was procured from a quarry in Lee, Massachusetts. The columns are all of white marble obtained from Maryland.

"The principal story of the Capitol rests upon a rustic basement, which supports an ordonnance of pilasters rising to the height of the two stories above. Upon these pilasters rests the entablature and beautiful frieze, and the whole is surmounted by a marble balustrade.

"The main entrances are by the three eastern porticoes, being made easy of access by broad flights of stone steps with massive cheek-blocks, and vaulted carriage-ways beneath to the basement entrances."

The building faces the east, and the rear is in the direction of the principal part of the city. This location was made under the impression that the neighborhood of the Capitol would be first settled up in the growth of the new city, but the designs of the projectors not having been realized, the building now faces the wrong way.

Standing in front of the edifice, and at a distance sufficient to take in the whole view, the effect is indescribably grand. The pure white marble glitters and shines in the sunlight, and the huge structure towers above one like one of the famed palaces of old romance. The broad flights of steps of the wings and central buildings have an air of elegance and lightness which is surprising when their massive character is considered. The pediments of the porticoes will contain magnificent groups of sculpture. The central pediment is decorated with a group sculptured in alto-relievo. The Genius of America, crowned with a star, holds in her right hand a shield bearing the letters U. S. A., surrounded with a glory. The shield rests on an altar inscribed with the date, "July 4, 1776," encircled with a laurel wreath. A spear is behind her within reach, and the eagle crouches at her feet. She is gazing at Hope, who stands upon her left, and is directing her attention to Justice, on her right, who holds in her right hand a scroll inscribed, "Constitution of the United States," and in her left the scales. The group is said to have been designed by John Quincy Adams, and was executed by Signor Persico.

The northern pediment contains Crawford's famous group, representing the progress of civilization in the United States. America stands in the centre of the tympanum, in the full light of the rising sun. On her right hand are War, Commerce, Youth and Education, and Agriculture; on her left the Pioneer, Backwoodsman, the Hunter, the Indian and his Squaw, with an infant in her arms, sitting by a filled grave.

The southern pediment has not yet been filled; but the design is said to have been selected, and to represent the discovery of America by Columbus. The sculptor is William R. Barbee.

The cheek-blocks of the steps to the central portico are ornamented by two fine groups of statuary. The group on the right of the steps represents the discovery of America, and is by Persico. Columbus, landing in the New World, holds aloft in his right hand a globe, symbolic of his discovery. He is clad in armor, which is said to be a faithful copy of a suit worn by him. An Indian maiden crouches beneath his uplifted arm, her face expressive of the surprise and terror of her race at the appearance of the Whites.

The group on the left is called "*Civilization,*" and is by Greenough. A terror-stricken mother, clasping her babe to her breast, crouches at the feet of a stalwart Indian warrior, whose arms, raised in the act of striking her with his tomahawk, are seized and pinioned by the husband and father, who returns at the fortunate moment, accompanied by his faithful dog, which stands by ready to spring to the aid of his master.

The estimated cost of the Capitol and the extension is twelve millions of dollars, but improvements have been ordered, and are contemplated by Congress, which will greatly increase the actual cost of the edifice.

We pause for a moment to admire the magnificent portico of the North Wing, and then ascend the broad marble steps to the platform of the portico. The doorway leading into the main hall of entrance of this wing is provided with a pair of magnificent bronze doors, the work of the gifted American sculptor, Randolph Rogers. The panels are occupied with representations of events in the life of General Washington, and each tells its own story.

From the portico, we enter a beautiful hall or vestibule constructed of marble. The floor and ceiling are of this material, and the latter rests upon a double row of marble pillars. The marble is variegated, and the general effect is fine. The hall is massive and elegantly proportioned, and is well worthy of the attention of the visitor.

On the right of the hall is a door leading to the Post-office of the Senate, a large and handsomely frescoed apartment, the principal feature of which is a small and tasteful post-office constructed of black walnut and plate glass. Each Senator and officer of the Senate is assigned a private box in this office, in which his letters, papers, and other mail matter are placed, subject to his order. Letters and papers from any member or officer of the Senate are mailed here. The office has its own Postmaster, who is appointed by the Senate. Mails are received and despatched from here direct, at stated times.

Adjoining the Post-office, and opening into it, is the office of the Sergeant-at-Arms of the Senate.

Returning from the Post-office to the entrance hall,

we notice a room at the side opposite the Post-office. This is the Stationery Department of the Senate, from which Senators, attachés, etc., are furnished with stationery, at the expense of the Government.

At the end of the hall is a door leading into the Senate Chamber. While that body is in session, this door is always in charge of an official, whose duty it is to prevent the intrusion of strangers upon the floor of the Senate.

The door on the right, at the lower end of the hall, opens into the Ladies' Reception Room, an elegant apartment, magnificently furnished, and beautifully frescoed. The carpets and hangings are of the richest materials. Marble columns support the ceiling, and splendid mirrors adorn the walls. The furniture is elegant and luxurious, and a costly chandelier hangs in the centre. A door leads into the private passage in rear of the Senate Chamber, so that Senators can reach the apartment without passing through the public halls. Ladies wishing to speak with a Senator, present their cards to the doorkeeper of this room, and await his pleasure in the reception room. The apartment is much frequented by "female lobby members," and by loungers in general.

Passing into the hall again, we cross it, and find ourselves at the foot of the stairway leading to the third floor. On our right hand is the famous statue of Benjamin Franklin, by Hiram Powers, a fine and life-like work. Passing by the stairs, we enter the south corridor of the Senate, which is spacious and handsomely ornamented. Half way down the corridor are two doors; the one on the right being the principal entrance to the Senate Chamber, and the other leading off to the old building. At the west end is a fine portrait of Mr. Lincoln, by Coggeswell. A bust of Chief-Justice Taney stands at the eastern end. An iron doorway admits us to the western corridor. The Senate Chamber is still on our right. The rooms on the left are the offices of the Secretary of the Senate and his clerks.

From the north end of the corridor, on the right, a private passage leads to the suite of rooms in the rear of the Senate Chamber, which are the handsomest in the Capitol. The first of these is called *The President's Room*, so called in consequence of its being set apart for the use of the Chief Magistrate of the Republic, during his visits to the Capitol. The President does not often occupy it during the session of Congress. During the last day of the session, however, he is present here, for the purpose of signing such bills as may be hurried through the two Houses at the close of their labors.

The apartment is small, square in form, and is one of the gems of the Capitol. The walls are adorned with portraits in fresco, and the ceiling is ornamented with representations of fruits and gilding. The ceiling is vaulted, and in the corners are portraits of Christopher Columbus, Benjamin Franklin, Americus Vespucci, and William Brewster. There are other figures on the ceiling, one of which typifies the strength and glory of the Union. The furniture is elegant and tasteful. There are several large mirrors set into the

THE SPEAKER OF THE HOUSE COUNTING THE VOTES.

walls, and a chandelier of vast proportions hangs from the centre of the ceiling, affording a pleasant light at night.

The portraits on the walls are those of President Washington and his first Cabinet, good men and true, and who deserve to be ever held in grateful remembrance by their countrymen. Mr. James Parton, in his biography of Mr. Jefferson, draws this pleasant picture of the assembling of this Cabinet:

"Such were the gentlemen who were gathered round the Council table at the President's house in New York, in 1790. How interesting the group! At the head of the table, General Washington, now fifty-eight, his frame as erect as ever, but his face showing deep traces of the thousand anxious hours he had passed. Not versed in the lore of schools, not gifted with a great sum of intellect, the eternal glory of this man is that he used all the mind he had in patient endeavors to find out the right way; ever on the watch to keep out of his decision everything like bias or prejudice; never deciding till he had exhausted every source of elucidation within his reach. Some questions he could not decide with his own mind, and he knew he could not. In such cases, he bent all his powers to ascertaining how the subject appeared to minds fitted to grapple with it, and getting them to view it without prejudice. . . . His glory is, that he was not richly endowed, not sufficient unto himself, not indifferent to human rights, opinions, and preferences; but feeling deeply his need of help, sought it, where alone it was to be found, in minds fitted by nature and training to supply his lack. It is this heartfelt desire to be right which shines so affectingly from the plain words of Washington, and gives him rank so far above the gorgeous bandits whom hero worshippers adore.

"On the right of the President, in the place of honor, sat Jefferson, now forty-seven, the senior of all his colleagues; older in public service, too, than any of them; tall, erect, ruddy; noticeably quiet and unobtrusive in his address and demeanor; the least pugnacious of men. Not a fanatic, not an enthusiast; but an old-fashioned Whig, nurtured upon 'old Coke,' enlightened by twenty-five years' intense discussion—with pen, tongue, and sword—of Cokean principles. Fresh from the latest commentary upon Coke—the Ruins of the Bastille—and wearing still his red Paris waistcoat and breeches, he was an object of particular interest to all men; and, doubtless, often relieved the severity of business by some thrilling relation out of his late foreign experience.

"Opposite him, on the President's left, was the place of Hamilton, Secretary of the Treasury, in all the alertness and vigor of thirty-three years. If time had matured his talents, it had not lessened his self-sufficiency; because, as yet, all his short life had been a success, and he had associated chiefly with men who possessed nothing either of his fluency or his arithmetic. A positive, vehement, little gentleman, with as firm a faith in the apparatus of finance, as General Knox had in great guns. He was now in the full tide of activity, lobbying measures through Congress, and organizing the Treasury Department—the most conspicuous man in the Administration, except the President. As usual, his unseen work was his best. In organizing a system of collecting, keeping, and disbursing the revenue, he employed so much tact, forethought, and fertility, that his successors have each, in turn, admired and retained his most important devices. He arranged the system so that the Secretary of the Treasury, at any moment, could survey the whole working of it; and he held at command all the resources of the United States, subject to lawful use, without being able to divert one dollar to a purpose not specially authorized. He could not draw his own pittance of salary without the signatures of the four chief officers of the department—Comptroller, Auditor, Treasurer, and Register.

"Henry Knox, whom President Washington appointed Secretary of War, had been, before the Revolution, a thriving Boston bookseller, with so strong a natural turn for soldiering, that he belonged to two military companies at once, and read all the works in his shop which treated of military things. From Bunker Hill, where he served as a volunteer aid to General Artemas Ward, to Yorktown, where he commanded and ably directed the artillery, he was an efficient, faithful soldier; and, after the War, being retained in service, he had the chief charge of the military affairs of the Confederacy, high in the confidence of the disbanded army and its chief. He was a man of large, athletic frame, tall, deep chested, loud voiced, brave, delighting in the whirl and rush of field artillery, and the thunder of siege guns.

General Knox had much faith in the tools he was accustomed to use. His original remedy for the ills of the Confederacy was as simple and complete as a patent medicine: Extinguish the State Governments, and establish an imposing General Government, with plenty of soldiers to enforce its decrees. In the Cabinet of President Washington, he was the giant shadow of his diminutive friend Hamilton. When Hamilton had spoken, Knox was usually ready to say in substance, 'My own opinion better expressed.'

"Edmund Randolph, who accepted the post of Attorney General, besides being a Randolph and a Virginian, had this claim to the regard of General Washington: he had been disinherited by his father for siding with the Revolution. He was a rising lawyer, twenty-two years of age, when his father, the King's Attorney General, withdrew to England—an act upon which the son commented by mounting his horse and riding by the side of General Washington, as his volunteer aid, until the General could organize his military household. This marked 'discrepancy' cost the young man his estate, and made his fortune. The next year, young as he was, Virginia sent him to the convention which called upon Congress to declare independence. At twenty-six, he was a member of the War Congress, in which he served three years, and at thirty-three was Governor of Virginia. Being a Randolph, we might infer, even without Mr. Wirt's full-length portrait of him, in the British Spy, that he was a man of great but peculiar talents, resembling his eccentric kinsman, John Randolph, of a later day, but sounder and stronger than that meteoric personage. Tall, meagre, emaciated, loose-jointed, awkward, with small head, and a face dark and wrinkled, nothing in his appearance denoted a superior person except his eyes, which were black and most brilliant. Mr. Wirt, who knew him some years later, when, after much public service, he had resumed the leadership of the Virginia bar, tells us that he owed his supremacy there to a single faculty, that of seeing and seizing at once the real point at issue in a controversy.

"Age had not quenched the vivacity of either of the four secretaries; Jefferson, forty-seven; Knox forty; Randolph thirty-seven; Hamilton thirty-three. When, in the world's history was so young a group charged with a task so difficult, so momentous?"

The *Vice-President's Room* is at the opposite end of the private passage way. It contains a large portrait of Washington by Rembrandt Peale, and is handsomely ornamented and frescoed. It is much larger than the President's Room, but is more simply furnished. It is used by the Vice-President of the United States, (or, in his absence, by the presiding officer of the Senate,) who receives his friends and transacts much of his official business here.

Lying between the President's and Vice-President's Rooms is a suite of sumptuous apartments—the most magnificent in the building—known as the Marble Room. The total length of the three rooms is about 85 feet, the width 21½ feet, and the height 19½ feet. The floor is an exquisite piece of mosaic in marble, and the ceiling is in panels of slightly colored Italian marble, and rests upon a series of magnificent white Italian marble pillars with elaborate capitals. The walls are adorned with large and superb mirrors, and are veneered with the finest specimens of Tennessee marble in the country. The windows are richly curtained, the furniture is exquisite, and the apartment is lighted by a large brass chandelier. The suite is used by the Senators as a retiring and private reception room. They are not altogether worthy of so much magnificence, as it is not uncommon to see cigar stumps on the floor and tobacco stains on the marble.

The private apartments of the two Houses of Congress are not open to any but invited guests during the sessions of those bodies, but visitors are permitted to examine them during the recess of Congress.

Returning to the west corridor, we notice near the foot of the stairway Stone's fine statue of John Hancock.

There are two stairways in each of the new wings, leading from the main floor to the gallery. They are amongst the chief beauties of the building, and are constructed of a fine quality of white and variegated marble, with massive balustrades of the same material.

Ascending the western stairway of the Senate wing we pause to notice the large painting on canvas, by Walker, representing the storming of the Castle of Chapultepec by the American army under General Scott, on the 13th of September, 1847. The scene represents the grim old castle in the background, which, together with its formidable outworks, is wreathed in smoke. A heavy fire is being maintained by the defenders, and the Mexican tricolor floats defiantly above the seemingly impregnable lines. The American forces are struggling, in the foreground, through the dense chaparal, and are steadily winning their way, step by step, towards the castle. The dead and wounded, and broken guns and artillery carriages lie about. An Indian woman with her babe strapped to her back, is seen supporting the head of her dying husband, unmindful of the storm of battle which is raging around her. The picture represents the battle at the moment of the consultation held between General Quitman and several of the officers of his advanced division, when the troops had carried the outworks at the foot of the castle, and opened the way along the aqueduct towards the Garita de Belen. The conception is brilliant, and the execution fine. The painting cost $6000, and was designed for the room of the Senate Committee on Military Affairs. This fact explains the singular shape of the canvas.

The upper corridor on the third floor extends around the entire wing. Opening into it are the doors of the rooms of Committees, a Document Room, and a ladies' retiring room. It is handsomely ornamented and tiled. The doors on the inner side lead into the galleries of the Senate Chamber.

This magnificent chamber is 112 feet in length, 82 feet wide, and 30 feet high. The ceiling is constructed entirely of cast iron, deeply panelled, with stained glass skylights, and ornamented with foliage, pendants, and drops, of th richest and most elaborate description

The walls and ceiling are painted with strong, brilliant colors, and all the iron work is bronzed and gilded. A cushioned gallery extends entirely around the hall. That portion immediately over the chair of the Vice-President of the United States is assigned to the reporters of the press, and a section enclosed by handsome iron railings, and immediately facing the Chair, is for the use of the members of the Diplomatic Corps. The rest of the gallery is divided into sections for ladies and gentlemen. A fine view of the hall can be obtained from any part of it. The space under the gallery is enclosed and used as cloak rooms, etc. The gallery will seat one thousand persons.

Immediately opposite the main door of the Chamber is the chair of the Vice-President of the United States, who presides over the Senate. It is placed on a platform of pure white marble, and behind a desk of the same material. Just below this is a similar but larger desk, used by the Secretary of the Senate and his assistants, and at the foot of this table are the chairs of the short-hand reporters of the debates.

The floor rises in the form of an amphitheatre from the space in front of the Secretary's desk to the rear. Along these rows of steps, the registers are built in the floor, and keep the temperature of the Chamber at a fixed heat. The desks of the Senators are of oak, of a handsome and convenient pattern, and are arranged in three semicircular rows facing the Chair. A comfortable armchair is provided for each desk; and sofas and chairs for the convenience of Senators and those entitled to the privileges of the floor, are arranged around the sides of the hall. The choice of seats is determined by drawing lots.

During the day the glass ceiling allows a soft and pleasant light to pass into the chamber, and at night the gas jets, which are arranged above the skylights, shed through the beautiful hall a radiance which can scarcely be distinguished from the light of the sun.

Leaving the galleries, we pass around to the eastern stairway and admire its beauty. Our attention is called to a painting by Rembrandt Peale, which adorns the first landing of the stairway. It represents Washington on horseback, reconnoitring the position of the British Army at Yorktown, previous to opening his lines of approach. He is accompanied by Lafayette, Hamilton, Lincoln, Knox, and Rochambeau. This painting does not belong to the Government, though the Senate once voted $4500 for its purchase.

We leave the North Wing by the south door, and stroll through the corridor connecting this wing with the central building. We are soon in the dark, circular lobby of the old Senate Chamber, and from this we pass into the magnificent Rotunda, to which we shall soon return. At the south side of the Rotunda is a door leading directly to one of the most interesting and memorable apartments in the building—the old Hall of Representatives.

This beautiful chamber is semicircular in form, and the ceiling is vaulted. It is 95 feet long, and the height from the floor to the apex of the ceiling is 60 feet. The ceiling is panelled and beautifully painted in imitation of that of the Pantheon at Rome. It is supported by twenty-four magnificent columns of American marble, which extend around the western side of the hall, and behind which are the galleries. A handsomely painted cupola rises from the centre of the ceiling and admits the light. At the south side of the tympanum of the arch, is a colossal statue of Liberty, executed in plaster by Signor Cansici, and beneath it is an American eagle in sandstone, modelled from life by Signor Valaperti. The speaker's chair was formerly placed under this eagle. Over the door leading into the Rotunda is Franzoni's beautiful statue representing History, with listening ear, recording the passing events in an open volume. She is standing in a winged car, the wheel of which rests on a globe ornamented with the signs of the zodiac. The wheel forms the face of a clock, the works of which are placed back of it. The whole is cut out of pure white marble, and forms one of the most beautiful ornaments of the Capitol.

The House of Representatives held its sessions here from 1825 until the completion of the new Hall, in 1859, and it was the scene of some of the most interesting events in the history of the country. A general desire was expressed throughout the country that the Hall should be preserved unchanged as a reminder of the past, and in 1864, Congress set it apart as a gallery of statuary. By the terms of this law each State is to have the privilege of sending hither the statues of two of her most eminent sons. In this way a national collection will be gradually formed, and it is to be hoped that it will be worthy of the nation and the illustrious dead it is to represent. The Hall has been fitted up for its present purpose, and statues are already beginning to take their places. Among these are Vinnie Ream's statue of Abraham Lincoln, Hablot K. Browne's fine statue of General Nathaniel Greene, and Emma Stebbins's statue of Roger Williams.

Passing under the eagle's outspread wings, and leaving the hall by the south door, we reach the corridor leading from the old building to the new South Wing. At the entrance we behold the famous Bronze Door, which is intended for the main entrance to the South Wing. This magnificent work of art, the most superb of its kind in the world, was designed and modelled in Rome, in 1858, by Randolph Rogers, the American sculptor, cast at the Royal Foundry at Munich, by F. Von Müller, and completed in 1861. It weighs 20,000 pounds, and cost thirty thousand dollars. It is seventeen feet high, nine feet wide, and is folding or double. The casing is semicircular at the top, and projects about a foot in front of the leaves of the door. Around the casing extends a handsome border, emblematic of conquest and navigation. The key of the arch of the casing is ornamented with a fine head of Columbus, beneath which is the American Eagle with outspread wings. Four figures, representing Asia, Africa, Europe, and America, stand at the top and bottom of the casing. The upper right-hand figure represents Asia, the upper left-hand figure Africa, the lower right-hand figure Europe, and the lower left-hand figure America.

There are eight square panels in the door, besides

the semicircular transom panel. Between these panels are ten heads, five on each leaf of the door, "representing historians who have written on his (Columbus') voyages, from his own time down to the present day, ending with Irving and Prescott." On the right and left of the panels are sixteen statuettes, set in niches, representing the most eminent of the contemporaries of the great discoverer. The names of these worthies are marked on the door, and the figures can be easily recognized. In describing them we shall begin with the lower right-hand figure, which is opposite the first part of the story told by the door.

The figure is that of JUAN PEREZ, Prior of the Convent of La Rabida, the most faithful of all Columbus' friends, and through whose influence he was enabled to state his scheme to the Spanish Queen.

The next above is CORTEZ, the Conqueror of Mexico.

The third is DON ALONZO DE OJEDA, a distinguished but unfaithful follower of Columbus.

The top figure is AMERIGO VESPUCCI, after whom the Continent is named.

At the top of the double row, between the two leaves of the door, are PEDRO GONZALES DE MENDOZA, Archbishop of Toledo, and Grand Cardinal of Spain, sometimes called, on account of his immense influence, the "third King of Spain," and POPE ALEXANDER VI. The Cardinal, who was an early patron of Columbus, stands on the right, and the Pope is on the left.

The figures immediately below them are FERDINAND and ISABELLA, King and Queen of Spain, the queen being placed on the right.

Below them are DONNA BEATRIZ DE BOBADILLA, Marchioness of Moya, one of the fast friends of Columbus, and CHARLES VIII., King of France. The artist was unable to find a likeness of the noble lady here represented, and gave to her the features of Mrs. Rogers, his wife.

HENRY VII., of England, and JOHN II., of Portugal, form the lowest pair, the English monarch being on the right. John of Portugal would not listen to Columbus' proposals; but Henry carefully weighed the scheme, which was presented to him by the brother of the discoverer. Before his answer was ready, however, the New World was found.

MARTIN ALONZO PINZON stands at the bottom of the left row. He was the captain of the "Pinta," one of the little squadron of Columbus, and enjoyed the honor of being the first to see the "land" of the Western World. Eventually, he betrayed his friend and commander, and died from grief and mortification.

Above him is BARTHOLOMEW COLUMBUS, the brother of the great man, and appointed by him Lieutenant-Governor of the Indies. This figure wears the face of the artist, Mr. Rogers, as it was impossible to procure a likeness of the subject.

Above him is VASCO NUNEZ DE BALBOA, who, crossing the Isthmus of Darien, with his followers, discovered the Pacific Ocean on the 29th of September, 1510.

FRANCISCO PIZARRO, the cruel conqueror of Peru, fills the topmost niche, and completes the group.

We now come to the exquisite pictures embraced in the panels of the door. The work is in *alto relievo*, the figures standing out boldly from the surface. Every detail is perfect, and the gazer's emotions of admiration are strongly mingled with wonder that such an elaborate design has been so faithfully and minutely executed. An oil painting or steel engraving could not more forcibly or perfectly tell the story.

The lowest right-hand panel begins the tale, the transom panel being the central scene.

PANEL I. Columbus is expounding his theory of finding the Indies by sailing due west, to the Council of Salamanca. This Council gravely deliberated the subject, and solemnly concluded that the project was "vain and impossible, and not becoming great princes to engage in on such slender grounds as had been adduced."

PANEL II. Weary and heart-sick, on foot, and leading his son, Diego, a mere lad, by the hand, Columbus sought shelter in the Convent of La Rabida, near Palos. He was without friends or money, and was in despair of having his grand scheme of discovery adopted by any potentate. The monks of the convent received him kindly, and induced him to remain with them a long time. While here, he stated his plan and hopes to the prior, Juan Perez, who had been Queen Isabella's confessor. Here he also met Alonzo Pinzon, who accompanied him in his subsequent voyage. The prior at once became warmly enlisted in the scheme, and mentioned it to Donna Beatriz de Bobadilla, an attendant and favorite of the queen. The two brought the matter to the queen's notice, and pressed it so thoroughly that her Majesty sent Columbus a sum of money sufficient to enable him to appear at Court, and plead his cause in person. The scene embraced in this panel represents him setting out from the convent to wait upon the queen.

PANEL III. Represents Columbus laying his plan before the King and Queen of Spain. The queen leans forward with eagerness, but the king holds back coldly and doubtingly. The courtiers in the background regard the bold adventurer with looks of mingled scorn and incredulity.

PANEL IV. Is at the top of the right leaf of the door, and represents "The Departure from Palos." The admiral's ships lie waiting in the harbor, while he is standing on the shore, bidding farewell to his son, and confiding him to the care of his friend, the prior.

THE TRANSOM PANEL. This extends across the whole door, is semicircular in form, and represents the admiral and his companions landing at San Salvador, and taking formal possession of the island. The banner of Spain is held aloft by Columbus, whose other hand holds a sword. Boats are coming in from the ships in the offing, and a group of natives crouch at the foot of a large tree, gazing at the new-comers with wonder and fear.

PANEL V. Is at the top of the left leaf of the door, and represents the first intercourse between the Indians and the discoverers. One of the sailors is seen approaching the admiral, bearing on his shoulders an Indian girl whom he has captured and bound. Columbus sternly rebukes him for his cruelty, and orders the instant release of the girl.

PANEL VI. Represents "The Triumphal Entry into Barcelona." Columbus, having returned from the New World, bringing with him the proofs of his discoveries, is entering the City of Barcelona, amidst the plaudits and cheers of the assembled multitude. The admiral, on horseback, is seen in the foreground.

PANEL VII. Represents the wrongs of Columbus. Don Francisco de Bobadilla, having been sent to the New World, to investigate the charges brought against the admiral by his enemies, took sides against him, and sent him back to Spain in chains. The panel represents the arrival of the admiral in chains, on board the vessel which was to convey him to Europe. The officers of the ship, filled with generous indignation, desired to relieve him of his fetters, but he replied, "No; I will wear them as a memento of the gratitude of princes."

PANEL VIII. Represents "The Death of Columbus." On the voyage home, Don Francisco de Bobadilla, and all his crew, were drowned, but the admiral reached Spain in safety, to find the charges against him cleared away. The queen was dead, however, and King Ferdinand was ungrateful to the man who had given a new world to Spain. The admiral was thus left without friends at court.

Landing near San Lucas, Columbus proceeded to Seville. He was poor in purse, and broken down in health, besides being feeble from age. He made repeated efforts to obtain redress for the wrongs done him, but failed in all. He died at Valladolid, May 20th, 1506, being about seventy years old.

The picture represents the chamber in which he died. His friends are gathered around his bed, the last rites of the Church have been received, and a priest holds aloft a crucifix, in order that his last earthly gaze may be fixed upon the symbol of his redemption. The world fast recedes from the dying eyes, the weak lips murmur, " *In Manus tuas, Domine, commendo spiritum meum*," " Into Thy Hands, O Lord, I commend my spirit," and the great, grand soul passes into a blessed eternity.

Columbus was buried with great pomp in the Convent of St. Francis, in Valladolid. In 1513 his remains were removed to the Monastery of Las Cuevas, at Seville. In 1536, they were removed from Spain to St. Domingo, where they rested until 1796, when they were carried to Cuba, and interred with magnificent display, in the Cathedral at Havana.

Not yet, however, have they found their proper resting-place. That place is under the dome of the Capitol of the Great Republic of the New World.

The door is indescribably beautiful, and an accurate description of it is an impossibility. It must be seen to be appreciated.

We pass by the door, whose beauties tempt us to linger over it, and through the corridor connecting the new South Wing with the main building. A telegraph office on our left affords communication with all parts of the country, and guide-books and photographs are offered for sale at a stand on our right. Leaving this, we enter the north corridor of the House wing. It is handsomely tiled and frescoed. Immediately in front of us is the principal entrance to the Hall of the House, in charge of the efficient and accomplished door-keeper and his assistants. Turning to the left, we pass into the East Corridor, and find ourselves at the foot of one of the marble stairways leading to the gallery. Here stands Powers' famous statue of Jefferson. It is claimed to be an excellent likeness, and is wonderfully like the late General Randolph, of Virginia, who was his grandson, and said to be the image of him. Beyond it we find ourselves in the vestibule communicating with the magnificent Southeast Portico. This is the principal entrance to the wing, and will soon be ornamented with the beautiful bronze door we have described.

On the right of the vestibule is the Post-office of the House. This establishment is similar to that of the Senate, but is larger and handsomer. It is conducted in the manner we have described in connection with the Senate Post-office. It opens into the East Corridor, and not into the vestibule.

The South Corridor, immediately in rear of the Hall of the House, is for the private use of Members, and is railed off from the other passages. It is carpeted, and has an air of comfort and elegance. Bronze stairways, similar to those of the Senate wing, lead from this passage to the basement, for the convenience of "Members only." The apartment at the eastern end of this passage is the ladies' reception room. It is beautifully furnished and carpeted, and the walls and ceilings are ornamented with fine frescoes. Ladies having business with Congressmen are shown into this apartment, while their cards are sent to the Member's seat in the Hall.

If he desires to see the lady, he seeks her in the reception room. Lobbyists are well known to the attachés of the chamber, and could the silent walls speak, their revelations would create a sensation in the Federal City, and elsewhere.

The Office of the Sergeant-at-Arms of the House adjoins the reception room. It is handsomely ornamented and comfortably furnished.

The Speaker's room is immediately in the centre of the South Wing, and faces the south. It is entered by two doors leading from the private passage. It is a large, elegant apartment, and is for the private use of the Speaker of the House of Representatives. Its carpets and draperies are rich and elegant, and the furniture is costly and tasteful. The ceiling is frescoed, and the walls are adorned with portraits of nearly all the distinguished men who have been speaker of the House since the first organization of Congress.

The adjoining apartment on the west is for the private use of Members of the House. It is elegantly fitted up, and is used as a private reception room.

The western end of the wing is occupied with offices of the Clerk of the House of Representatives. Visitors are not admitted to these offices, or to those of the Secretary of the Senate, at any time, as the officials engaged therein are always busy with the discharge of their duties. Committee Rooms open into the various corridors, and are handsomely furnished and elaborately frescoed.

At the north end of the west corridor is a splendid marble stairway leading to the third floor and the galleries. The wall, from the first landing to the ceiling is ornamented with Leutze's great painting, entitled, "Westward the Course of Empire Takes Its Way." It is lighted from a skylight in the roof, and is seen to the best advantage from the upper corridor.

The picture is painted in fresco, but the coloring is softer and more life-like than is often seen in such paintings. The surface is rough, but the work has been done with such a master-hand that it seems as if it were real life. Gaze at it for hours, and the eye will discover some new beauty every hour. However minute it may be, every detail is brought out with the utmost fidelity. The painting is the greatest work of art in the possession of the Government, and one of the grandest in the world.

The scene represents a train of emigrants crossing the Rocky Mountains. They have reached the summit of the range, from which a glorious view stretches out before them to the westward. The adventurers consist of the usual class of emigrants, men, women, and children. There are several wagons and a number of horses in the train. The faces of the emigrants express the various emotions which fill their hearts as they gaze upon the glorious scene before them. Some are full of life and vigor, and hope beams in every feature, whilst others are struggling with sickness and despair. The advance of the train has been momentarily checked by a huge tree which has fallen across their path, and two stout men, under the direction of the leader of the party, who is sitting on his horse, are engaged in hewing it away with axes. Two men have climbed to the summit of a neighboring rocky crag, on which they have planted the banner of the Republic, which is seen flapping out proudly from its lofty perch. In the foreground stands a manly youth, clasping his father's long rifle with a firm grasp, and gazing towards the promised land with a countenance glowing with hope and energy. His sister, hopeful as himself, is seated by her mother's side, on a buffalo robe which has been thrown over a rock. The mother's face is sad, but patient. She knows well the privations, toil, and hardships which await them in the new home-land, but she tries to share the enthusiasm and hope of her children. She clasps her nursing infant to her breast, and listens to her husband, who stands by and points her to the new country where they will all have a home of their own. Her face is inexpressibly beautiful. The rich, warm light of the rising sun streams brightly over the whole scene, and lends to it a magical glow. The legend, " Westward the Course of Empire Takes Its Way," is inscribed over the painting in letters of gold.

An elaborate illuminated border, illustrative of the advance of civilization in the West, surrounds the painting. It is in itself one of the most elaborate works of art in the Capitol.

Beneath the painting, and detached from it, is a view of "The Golden Gate," the entrance to the harbor of San Francisco.

On the right of the picture is a portrait of Daniel Boone, below which are the lines:

"The Spirit grows with its allotted Spaces :—
The mind is narrowed in a narrow Sphere."

On the left of the painting is a portrait of Captain William Clarke, and the lines:

> "No pent up Utica contracts our powers;
> But the whole boundless Continent is ours."

From the "guide" of Mr. Wyeth, we learn that the process of affixing the painting to the wall is termed *Stereochrome,* and is sometimes called "Water-glass painting." "The wall is coated with a preparation of clean quartz sand mixed with the least possible quantity of lime; and after the application of this the surface is scraped to remove the outer coating in contact with the atmosphere. It is then washed with a solution of silesia, soda, potash, and water. As the painter applies his colors, he moistens his work by squirting distilled water upon it. When finished it is washed over with the silesia solution. The picture also in its progress is washed with the same solution, and the colors thus becoming incorporated in the flinty coating, the picture is rendered hard and durable as stone itself." Leutze was paid $20,000 for this magnificent work.

We leave the painting with regret, and pass into the upper corridor, which extends entirely around the third floor. The doors on the outer side lead to rooms used by the Committees of the House, and those on the inner side to the galleries of the House. There are nine Committee Rooms opening into this corridor, all of which are splendidly fitted up. The only door on the north side leads to the Library of the House. This apartment is situated over the corridor connecting the South Wing with the old building. It contains nothing but documents published by order of the House of Representatives, and is for the exclusive use of members.

Passing through one of the inner doors, we enter the galleries of the magnificent Hall of the House of Representatives, and pause for a while to admire the beauty of its design and the comfort of its arrangements.

The hall is 139 feet long, 93 feet wide, and 36 feet high. It is of sufficient size to afford comfortable accommodations for the increased number of members a century hence. It has an area of 12,927 square feet. The galleries extend entirely around it, and will seat 1200 persons. The seats are cushioned, and present a handsome appearance. That portion opposite the Speaker's chair is ornamented with a magnificent bronze clock. Immediately over the Speaker's chair, is the Reporters' Gallery, which is for the exclusive use of the Press. It is furnished with handsome private desks, one of which is assigned to the accredited Reporter for some particular journal for the entire session. Some twenty-five or thirty of the leading newspapers of the land are represented here.

The rest of the gallery is divided into sections for the members of the Diplomatic Corps, for ladies, and for gentlemen unaccompanied by ladies. These are separated from each other by iron railings.

The ceiling is of cast-iron, and is similar to that of the Senate Chamber, but handsomer. In the centre is a large skylight containing a number of panels ornamented with the coats of arms of the various States and Territories of the Union. The hall is lighted by means of this skylight. "An arrangement of movable metallic plates, on the principle of Venetian blinds, is placed under the sunny side of the respective roofs of the House and Senate, so that the same amount of light may be admitted all the time." The arrangement of the gas-lights is similar to that of the Senate Chamber. Fifteen hundred burners are placed over the glass of the ceiling, at a distance of an inch apart. Over each one of these passes an incombustible wire. The gas is turned on, an electric current flashed along the wire, and in an instant the hall is filled with a soft, pleasing light, which resembles that of the sun.

Opposite the principal door, are three desks of pure white marble, ranged one above the other. The highest is occupied by the Speaker of the House, the next by the Clerk of the House and his assistants, and the lowest by the official reporters of the debates.

The registers for warming the hall are built in the sides of the different steps into which the floor is divided, and openings in the wall permit the heated air to pass off. The engines which work the heating and ventilating apparatus, are situated in the basement.

The ceiling is magnificently painted, and the walls below the galleries are laid off in large panels, which are to be ornamented with paintings in fresco illustrative of the principal events of the history of the country. One of these panels has already been filled with a magnificent fresco, by Brumidi, illustrating an event which occurred at the Siege of Yorktown.

On the right and left of the Speaker's chair are full length portraits of Washington and Lafayette. The portrait of Washington was painted by Vanderlyn, by order of Congress, and that of Lafayette was presented to Congress by the great Frenchman himself, on the occasion of his visit to the United States in 1825. Both pictures were among the ornaments of the old Hall of Representatives.

The floor rises from south to north, like an amphitheatre. The seats and desks of the members (which are similar to those of the Senators) are arranged along this amphitheatre, in successive circles, facing the Speaker. There are at present 236 of these desks and seats in use. The desks and chairs are all of a handsome pattern, and make a very showy appearance. Seats are chosen by lot at the beginning of every session. The desk of the Sergeant-at-Arms is on the Speaker's right, that of the Door-keeper on his left.

The space under the galleries is enclosed and occupied by two cloak rooms for Members, a Barber Shop for Members, a Folding Room, and Document Room.

There is also a private room for the use of ladies, at the southeastern end of the ladies' gallery.

Leaving the gallery, we descend to the main floor by the eastern stairway, which is constructed of polished Tennessee marble, with splendid columns and balustrades of the same material. It is exactly similar to the western stairway, by which we reach the galleries. On the first landing hangs a fine portrait of General Scott, mounted on his war-horse, by Mr. Edward Troyes. It was painted by order of the Legislature of Virginia, but being unfinished at the time of the breaking out of the Rebellion, was left on the artist's hands. It is to be hoped that Congress will purchase it, as it is the best portrait of the old hero in existence.

Continuing our descent of the marble stairs, we find ourselves in the basement of the South Wing. We enter a handsome corridor running north and south, lighted by the windows at each end. To the left of the stairway is the vestibule leading to the carriage-way under the southeast portico. Passing westward, the first room across the corridor containing the stairway is fitted up with a row of water closets for gentlemen. The next room contains the Members' baths. These consist of a row of handsome closets, finished in black walnut, each of which contains a large bath tub, with hot and cold water for both plunge and shower baths, a wash-stand, and a water closet. The floor is laid with marble tiles, and every thing is upon the handsomest and most comfortable plan. The room is for the use of the members and officers of the House alone, and is one of the most luxurious establishments of its kind in the world. When not in use, it is always open to the inspection of visitors. The next door on the right of the passage leads into the restaurant.

This establishment occupies two rooms, and is entered from the passage we have been traversing, and from the central corridor. It is handsomely fitted up, and is carried on for the accommodation of the members, officials, and visitors.

The central corridor traverses the basement from north to south, and joining the corridors of the old building, which communicate with those of the Senate wing, affords a continuous passage from one end of the Capitol to the other. In the House wing it is 24½ feet broad, and contains thirty monolithic fluted columns of white marble, with capitals foliated with tobacco leaves and buds, which support a panelled ceiling of cast iron.

The Committee Rooms on this floor are large and beautiful. There are thirteen of them. That on the south of the western entrance is the room of the Committee on Agriculture, and is one of the most beautiful apartments in the Capitol. It is magnificently furnished. The ceiling is arched, and is divided into four compartments, containing representations of the four seasons. In the east is Flora, scattering the flowers of Spring; in the south, Ceres holds sheaves of ripe grain; in the west, Bacchus is sporting amidst clusters of the vine; and in the north, Boreas brings storms of wind and rain.

The eastern wall is ornamented with a painting in fresco, representing " Cincinnatus Summoned from his Plough to be Dictator of Rome," and on the opposite wall is a companion picture, " Putnam Leaving his Plough to Fight for Independence." The paintings are all by Signor Brumidi.

In Room 34 of this wing, is the entrance to the " Heating and Ventilating Apparatus." A long passage way leads to the machinery, which is both novel and interesting.

There are two small engines, one on the right and the other on the left of the passage, which are placed in rooms of a slightly lower level. The cylinders are upright, and the steam is supplied from the boilers in the furnace room. They work with a droning sound, and the click of the piston rods and cranks is deadened by an abundance of oil. These engines turn large fan-wheels, one of which is eighteen and the other twenty-four feet in diameter, and from which they are separated by glass windows. A door communicates with the fan chamber, to which visitors are admitted, if they desire it; but the draught of air is so strong in this room, and the revolutions of the fan are so rapid, that one does not care to remain long in it. Opposite the engines are immense iron cases, or chambers, containing miles of coiled iron pipes. Steam is generated in boilers placed in another apartment, and is forced through these pipe coils, thereby producing a certain and regular degree of heat. By means of the fans, a current of fresh air is drawn into the chambers from without, and driven across these hot pipe coils until it is thoroughly warmed. Huge pipes then conduct it to all parts of the wing, the fan being sufficiently powerful to create a strong draught in the highest story of the building. In this way, an even and regular temperature is maintained in all parts of the Capitol. The fresh air, after being warmed, is constantly passing into the rooms and corridors through the registers, and it was hoped that the strong draught would produce a thorough and perfect ventilation of the entire building.

The boilers and furnaces for generating the steam are located in an adjoining vault, which is placed at a lower level than the engine rooms, and which opens (in both wings) into the western court of the old building. The vaults would be insufferably hot at all times, and especially in warm weather, but for an excellent arrangement which keeps a current of cool air constantly passing through them.

In the summer, the building is kept cool by shutting off the steam, and forcing the fresh air through the registers. The excellence of this system is manifest in every part of the Capitol. Many of the principal rooms have no natural means of ventilation, and would be damp and unhealthy but for this most ingenious arrangement.

Every thing is kept scrupulously neat and clean in this department. The machinery shines like polished gold and silver, and you might rub your pocket handkerchief over the floors of the engine-rooms without soiling it. The engineer has several assistants, and is provided with a handsomely fitted-up office, the perfect order and neatness of which attests the care and regularity with which his duties are discharged.

There is an apparatus in the Senate-wing basement, in Room 59, exactly similar to that we have described above. Besides warming their respective wings, these engines also supply heat and ventilation to the principal portions of the old building.

Powerful as these engines are, they have fallen short of the expectations of the Architect of the Capitol, who believed that they would supply a perfect ventilation to all parts of the building. They fail, however, to accomplish this in the most important portion of the South Wing—the hall of the House of Representatives. The Washington correspondent of the New York *Tribune*, writing December 15, 1872, says:

"The ventilation of the House is excessively bad this season. The air frequently becomes so foul that it assumes an appreciable color, and settles in cloudy, blue masses in the corners of the room. People in the galleries appear to suffer more than members upon the floor, and persons of weak lungs or delicate constitutions find it impossible to breathe the poisonous atmosphere for the few hours occupied by the daily session, without headache or more severe indisposition. The effect upon the members is in the long run more serious, however, because they are obliged to breathe the impure air day after day. Two or three die every year, whose deaths may be indirectly, if not immediately, traced to this cause; and many find their health ultimately wrecked after a few years' service. Theoretically the fans in the basement force up more fresh air than can possibly be consumed by the two hundred people on the floor, and the two or three hundred spectators ordinarily in the galleries; but practically, not nearly enough air is supplied, so that the same air must be breathed over and over again, until it has barely vitality enough to support life. The defects of the system employed for ventilating the hall are recognized by every member. Scarcely a session passes without an agitation of the subject, and numerous committees of investigation have been appointed within the past ten years. Nothing ever came of the agitation and investigation. There seems to be but two practical solutions of the difficulty. The hall must be remodelled, so as to have windows opening out-of-doors, or a new hall must be built. The former plan would necessitate the addition to the House of the hall known as the lobby, the Speaker's room, Sergeant-at-Arms' office, and the committee room, and the galleries above these rooms would have to be taken down or supported by columns. A project begins to be broached for erecting a building in the East Capitol Park for the Senate and House, and their committee rooms, only leaving the Capitol for the uses of the courts, the library, and for the great National Museum and Gallery of Art which some people dream of, as a thing that will be established in the near future. The ventilation of the Senate Chamber has been greatly improved within the past two years. During the summer of 1871, ventilators were placed under every desk, through which hot, fresh or cold air can be forced, and which can be closed at will. One of the greatest defects that then remained was the bad air in the galleries. This has been greatly remedied during the past summer, when similar ventilators to those mentioned above were put in. The difficulties to overcome in the House are much greater than those in the Senate, owing to the greater size of the hall."

From the South Wing, we pass back to the central or old building. Entering it at the basement, we find ourselves in a large crypt, whose vaulted ceiling is supported by two concentric peristyles, of forty Doric columns. It was the intention of Congress to place the remains of Washington in a mausoleum, in the sub-basement below this crypt, and Mrs. Washington consented to the removal of the body; but when the Capitol was ready to receive the precious trust, the Legislature of Virginia protested against the removal, and John A. Washington, Esq., the proprietor of Mount Vernon, refused to allow the body to be removed, on the ground that it was Washington's wish that his ashes should rest with those of his family.

The vaults are massive, and are models of strength and durability, and form decidedly one of the most interesting parts of the edifice.

Under the old Senate Wing are a series of rooms used for storing away books and documents belonging to the Supreme Court of the United States. The room immediately under the old Senate Chamber was formerly used by the Supreme Court. It is now the Law Library. The rooms under the Library of Congress in the western end of the building are occupied by the Court of Claims.

In the basement of the South Wing are the Folding Rooms of the House. The entire ground floor of this wing, consisting of twenty-two rooms, is devoted to storing, folding, and mailing of the House Documents. The whole department is in charge of a superintendent, whose business it is to receive, register, and store the various publications of the House, as they come in from the Government Printing Office. The speeches of members are also received and prepared for mailing here. The folding is generally done by boys, but men are required for the heavier work. Several tons of mail-matter, from a single copy of *The Globe* newspaper to a thousand-page folio book, are sent off daily by the members to their friends and constituents. Many of these publications are both useful and important, but the majority of them are used merely as waste paper by the persons to whom they are sent. Thousands of books already wrapped and sealed for mailing, are stored away in the vaults. Lists of their titles are affixed to the inner-side of the doors of the rooms in which they are kept, so that they can be easily found at any moment.

During the former great political contests of the country, publications and newspapers of all kinds were sent off from this room by members; and the expense of this means of electioneering fell on the whole people.

Leaving the vaults of the old building, one may either climb the inner stairway at the western entrance, or, passing out into the grounds again, mount the broad stairs, and enter by the main, or eastern door. Let us avail ourselves of the latter means, and pause a moment as we reach the splendid colonnade which is the chief ornament of the portico. It is from this portico that the President of the United States delivers his inaugural address, in the presence of his assembled countrymen, upon the occasion of his accession to power. Only a few weeks from the time these lines are written, and the grounds below will be thronged with anxious thousands, who will flock thither from all parts of our broad land, to hear our Silent Warrior declare the policy which is to guide him as a statesman.

Passing through the massive doors, we enter the Rotunda.

This immense chamber occupies the central portion of the old building, and lies immediately beneath the dome. The floor is of freestone, and rests upon the arches of the crypt below. A line drawn across it from wall to wall would measure ninety-five and a-half feet, and the distance from the floor to the frescoed canopy is one hundred and eighty feet three inches. The room is handsomely panelled and frescoed, and is surrounded by an ordonnance of fluted pilasters thirty feet in height, supporting an entablature, and cornice of fourteen feet, a piece of skilful and tasteful workmanship.

"Above this cornice, a vertical wall will be raised, with a deep recessed panel nine feet in height, to be filled with sculpture, forming a continuous frieze three hundred feet in length, of figures in alto relievo. The subject to be the History of America. The gradual progress of a continent from the depths of barbarism to the height of civilization; the rude and primitive civilization of some of the ante-Columbian tribes; the contests of the Aztecs with their less civilized predecessors; their own conquest by the Spanish race; the wilder state of the hunter tribes of our own regions; the discovery, settlement, and wars of America; the advance of the white and retreat of the red races; our own revolutionary and other struggles, with an illustration of the higher achievements of our present civilization, will afford a richness and variety of costume, character, and incident, which may worthily employ our best sculptors in its execution, and which will form for future ages a monument of the present state of the arts in this country."

Above the portion reserved for this frieze, is a series of attached columns, the spaces between which are filled with large, handsome windows, which admit a sufficient light to the Rotunda.

Above this colonnade rises the dome, which contracts to a space of sixty-five feet in diameter, and reveals another and a lighter colonnade at a much higher level. The whole is closed in at the base of the lantern, but just below the lantern a large canopy obstructs the view, and is covered with a magnificent fresco, by Brumidi, which we shall have occasion to notice shortly.

The walls of the Rotunda, between the pilasters below, contain eight paintings on canvas, set in panels, each painting being eighteen feet long and twelve feet high. Four of these are by Colonel John Trumbull, who was an aide-de-camp to Washington during the Revolution. These are "The Declaration of Independence," "The Surrender of Burgoyne at Saratoga," "The Surrender of Lord Cornwallis at Yorktown," and "The Resignation of Washington as Commander-in-chief of the Army in 1783." These paintings were ordered by the Government at an expense of $8000 each. They are faithful representations of the scenes and events they depict, and contain accurate portraits of the personages represented. This fact alone renders them amongst the most valuable of the national possessions.

The other four are "The Embarcation of the Pilgrims in the 'Speedwell,' at Delft Haven," by Robert

W. Weir; "The Landing of Columbus," by John Vanderlyn; "De Soto Discovering the Mississippi River," by William H. Powell; and "The Baptism of Pocahontas," by John Gadsby Chapman. They were painted by order of Congress, and cost the Government from $10,000 to $20,000 each. They are all faulty—the whole eight—in many respects, but are still great works of art, and merit a careful study. To our mind, "The Departure of the Pilgrims," by Weir, is the best in the Rotunda. No finer specimens of manly and female beauty are to be found anywhere, than in the characters of this painting. New England still retains a few women who are blessed with the loveliness which makes Rose Standish so attractive to the gazer, and seems to have been given what is left to us of such men as those whom Weir has chosen for his heroes. This type of masculine beauty is found chiefly in Connecticut.

Panels of arabesque, in bas-relief, ornament the walls above these paintings. Four alternate panels contain heads of Columbus, Sir Walter Raleigh, La Salle, and Cabot. Over the four doors of the Rotunda are the following alto-relievos in stone:—"Penn's Treaty with the Indians," by M. Gevelot; "The Landing of the Pilgrims at Plymouth," by Causici; "The Conflict of Daniel Boone with the Indians," by Causici; and "The Rescue of Capt. John Smith by Pocahontas," by Capellano.

A marble statue of Alexander Hamilton stands in the centre of the Rotunda, and is an object of much curiosity.

Leaving the Rotunda by the north door, we enter the lobby of the old Senate Chamber. The first door on the left swings ajar, and we open it, mount the stone stairway, and soon find ourselves on an iron platform in a small court between the Rotunda and the North Wing. An iron stairway, winding around the outer side of the base of the dome, conducts us to a second door. Entering it, we find ourselves at the base of the dome, in a handsome gallery, which encircles the walls of the Rotunda, and affords an excellent and picturesque view of the room below. The dome rises from the level of this gallery, and is constructed entirely of iron. It consists of an inner and an outer shell, joined and held together by an infinity of bars and bolts, and between which an iron stairway leads to the lantern. Half way up the dome is a gallery, running around the exterior of the outer shell, from which a fine view of the city and surrounding country may be obtained. Mounting still higher by the stairway, we enter the gallery just beneath the canopy and look down on the floor beneath, nearly two hundred feet distant. The persons moving about below seem like so many pigmies, and their footfalls and voices sound far off. Above us is Brumidi's allegorical picture. The painted figures which appeared so small from the floor beneath, now seem colossal, and the work which was so soft and delicate as seen from below, looks coarse and rough. The picture is well worth seeing, and the view from the various heights is very fine.

Washington is seated on the rainbow in glory, surrounded by bright-colored clouds. The Goddess of

Liberty on his right holds a scroll towards him, and on his left is the winged representation of Fame and Victory. Before the three are thirteen maidens with joined hands, representing the thirteen original States, and forming a semicircle. They hold aloft a bright-colored scarf, on which is inscribed the legend "*E Pluribus Unum.*" They are arranged geographically, and not historically. Beginning on the left of Washington, they occur in the following order: New Hampshire, Massachusetts, Rhode Island, Connecticut, New Jersey, New York, Pennsylvania, Maryland, Delaware, Virginia, North Carolina, South Carolina, and Georgia. The States are distinguished by the coloring, drapery, attitudes, and the leaves and blossoms worn by the maidens. The prevailing hue of the Northern States is here a delicate green, which grows stronger and richer as the South is approached. The staple productions of the States are used as ornaments, and aid in distinguishing them.

This constitutes the central croup. Around it are six other distinct and characteristic groups. We shall begin with that on the west, and proceed in discribing them from left to right, taking the position of Washington in the central group as our standpoint.

1*st Group.* WAR.—Freedom, with drawn sword and in full armor, has smitten down Tyranny and Oppression, and is driving them away. By her side an eagle fights with his beak in the same cause. Her enemies are overcome with terror, and are fleeing from her presence in hot haste; and with them Anger, Revenge, and Discord are driven away.

2d Group. AGRICULTURE.—In the centre sits Ceres, the Goddess of the Harvest, holding the horn of plenty in her left hand. America, with her head crowned with the liberty-cap, grasps the reins attached to a pair of fiery horses which are hitched to an American reaper and held in check by two stout laborers. Pomona with a basket of fruit stands by the side of Ceres, and Flora kneels near the reaper, gathering flowers, while a child sports by her side. The background is a tasteful arrangement of American vegetation.

3d Group. MECHANICS.—Vulcan stands with his right foot resting on a cannon, and his right hand grasping a hammer which he leans on his anvil. Machinery, cannon balls, mortars, and other mechanical contrivances are scattered around, and five attendants are busy in preparing them for use.

4th Group. COMMERCE.—Mercury, the patron of travellers and merchants, is seated on a pile of bales and boxes, holding up a bag of gold to the gaze of Robert Morris, the Financier of the Revolution. On the right of the swift-winged deity are laborers engaged in loading a truck, and on the left two sailors point to a distant gunboat. There is a bitter sarcasm about this picture, which symbolizes not only the country's commercial greatness, but also its ingratitude. One seems to detect a wild yearning in the gaze which Robert Morris fixes upon Mercury's gold. The poor man needed the money badly, for after guiding his country safely through its pecuniary difficulties, he fell a victim to his own embarrassments, and died a bankrupt, in a debtor's prison, in which his grateful countrymen allowed him to languish.

5th Group. THE MARINE.—Neptune, in royal state, is seen emerging from the deep, gazing about him as if to seek some explanation of the mighty events which are going on upon the land and sea. Below him, Aphrodite, half risen from the waves, is about to drop into the ocean the Atlantic cable, which she has received from a winged cherub which hovers near her.

6th Group. THE ARTS AND SCIENCES.—Minerva, armed with helmet and spear, stands in the centre, instructing a group on her left, collected around an electrical machine. These are Benjamin Franklin, Robert Fulton, and Professor Morse. They listen with rapt attention to her teachings. On her left is a group of school-boys being instructed by their teacher.

The painting covers an area of 4664 square feet, and was executed by Signor C. Brumidi, a native of Italy, and a naturalized citizen of the United States. It cost the Government forty thousand dollars.

A stairway leads from the gallery below the picture to the base of the lantern, beyond which visitors are forbidden to ascend. A door admits us to the highest outer gallery of the dome. It requires a fatiguing journey to reach it, but the magnificent view to be obtained from it fully repays us for all our trouble. The air blows keen as we pass out upon the narrow balcony, for we are nearly three hundred feet above the ground. The view is magnificent. The whole city is at our feet, with its long lines of streets, its splendid public buildings, its parks and gardens, and beyond is a panorama of unsurpassed beauty.

To the northwest the high hills in Virginia and

beyond Georgetown stretch back to the horizon. The river, breaking from them, sweeps away to the southeast, and is crossed by the canal bridge at Georgetown and the Long Bridge at the foot of Maryland Avenue. On the Virginia side the heights are bold and picturesque. Arlington, once the home of the Rebel General Robert E. Lee, and now a Freedmen's village and National Cemetery, stands near the Virginia end of the Long Bridge. The heights here are crowned with massive earthworks, which were erected for the protection of the Capital during the war. They are very distinct to the eye, and with a good glass every detail of construction can be made out. Pennsylvania Avenue stretches out grandly before us, and at our feet, that portion extending from the Capitol to the President's house being handsomely built up. The various objects in the city can be distinctly made out, for the whole town is splendidly mapped out below us. To the westward the eye ranges over a vast tract of country in Virginia, and to the southwest the city of Alexandria, eight miles distant, is in full view. The Potomac, here over a mile wide, sweeps majestically by the city, and disappears amidst the southwestern woods which shut in the view. To the south are the Eastern Branch, the Navy Yard, the Insane Asylum, and beyond, the hills crowned with the red earthworks. To the north, the Baltimore Railroad is seen emerging from the woods and descending a steep grade towards the city. On all sides, long lines of fortifications greet the eye, each telling its mute but eloquent story.

In the early months of the war, when the Southern

army occupied Mason's and Munson's hills, in Virginia, their colors could be seen from this balcony, and during the desperate struggles on the early Potomac the smoke of battle frequently hung over the distant woods, and the dull throbbing of the guns could be distinctly and painfully heard.

Descending as we came, we pause in the gallery under the fresco to notice the ingenious arrangement of the gas-lights. Four hundred and twenty-five burners are arranged in a circle around the base of the canopy, at distances of one inch apart, and over each one passes an incombustible wire connected with an electrical battery placed between the outer and inner shells of the dome, near the stairway, on our right as we go down. Upon reaching the old Senate lobby, after descending from the canopy, we pass into the Rotunda again, and pause in the doorway to notice a large metal plate in the side of the wall, containing a number of knobs, each of which has its appropriate label cut in the plate immediately over it. These control the lighting apparatus of the dome and the two Houses of Congress. A pressure on one of the knobs opens a valve, and allows the gas to flow up to the burners, and a touch upon an adjoining knob causes an electric current to flash along the copper wire over the burners, and in an instant the whole dome is in a blaze of light. The effect of this illumination is very fine. The light falls brightly over every object, and when seen from without the dome seems almost on fire.

Leaving the Capitol, which we have now explored, we pass out into the grounds, from which we can obtain a fine view of the magnificent bronze Statue of Freedom, which surmounts the lantern of the dome, at an altitude of 300 feet above the ground. The statue was finally placed in its present position at 12 o'clock on the 2d of December 1863, and was greeted with a salute of 35 guns from a field battery on Capitol Hill, and with similar salutes from all the defences of the city. It is 19 feet 6 inches high, and weighs 14,985 pounds. It cost the Government, before being raised to its present position, $23,796.82.

This magnificent statue was the last conception of the lamented Crawford. It represents a female figure in a royal robe, on whose head is placed a helmet cap ornamented with the wings and beak of an eagle. Her right hand rests upon a sheathed sword, the point of which touches the ground at her feet, and her left holds a wreath over a shield ornamented with the Stars and Stripes. Her face is uplifted, and her brow is encircled with a wreath of stars. The face is pure and queenly, and seems glowing with life and noble thoughts. It is one of the noblest works of its kind in the world.

The bronze cast was made by Mr. Clark Mills, at his foundry near Washington.

Greenough's statue of Washington is placed in the Capitol Park, opposite the Central Portico, east of the building. It represents Washington seated in majesty, his left hand holding a sheathed sword, and his right pointing to Heaven. His figure is naked to the waist, but the right arm and lower part of his body are draped The figure is about twelve feet high, and the features are massive, but the likeness is correct. Lions' heads and acanthus leaves ornament the chair, against the back of which leans a small figure of Columbus, and one of an Indian Chief. The former suggests the origin and source of our civilization, the other our country in its primitive days.

On the right of the chair, in *basso-relievo*, Phaeton in his chariot, with its steeds, symbolizes the rising sun, with the crest representing the arms of the United States.

The following design, also in *basso-relievo*, ornaments the left side of the chair. The Genius of North America, in the guise of the young Hercules, is strangling the Serpent of Despotism. That of South America, as Iphiclus, crouches to the ground, fearing to enter upon the struggle.

On the back of the chair is the following inscription:

"SIMULACRUM ISTUD

MAGNUM LIBERTATIS EXEMPLUM,

NEC SINE IPSA DURATURUM."

HORATIUS GREENOUGH,
FACIEBAT.

which has been tanslated:

"This statue cast in Freedom's stately form,
And by her e'er upheld."
HORATIO GREENOUGH, Sculptor.

The statue is of one piece of marble, but is not pure white. Together with its pedestal, it weighs fourteen tons. On three sides of the pedestal are inscribed the lines, "First in War—First in Peace—and First in the Hearts of his Countrymen."

The statue has been much admired, and much abused. Edward Everett considered it one of the greatest works of sculpture of modern times. Others have denounced it as unworthy of its place; and it is hard to say which are the more numerous, its admirers or those who condemn it.

It was finished in 1843, having been executed in Italy, and was brought to the United States in the ship of the line, Ohio, no merchant vessel being able to transport so large a single bulk. It cost Congress twenty-five thousand dollars.

The Capitol Park covers an area of several acres. Entering it at the western gate, on Pennsylvania Avenue, the broad walks lead us up several flights of stone stairs, by which we mount from terrace to terrace, until we reach the level of the basement of the building. The hill on which the Capitol stands is between eighty and ninety feet higher than the level of the western entrance. The terracing is handsomely finished in freestone, and gives to the grounds a very elegant appearance. That portion in front of the building is level, and is well laid off. The entire park is ornamented with handsome shrubbery and fountains, and enclosed with an iron railing.

The Capitol, as well as all the other public buildings of the city are in charge of the Commissioner of Public Buildings, who has the care also of all the squares, parks, streets, and avenues, under the control of the Government. He is appointed by the President, and it is customary for him to attend at the White House as usher at receptions and State occasions. His office is in the west front of the old building of the Capitol, and he is assisted in his duties by several clerks. The position is one of great responsibility, and is always filled by a man of character.

The Capitol police form a force distinct from that of the city. They are uniformed, and are on duty in the building and through the grounds, day and night. They are charged with the peace and safety of the establishment, and are required to exercise the utmost vigilance over all parts of it. They are courteous and obliging to strangers, and readily furnish any information desired of them. They have their headquarters in the basement of the old building, where they have also a guard-room for the detention of offenders.

CHAPTER V.

THE SENATE OF THE UNITED STATES.

Organization of the Legislative Branch of the Government—The Senate—Its Organization—Its Character—How Senators are chosen—Contrast between the old time Senators and those of to-day—The Senate in Session—Scene in the Chamber—Conduct of Senators—Untimely Applause—Pen and Ink Sketches of Senators—Vice-President Colfax—Senator Hamlin—Senator Patterson, of New Hampshire—Charles Sumner—Sketch of his Career—Henry Wilson—A self-made Man—The new Vice-President—Senator Sprague—The "handsome Senator Conkling"—Simon Cameron—A Veteran—"Parson Brownlow"—John Sherman, of Ohio—The Western Statesman—Senator Morton—Senator Trumbull—"Fighting Johnnie Logan"—A brilliant record—Senator Harlan—Senator Blair—A good Story—Carl Schurz—His romantic history—A daring Adventure—Senator Pomeroy—"Old Subsidy"—A crushing Downfall—Scene in the Kansas Legislature—Indignant Virtue—Pomeroy's Defence—Senator Caldwell—How they make Senators in Kansas—The Commercial Value of a Legislature—Report of the Committee of the United States Senate—"A Novice in Politics."

THE Constitution of the United States divides the Federal Government into three distinct parts—the Legislative, the Executive, and the Judiciary. Each is dependent upon the others, and each acts as a check upon the others in the workings of the Federal system, yet each is separate and distinct in itself, and in the exercise of its particular duties and rights is independent of the others. The Legislative branch originates and enacts the laws for the government of the **country**, the Executive is charged with the duty of seeing that these laws are properly executed and obeyed, and the Judiciary is assigned the task of determining the constitutionality of these laws when called upon to do so by the other branches of the Government.

The Legislative branch of the Government consists of the Congress of the United States, which body is composed of a Senate and House of Representatives. The Senate consists of the accredited Representatives of the *States* of the Union; while the members of the House of Representatives represent the *people* of the United States. The two Houses of Congress are required by the Constitution to assemble, in the Capitol, at Washington, at least once a year, on the first Monday in December, unless they shall by law appoint some other day of meeting. Every Congress expires by law at 12 o'clock on the 4th day of March, next following the commencement of its second Session. A majority of each House is necessary to constitute a quorum for the transaction of business, but a smaller number may adjourn over from day to day. Either House may adjourn at pleasure, for a period not exceeding three days, but for a longer time, it is necessary for the consent of the other House to be given. The members of both Houses swear to support the Constitution, and, during their terms of office, are privileged from arrest, except for treason, felony, or breach of the peace.

The Senate is the higher branch of Congress, and is generally held in higher esteem by the people of the Union than the Lower House. The Senators are in fact the ambassadors from the States forming the great Confederation, and thus occupy a higher and more responsible position than the Representatives, for while a Representative is the mouthpiece of but a section of a State, the Senator is the mouthpiece, or accredited agent of the Commonwealth, in its sovereign capacity as one of the members of the Union.

The Senate is composed of two Senators chosen from each State by the Legislature, for six years; or, in case of a vacancy, appointed by the Governor, to serve until the next session of the Legislature. It is provided by the Constitution that, "No person shall be a Senator who shall not have attained to the age of thirty years, and been nine years a citizen of the United States, and who shall not, when elected, be an inhabitant of that State for which he shall be chosen." The Senators are usually men of more weight in their own States than the Representatives, and it was once the ambition and the pride of every State to send to the Senate of the United States its purest and most illustrious citizens. Then the Senators were chosen more for their actual worth than for mere political reasons, and the past history of this body is adorned with the brightest and purest names of which the Republic can boast. Now, alas, Senators are no longer chosen from the good and great. The chief qualification demanded of the aspirant for Senatorial honors is devotion to a party; and men who are not fit, either by reason of intellectual gifts, or the admiration and confidence of the people, to represent the great States of the Union, have found their way into the Senate, and the high standard of fitness for the position once set up by that body has been effectually, and most unfortunately lowered.

The Vice-President of the United States is, by virtue of his office, the President of the Senate, and occupies the chair during the deliberations of that body; but the Senate also chooses a president *pro tempore*, who presides in the absence of the regular chairman. The Vice-President has no voice in the deliberations of the Senate, and cannot vote except in case of an equal division, when he has the casting vote. The deliberations of the body are open, except when some special occasion renders it desirable to sit with closed doors. In such case, a Senator offers a resolution that the galleries be cleared, and that the Senate go into secret session. The resolution is then submitted to a vote, and, if carried, the presiding officer warns all persons not connected with the body to leave the hall. Twelve o'clock, noon, is the regular time of meeting, but, late in the session, an earlier hour is generally appointed, in order to accomplish all the business before the House. The officers of the Senate are, a secretary, a sergeant-at-arms, a door-keeper, and assistant door-keepers. They are chosen on the second Monday of the first session of every Congress, but it is not usual to remove officers who have given satisfaction.

The Senate has the sole power to try impeachments, to confirm or reject the nominations of the Executive of persons to fill the various offices under the Government, and to ratify treaties with foreign powers. The Senators are generally men of middle age or advanced in years, and who have filled offices and positions of prominence and trust in their own States and in the Federal Government. The Senate cannot originate bills for the raising of the revenue or the levying of taxes, that privilege belonging by the provisions of the Constitution exclusively to the House of Representatives, but it may originate any other bills. Before a measure can become a law, it must receive the consent of both Houses and the approval of the President. Should the President veto a bill, he must return it to the House in which it originated, and the measure must then receive the approval of two-thirds of each House before it can become a law. Each House prescribes the rules for its government, and is the sole judge of the qualifications of its members.

The Senators during their deliberations afford a marked contrast to the members of the Lower House. Their proceedings are usually quiet and dignified, though sometimes the heat of party quarrels will burst through the restraints of the Chamber, and then the Senate can be as detestable as the veriest back-woods political meeting; but usually the Chamber is a model of decorum and dignity. Perhaps the Senators do not deserve much credit for this after all, for being, as a rule, men who have passed beyond the frivolities of their younger contemporaries, and having arrived at that period of life when gravity and dignity are natural to men, and, above all, being sure of their positions for a longer period than the Representatives, they are not subject to the temptations of the Lower House. Taken as a whole, the Senate is not an extraordinary-looking body. There are some fine-looking men in it, but as a rule, the present Senators do not in any personal manner indicate their exalted positions.

As the hour for meeting approaches, the lobbies or corridors of the Chamber begin to fill up, the galleries present an array of strangers, and Senators begin to straggle into their seats, or stand in groups about the Chamber conversing. At length the Vice-President appears in his seat, and is at once surrounded by members who are eager to secure the brief opportunity thus afforded for a chat with him. The present incumbent of the office is personally popular with both parties, and you may see the bitterest political opponents gathered in friendly converse around the second officer of the Government. At the moment for assembling the Vice-President rises, strikes the marble desk sharply with his gavel, and calls the Senate to order. The proceedings are opened with a prayer by some clergyman, and then the business of the Senate begins with the reading by the clerk of the journal of the previous day's session.

The Senators at once fall to work at their task of paying no attention to what is transpiring in the hall. Some are engaged in conversation, some in writing, some in reading newspapers, the constant rattle of which must make any but old hands nervous.

A number of pages are scattered about the hall. They are sent to and fro by Senators at all times, without regard to what is going on. A Senator wishing to summon a page claps his hands together smartly, with a ringing sound which is heard all over the hall. It is said that a stranger to the place and its customs was once sitting in the gallery, absorbed in the debate, which was warm and rather personal. Suddenly a Senator struck his hands together for the purpose of summoning a page. Our innocent friend immediately supposed that this was designed for applause of the Senator speaking, with whose cause he sympathized warmly, and bringing his hands into play he made a vigorous clapping, which threw the whole Senate into a roar of laughter.

A person unaccustomed to the scene is overwhelmed with astonishment at the utter indifference manifested by Senators towards the business of the House. Unless something of more than usual interest is transpiring, little or no attention is paid to any Senator who may have the floor. So deeply does every one seem to be interested in his own affairs, that it is surprising that any Senator should ever be able to vote intelligently on the majority of the questions presented to the House. Indeed, it is no uncommon thing to see Senators so much absorbed in their private affairs, or in conversation, as to forget to answer to their names when the vote is taken by a call of the House.

Visitors to the Capitol are admitted to the galleries of the Senate during the public sessions of that body, and those who are personally acquainted with Senators may through them secure admission to the floor of the Senate; but the galleries are the best places for seeing the "grave and reverend" body, and watching its proceedings. Diagrams of the Chamber, indicating each Senator's seat, are sold in the corridor leading from the old building to the North Wing, and by means of these visitors can distinguish the various Senators, providing they are in their proper seats. A few pen portraits may not be out of place here.

The occupant of the chair behind the marble desk, is, and will be until the 4th of March, 1873, the Honorable SCHUYLER COLFAX, the Vice-President of the United States. Mr. Colfax is so well known to the public that it is almost useless to say anything concerning him. None of his portraits do him justice. They make him too dark, for the sunny, genial expression of his face, which is enhanced by the light color of his hair and beard, is his greatest outward attraction. This peculiar expression has won him the nick-name of "Smiler." He generally dresses in black broadcloth, a style much affected by Congressmen, and which gives to that body the appearance of an assemblage of undertakers. His personal dignity is very great, in spite of his everlasting smile. He is nearly fifty years old. He is a native of the City of New York, and has climbed to his present lofty position by his own efforts. He has had an extensive experience in public life, and has been in Congress for many years. He was Speaker of the House for several sessions, and won great credit for the able and impartial manner in which he presided over the deliberations of that unruly body. Personally he is popular with all parties, but he has been unmercifully handled by his political opponents. Concerning his intellectual qualifications, people are divided. His political opponents, while conceding his amiability and popularity, assert that his talents exhaust themselves in his "eternal smile;" while his friends—and he has hosts of these—claim that he is intellectually superior to the average Congressman, and in every way worthy of the exalted position he holds. It is Mr. Colfax's misfortune to close his official career under a cloud. His name has been connected with the unpleasant scandal of the *Crédit Mobilier*, and he has not enjoyed his usual good fortune in connection with it.

HANIBAL HAMLIN, Senator from Maine, is one of the marked men of the Senate. He is a native of Paris, in Oxford County, Maine, and was born on the 27th of August 1809. He is a lawyer by profession, and became a member of the Legislature of his native State at the age of twenty-seven. He was elected to Congress in 1843, and served two terms in that body, after which he returned to the Maine Legislature in 1847. In May 1848, he was elected to the Senate of the United States, to fill a vacancy, and was reëlected for six years in 1851. In 1857, he was elected Governor of Maine, and resigned his seat in the Senate to accept the office. He served as Governor for only a few weeks, being reëlected to the United States Senate in January, 1857. In 1860, he was nominated by the Republican Party for the office of Vice-President of the United States, on the ticket with Abraham Lincoln, and was elected to that position in November of that year. In March, 1861, he resigned his seat in the Senate to enter upon the Vice-Presidency, which he held until the 4th of March, 1865. In 1869, upon the death of Senator Fessenden, he was returned to the Senate. Mr Hamlin is regarded as one of the leading members of the Senate, and his opinions carry great weight with them in that body. In appearance he is dark and swarthy, and is reserved and dignified in his demeanor.

Another prominent New England Senator is Mr. JAMES W. PATTERSON, one of the Senators from New Hampshire. He has been brought into anything but pleasant notoriety by the revelations in the *Crédit Mobilier* Case, and as we shall have occasion to refer to him in connection with that affair, we pass him by for the present.

Two of the most noted occupants of the Chamber are the Senators from Massachusetts.

The senior member from that State is CHARLES SUMNER. He is also one of the oldest members of the Senate, as regards his term of service, having been a Senator for twenty-two years. He is in his sixty-third year, having been born on the 6th of January, 1811. He is a native of Boston, and a graduate of Harvard University. He is confessedly the most accomplished member of the Senate, but the merits of no other Senator have been disputed as warmly as those of Mr. Sumner. His enemies charge him with being lacking in practical sense, and in natural ability — qualities which his friends claim for him in the highest degree. The late Count Gurowski said of him: "Sumner is a little afraid of losing ground with the English guardians of civilization. Sumner is full of good wishes, of generous conceptions, and is the man for the millennium. Sumner lacks the keen, sharp, piercing appreciation of common events. . . . . Sumner attributes to envy his anomalous position with the best men on the Republican side. He cannot understand that it is his scholarly pretensions which render him unpalatable to his colleagues. His cold rhetoric falls powerless at their feet, and no Senator envies him his fertility in random quotations."

Mr. Sumner served for many years as the Chairman of the Senate Committee of Foreign Relations, and during his occupancy of this position rendered good service to the country. He is credited with being the best informed man with regard to the affairs of other nations in the Senate, and he enjoys on the other side of the Atlantic a reputation of which he is justly proud, and, in this respect at least, he is superior to his contemporaries. He was a warm friend of the late President Lincoln, and, to his honor, did not, like so many others, turn his back upon the widow and children of the Martyr when power and patronage had passed from them.

Mr. Sumner has, for reasons which he has ably set forth, taken a position of decided hostility to the Administration of President Grant. The gossips of Washington asign a thousand reasons for his course, all of which savor of spite and envy; but there can be little doubt that in this, as in the other acts of his public life, the Massachusetts Senator has been governed by a sense of duty. He has been, personally, a sufferer by his course, for the Chairmanship of the Committee on which he served so long and honorably has passed from him to Senator Cameron. During the late Presidential Campaign, although absent from the country, in consequence of the feebleness of his health, he supported

Mr. Greeley for the Presidency, and was universally recognized as one of the Liberal Republican Leaders.

Mr. Sumner's career in the Senate has been an honorable as well as a long one, and it is his fortune to be able to look back upon it with pride and satisfaction. During his long term of office, though he has been hotly opposed by his political enemies, no one has ever been able to charge him with any private or official delinquency. He is one of the few incorruptible men left to the country. Mrs. Stowe has well said of him: "Sumner's mind is particularly remarkable for a nice sense of moral honor. He had truly that which Burke calls 'the chastity of honor which felt a stain like a wound.'"

In person Mr. Sumner is tall, squarely built, with a handsome and intellectual face. He is faultlessly neat in his dress, and though reserved, and even cold in his manner, is a fair specimen of what the old time Senators were, and what the present Senators should be.

HENRY WILSON, the other Senator from Massachusetts, is also one of the most prominent men of the Chamber. He is tall, squarely built, with an inclination to stoutness, and is decidedly one of the "heavy weights" of the Government. Seen from the galleries, Mr. Wilson has rather a sombre appearance, due no doubt to the immense amount of black broadcloth in which he shrouds himself, but he is far from being sombre in reality, for he is one of the most genial and best natured members of the Senate. He is very popular with his brother Senators, and is more accessible and free spoken than Mr. Sumner.

He is a native of New Hampshire, and was born at Farmington on the 12th of February, 1818, of very poor parents. "At the age of ten," says Mrs. Stowe, "he was bound to a farmer till he was twenty-one. Here he had the usual lot of a farm boy—plain, abundant food, coarse clothing, incessant work, and a few weeks' schooling, at the district school in the winter. In these ten years of toil, the boy by twilight, firelight, and on Sundays, had read over one thousand volumes of history, geography, biography, and general literature, borrowed from the school libraries and from those of generous individuals.

"At twenty-one he was his own master, to begin the world; and in looking over his inventory for starting in life, found only a sound and healthy body, and a mind trained to reflection by solitary thought. He went to Natick, Mass., to learn the trade of a shoemaker, and in working at it two years, he saved enough money to attend the academy at Concord and Wolfsborough, New Hampshire. But the man with whom he had deposited his hard earnings became insolvent; the money he had toiled so long for, vanished; and he was obliged to leave his studies, go back to Natick, and make more. Undiscouraged, he resolved still to pursue his object, uniting it with his daily toil. He formed a debating society among the young mechanics of the place; investigated subjects, read, wrote, and spoke on all the themes of the day, as the spirit within him gave him utterance. Among his fellow mechanics, some others were enkindled by his influence, and are now holding high places in the literary and diplomatic world."

He entered public life in 1840, as a supporter of the Whig party, and was elected in that year to the Legislature of Massachusetts. He was one of the earliest Anti-Slavery men, and from the first took a prominent part in the efforts to put a stop to negro slavery. He gained great popularity by his course, and was soon promoted to the State Senate, of which body he was twice elected President. In 1855, he was elected to the Senate of the United States, as the successor of Edward Everett, and has since served his State at Washington with credit and diligence.

"Wilson went to Washington," says Mrs. Stowe, "in the very heat and fervor of that conflict which the gigantic Giddings, with his great body and unflinching courage, said to a friend, was to him a severer trial of human nerve than the facing of cannon and bullets. The Slave aristocracy had come down in great wrath, as if knowing that its time was short. The Senate Chamber rang with their oaths and curses, as they tore and raged like wild beasts against those whom neither their blandishments, nor their threats, could subdue. Wilson brought there his face of serene, good nature, his vigorous, stocky frame, which had never seen ill health, and in which the nerves were yet an undiscovered region. It was entirely useless to bully, or to threaten, or to cajole that honest, good-humored, immovable man, who stood like a rock in their way, and took all their fury as unconsciously as a rock takes the foam of breaking waves. In every anti-slavery movement, he was always foremost, perfectly awake, perfectly well informed, and with that hardy, practical business knowledge of men and things which came from his early education, prepared to work out into actual forms what Sumner gave out as splendid theories.

"Wilson's impression on the Senate was not mainly that of an orator. His speeches were as free from the artifices of rhetoric as those of Lincoln; but they were distinguished for the weight and abundance of the practical information and good sense which they contained. He never spoke on a subject till he had made himself minutely acquainted with it in all its parts, and was accurately familiar with all that belonged to it. Not even John Quincy Adams, or Charles Sumner, could show a more perfect knowledge of what they were talking about than Henry Wilson. Whatever extraneous stores of knowledge and *belles lettres* may have been possessed by any of his associates, no man on the floor of the Senate could know more of the *United States of America* than he; and what was wanting in the graces of the orator, or the refinements of the rhetorician, was more than made amends for in the steady, irresistible, strong tread of the honest man, determined to accomplish a worthy purpose.

"Wilson succeeded Benton, as Chairman of the Military Committee of the Senate, and it was fortunate for the country that when the sudden storm of the War broke upon us, so strong a hand held this helm. General Scott said that he did more work in the first three months of the War than had been done in his position before for twenty years. Secretary Cameron attributed the salvation of Washington, in those early days, mainly to Henry Wilson's power of doing the apparently impossible in getting the Northern armies into the field in time to meet the danger."

At the last Presidential election, Mr. Wilson was chosen Vice-President of the United States, and on the 4th of March next, he will leave the Senate to assume the high office to which he has been chosen.

Senator SPRAGUE, of Rhode Island, is one of the youngest members of the Senate. He wears eye-glasses, but this does not alter the boyish expression of his countenance; and even the nice little moustache he sports, fails to bring him up to the popular ideal of a Senator. He is only forty-two, and is rather dissipated, *blasé* looking. They tell hard stories about the capers of this "grave and reverend seignior" in his wild days, and if the half of them are true, he must have been "a broth of a boy." He is a member of the Sprague family of Rhode Island, who are popularly believed to carry the little Commonwealth in their breeches pockets. The immense wealth of this family, and their great interests in the State, make them supreme in "Little Rhody." When William was thirty-one years old, it was thought to be a good thing for the family to make the young man Governor of the State, and consequently he was elected. During the first Campaign of the late War, he took the field, and served as Colonel of the First Rhode Island Regiment, thus illustrating nobly the patriotism of the Sprague family. Later still, the Sprague family came to the conclusion that they would like to have a representative in the United States Senate, and accordingly

William was sent to Washington as Senator from the family possession of Rhode Island. Later still, the young man came to the conclusion that he would take a wife, and his usual good luck attended him here. Whether it was the Sprague family that did it—no one exactly knows—but William succeeded in winning the hand of one of the prettiest and most accomplished women in Washington—Miss Kate Chase, the eldest daughter of the present Chief Justice of the United States. During the late canvass, William gave his support to the Liberal Republican Cause, and, as a consequence, has lost the chairmanship of the Senate Committee on Manufactures, a position he was well qualified to hold, being one of the wealthiest and most prominent factors in the country.

ROSCOE CONKLING, Senator from New York, is one of the leaders of the Administration party in the Senate. He is slow and heavy as a speaker, but is regarded as one of the working men of the Senate. He deserves credit for one thing if no other—for his independence in dropping the undertaker's dress so popular with the Senators. He is tall, well made, and has a florid complexion, with light sandy hair and beard. In short, Mr. Conkling is a very good-looking man—a fact of which he is not at all ignorant. When the galleries are full of ladies, the New York Senator is supremely happy, as he is fully aware that "the handsome Senator Conkling" is sure to come in for a fair share of their regards. He resides in Utica, New York, and is a brother-in-law of Ex-Governor Horatio Seymour.

SIMON CAMERON, Senator from Pennsylvania, is another of the marked men of the Senate. He is seventy-four years old, and his head is one of the whitest in the Chamber. He bears his age well, however, and is tall, erect, and cold and defiant looking. He began life as a poor, friendless boy, and raised himself to his present position by his own unaided exertions. He has had very great experience in political affairs, and has served in the Senate about twenty years. He was Mr. Lincoln's first Secretary of War. Being an active and daring politician Senator Cameron has hosts of enemies as well as friends, and the latter are bitter in their hatred of him. His friends esteem him highly, and declare that the attacks upon him are due solely to political malice.

WILLIAM G. BROWNLOW, Senator from Tennessee, is an object of much curiosity to visitors to the galleries when his feeble health permits of his appearance in the Senate. To the world at large he is best known as "Parson Brownlow," formerly the fighting editor of the *Knoxville Whig*. He has always been known as one of the bitterest and most violent partisans in the country, and when possessed of power has not scrupled to make his enemies feel his vengeance. He was at one time connected with the ministry of the Methodist Episcopal Church South, and was, until the Rebellion, a warm advocate of slavery. He remained faithful to the Union during the Civil War, and was made Governor of Tennessee at the close of the struggle. At the expiration of his term he was sent to represent his State in the United States Senate. It is a matter of congratulation among those who have an interest in the reputation of their country that Mr. Brownlow is without a peer in the august body of which he is a member.

JOHN SHERMAN, of Ohio, is a young Senator, but one of the leaders of that body. He is a vigorous thinker, and a statesman of cool, clear head. He is the chairman of the Finance Committee of the Senate, and is regarded as the best qualified member for that position. He is a brother of General W. T. Sherman, and resembles him so much that a stranger will have no difficulty in recognizing one after having seen the other.

OLIVER P. MORTON, of Indiana, is easily recognized by his immense head, and his dark, thoughtful face. He has great influence in the Senate, and is one of the recognized leaders of the Administration party.

LYMAN TRUMBULL, of Illinois, is soon to be lost to the Senate, his term of office expiring on the 4th of March next. He is one of the ablest and most upright members of the Senate, and his loss will be felt by that body. He was one of the original Republicans, when to bear that name required more courage than it does now. He was the colleague of Stephen A. Douglas, and many a tilt have these two intellectual giants had in this beautiful Chamber. He is a native of Connecticut, but removed to Illinois when a. young man. During the late Presidential Campaign Mr. Trumbull supported the claims of Mr. Greeley. Hence his failure to secure a reëlection.

JOHN A. LOGAN, the other Senator from Illinois, is a

new member of the Senate, having been elected to his present position in 1871. He rejoices in a multitude of nick-names, such as "Black Jack," in consequence of his swarthy complexion, and "Fighting Johnnie Logan," in consequence of his brilliant services in the field during the Rebellion. General Logan has yet to make his reputation in the Senate, but, judging his future by his past, it will no doubt be brilliant. Logan is of Irish parentage, and has had a long and varied experience in political life. He was a member of Congress before the War, and a devoted friend and follower of the gifted Stephen A. Douglas. He was an old Democrat, and a hard worker for the success of his party. Some of his enemies have asserted that, at the beginning of the Rebellion, he offered his services to Jefferson Davis, and was refused in consequence of Davis's personal dislike for him; but the best contradiction of this story is the fact that Logan was one of the first to volunteer for the defence of the Union after the fall of Fort Sumter. He served in the army throughout the War, and with great distinction, and rose to the rank of Major General of Volunteers. He commanded the Fifteenth Army Corps during Sherman's campaigns, and was regarded by the great soldier as one of his best and most promising lieutenants. At the close of the War he resigned his commission, and returned to Congress, where he at once took his position as one of the leaders of the Republican party. He acted as one of the managers in the trial of President Johnson. Logan is an ardent partisan, extremely bitter toward his enemies, but as generous to his friends.

He is an eloquent speaker, and a man who has an eye to dignities beyond the Senate. He is a large man, well made, as dark as an Indian, with a keen, flashing eye, a military air, and is decidedly one of the handsomest men in the Senate. He is forty-seven years old.

JAMES HARLAN, Senator from Iowa, is another of the prominent men of the Senate. He has been a Senator since 1854, with the exception of a brief period during which he served as Secretary of the Interior under President Johnson. Mr. Harlan is to leave the Senate in March, 1873, and has, in order that he may retain a voice in the affairs of the country, become the editor and proprietor of the Washington *Chronicle*.

Mr. Harlan has come into very unpleasant notoriety since the revelations of the *Crédit Mobilier* scandal were begun. During the course of the investigation, Dr. Thomas C. Durant, the President of the Union Pacific Railroad, testified that he had contributed the sum of ten thousand dollars to secure the election of Mr. Harlan as Senator from Iowa. Mr. Harlan denied that he knew anything about the sending of this money at the time; but Dr. Durant met this denial by stating that he had sent the amount to Mr. Harlan himself, in two New York checks of $5000 each, payable to Mr. Harlan's order. So the money was payable to Mr. Harlan direct. Says the *New York Tribune:* " Why did he not know of the alleged expenditure ' until some time after?' The question is a painful one, and is thus met by the *Chronicle* (Mr. Harlan's own paper), of January 6th :

"'The testimony which was drawn out before Committee No. 2, on yesterday, discloses no new fact, except that the check or checks for the funds were made payable, as the witness supposed, to the order of Mr. Harlan at the counter of the donor's bank, in New York City. The main facts remain as before. Dr. Durant states that the funds used by him were his own money, and not the money of the Union Pacific Railroad Company, or of the *Crédit Mobilier;* that the contribution was voluntary on his part; that his motive was "personal friendship toward Mr. Harlan;" that he "had an interest in Iowa, and wanted a good man in." This settles the question, if Dr. Durant's testimony can be relied on: First, that the doctor wanted Mr. Harlan elected on two grounds—personal friendship and his Iowa interests; second, that he voluntarily contributed to aid in that result; third, that he used his own private means, and not the funds of the company. The only remaining question to be settled in this connection is, were the funds used for any purpose of corruption? This will be decided when the Committee shall be able to state how the money was applied. That it was not intended to corrupt a member of Congress is clear, as Mr. Harlan was not at the time a member of either House. But whether it may not have been intended to be used to corrupt the people of Iowa, or members of the Iowa Legislature, seems to be a question that this Committee is disposed to solve, and we await additional testimony on this point.'

"The *Chronicle* then argues that as none but an imbecile could suppose that a Senatorial contest could be (even legitimately) conducted without expense, the use of Dr. Durant's friendly $10,000 was not, or need not be, a corruption fund. He adds:

"'This charge of the corrupt use of money by the Union Pacific Railroad Company to influence his election was first brought forward in his own State during the Senatorial contest one year since, under the apparent auspices of the friends of ex-Senator Grimes, Senator-elect Allison, and ex-Member James F. Wilson; the two latter being his chief competitors for the shining prize. It was published in their partisan journals. It was bandied about by their friends, and said to be capable of proof by "a distinguished ex-Senator," whom everybody knew to mean Senator Grimes. Mr. Harlan had the evidence at the time proving the falsity of the charge, so far as it could be supposed to smack of corruption; and that all three of these parties were themselves largely interested pecuniarily in the *Crédit Mobilier* and the Union Pacific Railroad or branches.'

"This does not seem to meet the case. Does it follow that Mr. Harlan is innocent of any improper use of money in the Senatorial canvass because the charge that he has is an old one? Has he disproved it before? Will he disprove it now? It will strike most people that $10,000 is a large sum to use in the ordinary and legitimate expenses of an election pending in a State Legislature; and it is by no means certain that Dr. Durant's cash is all that Mr. Harlan used in his canvass. Nor do we see how Mr. Harlan's statement that the money furnished by Dr. Durant was from that gentleman as 'a personal friend,' not as an officer or agent of a corporation, helps the case. Dr. Durant expressly said of Mr. Harlan that 'he lived, to be sure, on a rival line of road, but I thought he understood the wants of the State, and that he had been in Washington long enough to know how to look after the interests of the State.' If it was a mere matter of personal friendship between Dr. Durant, who is a New York Democrat, and Mr. Harlan, who was a Republican candidate in Iowa, why was this matter of 'a rival line of road' brought into the case at all? Did Dr. Durant give Mr. Harlan $10,000 to help him into the United States Senate as a friend? Or did he give it as any man interested in railroad matters in Congress would give it? Did Mr. Harlan ask for this money because Dr. Durant was his friend, or because he was a representative of certain railroad interests? Really, these questions have not been answered."

Clearly the questions of the *Tribune* are well put. Mr. Harlan has gotten into a most unfortunate predicament, from which he will need greater dexterity than he has yet shown to extricate himself. The public are not satisfied with the explanations he has offered.

FRANCIS P. BLAIR, Senator from Missouri, will also retire from the Senate in March. He is a native of Lexington, Kentucky, a son of Francis P. Blair, Sr., or, as he is better known, "Old Frank Blair," and a member of the well known "Blair Family," which has played a prominent part in our political history for the last half century. He is fifty-two years old. He entered the Lower House of Congress, from Missouri, in December, 1857, and continued to serve in that body until the breaking out of the Civil War. He was one of the early leaders of the Republican party, and took rank as one of the boldest and most determined anti-slavery champions in Congress. He was an able opponent of the Secession movement, and it is due to him, more than to any other man, that Missouri remained in the Union when the rest of the Slave States withdrew. The Missouri *Democrat*, in its issue of June 26th, 1861, thus sums up the efforts of General Blair, at this period of his career: " It is but just to Colonel Blair to record that, on his return to this city in April last, his talents were subjected to a most severe and trying experiment. The grand object before him, at that time, was to arrest the State of Missouri, then trembling on the verge of Revolution, and bind her fast to the Union. The means by which this great and patriotic end was to be accomplished, were of the most difficult and delicate nature. They consisted in the organizing and arming in this city of a military force, sufficient to protect its loyal inhabitants against armed bands of secessionists, already organized and officered and drilled, and backed up by a traitorous State Government, and a City Government, which, if not traitorous in fact, was hostile to the Union, and sympathizing strongly with secession. Who does not remember the haughty bearing of the secessionists at that time (so chopfallen withal and humbled now)? Our Commissioners of Police had discovered that Captain (now General) Lyon, who had only some two hundred men in the Arsenal, had no authority to bring his men outside its walls. They had procured the opinion of a certain traitor lawyer, that to do so was unconstitutional. They had posted sentinels around the Arsenal to spy out the movements there, and bring into contempt the national flag, and put under the law of a Rebel City Police the men who bore it. Brigadier General Frost, who has 'since melted quite away,' had announced his purpose to plant batteries on the high grounds commanding the Arsenal, and General Harney had decided that it would be '*prudent*' in Lyon to take any step to prevent it, and that *no such attempt should be made*. St. Louis trembled, and cowered beneath the overwhelming power of secession.

"The difficulty of organizing such a military force as Blair desired, was threefold. There was difficulty in overcoming the fears of the rank and file of the Union men, who knew their motions were watched by a sharp and hostile police. There was danger that the first small body of Union men who might initiate the work might be set upon, and cut to pieces by the 'Minute Men,' who had garrisoned and fortified with cannon the building on the corner of Fifth and Pine, or by Frost's brigade, who were at that time quartered in the city.

"But another most imposing difficulty to be overcome, lay in the hesitation and timidity of many men of influence among the Union men themselves. It was dangerous, said these, to organize; it was rash to arm; it would excite secessionists, provoke attack, draw down upon us the city police, and lead to bloodshed. But all these difficulties were surmounted; it was in the genius of Colonel Blair to overcome them all. He moved right on. His quiet, steady, and unpretending courage inspirited the faltering Union men. His discretion and celerity of action overreached both the police and the 'Minute Men,' the organization was perfected with so much secrecy and dispatch that an army seemed to have been created in an hour. It was in this way that Colonel Blair held up and sustained the Union men with one hand, while with the other he smote and discomfited the secessionists.

"The rest is known. The capture of Camp Jackson, that nucleus of the secession army, which was to take Missouri out of the Union, the most gallant feat in the history of the War, was but one of the results of the wisdom we have been attempting to portray.

"The battle of Boonville, another brilliant feat of arms, whose splendors have covered our little army as with a mantle, might have been won by any officer with less than a tithe of the credit for talents which rightfully belong to Colonel Blair. These victories were won, in fact, last winter and spring, when Frank Blair, and the friends who followed after him in their self-denying work of patriotism, threaded the streets and alleys of St. Louis by night, and met with secrecy in halls and garrets, and collected, and officered, and drilled, and formed, and moulded into shape by slow degrees the Union army of St. Louis, six thousand strong, soon after to be swelled by contributions from the country to nearly thrice that number. . . . . The State is safe, and has been saved by a stroke of genius, with little bloodshed, from the horror of a protracted conflict. The indiscretion of a far reaching sagacity and a lofty courage in a single man has done the work."

Colonel Blair entered the army at the outset of the War, and served throughout the entire struggle. He rose to the rank of Major General of Volunteers, and was regarded as one of the most brilliant and successful officers of the Western army. During the latter part of the War he commanded the Seventeenth Corps, in Sherman's army. He resigned his commission at the close of the struggle, and retired to civil life. He became one of the leaders of the Liberal Movement in Missouri, and in 1868 was nominated for the Vice-Presidency of the United States by the Democratic party. He was defeated, and resumed the practice of his profession—the law—in St. Louis. In 1871, he was elected to the Senate of the United States.

In person, General Blair is tall, squarely built, and, though by no means a beauty, is one of the most manly looking members of the Senate. His lack of beauty has often been the source of amusement to his friends. A gentleman not long since, an ardent admirer of General Blair, met him for the first time at the Jerome Park Races in New York. A friend of the Senator who had witnessed the meeting asked after he had withdrawn, "Well—what do you think of Frank Blair, now?" "I am agreeably disappointed," was the reply. "Indeed!" asked the friend; "in what respect, pray?" "Why," said the other," Blair isn't so d—d ugly after all."

The other Senator from Missouri, CARL SCHURZ, is well known to the country. He is also one of the ablest members of the Senate. He is thoroughly educated, deeply read in political lore, and is one of the most brilliant and effective orators in the Senate. He is a native of Germany, and was born at Liblar, near Cologne, March 2d, 1829. He received a thorough education, and passed through the University of Bonn, but his career there was interrupted by his taking part in the Revolution of 1849. Being unsuccessful, he was obliged to fly from Germany to Switzerland. His former tutor, and fellow agitator, Dr. Gottfried Kinkel, was not so fortunate. He was captured, condemned to twenty years' imprisonment, and shut up in the fortress of Spandau. Schurz, upon hearing of this, determined to attempt the rescue of his friend, to whom he was much attached, "and for this purpose made his way secretly back to Germany, in May, 1850, spending much time in preparations in Cologne and Berlin, and remaining in the latter city for three months engaged in endeavors to establish relations with the guards who watched the prisoner. The rescue was finally accomplished in the night of November 6th, 1850, Kinkel's cell being broken open and he brought upon the roof of the prison, whence he was successfully lowered to the ground. The fugitives escaped the same night across the frontier into Mecklenburg, and thence made their way to Rostock, and, after remaining some time in concealment, took passage in a small schooner for Leith, where they arrived about December 1st. Schurz then went to Paris, where he remained as a correspondent of German journals till June, 1851, when he went to London, and lived as a teacher till July, 1852. He then married and removed to America. He remained three years in Philadelphia, engaged in legal, historical, and political studies, made a short visit to Europe, and then settled at Madison, Wis. In the Presidential Campaign of 1856 he became known as an orator in the German language. In 1857, he was nominated by the Republican State Convention as a candidate for the office of lieutenant governor of the State, but was not elected. In 1858, on occasion of the contest between Mr. Douglas and Mr. Lincoln for the U. S. Senatorship of Illinois, he delivered his first English speech, which was widely republished by the journals in various parts of the country." About the year 1859, he removed to Milwaukee and entered upon the practice of the law. From this time, he took a prominent part in Western and Federal politics. Upon the inauguration of Mr. Lincoln, he was appointed U. S. Minister to Spain. He returned from Madrid in December, 1861, resigned his position as Minister, and entered the army as a Brigadier General. He was subsequently promoted to the rank of Major General of Volunteers, and served with distinction throughout the War. After the close of the War he removed to St. Louis. In 1869, he was elected to the Senate of the United States. Mr. Schurz was one of the first and most prominent leaders of the Liberal movement in Missouri, and one of the creators of the Liberal Republican party, whose cause he supported during the recent Presidential Campaign.

In person Mr. Schurz is tall and thin, with a thoroughly German face. He is near-sighted and wears eye-glasses. He has the face of a student and a thinker, differing in this respect from the majority of his associates.

The State of Kansas has the misfortune to furnish two of the most unhappy scandals of the session. Both of its Senators stand charged with the shameful crimes of bribery and corrupt practices.

SAMUEL C. POMEROY has been a member of the Senate for twelve years. He is a large, fleshy man, with a bold, high forehead and a bushy beard. He is a native of Massachusetts, and went to Kansas in 1854, in charge of a colony, as the agent of the New England Emigrant Aid Society. He has figured very prominently in the politics of his adopted State since that time. His term of office expires March 4th, 1873. Mr. Pomeroy was very anxious to continue in his seat as Senator during the next Congress, and made energetic efforts to carry the Kansas Legislature in his favor. Being a man of ordinary talents, he relied upon other things than his influence in his State to carry the Legislature in his favor. For a long time it had been charged in Kansas and elsewhere, that Mr. Pomeroy's virtue was not like that of Cæsar's wife, and it was hinted broadly that he had used his political position to make money; that he had gone to Kansas a poor man, and had made a fortune by the corrupt use of his influence and position in the State. His friends denied these charges, and claimed that he had made his money honestly; but it is certain that the nickname of "Old Subsidy," by which he was popularly known in his State, was bestowed upon him because of the general belief that every subsidy which he procured for enterprises in his State and section was, directly or indirectly, the means of adding to his own wealth.

When the contest for United States Senator began, during the present winter, it was openly announced that Mr. Pomeroy would endeavor to secure his election by buying up the State Legislature. Mr. Pomeroy's friends indignantly denied this charge, and declared that it was not possible to buy up the Legislature of a State like Kansas. The matter was discussed with considerable feeling on both sides. The election took place on the 29th of January, and Mr. Pomeroy was signally defeated, owing to the charge brought against him by Mr. York, that he had endeavored to bribe the Legislature. Senator York supported his charge by producing the money paid him by Mr. Pomeroy, and handing it over to the Clerk. A letter from Topeka, thus describes the scene in the Legislature:

"Yesterday much surprise was expressed among Senator Pomeroy's opponents at the strength that he showed in the Legislature; to-day, in the light of the developments contained in Senator York's speech, the cause of his strength is well understood. In a vote in the two Houses yesterday, out of 130 votes cast, Pomeroy received 50 votes for Senator, to 24 for Governor Harvey, 18 for Judge Lowe, and 13 for Dr. Logan. The friends of the other candidates named had conceded Pomeroy between 35 and 40 votes, and this exhibit startled them. Pomeroy's partisans were jubilant, and were profuse in their boasts that he would be elected on the first ballot to-day. Whether or not they knew what means had been employed to make sure of his election cannot be stated with certainty, but doubtless many of them—those who were 'behind the scenes'—went to their beds last night satisfied that ere another night should supervene the bribe-money that had been lavishly expended would do its expected work, and that Samuel C. Pomeroy would be declared the choice of the Kansas Legislature for Senator of the United States. But there was fortunately for Kansas and the nation, a man who, like Sergeant Champe of the Revolutionary War, was willing to make an apparent sacrifice of his fidelity to his trusts for the sake of justice and honesty; and through this man (Senator York) the whole nefarious plot was exposed, and amid a tempest of indignant denunciation—honest from those who knew the man and despised him, and affected from his tools, who feared not to join in the rebuke administered to the exposed suborner of legislatures—S. C. Pomeroy met with his crushing defeat and disgrace.

"For several days past, according to this exposure, it had been known among the opposition to Pomeroy that he had so arranged matters after his peculiar fashion that a counterplot was necessary to defeat him, or rather to prevent the successful consummation of the bargain and sale by which he was to be declared elected. It was therefore decided upon that the easy-virtued Senator should be led to bribe, as he would suppose, a leading opponent of his in the Legislature, who would, when the proper moment should come, denounce him for the attempt and show to the assembled Legistators the material evidence of Pomeroy's corruption in the shape of the greenbacks which had been paid by him to effect his end. This was done, and with what successful results will be shown.

"Senator York, the self-appointed instrument of this retributive justice upon the chief of the subsidy ring, came, he says, to this city to assume his duties in the State Senate an earnest and sound anti-Pomeroy man, and determined, by allying himself with the party in the Legislature that opposed Pomeroy, to do all in his power to regenerate the State and his party from the incubus of Pomeroyism. The well-known Pomeroy-Ross letter, having reference to certain profits in Indian goods which were, it is alleged, to have been shared between the writer of the letter, Pomeroy, and the receiver, Ross, had done infinite damage both to the reputation of Pomeroy and to his chances, among members of his own party in the Legislature, for the United States Senate. At an anti-Pomeroy caucus held not long since a man named Clark exhibited $2000, with the declaration that he had been paid that amount to sign a confession to the effect that he had forged the letter in question and the signature of Pomeroy attached to it. The charges thus brought against Pomeroy still more prejudiced Senator York against him, but, at the solicitation of several friends of Pomeroy, he consented to an interview with that person. The interview took place on Friday last in the presence of three friends of Mr. York. At that meeting Mr. York asked Pomeroy point-blank whether he had written the Ross letter. After some evasion of the question, and being pressed by the questioner, Pomeroy replied that he had not written it. Mr. York then responded in these words: 'Mr. Pomeroy, you are the most infamous scoundrel that ever walked the earth, or the worst defamed man that ever stepped on Kansas soil.' With this remark the interview ended.

"It was about this time that the question of the counter-plot against Pomeroy was marked as a bar to his successful use of criminal and illicit means in attaining the Senatorship, and it was also at this time that Senator York offered himself as the Nemesis to bring Pomeroy to that justice which he was prepared to defy. After consultation with several friends in whom he had every confidence, and who were also in the movement to expose Pomeroy, he again called upon the latter. The subject of money for his vote was broached, and Mr. York affected to be not averse to entering into an arrangement by which, 'for a consideration,' his vote and influence should be given to Pomeroy at the election to-day. On Monday—day before yesterday—night he again had an interview with Pomeroy, and there he says the 'bargain' was clinched, and Senator York was paid a portion of the money on the same evening. This was the closing episode of the prologue to the, for Pomeroy, tragedy that was enacted in the Legislature to-day, and this brings us immediately to the grand climax.

"Pomeroy went into the joint session of the Legislature to-day with sixty-eight votes pledged to him, with confidence in his heart and with the calm assurance that as his plans had been well laid so was his success insured; he left the Legislature with a Waterloo defeat crushing him down, with a deputy sheriff at hand to receive him with a warrant for his arrest for bribery, and with his reputation smirched, it now seems, beyond recovery. When the balloting for United States Senator for the full term, beginning March 4, 1873, commenced, Senator York slowly rose from his seat and demanded the floor on a question of privilege. This was granted. Mr. York then walked to the desk of the Speaker, drew from his pocket two packages of money containing $7000 in currency, placed them in front of the Speaker, and asked that the money be counted by the Secretary. While the Secretary, acceding to his request, was counting the money, amidst the restrained excitement of the two Houses, Mr. York returned to his seat. Having reached it he commenced to address the Legislature. He detailed the incidents of his interviews with Pomeroy, the substance of which I have given above. At the following passage, explaining Pomeroy's attempt to bribe him, of which attempt the evidences were then in the hands of the Speaker, the excitement was intense:

"'I visited Mr. Pomeroy's rooms in the dark and secret recesses of the Tafft House on Monday night, and at that interview my vote was bargained for a consideration of $8000—$2000 of which were paid to me on that evening, $5000 the next afternoon, and a promise of the additional $1000 when my vote had been cast in his favor. I now, in the presence of this honorable body, hand over the amount of $7000, just as I received it, and ask that it be counted by the Secretary.'

"As Mr. York continued his developments and his denunciations of Pomeroy, the excitement increased to a dramatic pitch, and the mention of Pomeroy's name was received with emphatic expressions of indignation. The scene was one rarely witnessed in the halls of legislation—one that it is to be hoped may never be seen again under the same circumstances. 'I ask, Mr President,' he said, 'that that money be used to defray the expenses of prosecuting the investigation of S. C. Pomeroy for bribery and corruption, as my limited influence extends in deed as well as in thought. I have an aged parent whose life has been spared to bless me with her love and her approval of the conduct of my life. I have a wife and little ones to whom I hope to bequeath a name which, however obscure, they may have no reason to blush to hear pronounced. Yet this corrupt old man comes to me and makes a bargain for my soul, and makes me a proposition which, if accepted in the faith and spirit in which it is offered, will make my children go through life with hung heads and burning cheeks at even mention of the name of him who begot them.'

" He demanded that the Legislature take measures to thoroughly examine the actions of S. C. Pomeroy in the contest, and that the alleged corruption money then in the Speaker's hands should be used to bring him to justice. He stated that in the hour or two he had passed in 'the den of infamy, the Tafft House'— Pomeroy's headquarters—he gained a knowledge of the detestable practices of the Kansas politician—of the depth of degradation a pure Republican government has reached—that no words of his could express. Disclosures made there made him aware that some of the most prominent and respectable men in Kansas were implicated in disgraceful schemes. From Pomeroy's own lips he learned that his spies and emissaries were working in the caucusses of the opposition to find out the candidates who had been brought against Pomeroy. He closed his nervous, impassioned address with these damning accusatory words :

"'These disclosures I will not now make; they are sufficient to satisfy me that the most conscienceless, infamous betrayer of the solemn trust reposed in him by the will of the people is S. C. Pomeroy. I have been actuated by no motive personal or vindictive in my action here to-day. I have not made the fight on Mr. Pomeroy in Mr. Ingalls's interest, in Mr. Lowe's or Mr. Harvey's interest, but in behalf of the betrayed and long-suffering people of this Commonwealth, and in furtherance of the solemn oath I took when I entered these halls as a representative of the people. As to the truth of what I have stated in the presence of this august and honorable body of representatives of the sovereign people, and before the Almighty Ruler of the universe, I solemnly declare and affirm that every word I have spoken is God's truth, and nothing but the truth.'

"The speech at the close was received with loud cheers and with fierce epithets hurled at Pomeroy, and with exclamations from the members which showed that his action was vindicated by the body, and that he was exonerated from all blame. The shouts in the hall and in the galleries were deafening as he sat down.

"When order had been somewhat restored the balloting commenced. If Pomeroy had any friends in the house they did not manifest themselves. Everybody voted for Ingalls—the whilom Pomeroy men in a feeble and cringing way that was painful to witness. Pomeroy was deserted to a man, and the ballot showed that Ingalls, who had been made the choice of the anti-Pomeroy caucus the evening before, received 118 votes out of the 132 cast. Pomeroy scored 0.

"Shortly after the result of the election in the Legislature was known a deputy sheriff proceeded to the Tafft House and arrested Pomeroy on a charge of bribery. His examination is fixed for Friday. At first he professed to be indifferent to the revelations made by Senator York, declaring that he was not demoralised, though his friends were, and that he was the victim of a foul conspiracy. But as time passed he began to realize his situation and the damage to his reputation, and completely broke down. Great as was his offence, there is something sad and pitiful in the spectacle of this dishonored old man.

"The excitement in the city to-night takes the shape in some quarters of threats to lynch Pomeroy, but these are merely temporary ebullitions of a transient passion. The law will take its course, and from present appearances Pomeroy will be prosecuted to the full penalty, which is seven years in the Penitentiary. From the United States Senate to the Kansas Penitentiary—what a spectacle!"

Mr. Pomeroy has denied the charges brought against him, and has asserted that he is the victim of a conspiracy on the part of his enemies. He has asked an investigation on the part of the Senate of the United States into the matter. It must be confessed, however, that the people of the country at large attach more importance to Mr. York's charges than to Mr. Pomeroy's denial. In plain English, Mr. Pomeroy is popularly believed to be guilty, and he has before him the task of convincing the people of his innocence. As for the Senate Investigation, it will amount to nothing, for before it can be had, or can determine anything, the Forty-Second Congress will expire, and Mr. Pomeroy will be no longer a Senator.

The New York *Tribune*, commenting editorially upon this matter, says: "Men who regard politics as a mere matter of trade acquire, in the course of a successful career, a contempt for human nature which sooner or later proves their ruin. They judge the public by themselves and their chattels. They think every man has his price, and sometimes make the mistake of putting the price too low. Public distrust or public indignation they think very little of. They defy the first and feel sure that the second when it comes will soon blow over. The basis of their confidence is that honest people have no such interest in fighting them as they have in holding to place and power. Fortified by this reflection they grow continually more impudent and careless, until at last they positively force the community to rise against them and rend them.

"Who would have imagined it possible for any Senator to have shown so brutal a contempt for public intelligence and virtue as to go to Kansas, while the

State and country were all alive with indignation over the man-traffic of Caldwell, and attempt to buy another Legislature? Yet this is what Senator Pomeroy seems to have done. He had no other means of working. He saw his hold on the State was weakening. His popularity was gone. He was without those personal qualities which attract men. His career in the Senate had been marked by nothing but a participation in a series of enormous jobs—by which many men of his kind prospered, and none of them were grateful. His only weapon was his money. He had enough of that, acquired in many ways, and he went to work to use it in the old manner. He had no more sagacity than to go into the open market for votes, at the very moment when the Caldwell case was throwing a broad shaft of light into all such shady places. As might be expected, he was caught in his iniquity. Yesterday morning, Mr. York, a State Senator, sent to the Clerk's desk $7000, which he said he had received from Mr. Pomeroy for his vote. We are told the effect was enormous. We are prevented by previous events from inferring that the mere mention of a bribe proved so startling to Kansas legislators. But perhaps there was something in the amount which roused their dormant virtue. Perhaps 'Old Subsidy,' as they playfully call their great man, had acquired the rest of them on more reasonable terms. At all events they were greatly outraged, and immediately elected the Hon. John James Ingalls gratis, and had their favorite statesman arrested.

"There is little reason for regret and much for congratulation in this disappearance of the Kansas Senator from the field of his activity. Among all the wrecks that lie along the shore, tossed there by the storms of the last few months, there is probably not one so sordid as he. Like Mammon, he was 'the least erected spirit that fell.' From his first entry into public life he has weighed everything by a money standard. He has judged all public measures by the cash that was in them; and estimated all men by the amount it would take to buy them. Other considerations he regarded with a dull and phlegmatic scorn. He found success and comfort in his way of life, and doubtless imagined it was to last forever. The sum he is said to have squandered in this election proves sufficiently what confidence he had in the final triumph of his greenbacks. He was not a man to throw-away a hundred thousand dollars on a forlorn hope. We cannot therefore but be glad that he made the trial, and that the country can have the benefit of the lesson his failure can teach. There is, after all, a quickening of the public conscience, which demands a decent respect for honesty from public men. Even in Kansas the effect of the exposure of Caldwell is plainly seen in the drama of yesterday. Two years ago, when the Kansas lawgivers heard Caldwell was in the market, they carried him their votes like merchandise. To day, when they learn that Pomeroy is engaged in the same traffic, they show him the door and then send a constable after him."

ALEXANDER CALDWELL, the other Senator from Kansas, has been brought into great prominence during the present session by being charged with practices similar to those of Mr. Pomeroy. The history of this case was so well summed up by the New York *Tribune* at the time, and the relation exhibits so well the popular feeling on the subject, that we insert it here in place of any remarks of our own.

"The testimony of ex-Governor Carney in the Caldwell case is enough to make one doubt whether such a thing as legislative honesty exists any longer in the United States. When Mr. Caldwell made up his mind to go into the contest for the Senatorship, he vowed that he would win if it cost him $250,000. His first operation was to buy off his competitor, Mr. Carney, for the sum of $10,000 down, and $5000 conditional upon his (Caldwell's) election; and then he began the systematic purchase of the honorable gentlemen whose votes in the Legislature were to confer upon him the coveted honor. To one he paid $1000, to another $2500, to a third as much as $5000—but this member seems to have been uncommonly high-toned. One he secured by paying off a note that troubled him. Another was tempted with a saddle horse, and a large amount of money besides. The whole Doniphan County delegation was fixed for $7000, and at times the market was so flat that Kansas legislators could be had for the ridiculously low price of $500 a head. Nor was there much difficulty or delicacy in conducting the negotiations. When the gentlemen 'heard that Caldwell was buying,' they came forward with a rush to offer themselves for sale. The editor of the Leavenworth *Times* testifies that Mr. Caldwell obtained the support of that fearless and independent paper for $2000. It is usual, we believe, in transactions of this sort, for those who receive the money to give some sort of explanation to their own consciences. Some of the legislators considered the sums paid by Caldwell as reimbursement of their election expenses; others were complimentary enough to say that as Mr. Caldwell was a very unpopular and discreditable person, they could not afford to go home and defend their course in voting for him unless he offered compensation for the strain upon their conscientiousness and the damage to their standing among their constituents. The prevalent readiness to sell must have kept down the prices; for it turned out that Mr. Caldwell got into the Senate for only $60,000—although one of the legislators whom he had purchased failed to vote according to agreement, and ran away with the money in his pocket.

"The question has of course occurred to a great many people, what return did Mr. Caldwell expect from an investment into which he went so heavily? Men of his stamp are not usually willing to spend $250,000 without some tangible equivalent for their money. Perhaps certain facts which have been developed in one committee-room of the Capitol while ex-Governor Carney has been enlightening a select company in another, may throw some light upon the answer. A great deal can be made in Congress when 'good things' are urged upon Congressmen in consideration of their influence; when railroad companies want Senators and Representatives to take 'a friendly interest' in their schemes, and all sorts of enterprises are anxious not to be interfered with or investigated. *Crédit Mobilier* stocks, which pay 1500 per cent. dividends in a year and a half, are not to be picked up every day; but we have Oakes Ames always with us, either in person or in some of his many imitators and successors, and the yawning pocket need not be long unfilled. The railways probably furnish Congressmen of a business turn of mind with all the trade they can desire, and if the truth were told we should doubtless find on the books of a good many corporations a 'suspense account,' like Mr. Durant's $435,000, which has been audited without a very close examination of the items. Mr. Caldwell declared, according to Mr. Carney, 'that the Kansas Pacific Company had promised to pay him some money to assist in his election, and so far as he was concerned they would get no legislation until they kept their promise.' Mr. Bushnell, on behalf of the Union Pacific and *Crédit Mobilier*, confessed to contributing to 'general political purposes,' because it was every man's duty to do something 'to save the country,' and the particular method by which the country was to be saved in his case was the contribution of $5000 to the 'election expenses' of Senator Thayer. This was a pretty large sum, but Mr. Bushnell said he was in the habit of paying from $1000 to $2500 for such purposes, 'just as he would pay taxes.' Even the excellent Mr. Harlan, when he was Secretary of the Interior, came upon the Union Pacific for $10,000 to defray the cost of electing him to the United States Senate, though what cost there could be in such an election, unless it was managed like Mr. Caldwell's, has yet to be explained.

" With these instances before us, we can understand

how corruption at the State capitals is the natural result of the loose morality and debased sense of honor which prevail at the national seat of Government. If six years in the Senate are equivalent to a handsome fortune, we shall have mercenary adventurers buying their way into the seats of Monroe, and Clay, and Webster. If a member of the House is permitted to make money out of his position, the House will inevitably be overrun with scamps, and the honest men will be driven out. There must be thorough work with the cases now before Congress, or we shall never have a reform. Whatever may be said of the guilt or innocence of individual members, there can be no doubt that the three Investigating Committees now in session are on the track of shameful corruption. Let each make a searching inquiry and a just report; and then we shall look to Congress for a salutary example."

The Committee of the U. S. Senate appointed to investigate the charges against Mr. Caldwell, on the 17th of January submitted a report sustaining these charges, and declaring that, in consequence of the practices resorted to by him, Mr. Caldwell was not legally elected. They closed their report with a recommendation that the Senate declare his seat vacant, ending the document with these words:

"The Committee remark that while Mr. Caldwell did things to procure his election which cannot be tolerated by the Senate, they believe that he was as much sinned against as sinning. *He was a novice in politics, and evidently in the hands of men who encouraged him in* the belief that Senatorial elections in Kansas were carried by the use of money."

CHAPTER VI.

THE HOUSE OF REPRESENTATIVES.

Organization of the House—Apportionment of Members—The House in Session—A Characteristic Scene—Rivalries—Partisan Outbreaks in the House—Mr. Toombs's idea of Free Speech—A very "Personal" Explanation—A Free Fight in the House—Disgraceful Scenes—Party Discipline—Recollections of "Old Thad"—Party Leaders—How to keep an Obnoxious Member out—Speech Making—A happy Expedient—Congressional Salaries—A Glance at the "Perquisites"—Abolition of the Franking Privilege—A Triumph of Public Opinion—Pen and ink Portraits—Mr. Speaker Blaine—Ben Butler—A Scotchman's Opinion of Butler—A Good Story—N. P. Banks—Horace Maynard—General Garfield—W. D. Kelley—The Champion of Pig Iron—James Brooks—Fernando Wood—Oakes Ames—The Chief Engineer of the Crédit Mobilier.

THE House of Representatives, or, as it is sometimes called, the Lower House, is the popular branch of Congress, and is composed of Representatives chosen once in two years by the people of the various States of the Union. The Constitution provides that "No person shall be a Representative who shall not have attained to the age of twenty-five years, and been seven years a citizen of the United States, and who shall not, when elected, be an inhabitant of that State in which he shall be chosen." The number of Representatives is limited by law to 233, and the apportionment of members to the various States is made according to the population of those States. This apportionment is revised and changed every ten years, immediately after the results of each Census are known. The various Territories of the United States send Delegates to the House of Representatives, each Territory sending one Delegate. These are admitted to seats in the House, and are privileged to take part in the debates, but have not the right to vote. The House of Representatives is accorded by the Constitution the exclusive privilege of originating bills for raising revenue, and the sole power of impeaching the officers of the General Government.

The House in session presents an interesting scene, and its galleries are usually well filled with strangers eagerly watching the proceedings. Many years ago an English traveller drew the following picture of the House in session, which is a fair description of it to-day:

"Except when some remarkably good speaker has possession of the floor, the members, instead of attending to what is spoken, are busy in conversation, writing letters, rapping the sand off the wet ink with their knuckles, rustling the countless newspapers which deluge the House, locking or unlocking their drawers, or moving up and down the avenues which divide the ranges of seats, and kicking before them, at every step, printed reports, letter covers, and other documents strewed on the floor. A couple of active little boys are always seen running to and fro with armfuls of papers, or carrying slips of writing from members to the Chair, or from member to member. Whenever any one rises to speak, who, there is reason to infer, from experience or from internal evidence, will be lengthy, one of these little Mercuries flies off for a glass of water, which he places on the orator's desk."

What Congress was then, it is now, except that the confusion and noise in the hall have increased. The number of pages has been multiplied several times, and are still kept quite busy. Sometimes the Speaker has hard work to preserve order in the House. Members are very unruly, and give the Chair a world of trouble. You see them obstructing the aisles, talking and laughing in a tone which is audible in any part of the hall, or sitting with their feet elevated on their desks, oftentimes fast asleep. If any thing of interest attracts them away from the hall, they leave it in such numbers that the House is often without a quorum, and the Speaker is forced to compel their attendance by the Sergeant-at-Arms.

There are bitter rivalries and heart-burnings between the members, and these often lead to outbreaks as fierce and disgraceful as those which marked the old slavery contests before the War. As a rule, the disputes end where they began, on the floor of the House, and political enemies are often warm personal friends, but sometimes the tilts in the House are followed by the fiercest and most uncompromising hostility at all times and in all places. The lie is given freely on the floor of the House, and members bandy the most insulting epithets with true bar-room proficiency. Matters get especially lively when some member denounces Judge Bingham as the "assassin of Mrs. Surratt," or calls

Ben Butler, to his teeth, an "appropriator of other people's spoons." Perhaps, we cannot better illustrate this than by introducing three characteristic scenes in the House. The first occurred on the first Monday of December, 1849, at the organization of the House for that session.

"The slavery question was prominent in the legislative halls. Northern members were determined not to be driven from their 'free soil' position, while the Representatives of the South clamorously insisted upon being allowed the right of carrying their slaves into all the Territories of the United States. The issue had been fairly joined; neither side was disposed to yield anything; and under this condition of affairs, members sternly met face to face.

"The first business was to organize the House. Frequent votes had been taken for the election of a Speaker, but without success. Members desired to open up discussion before this necessary preliminary was effected, and Mr. Toombs, of Georgia, was loudly in favor of latitude of debate. He considered that the House, at the time, was nothing more than a town-meeting, or a mob, and vociferously declared, with extravagant gestures, that the Union was at an end! Practically, however, we had not reached the catastrophe.

"The House adopted a resolution that no debate was in order previous to the election of a Speaker and other officers.

"Mr. Toombs determined to speak. He denied the right to pass any order prohibiting debate. He *would* exercise his right of discussion! He was saluted with deafening cries of 'Order!' 'Order!' to which he responded: 'You may cry order, order, till the heavens fall, but you cannot take this place from *me!*' He had a right, he said, to protest against such a gag!

"While Toombs was engaged in declamation, some one moved to rescind the anti-speaking rule; when the Clerk proceeded to call the roll on that question, amid the combined noise made by 'the gentleman from Georgia' and the repeated calls to order.

"'I know my right,' he repeated for the twentieth time; 'you may call the roll, but you cannot *silence me*. I stand on the constitution of my country, and on the liberty of speech. [Cries of 'Order!'] You have treacherously violated and opposed the rights of my constituents, and your fiendish yells may well be raised to drown an argument which you tremble to hear! I ask by what authority *that* man (pointing at the Clerk) stands there and calls the roll? A member in defending his constitutional rights must not thus be interrupted.'

"Mr. Toombs was becoming weaker and weaker. No one seemed to have any 'constitutional right' but himself; at last, exhausted, hoarse, and panting for breath, from his violent oratorical effort, he sank into his seat, apparently satisfied that he had indulged in 'freedom of debate.'

"Members from the North had no disposition to come in personal collision with Mr. Toombs and his partisans, for they knew that he was earnestly seeking an opportunity to break up the assemblage altogether, if he could, and thus give practical effect to his declaration that the Union was at an end!

"The Clerk was finally allowed to call the roll, when the announcement was made by him that the House had refused to rescind the rule forbidding debate."

The next interesting episode was in June, 1854:

"Mr. Churchwell, of Tennessee, felt compelled to throw himself on the charity of the House for one moment.

"The Speaker reminded him that half a dozen members objected.

"Mr. Washburne, of Illinois, hoped the gentleman would be allowed the privilege he asked. He wished to propound a question.

"Consent having been given—

"Mr. Churchwell said it would be recollected that through the whole of the peculiar debate yesterday good humor prevailed. The point made by the gentleman (Cullum) was, a few words, not of an offensive character, had been inserted in his previous speech. He regretted to find a liberty had been taken by the gentleman to insert language, after the close of the debate, which was not uttered on this floor.

"The language referred to by Churchwell, as attributed in the *Daily-Globe*, to Cullum, was as follows:—

"'I positively deny that I was congratulated by a single Abolitionist on this occasion, and the gentleman should learn to be a little more particular in making this sweeping and random charge, intended to affect others, without the semblance of truth or fact to sustain them. Being untrue, those charges all fall to the ground.'

"There was much confusion during these proceedings.

"Churchwell pronounced the language infamously false.

"Cullum, who sat about fifteen feet from Churchwell, before the last word was pronounced, sprung from his seat, with fists upraised, and exclaiming, 'G—d d—n you,' and 'd—n rascal,' made a desperate effort to reach Churchwell. He was instantly seized by the coat-collar, legs, and body. Several voices called out, 'No words, Cullum'—'Separate them,' 'Sergeant-at-Arms,' etc.

"Churchwell, too, was restrained from advancing toward his colleague. The persons in the main aisle formed an impassable barrier, apart from those who held the belligerents. A crowd quickly gathered round them. The greatest possible excitement prevailed, both on the floor and in the galleries. The Speaker banged and rapped to order, loudly calling on gentlemen to take their seats. The Sergeant-at-Arms rushed first to Cullum, and next to Churchwell, and held up his emblem of office—the mace.

"Cries of 'Order! Order!' were resumed, the Speaker still endeavoring to restore quiet.

"Mr. Seward, of Georgia, moved that the House adjourn.

"The Speaker said he would entertain no question until quiet was restored, and again and again requested gentlemen to be seated.

"Quiet was finally restored. Cullum returned to his seat, and Churchwell to the lobby."

Scene Third occurred in February, 1858:

" On the 1st of February, 1858, President Buchanan transmitted a message to Congress, enclosing and indorsing a copy of the Lecompton Constitution, which had been brought to Washington by John Calhoun. He alluded to 'the dark and ominous clouds now pending over the Union,' and conscientiously believed 'they would be dissipated with honor to every portion of it by the admission of Kansas during the present session of Congress; whereas, should she be rejected,' he greatly feared, 'those clouds would become darker and more ominous than ever yet threatened the Constitution and the Union.'

" The House was thrown into great disorder by this message, and various propositions were made concerning it, including one of reference. During the night session of Friday, the 5th of February, a gentleman in the crowd asked whether he could move that a daguerreotypist be sent for to take a view of the scenes. (Laughter.)

" The Speaker said: 'That is not exactly in order at this time.' (Much merriment.)

"A voice was heard: 'How in the devil can they take pictures by gaslight?' (Ha! ha! ha!)

" Motions to delay action were made, and all questions decided by yeas and nays. Clerk after clerk broke down, in the exercise of calling the roll.

"'Come,' said one, 'let's adjourn; what is the use of continuing this farce?' Another replied: 'I'll bring my bed and stay here till Monday, before I give way to these Lecomptonites.' The dilatory motions continued.

"Mr. Warren, of Arkansas, suggested, as they had been so long engaged on Kansas, they had better do a little for his State of *Ar*-Kansas. (Loud laughter.) Mr. Warren was called to order from the Republican side.

"Mr. James B. Clay, of Kentucky, asked: 'Suppose a gentleman occupies another's seat, what then?'

"The Speaker replied: 'He can be ousted.'

"Mr. Letcher, of Virginia, asked whether that could be done by legal process. (Laughter.)

"Mr. Reuben Davis, of Mississippi, appealed to the Republicans for liberty to speak an hour. He said if this privilege should be denied, his personal popularity would be sacrificed. (Laughter.) He afterward rose to a privileged question, saying, 'that the heat from the gas above was blistering his head, (which was bald,) and he asked unanimous consent to wear his handkerchief on it. (Laughter.)

"Mr. Florence (the top of whose head was also bald) objected, causing renewed laughter.

"It was now half-past twelve o'clock; the sofas were occupied by fatigued Congressmen, while others slept in their seats. The proceedings became exceedingly dull, one-third of the members being asleep, or nodding at their desks; a few were smoking cigars, while others were going to or returning from the restaurant, or 'hole in the wall'—a private drinking-place.

"Mr. Quitman, of Mississippi, re-opened the speaking part of the entertainment, saying, it was now manifest that the present proceedings would come to no practical result. He had no authority to speak for his friends, but he suggested that they come to an understanding that all motions subsequent to the previous question should be withdrawn.

"Just at this point the House was thrown into the most violent excitement, and a fearful scene of confusion was presented.

"Mr. Grow, of Pennsylvania, was walking down the aisle on the Democratic side of the House, when Mr. Keitt and a friend approached him. A scuffle took place between Grow and Keitt; the latter struck him, when the parties were separated. They then exchanged words in an evidently excited manner, when Keitt again dealt a blow at Grow, who knocked Keitt down. Their respective friends rushed to the rescue.

"Various members on each side engaged in a general fight, which took place in the area fronting the Clerk's desk.

"Conspicuous among the belligerents were Messrs. Washburne, of Illinois, and Potter, of Wisconsin. They dealt their blows right and left. The comic feature in the exhibition was: Mr. Covode, of Pennsylvania, seized a heavy spittoon, and raised it to strike Mr. Barksdale, of Mississippi, who had approached him in a menacing attitude. Just at this point, Barksdale's wig fell off. Covode dropped his weapon; he could not strike a man's head which was bald as his hand!

"The Speaker, in a loud and imperious manner, demanded order, and excitedly called upon the Sergeant-at-Arms to interfere. That functionary, carrying the mace of office, together with his assistants, hurried to the scene and penetrated the crowd of combatants. Some minutes elapsed before this beautiful contest was quieted.

"A proposition was made that the vote on the Kansas question be postponed till Monday next. There was a general response from the Republicans of No, no.'

"The confusion began to break out afresh, when the Speaker said he had directed the Sergeant-at-Arms to put under arrest those who disregarded the order of the House.

"Mr. Campbell, of Ohio, said he had foreseen that a disagreeable feeling would result here from the exciting questions connected with Kansas.

"Mr. Barksdale called the gentleman to order.

"Mr. Campbell wished to let the gentleman from Mississippi know that he was his peer.

"And thus the proceedings progressed, amid much disorder.

"A member on the floor of the House, who was near to Grow and Keitt at the time of the outbreak, kindly furnished me, at my request, with the following particulars, I not having been near enough to ascertain them:

"Grow objected to Quitman's making any remarks. Keitt said: 'If you are going to object, return to your own side of the House.' Grow responded: 'This is a free hall; every man has a right to be where he pleases.' Keitt then came nearer to Grow, and said: 'I want to know what you mean by such an answer as that?' Grow replied: 'I mean just what I say; this is a free hall, and a man has a right to be where he pleases.' Keitt seized Grow by the throat, saying: 'I will let you know that you are a damned Black Republican puppy.' Grow knocked up his hand, exclaiming, 'I shall occupy such place in this hall as I please, and no negro-driver shall crack his whip over me.' Keitt again grasped Grow by the throat, and Grow knocked his hand off. Keitt came at him again, when Grow squarely knocked him down. The fight took place at twenty minutes to two o'clock in the morning. Of course, all the sleepers were awakened to the combat. The House continued in session till half-past six o'clock on Saturday morning, and agreed that the vote should be taken on the next Monday, when the message was referred to a committee of fifteen." *

Let no one suppose that these scenes were peculiar to the *ante bellum* days of the House. Others, quite as characteristic, have occurred since then. The sharp passages between Messrs. Washburne and Donneley, and Rousseau and Grinnell, are still fresh in the minds of the public, and the present House has in this respect done some things towards maintaining the traditional reputation of the body.

Party lines are drawn very deeply in the House, and party discipline is very strict. Each party has a recognized leader, who, to some extent, directs its move-

---

* Gobright's *Recollection of Men and Things at Washington.*

ments, and is the most prominent in attacking or resisting the other party. Old Thad Stevens was a real leader, and he made his followers feel his power. His will was their law, and woe to the politician who dared to oppose him. When Thad "cracked his whip," as the phrase of the time had it, the Representatives who followed his leadership came crowding to his side, to do his bidding, as meek as a parcel of lambs. The present leader of the Republican party in the House is undoubtedly the Honorable John A. Bingham, of Ohio; and the leadership of the Democratic party is believed to belong to Mr. James Brooks, of New York.

The men acting as leaders of their respective parties, are always on the alert. It is their business to prevent strife amongst their followers. For the sake of success, they exert themselves to heal these breaches when made, and are usually successful in preserving at least an outward appearance of harmony. The reader will remember the fierce quarrel between Messrs. Butler and Bingham, which was smoothed over for the sake of success in the impeachment trial.

Party is supreme in both Houses of Congress, and legislation is shaped entirely with a view to perpetuate that supremacy. Congressmen support men and measures they dare not defend to their constituents, because they think such measures will benefit the party. No matter how injurious to the country at large a measure may be, if the party in power needs it, it is passed. Democrats and Republicans are alike guilty of such conduct. Members elect, fairly chosen by their constituents, not unfrequently find their seats contested by the beaten candidate, who is in sympathy with the party in power. Feeling sure that the lawfully expressed wishes of the district they represent will not be disregarded, they do not concern themselves about the effort to turn them out, and are startled by a report from the Committee on Elections that they are not entitled to their seats. The result is that they are unseated, and the contesting member, fairly beaten at the polls, put in their places, not because Congress wishes to enforce the will of the people sending Representatives to Washington, but because it wishes to secure one more vote for the party in power. Again, when the case is too clear to be decided on mere party grounds, the same result is accomplished by delaying the report until within a week or two of the close of the session, thus really excluding the rightfully chosen Member from his seat.

Speech-making is a weakness of Congressmen. Every Senator or Member must make one speech during the session, if no more, in order that he may have it printed and sent home to his constituents; and every possible occasion is seized upon with avidity. For the honor of the country, nine out of ten of these speeches had better be unspoken. They are so many empty words; for the Congress of the United States, though it has many able men, does not, as a whole, represent the intelligence or the eloquence of the nation. There are not many really good speakers in either House, and it is a great mistake to think that a Congressman is *ex-officio* an orator. Many of the speeches to be found in the *Globe*, which is the official record of the proceedings, are never spoken at all. The House, in order to escape the infliction, gladly consents to the printing of the speech in the *Globe*, and the Honorable Member is, on the whole, very much better off for the privilege thus accorded him.

The pay of a Member of Congress has just been increased from five thousand to seven thousand five hundred dollars—and mileage. The latter item is intended to cover all the expenses of the regular journeys between Washington and the member's home, which consist in coming to the Capital at the beginning of the session, and returning home at the end of it. This often amounts to a considerable sum, and is paid to members should they remain the whole year in Washington.

The perquisites of members form a considerable item in their compensations. Each one may order large quantities of stationery for his private use; and in this term "stationery," are embraced many articles of luxury and extravagance. Members receive knives, toothpicks, fans, combs, pocket-books, and a variety of other things; and it is even said that articles of clothing have been drawn by unprincipled members "as stationery." A recent report made in Congress, showed that the total cost of these luxuries to the taxpayers of the country amounts annually to an enormous sum; and it is difficult to understand how so much "stationery" can be conscientiously used by Congress, during a single session. In the single item of pocket-knives, it was shown that the number issued to members was sufficient to supply each one with a new knife, of the finest pattern, every week during the session.

Whole tons of writing materials are issued—more, in fact, to each member, than it seems can possibly be used by him. Indeed, the waste and extravagance of members, in articles of "stationery" is abominable, and imposes a heavy load upon our already overburdened people. Members seem to think they are bound by no obligation to be economical of the public funds; and while they are careful to deny appropriations to really deserving objects, on the ground of economy, they never fail to minister to their own luxurious fancies, at the public expense. Not long since the idea was seriously advanced, that it was the duty of the Government to build residences in the city for the Senators, and it is probable that the scheme would have grown in favor, had not the indignant whirlwind of public sentiment swept it away, at its birth.

Congress has just relinquished one of its most cherished and important privileges. In July next, the Franking Privilege will expire by law, and henceforth each M. C. must pay the expense of his correspondence out of his own pocket. The Franking Privilege was originally designed to enable Members of the two Houses of Congress, and certain officers of the Government, to send through the mails their official correspondence and other legitimate mail matter free of charge. For many years it has been so shamefully abused, by Congressmen more than any others, that it has been a serious burden to the Postal branch of the Government. Whole tons of matter have been sent in this way through the mails. Packages occupying an entire mail bag have been sent by Congressmen with tough consciences as franked matter. It is said that sewing-machines have been thus sent by members to their wives at home, and that certain members have sent home their dirty linen to be washed, under the cover of their franks, in order to save expense. However, the great swindle has been brought to an end, and in July next no free matter will be sent through the mails. From the President to the humblest official, every one hitherto enjoying the privilege of franking, will be obliged to prepay his mail matter. This sudden effort at retrenchment is a matter for which Congress deserves no credit whatever. The measure had its origin among the people of the United States, whose taxes went to pay the cost of transporting franked matter, and their demand for the abolition of the privilege was resisted until it was plain to the Honorable Members that the people would send to Washington men who *would* execute their will if a change was not speedily made. Hence the passage of the new law.

The presiding officer of the House is called the Speaker. He is addressed by Members as Mr. Speaker. He finds it no easy task to rule such an unruly body as the House, and his ability to do this is usually accepted by Members and by the country as evidence of genius of a high order. As a matter of course, the Speaker being elected by a majority of the votes of the Members, belongs to the party in power.

The present Speaker is Mr. JAMES G. BLAINE, of Maine. He is a large, fine-looking man, and has served as Speaker during two sessions of Congress, or since 1869. Mr. Blaine had the misfortune to be "mixed up," in the *Crédit Mobilier* Scandal, but the good fortune to emerge from it with less damage than any of those concerned in it, except, perhaps, Senator Logan, of Illinois. As the Speaker and as a man, Mr. Blaine is very popular with the House, and is much liked by his political opponents, who rarely find fault with his rulings He shows to advantage in the Speaker's chair, and presides over the House with dignity and firmness. As a general rule, he follows the example of the Members of the House, and engages in conversation with some one. His inattention is only seeming, however, for he is closely watching the House all the while. A member no sooner rises then the Speaker's quick eye discovers him and announces his name. Let a dozen rise together, and the Speaker, although apparently engrossed in his conversation, will in nine cases out of ten single out the right man and assign the floor to him. Members rarely quarrel with his decisions, as they know them to be just. Long experience has taught the Speaker patience in dealing with the humors of the House. A moderate amount of disorder and confusion will draw from him only a slight rebuke, but frequently the noise increases to such a degree that the Speaker is obliged to reprove the offending members by name.

BENJAMIN F. BUTLER, of Massachusetts, is a burly, heavy man, who waddles as he walks, and carries his head slightly bent forward. He is the best abused, best hated man in the House. It suits some persons to imagine that Ben Butler, as he is popularly called, is simply a blustering, swaggering politician without much ability of any kind. The truth is that Butler's big head contains a good share of the brains of the House, and he possesses qualities which would make him a leader in any cause he might espouse. He failed signally as a soldier during the Rebellion, but as an administrative officer he " was a success." He is a man of extensive, patiently acquired, and thoroughly digested information, and has the courage to form and hold opinions of his own. His share in the impeachment trial of President Johnson was marked by an extraordinary amount of vigor and ability, made all the more striking by the strong personal hostility which characterized it. Butler is much of a philosopher. He is a man of strong feelings, but he has learned to control them, and, when it suits him, he can pocket his grievances, and work with a smiling face by the side of the men whom he hates with all the intensity of his nature. Giving him credit for patriotism, it cannot be denied that he has a thorough appreciation of the interests of Benjamin F. Butler, and those who know him feel sure that his acts, which sometimes seem inexplicable to the outside public, are all directed to the permanent advancement of these same interests. A Scotch writer, who recently visited this country, has drawn the following picture of him:

" A short, stout man, with large bald head, a round body and short spindle legs, stood at the front of the platform, speaking in a somewhat harsh but very fluent and articulate voice. It was easy, even at a glance, to see how this man had the power to make himself an object of deadly hate to a whole people. There was a power in the big bald head, in the massive brow, in the vulture nose, in the combatively bullying face, in the heavy eyelids, and in the keen, scrutinizing eye. It was literally eye, not eyes, for the right eyeball seemed to be engaged in some business of its own, as if relieved from regular duty, while the spirit of the man when he looked at you seemed to crouch at the other, and (from under the heavy eyelid) glare out keenly and warily. He had in his left hand a pamphlet or bit of paper—I could not see which—but once or twice he brought this paper up to the side of the head, within two or three inches of his eye, as if for reference. Tastes differ, but I confess Butler's face was not pleasant to me. His speech, as far as I heard it, was clear, logical, and full of practical wisdom, but was delivered with an audacity of manner that made one reluctant to admire even what deserved admiration."

The same writer is responsible for the following story, which is too good to be lost:

"The character written in Butler's face seems to have developed itself at an early age. When a lad at college, it was binding on the students to attend the college church—a duty which to Benjamin was very irksome. On one occasion he heard the college preacher (who was also a professor) advancing propositions like the following: 1. That the elect alone would be saved. 2. That amongst those who by the world were called Christians, probably not more than one in a hundred belonged really and truly to the elect. 3. That the others, by reason of their Christian privileges, would suffer more hereafter than the heathen who had never heard the Gospel at all.

"Butler, whose audacity was always more conspicuous than his reverence, made a note of these positions, and on the strength of them drew up a petition to the Faculty, soliciting exemption from further attendance at the church, as only preparing for himself a more terrible future.

"'For,' said he, 'the congregation here amounts to 600 persons, and nine of these are professors. Now, if only one in a hundred is to be saved, it follows that three even of the Faculty must be damned.' He (Benjamin Butler) being a mere student, could not expect to be saved in preference to a professor. Far, he said, be it from him to cherish so presumptuous a hope! Nothing remained for him, therefore, but perdition. In this melancholy posture of affairs he was naturally anxious to abstain from anything that might aggravate his future punishment; and as church attendance had been shown in last Sunday's sermon to have this influence upon the non-elect, he trusted that the Faculty would for all time coming exempt him from it."

General NATHANIEL P. BANKS, of Massachusetts, is one of the noted men of the House. He is a tall, handsome man, about fifty-seven years old. He has a long and honorable public career to look back upon. He is emphatically a self-made man, as he was the son of parents too poor to do more than educate him at the free schools. From a poor apprentice boy, he rose to be the editor of a newspaper, published first in Waltham, and then in Lowell, in his native State. His next step was into the Legislature, in 1848, at the age of thirty-two. He served in both Houses, and was chosen Speaker of the Lower House. He presided over the Convention of 1853, which revised the Constitution of Massachusetts, and for the next four years represented his State in Congress. He was elected Speaker of the House in 1855, and presided over the deliberations of that body with a grace and dignity which have never been surpassed. In 1857, he was chosen Governor of Massachusetts, and was reëlected to that office for three successive terms. He was a Major-General of Volunteers during the Rebellion. General Banks is the Chairman of the important Committee on Foreign Affairs. He was formerly possessed of great influence in the House, but his espousal of the Liberal Republican cause during the recent Presidential Canvass, injured him very greatly, and caused his defeat at the last Congressional election. In consequence of this, he leaves the House in March. Personally he is one of the most popular members of the House, and socially is one of the most brilliant ornaments of the Capitol.

HORACE MAYNARD, of Tennessee, is a tall, dark, wild-looking man, nearly sixty years old. He is gaunt in figure, and looks very much like an Indian. He is one of the few Southern Congressmen who remained faithful to the Union during the Rebellion. He suffered great losses because of his loyalty. He had considerable difficulty in procuring the readmission of his State into the Union after the War, and was refused his seat at the assembling of the Thirty-ninth Congress. He is a native of Massachusetts, and went to Tennessee about 1840, as Professor of Mathematics, in the University of East Tennessee. He is a fierce partisan, and is a man of ability.

JOHN A. BINGHAM, of Ohio, is one of the ablest men in the House. He is nearly fifty-eight years old, sixteen years of his life having been spent in Congress. He is generally regarded as the leader of the Republican party in the House, and is a staunch supporter of the Administration. He is a profound lawyer, and was retained by the Government as Assistant Judge Advocate in the trial of the Assassination Conspirators, in May, 1865. He was prominent in bringing about the impeachment of President Johnson, and served with great credit as one of the Managers of the Prosecution during the trial.

JAMES A. GARFIELD, of Ohio, is another of the marked men of the House. He is thirty-seven years old, is a native of Ohio, and began life as a teacher. He made a brilliant record in the Western army during the Rebellion, and rose to the grade of Major-General of Volunteers. He is an eloquent speaker, and is in high favor with the President. His name has been connected with the *Crédit Mobilier* Scandal, to which we shall refer in another chapter.

WILLIAM D. KELLEY, of Pennsylvania, is another of the self-made men of the House, and is regarded as one of its ablest members. He is fifty-five years old, and is a rugged, hard-featured man. He has fought his way up from his apprenticeship in a jeweller's shop, single-handed, and with no one to help him. He studied law after coming of age, and was admitted to the bar in his twenty-seventh year. He at once plunged into politics as a Democrat, but left that party in 1856, as he could not sustain the repeal of the Missouri Compromise. He is now one of the first men in the Republican party, and is the principal champion in Congress of the High Tariff Members. We shall refer to him again in connection with the *Crédit Mobilier*.

JAMES BROOKS, of New York, is generally regarded as the leader of the Democratic party in the House. He is about sixty-two years old, and is a native of Maine. He was a clerk in a store at the age of eleven, a school teacher at sixteen, and at twenty-one he graduated at Waterville College. After travelling and corresponding with the press for several years, Mr. Brooks found himself in the Maine Legislature at the age of twenty-five. The next year he removed to New York City, and established the *Daily Express*, of which he is at present an editor and proprietor, his brother being his associate. He has been actively engaged in political life since his removal to New York, and has served several terms in Congress. He is an able and vigorous speaker, and usually commands the attention of the House when he has the floor. Although not formally recognized as such, he is generally regarded as the leader of the Democratic party in the House, and is decidedly one of the soundest men in the hall. A Republican historian styles him the "most plausible and best natured of Democrats." Mr. Brooks will claim our attention again in connection with the *Crédit Mobilier*.

FERNANDO WOOD, of New York, may be easily recognized by his tall, commanding figure, and his heavy white moustache, which contrasts strikingly with his dark hair. He is one of the finest-looking men in Congress, a circumstance of which he is well aware, and in which he takes considerable pride. Mr. Wood is regarded as one of the most adroit and experienced politicians in the House. He has a host of enemies, who show him little mercy in their denunciations of him.

The member most largely sought out by strangers, and the one whose name is now oftenest in print and on people's lips, is

OAKES AMES, of Massachusetts, whom the New York *Herald* has dubbed "Hoax Ames." Mr. Ames is a native of Massachusetts, having been born at Easton in that State, on the 10th of January, 1804. He was educated at the public schools, and upon leaving them engaged in mercantile pursuits. "His first operations were directed towards building up the manufacturing interests of his section of the State; and it was while so engaged that he turned his attention to railroad matters. In 1860 he was elected a member of the Executive Council of Massachusetts for two years. His enterprise and progressive character combined to render him a prominent candidate for Congressional honors, and we find him elected successively to the Thirty-Eighth, Thirty-Ninth, Fortieth, Forty-First and Forty-Second Congresses. He represents the Third Congressional District of Massachusetts, comprising nine wards in the city of Boston, as well as Brookline."

Since the past summer, Mr. Ames has figured prominently in connection with the *Crédit Mobilier* Transactions. He has appeared as the Evil One who made his way into the Congressional Paradise, and tempted the, until then, innocent Congressmen to their fall. "Mr. Ames's further career," says Frank Leslie's newspaper, "as the prime mover of the *Crédit Mobilier*, is well told by the following anecdote:

"Everybody has heard of the man out West who was indicted and tried for stealing a large lot of smoked hams. He employed a lawyer to defend him, but when the evidence was all in, his legal adviser was so overwhelmed with its directness and force, that he sank down in despair. 'Get up and address the jury,' said the prisoner, 'and pitch into the witnesses for the prosecution, for I tell you it will come out all right.'

"The lawyer did as directed, and, to his amazement, the jury, without leaving their seats, rendered a verdict of 'Not guilty.' As they were retiring from the courtroom, the learned counsel, in a hoarse whisper, asked his client how on earth the jury could render such a verdict, in the very teeth of such positive proof that he stole the hams. 'Why, bless your soul,' replied the defendant, 'every man on that jury had some of the hams!'"

Mr. Ames's personal appearance is not prepossessing. He has a hard, rugged face, and one not calculated to win him the confidence of strangers. It is a determined face, and he looks as though he could be a dangerous man if pushed too far. Doubtless some of the members of Congress have already come to this conclusion.

CHAPTER VII.

A GLANCE AT THE LOBBY.

Natural history of the Lobby—"Deluded Souls"—Why Shrewd Men and Women go to Washington—The growing demand for Legislative Aid—The course of Monopolies—How Congress plunders the National Treasury—Popular demand for a Cessation of Subsidies—The true View of the Case—Congressional Breaches of Trust—How the Lobby is worked—Arrival of the Lobbyist in Washington—His Mode of Procedure—A Public Man's Foes are his own Household—A mild Form of Lobbying—Laxity of Public Sentiment upon the subject—Reckless Charges—Difficulty of Proof—The popular Suspicion—The Women of the Lobby—A startling History—Division of the Women of the Lobby—The Women of the Hotels—How they conduct their Operations—Sad State of Affairs—Scene in the Hotel Dining Room—The " Beautiful Woman's Private Table "—Who are caught by it—Susceptible Officials—A Spectacle of Roman Virtue—How to snare a Congressman—The office hunting Women—Humbugging a Secretary—A little Morning Call at the Department—The great Man fooled—Managing the Senate—How to secure a Confirmation—The Widows who have Claims—How to make a small Claim cover a large one—Preserving appearances—The Story of Mrs. Billpusher—Cheap Hospitality—Who pays for it.

It is a weakness of the good people of Washington to believe that they are politicians. Dwelling under the shadow of the General Government, they imagine that they inhale politics with every breath they draw. You will hardly find a male resident of the Capital but is firmly convinced that he has influence with some branch of the Government. He is diffident about exerting it, but is sure that he possesses it. As for the women, their confidence in their power is sublime. Of course they can accomplish what they undertake, for where is the Congressman or official that can resist them? Be he never so obdurate, they are sure they can win him over. How much of truth there is in this feeling, it is impossible to say, but it is certain that numbers of the residents of the city, of both sexes, do seek to exercise this influence, some making an actual business or profession of it. Every winter their ranks are swelled by the arrival of men and women from all parts of the country, who are equally sure that they either possess or can obtain a similar influence over the powers that be, and who are determined to exert it in behalf of the various schemes in which they are interested. These numerous persons make up the class that is commonly known as the Lobby. They constitute a real power at the Capitol, and their appearance is as regularly expected as are the arrivals of the members of the two Houses of Congress. The Lobby has a veritable and interesting history, and its leading members are as well known as any legitimate officer of the Government.

Pecuniary enterprises of all kinds are springing up in various parts of the country every day, and old ones are seeking new channels into which to direct their energies. Some of these are legitimate, and some are whatever you may choose to call them. It is getting to be the habit of capitalists now to expect and solicit aid from the General, or some State Government in everything they undertake, and, strange as it may appear, very few of the greatest schemes which apply to the Government for aid have vitality enough of their own to carry them through to success. The great majority depend upon subsidies of lands or money from the General or State Governments, or from both. In plain English, the men who organize and carry through these schemes, although they do so for their own private benefit, rely upon using the money of the whole people rather than their own. Consequently, men without means of their own, without possessing the confidence of the communities in which they live, without financial standing, or training, or experience, appear before the public as incorporators of some of the most gigantic schemes of the day. Their plan is very simple. If they can secure a grant from the General or State Government, the public funds thus placed in their hands will give them the means of carrying out their schemes. In other words, the people at large pay the cost of the undertaking and the profits go into the pockets of the persons referred to. To be still plainer—their plan is to rob the public treasury, with the aid or connivance of the guards to whom the nation has confided it, and to enjoy the plunder.

The people of the United States are not averse to the granting of aid and encouragement, by the Government, to legitimate enterprises which are for the public good, and which will render, at some time, an equivalent for the aid thus extended. It is both wise and expedient for the Government to foster by all means in its power such enterprises as are truly national in their character; but the American people are decidedly, and very sensibly, opposed to spending their money for the benefit of a private corporation, and are emphatically opposed to such a use of it by Congress. Just now they are very sore over the immense sums that have been squandered by Congress in this way. The Honorable Members are well aware of this, but they appear to entertain a lordly contempt for the will of the people, fancying that they are the masters rather than the servants of the nation. The public feeling has been expressed repeatedly, but the work of "subsidizing" still goes on. Congress appears to have come to the conclusion that it is the lawful owner of the wealth of the nation, and not the trustee holding it for the benefit of the people. The New York *World* commenting on this some time since, very cleverly expressed the popular sentiment on the subject as follows:

"Let us say that the property of the Government of the United States—meaning thereby of course the common property of the people of the United States—is worth $4,000,000,000, or $100 a head. In the management of this property by the few hundred men who make up what we call the Government, the implied trust is that the property will in all cases be managed for the benefit of the whole people, and that in no case shall one or two, or half a dozen, or a hundred citizens be given any portion to use for their own peculiar personal profit, to the exclusion of the remaining millions. Now if the Government—*i. e.*, the men under this trust, the trustees of the people in other words—give say $500,000,000 of this property to a score of men associated together as a railway or other company, to have and to hold and to use it as their own as much as if it were the product of their own toil, the implied trust is broken; the trustees betray the confidence reposed in them. This is not a fashionable view, we know, but still it is a true one. The wrong is the same in the few men called and calling themselves the Government as if they had committed it in their individual capacities and as private citizens. No man in any capacity has any right to betray a trust reposed. And yet, that such betrayal is not only not wrong, but that it is even nobly, gloriously, beautifully right, is the doctrine underlying the subsidy system. The Government, (so the subsidy doctrine runs,) may, and not only may but should, give the Union Pacific Railroad Company, and the rest, hundreds of millions of public acres and scores of millions of public money for the purpose of building up and operating a business for the exclusive profit of the said company, to the utter and eternal exclusion of any and all of the millions of other citizens whom the act of incorporation fails to recite. And as with this one particular donation so with scores of others; it is right and proper for the Government to give away to whom it will so much of the $4,000,000,-000 as it deems proper. It develops the country to do this; it is progress; it is in the line of the best patriotic thought; the wilderness is thereby made to bloom and blossom as a rose—there are, in short an infinite variety of fine phrases to conceal the real nature of the breach of trust. One particularly specious plea is that unless the millions were thus robbed in behalf of the scores, the scores could not provide great and beneficent instrumentalities for the use of the millions. It is forgotten that the scores charge the millions as much for the use of the instrumentalities as if they had not been built with the millions' own means, but had come bodily out of the bank accounts of the scores. If a man steal from me enough to buy him a horse and vehicle, and then insists he is doing me an immense service by charging me $5 for carrying me a mile on my own property, he does that on a small scale which subsidized corporations, railroad or any other, do upon large. Such then is the morality of the subsidy system which has been fostered into such magnificent proportions. The natural operation of the system is to generate about it a fine swarm of adventurers, of all grades, from the benevolent looking company president, whose gold-rimmed glasses would shrivel in the heat of his indignation did any one call him an adventurer, down to the professional lobbyist, whom he uses as the huntsman uses his hound, to run down the game. There being millions at stake, these adventurers, each in his sphere, are instant in action. They cajole, they seduce, they ensnare. All the arts of temptation ooze from their tongues in drops of honey, and fall from their hands in streams of gold. What wonder if success only too often rewards their nefarious efforts—if the not over-stubborn normal virtue of the Senator or Congressman succumbs? If the records of the *Crédit Mobilier* investigation reveal anything, they disclose this—that tactics of this kind were employed with exquisite skill and relentless tenacity; and, despite the half-frantic denials of the victims, it is perfectly evident the strategy of the subsidy adventurers won."

The parties interested in the schemes for which Government aid is asked, begin their operations by supposing that they must have some energetic, active agent in Washington, to keep the scheme before Congress and the Government, and urge upon the members and officials a compliance with their demands. Forthwith, an agent with full powers is despatched to the Capital. This person is generally a man, but is sometimes a woman. Almost all important schemes, however, have agents of both sexes, who are persons of education, intelligence, and great powers of insinuation and fascination. Women make excellent lobbyists, as they are more plausible than men, and cannot be shaken off as rudely.

Upon reaching Washington, the lobbyists are not slow in getting to work. Much is left to their own discretion; but much more is done in obedience to "instructions from headquarters." The aid desired may be from the Government, or from Congress, or from both; and all sorts of artifices are resorted to to secure it. Officials are approached in every imaginable way, and, if no direct bribe is offered, the intriguer endeavors, generally with success, to gain the confidence and friendship of the party against whom his arts are directed. This accomplished, he broaches his scheme so delicately, and presses it so skilfully, that the official is won over before he knows it. If the man fails, the female lobbyist is called in to exert her arts, which are more potent than those of the sterner sex. Congressmen and officials are famous as being the most susceptible men in the world, and the fair charmer is generally successful. Men in public life are very obliging when they choose to be, and these women know how to win favors from them.

It is very common for the lobbyists to approach public men through their families. Mrs. A. or Mrs. B. will receive magnificent presents from persons who are but little more than casual acquaintances. Their first impulse is to return the articles, but they are so handsome, and just what they have been wanting so long, without being able to afford them out of their husbands' incomes —for the lobbyists are careful to inform themselves what will be most acceptable—and so, after a little struggle, they decide to keep the gifts.

Of course some especial civility must be shown the givers of the presents. This is done, and the first point of the lobbyist is gained. In a little while the wife is won over. She thinks the scheme an excellent one—and honestly thinks it too—and will be so beneficial to the country! She does not like to meddle in her husband's affairs, but she will mention the matter to him. The better half of the official being thus secured, the remainder can and does make but a feeble resistance, and his aid is secured for the scheme.

This is lobbying in its mildest form, and official integrity has sunk to so low an ebb that it sees nothing wrong in it. Men's consciences are tough now, and that nice sensitiveness of honor which once marked the public men of our country, seems to have departed from us. Men go into public life now to make money, as they would enter upon a trade. The lobby offers them a fine opportunity for the gratification of their desires, and they are not slow to avail themselves of it. Alas for the country in the hands of such men!

Charges are plentiful in Washington, but it is very hard to get at the facts. Even a Congressional Investigation fails to elicit them. You will be told many things in confidence, but no one is willing to substantiate his charges. Much that you hear is simple scandal, but there is a sad foundation of truth for the rest.

The facts are, that both in Washington and throughout the whole country, the integrity of many men in public life is doubted. The public moneys are wasted. Measures are set on foot and carried out which do not commend themselves to the sober judgment of the people, and which ought not to be adopted by those in power, and the rumor is general throughout the whole country that these measures were carried through by bribery. It is furthermore believed throughout the country that men are sent to Congress, and put into the various departments of the Government for the especial purpose of carrying out the most iniquitous schemes, of preventing inquiry into them, and shielding from punishment those engaged in them. No one will deny that these feelings of distrust and suspicion do prevail all over the land. Their effects are very damaging to the country and to the cause of public morality. It is known that large sums of money are spent by the "rings," as they are called, for the purpose of securing Government aid for their schemes. It is rumored and generally believed that this money is spent in buying the aid of individual members of the Government. It is known that few public men above the position of clerks, can or do live upon their official salaries. They spend annually more than double the sum received from the Government, and many of them have no other visible source of income. It is said that the most of this splendor is paid for by the lobby, and that the majority of public men are always open to bribes. We make no charges against any one. We merely mention what is generally suspected and believed throughout the country at large; and that our statements are true, as to this popular belief, no one will deny. People know that shrewd men and women are sent to Washington every year, and bountifully supplied with money by parties and associations whose habit is not to be so liberal without receiving an equivalent, and the country is now indignantly demanding to know what use is made of this money at the seat of Government.

Mention has been made of the women who come to Washington for the purpose of "working the lobby." These constitute a distinct class which may be divided into various sections.

"The field of the force we are considering is the Lobby, but let the comprehensive term be clearly understood. It is bounded only in territory by the limits of the city itself, in the aspect of it here detailed. From the Capitol parlors to Georgetown, influences ramify and wires work, which draw their power from a common battery, and which discharge it into a common object— some measure which is to be worked up and worked through. Every hotel where 'Members' and 'Senators' (a distinction is always made) either board, or during the day and night do congregate from their in-town lodgings, is carefully colonized with reliable women, in the interests of projects seeking legislation. Several pretentious, unsuspicious, and even imposing houses are often rented in the most respectable quarters 'for the session,' and put in charge of considerate, accomplished, educated, and fascinating 'ladies,' conveniently provided with husbands *ad interim*, which latter have legitimate business to account for their presence and to fill out their time. Moreover, if 'no one can tell who these people are,' discreet and very proper persons stand ready to avouch that they have known them at Syracuse, Boston, New Orleans, or where not, for years; that they are eminently respectable, persons of culture, and friends of their particular friends—indeed, position and pedigree can be made to order, and these female foragers can be better fortified than many a darling, modest wife, whose reputation can never in human likelihood, and never in human justice, become the subject of debate or inquiry.

"While these rotten ones are thus made secure from any worse criticism than conjecture, and while they play many parts, which will be duly told, there is a corps of operators who act as bushwhackers between the line of conventionality and the verge of looseness. Women of spice and dash they are, so prudishly quick to interpret anything as an insult from those not within their circle, and to regard everything from those who are in it—no matter how familiar or impertinent—as only 'mischief,' 'fun,' and 'really meaning nothing.' She will flare up at a mere glance of curiosity from a stranger, and pardon a kiss red hot on the lips from a man who has a vote, on the promise that he will not do so again, or at least will not put her in a false position by talking about it.

Pretty sure it is that talk as he may about it, he will not succeed in putting her in a false position. These gaudy guerillas are at this point only mentioned in course.

"Another intermediate division of women workers are the lovely and patient sufferers. They work the mines of Representative and Senatorial sympathy. They are the weeping and winsome widows of the period. The dear departed one was, it may always be depended on, 'a general during the late War,' and his unrequited services are here pleaded as entitling his ripe and sorrowing relict to a 'claim,' or at least to a pension, on either or both of which 'the Committee has promised to act soon.' While there are bona fide cases of this character, at which he were less than a man who would sneer, the number of sham ones is notorious, and they can always be detected by the dependence which any claim submitted has for success upon some contemporary measures which are rank with possibilities, if not with direct evidences of jobbery. A widow, young, handsome, and seemingly modest, has a claim. She assures a member that she has been told that there will be no chance for the consideration of such a claim until such an one (always of a much larger kind) is got out of the way; and if this latter could be easily disposed of, then hers would go right through. These can be set down at once as agents of the big thing which is only incidentally mentioned.

"The women who do not work for the passage of bills, but who work for the procurement of nominations and confirmations, are quite a notable fraction of the force under review. Having to deal with a President, with Secretaries, and with the two Senators, and they alone, of all the Senate, from the State to which they wish the appointment accredited, they are always mighty clever persons, and except for the indubitable stigma which their very activity in patronage getting affixes to them, cannot be distinguished from the best demeaned and best charactered of all the women in Washington. They exist, and are potential within their pale. Conventionality itself has no little game which they are not up to. A stranger of either sex, casually at the Capital, cannot tell them from the real thing. That fatal facility for getting intimate with all the men of available influence, and of happily subsisting without the intimacy of very many of their own sex, betrays them, however, in the long run. But though seldom unruffled, they are never seriously soiled. So careful and so conventional are they, that the jury of Society rarely agrees on a verdict in their case. They are the cream of the cheese we are cutting into.

"First and most numerous are the Hotel Women of he Lobby. Under these are included both the general force who labor to effect legislation, and the finer, keener, warier sisterhood of office-hunters. They generally come some time before they are directly needed. That is, they flutter in the air before the prey is started. Till after the holiday recess, little is really done, or even proposed, in Congress. By the first Monday in December. however, these hotel haunters are present. Why they are so soon on hand is not hard to explain. They don't desire to emphasize their arrival by the simultaneous introduction of the very bills to which they are committed—rather for which they are procured. Moreover, they want to feel the ground, to renew old acquaintances, and to form such fresh ones as are, or may be, conducive to their ends. They believe that early birds catch not only the first worms, but all the worms. In the hotels they do not behave themselves unseemly. A Washington hostelry is eminently moral on the surface. You must have business or baggage, one or the other, to be able to negotiate for permanent board in any of them. In addition to these requirements, the lobbyesses generally hunt in couples. Mrs. Billpusher and her sister, intending to spend the winter in Washington, can very properly apply for modest fourth story apartments, 'bedroom and parlor adjoining,' and as they are refined looking people, with no lack of money, and with ability to refer to not a few Congressmen of the period, they are received at so much a month, and no questions asked. Sometimes Mrs. Billpusher does not bring on a sister, but a lady friend, Miss Memberhooker, for instance. It matters not which, and it matters not whether, after the lapse of a few initiatory weeks, the second leaves or not, which she frequently does. Once established in a fashionable hotel, the next step is to secure a 'regular' table in a commanding quarter of the dining-room. This table is at once a base of operations and a strategic point. It must be central, but not too near the main entrance, where the transient guests are herded. It must be accessible from the private stairs and from the public doors. It must be large enough to accommodate three or four persons besides those regularly at it. It must be in a good light, and it must be furnished with a quick, wide-awake, active darkey as waiter. In a day or two that table will lose its integrity as a piece of furniture. It will be sentiently identified with the persons who inhabit around it at meal time. They will be the feature of that scheming spot. For a few days Mrs. Billpusher and her sister, or friend, will come down to the aforesaid table alone. Inasmuch as the other permanent lady guests of the house will be probably from the first attended by their fathers, husbands, brothers, or some one else's brothers, this lack of an escort will attract a little notice, but any premature comment will be nullified by the beautifully retiring demeanor of the ladies in the case. They will come down after most of the people are through, will deport themselves with exemplary quietness and retirement, and will leave as modestly as they came in. A day or two thereafter, all the mild misses and the doubting dames adjacent will be envy-struck by the appearance at the solitary table of the most dashing of dashing men, his clothes perfectly *à la mode*, his manners the acme of possession and grace, and his frame compounded of that union of bulk with beauty, which fills at once the eye and the aspiration of a woman at first sight. The attentions he will pay to the lone, if not lorn, ladies, whose prior solitude has excited commiseration, will be all what they could desire, and everything which spectators of the same sex would covet, and compass if they could. 'Isn't he elegant?' 'Who is he?' 'When did he come?' 'Where did he come from?' 'I wonder if he's her husband?' 'Do you see anything singular about him?' 'Im going to get pa to find out at the office what his name is, and all about him!' These and similar sentences will sparkle round the tables concerning him. It never occurs to a single one of the talkers to suspect him to be this woman's keeper, instead of her loyal husband or her honorable friend.

"Through this morally noisome exquisite, Congressmen of political inexperience, loose social habits, or such as have, from their obscurity or crimes, never been admitted to regular circles, will be introduced to these women of business and mystery. In a little while a complete and a weekly reinforced cabal will be formed. The mask of ladyhood will still be maintained, but something or other will ere long make the mask transparent, and through it to sensitive eyes will peer and appear the painted features and the ice-cold forehead of those who graft on to the subtle sale of their characters the destinies of laws, made not for the people, but for a few, rendered inaccessible yet powerful under the name and form of a corporation. Each day in the dining-room the proprieties will grow limper Honorables who eat with their knives and come in with unkempt hair to dinner will be welcomed to the board with the set stage smile, and their greedy eyeballs will leave the perusal of the powdered face to roll coarsely down to and over the snowy shoulders as the swaying body from its chair bends forward to salute the man without a virtue but not without a vote. The meals will be more a revel than a repast. Before the first course is under way, hotel wines, which bloat coarseness, passion, fellowship, and corruption to high tide, are ordered, and the popping of corks makes the jeering jests inaudible, and all but unheard for the time is the hollow laugh of the prandial fools of to-night, who are also the Parliamentary knaves of to-morrow and yesterday. Wine begins, accompanies, and closes the eating; and from the table will the party adjourn to the private parlor to more wine, to cards, to flash music, to general chaff, and to such commerce of charms against votes as can be struck between a drunken, conscienceless man and a wily, willing woman.

"In any single 'first-class' hotel in Washington, at any time during mid-session, at least half a dozen of these lobbyesses are thus at work at once, each one roping in her dozen or ten of wild-cat Congressmen. The lever of lust is used to pry up more Legislators to the sticking point than money itself avails to seduce. Given a 'member,' with his family and all who can or would care to tell on him hundreds of miles away, and present to him all the delights and none of the dangers or expenses of wantonness, and ten to one he falls. The address and cunning with which he can pursue his path rob the vice of half its hesitation in shearing off its grossness. That a public and a respectable hotel should or would brothelize itself is not to be supposed. Moreover, unlike the Gospel, this thing is done in a corner; this lobbying is transacted under the guise and guild of social visits—open sesame to a Congressman any and everywhere in Washington. Tolerated if not caressed are a Congressman's friends, even if not more recently formed than Veeneering's oldest and best. Moreover, landlords can afford to be blind. In session, the field of guests is white unto the harvest. Money is power, and so long as the regular bills promptly paid are daily supplanted by costly extras equally quickly settled for, anything short of flagrante delicta will pass for Old School Presbyterianism. Nor is anything indictable. Guesses there may be. Indications, perhaps, abound. Moral conviction widely obtains. All the virgins and the married hens cry shame, and wonder who is Mrs. Billpusher's dressmaker, and if her diamonds are real. By this time the latter has grown bolder. Society not knowing either her grandfather or her business, will not receive her. So much the worse for society. She always did hate women—all of them but one. So she stuns the eye with her dresses, decollete or square in the neck; plays on the keys of the air with the scientifically negligent sweep of her train; queens it through her room to her table; takes her moselle as often as her Congressional friends, albeit it only flushes and never flusters her; glares down her sisterly critics; and repairs to her private parlor, followed by a wake of honorables, picking their serrate teeth on the way.

"Oh! she is a sharp woman. She knows what's what. Therefore it is that she takes all the New York dailies, and one way or another has yea and nay lists of both Houses always available in her rooms. The run of legislation is as familiar to her as to the unhappy man who has to-night to edit the manifold of Congress for the morning journals. The precise parliamentary effect of moving to reconsider a vote, and to lay the motion to reconsider on the table, is lucidly apprehended by her, and not three women out of every ten thousand who read this article can or care to know aught of this paradox, which to her is vital.

"She has her pleasures, too. It is her delight to be escorted to receptions on the arm of a Congressman of the coarser cast. An M. C. can, by the mere factitious force of position, assure her introduction to and attention from Presidents, Vice-Presidents, and Secretaries, who are nothing if not the dear public's most obedient, most humble servants. Then, too, the Jenkins of the small local papers is sure to put her costume down along with those of ladies who are as much angered as she is pleased at the juxtaposition. Besides, in so cosmopolitan a city, there is a constant flux of new comers, and on these can she disburse herself till she snares them in or they find her out. Rarely going to the Capitol, she is, however, when condescending to be there, scrupulous to occupy the diplomatic box, the dapper doorkeepers whereof have been directed to pass her in by honorable adulterers on the floor, from whom their bread and cheese are. The ensemble of the hotel lobbyess has thus been sketched. The details of her dodges can be inferred from what has been said.

"The office-hunting women are very like unto her. Theirs is a task of more unity, more concentration, but it is questionable if it is not of greater difficulty. What they seek is one thing, at least one thing at a time—one office for one man. The steps to this are a nomination and a confirmation. Lucrative, not especially prominent places are intrigued for in this way. Missions, judgeships, customs collectorships of large import in a double sense, are esteemed too high game to work for in this manner. These go to merit, or if not thatwise, are parcelled out to relatives or gift-bearers, or very prominent politicians. But revenue-officers, consulships, and the like, are constantly obtained by womanly effort for manly candidates. A would-be appointee who can retain a sensible and beautiful woman in his personal interest is reasonably certain of persuading or coercing a considerable slice of the public patronage. This is the most delicate kind of work. Cabinet members, or the equally powerful and equally respectable commissioners, must, in nearly every case, be influenced to advise the nomination which the President must ultimately make. There is no suggestion sought to be conveyed that any of these gentlemen are corrupt. That they can be and are imposed on in many of their selections will not be denied. And it is these women office-hunters who effect this exquisite imposition. A double deception falls to their lot: the palming off of themselves, and the making good of the spurious claims of those they work for. To Messrs. Grant, Boutwell, Delano, or Fish she must appear as a lady, and before them assume the virtues which she has not. Excuse must be adroitly established whereby to account for her appearing as an office-seeker The candidate to this end is made out to be her relative (which has a strong precedent in its favor), or her noble benefactor, in which latter case the delusions are easier and the scope for fabrication unlimited. A lady daily at the department or the White House soliciting this one thing—an office—is pretty apt to compel to address and to importunity what the coalition of a score of men would fail to accomplish. The lady has never done such a thing before; does not know how to go about at all; if wrong in coming direct to the Secretary, to whom she has letters of introduction, will he kindly pardon her inexperience and refer her to a proper subordinate, so that all may proceed in course; she knows the liability of being confounded with those horrid women of the lobby, of whom she has vaguely read; and again, she knows how frequent it is for these women themselves to disclaim exactly what she is now disclaiming; this is owing to her unfortunate position and to her exceptional interest in the fortunes of her noble benefactor; Washington is a horrid place, and any lady could well wish she was out of it; but she has intruded too much on the Secretary already, and would beg to call again to-morrow, so she must shake hands and bid him good-bye for the time; by the way, she forgot to mention that the chairman of the Committee on Commerce or Finance, to whom she was so fortunate as to be accidentally introduced last night, was kind enough to assure her there would be a favorable report were the name of her noble benefactor, who was well-known to the gentlemen of the committee, to receive the recommendation of the Secretary; but— ah, how time passed while she was rattling on; so, again and for the last time good day. A plump, throbbing hand in pressure; dark, large liquid and pleading eyes looking into the steel gray of the Secretary's for a minute; a horizon of classical features; the mingled sight, scent and suggestion of an elegant attire, elegantly inhabited—all this fires the fancy and soothes the senses for a brief while; then, after departure, inexorable routine, hard practical statistics, or harder Gradgrinds of men pass in business review, and the day becomes a desert of prose with a single oasis of poetry in it. If that woman can keep up appearances at the department, the chance is ten to one that she will get her nominee sent in. Hers is there only a work which in a sense is creditable to her as a woman and an artiste. Before the secretaries, who are gentlemen of virtue without exception, her task is simply the reflection or the simulation of sympathetic, cultivated, energized honorable womanhood. An office is a legitimate object of ambition. Office-seeking on a fair statement of claims and credentials is not unworthy work; nor is it at all intrinsically wrong to surcharge your friends with zeal for your interests. But the professional woman office-hunter has so grafted on to her role all the arts of simplicity, virtue, purity, seemingly headlong womanly zeal, which knows neither method, concealment, nor formality, that it is entirely literally possible for her to deceive the very elect. Her 'plant' is simple, and, with her, at the department, honesty (at least exterior honesty) is the best policy. If there is a weak carnal spot in a secretary's constitution, he will soon betray it, and gradually, but not precipitately, will she recognize and act upon it. But she generally carries her point without the suppression of her simulation of true womanhood. Virtue is her own reward in the nomination stage of the business.

"Then comes the task of confirmation. Now her 'lay' is the Senate. That body, smaller than the House, is by so much more measurable, if not manageable. It has a beautiful economy, too, of procedure in the matter of confirmation for minor offices. All the revenue nominations go to the Committee on Finance, which means John Sherman, of Ohio. All the consular nominations go to the Committee on Commerce, which means Zachariah Chandler, of Michigan. These Senators, as chairmen of these respective committees, are practically supreme in the article of favorable or unfavorable reports. All their colleagues in committee are glad enough to throw the general responsibility of the batch of nominees on these two. These two are too conservative of their accredited power to decline the assumption, or to indulge the exercise of this responsibility. They prefer officially to retain and personally to shift it. The committee have thrown it on them. Hoop la! They will devolve it deferentially and discreetly on some one else. Who so proper persons as the Senators from the State from which the nominee hails, and to which he is to be accredited? If the brace of Senators from that Commonwealth are both Republicans, then are they both conferred with, which means that the one of the two which is keener politician rules his colleague without the latter's knowing it, just as Morton, of Indiana, though not a large man in one sense, is big enough in another, utterly to shade into invisibility the obese bulk and the minimum mentality of his colleague, the pathetic and plethoric Pratt. If, as in the case of New Jersey, one Senator is Radical and the other Democratic, then has the former a soft thing, and he dominates the destiny of all the candidates from that province in the crucial concern of confirmation. Hence, Sherman and Chandler repose the rejection or commit the confirmation of the candidates in and to the option of these two Republican Senators, or this one Republican Senator, as the case may be. Therefore, is the course of the woman office-hunter plain. Not to euphemize, her 'lay' is to bring over the decisive Senators in question the moment after the name has been brought to the Senate by General Porter, or as soon after as possible. An experienced woman office-hunter will not infrequently be seducing a Secretary out of his moral eye-sight in the morning, and captivating a Senator each successive evening. Her tactics in this last event depend entirely on the character of the man. The Senate, on the whole, is a better body in social extraction and moral behaviour than even any equal number of men drawn from the House. It has its weak men and its wicked men in it, however, as it also has its statesmen, its sensible, brave men; and its loyal husbands and even virtuous bachelors. The man is confirmed. He withdraws his agents, and settles with them as he and they can agree on. If, however, as is not seldom, the woman office-hunter must secure to her interest upright Senators, she either wins them, as she had first won unsuspecting and sympathetic secretaries—which is not harder to do in the one case than the other—or, taking a different tack, she secures to herself another Senator by most questionable means, and then shows him how to secure the Senator whom she needs, in his daily interchange with him of personal and political courtesies. For a Senator to resist the request of an associate, whose motive he has no reason to suspect, is a very rare thing, especially when that associate is of the same party, and when the support solicited will compromise no party interests, and when the acceptance of the solicitation will only take the burden of considering the case off the Senator's shoulders, whereon it has been placed by equally derelict others. Sometimes, too, instead of securing a Senator to secure for her another Senator, the woman office-hunter plies her vocation on a member of the House intimate with the Senator wanted, if possible, a member of the delegation from his own State. If necessary, in stubborn cases, all the artillery of charms, finesse, entreaty, boredom, importunity, and lovely woman in suffering are opened on the badgered legislator, and he must indeed be a man of nerve who can stand before such broadsides.

"The hunter, or huntress, will accost him in the literal Lobby; will send in her card to him from the Senate parlor, or from the ladies' gallery; will call on him at his hotel; will deluge his mail matter with representations (often forged and always procured) from myriad parties, requesting his influence and favor;

will, in short, do any and every thing which a woman in earnest, to whom conscience, truth and honor are no let, can essay or effect. Although the Senator can promise one way and—in the presumed secrecy of executive or committee session—report, act, and vote another, he will find the next morning that true and trenchant tongues have borne the events of executive session to the ears of the woman office-hunter, and the way she will call him to account and threaten to acquaint the press with his double course, is not amusing or undamaging to endure. The odds in this dire diplomacy of Senator against determining woman, are in favor of the latter. If a legislator allows to himself the slightest access from the woman, from that time he either is won to her interest, or tied up from proceeding averse to it. It is indeed known that a refusal to report in favor of a candidate, would have exposure of the most shameless sort as its penalty. More votes than one are thus blackmailed in the affirmative. One vote, however—that of the controlling Senator from the State—is generally enough. In inconsiderable office matters, a flock of sheep does not more obediently follow their leader than the august Senate of this Republic follows the report of the Senator to whom the case is, in the wholesale footballing of responsibility, committed.

"Any one of the leading hotels here, part of the politico-socio strategy which we have been considering, will also contain in addition to the lobbyesses and woman office-hunters already photographed, a bevy of the weeping widows 'who have claims.' In the preliminary classification with which this article started out, these have been mentioned, but they were only mentioned. They are eminently worthy of introduction, and should have their pictures drawn from life, just as large and as natural as the lissome forms acting as purveyors of vital sap to the weeds which they wear. These widows, having all of them lost a dear departed in the late war, come on to Washington to submit claims of back pay or of incidental real damage, or to lay pipe for a pension which, through some hocus pocus, has not been granted on sight. That in many cases their object and aims are worthy is most probable. That in not a few other cases they are no widows at all, and that they have not dared submit a single paper or claim to the scrutinizing eye of any committee, is also true. Here, then, on false pretences, it remains true that they must be also here on some more substantial business which does not come to the surface until the time is propitious for their schemes to go a-ripening. They are often, mostly always in fact, acompanied by a child. A widow with a child is an interesting object. The child is a good sponge wherewith to absorb attention. He, she, or it, too, falls to playing with other children round the hotel corridors, and himself, herself, itself, *and* the mother do thereby become acquainted with other families; the offspring really doing much better than letters of introduction. Moreover, the very existence of the youngster is demonstrative of paternity, and proof presumptive of matrimonial maternity and subsequent widowhood, inasmuch as the responsible man in the premises never appears. In passing, it must here be submitted that, even if the widow be a *bona fide* widow and her claim a *bona fide* claim, it often happens that whether from straitened circumstances, large inducements, ripe opportunities, innate corruptibility, or from the very intoxication for affairs which her own claim-hunting implants, the real widow with the real child and the real claim will be very prone to tack her claims on as a rider to some much more imposing, well-lobbied job, and will find in its success either the success of her own proposition or such satisfactory compensation as will make up for the loss of it, till the next session allows her to renew it as before, perhaps renewing it in this indeterminate fashion perennially. One North Carolina vidual claim of this character was prosecuted feebly but profitably in this manner for forty years, being taken up by children of the third and fourth generation, and finally settled in 1859, with an interest which considerably exceeded the principal. These widows are very like other widows in tactics, although the designs of those we are considering are possibly more sinister than we should prefer to credit any of their contemporaries with. Grief, which is inconsolable until the arrival of a consoler; a demeanor which attracts observation by shunning it; habits which incarnate privacy and tantalize to its invasion; ability to talk a wife blind and look clear through her adjacent husband at the same time; the wearing of mourning both as a comfort and a coquetry; a gravity of manner which does not suggest frigidity, but only great warmth under strong control the cap which captivates and captures; the retention of the girl's ardor grafted on to the matron's invaluable experience;—all these little combinations and contradictions are played off by our subjects with eminent success. They stalk their deers. They do not hunt except alone. They do not pursue a herd. They draw off the best buck from the rest and him they bring to bay, often to a bay window of the public parlor; *tête-à-tête* in the deepening twilight, and while the halls are full of ebullient flirters and the carpets kissing the feet of merry dancers, the quiet, sorrow-stricken widow with a claim, in the concrete corner is fascinating by heroic humility and scientific assumption of sables and sincerity some very considerable statesman whose vote is all important on the particular job she has in hand. Any regular 'procurer of legislation' here will tell you that a smart, youngish widow is the best aid to have—if (a portentous if) she is to be depended on. Depended on means guaranteed against the probability of assaulting some distinguished and rich nobody and marrying him with lucre prepense before he can defend himself or call for assistance.

"Such base and cowardly attacks are successfully made here every winter. A widow, in the language of the procurer, needs watching from the first. She has no objection in the world to doing a good thing for her agents, albeit she never stops at doing a better thing for herself. If the lobbyist will support her during the session, well; but if the man whom the lobbyist selects for her to secure for him can be secured for herself, by herself, for life, and thereby secure more than support, position, and comfort—and even, may-chance, affection—through all the winters and all the summers of time which remains to her, probably that is better, and our widow sees it in the same light herself.

"Respect for truth exacts the concession that mostly these widows with claims do the cleanest work of the Lobby. Having been married, they know that the maintenance of at least their conventional repute, if not their real character, is the only barrier which they or any other woman can erect between self and hell, even on earth. They do not first conserve and then flout the proprieties. They do not keep that carnal convenience known as a private parlor. They affect and judiciously circulate in the public reception rooms. They breakfast not boldly, they dine decorously, and they tea tastefully. They do not take to wine, and they associate, when with men, with gentlemen. Neither are they tabooed by the ladies, as a whole. The more critical of society do not know them, but the unsuspicious and more tolerant take them on credit, and are not often called on to foreclose the social mortgage. They are careful of their hours, and generally move round in public places with a party of their own sex. Still their ability to assist the Lobby, and their retention by that Lobby, are patent, and the copyright is apt to be secured, as we have seen, by some susceptible single person who seconds them even as husband through life. Let us believe as well of them as we can, and, if they do even compass wrong votes by wrong means, let us conclude their poverty and not their will consents.

"Outside of the hotels, and on even more pretentious,

though less populous, thoroughfares than they occupy, can be pointed out a few unsuspicious, even imposing residences rented for the season or the session, which is a synonym of that term here. Those who live in them are not Washingtonians. They cannot be said to be known to any of our people, and even the oldest citizens' associations fail to recall ever having heard of them since the Capital was chained off by the surveyors at the beginning of the century. There is absolutely nothing exceptional or objectionable in any of the appointments or occupants of these houses. The inmates maintain style, and maintain it genteelly. They have coachmen, waiters, sometimes footmen, and nearly always pews in Dr. Newman's church, or some Episcopal religious edifice. A lady and her indubitable husband often come out and proceed in company to church, theatre, Capitol and other public resorts. He gives receptions, say as often as once a fortnight, and but for the preference he has to make every entertainment purely a stag-party, there would be no apparent difference between his and other people's social occasions. Not that no ladies call, for some of them do, and arrive in their own carriages at that, sending in their cards, and driving on, after a short interchange of courtesies and compliments. If inquisitive neighbors' servants pump, at the instigation of their curiosity and their mistresses, the domestics in the establishments we are considering, they certainly learn nothing against them, and the exact amount of what they do learn is not expressible by any existing fractional term. Perhaps the old adage, 'Tell me what company you keep, and I'll tell you what you are,' may assist to solve the problem of being and business in the case of our subject. Well, she who called at high noon was Mrs. Billpusher, and with her was Miss Memberhooker, whom we beg our readers not to forget. After them called the distinguished and versatile woman whom we saw hunting up nomination and confirmation incarnate in the person of a Secretary and a Senator. The gentlemen who constitute the guests at the stag-parties hereinbefore mentioned are notably all Senators and Representatives, with a very slight intermixture of newspaper correspondents and a man or two of the great number who come to and depart from Washington with Congress. Allow us, then, to introduce the public, to whom we look as unto the hills whence cometh our help, to the dinner-giving members of the ramified Lobby. That woman and that man may be wife and husband or not. They pass for such, and it serves their purpose here. It is their vocation to entertain the friends of the bill. The house and furniture, even to the table service, the coach and span, the church pew, the servants and their wages, are all provided for them by the Lobby, whose they are and whom they are bound to serve. In return for value received, they exercise and dispense prandial powers and conversational graces which would honor and would be rarely found in the most polished circles. The art of preparing a dinner is equal to that of upsetting a dynasty. The greater art of bringing the right sort of guests together, and of realizing in the succession of the courses the subtler but more powerful feast of reason and flow of soul, embodies a statesmanship which could render larger possibilities, hold up empires, and rear the republics which endure. This art—this great art—these people understand to perfection. Of course, of these two, the woman is the greater. In society she is bound to take the lead, and the hostess anywhere is the toast and the sun to which her lord is a satisfied satellite. These dinner-givers turn out well sometimes. Under Tyler's administration the son of a Senator married the daughter of a dinner-giver; that son is now a very distinguished military man, and a brother of his, who married a ballet-girl off the stage of New Orleans in a spree, has now the most showy wife at the Capital, to which he comes as a Senator of a proud State, and where recently he purchased a princely residence on the very site of the former one in which his father dined and his father's son married. There may be nothing worse than dinners at these places. Let us hope not. One cannot affirm otherwise, and the supposition is always on the side of toleration. They are elegantly equipped, and they wield that powerful influence which the table has always concentrated and radiated in conspiracy or politics—begging excuse for the tautology. All sorts of vague statements obtain concerning these establishments. If the events inside anything like earn the reputation attributed to them, then right in the midst of our political civilization exist orgies which make Pagan Rome and Christian France as the garden of the Lord. They are credited with being the most select and refined of the brothels of the period. It would be difficult to maintain this assertion, because the utmost local vigilance fails to discover more females than the mysterious woman and her harmless necessary servants as regular residents; and these no more make a bagnio than three swallows make a summer."

CHAPTER VIII.

THE CREDIT MOBILIER.

History of the Crédit Mobilier—Its connection with the Pacific Railway—The Oakes Ames Contract—Liberality of the Government towards the Road—A sharp Transaction—Bleeding the Government—Congressional Aid—The kind of Aid needed—"We want more Friends in Congress"—Ames undertakes to manage Congress—"Satan in Paradise"—How Ames let his Congressional Friends into a "Good Thing"—History of the Purchase of the Stock—The Crédit Mobilier cheats the Government again—Estimate of the Profits of the Crédit Mobilier—Where the Money came from—How to win Friends in Congress—Quarrel between McComb and Ames—Letting the Cat out of the Bag—Charges against Congressmen—Indignant denials of the Crédit Mobilier Congressmen—"We never owned any Stock"—Fatal Mistake of the Congressmen—A Lie out somewhere—Meeting of Congress—Demand for an Investigation—The real Issue—Report of the Committee—A pitiful Affair—Congressmen convicted of Falsehood—The Innocents in Congress—Detailed Statement of the Facts in the Case of each Congressman—The two Victims—A Congressional Committee trying to humbug the People—The Truth of the Matter—The Crédit Mobilier Senators—The Facts in each Case—The Evils of a bad Memory—Oakes Ames's Note-book—Senator Patterson's Documents—The Case of Mr. Colfax—Detailed Statement of it—Terrible Chain of Circumstantial Evidence—The Vice-President's Dilemma.

ONE of the great public works of the Union, of which the whole country is justly proud, is the Pacific Railway, extending from the Missouri River to the Pacific Ocean. The early history of the great road is a story of constant struggles and disappointments. It seemed to the soundest capitalists a mere piece of fool-hardiness

OAKES AMES.

to undertake to build a railroad across the continent and over the Rocky Mountains, and, although Government aid was liberally pledged to the undertaking, it did not, for a long time, attract to it the capital it needed. At length, after many struggles, the doubt which had attended the enterprise was ended. Capital was found, and with it men ready to carry on the work. In September, 1864, a contract was entered into between the Union Pacific Company, and H. W. Hoxie for the building by said Hoxie of one hundred miles of the road, from Omaha west. Mr. Hoxie at once assigned this contract to a company, as had been the understanding from the first. This company, then comparatively unknown, but since very famous, was known as the Crédit Mobilier of America. The company had bought up an old Charter that had been granted by the Legislature of Pennsylvania to another company in that State, but which had not been used by them.

"In 1865 or 1866, Oakes Ames, then and now a Member of Congress from the State of Massachusetts, and his brother Oliver Ames, became interested in the Union Pacific Company, and also in the Crédit Mobilier Company, as the agent for the construction of the road. The Messrs. Ames were men of very large capital, and of known character and integrity in business. By their example and credit and the personal efforts of Mr. Oakes Ames, many men of capital were induced to embark in the enterprise, and to take stock in the Union Pacific Company and also in the Crédit Mobilier Company. Among them were the firm of S. Hooper & Co. of Boston the leading member of which (Mr. Samuel Hooper) was then and is now a member of the House; Mr. John B. Alley, then a member of the House from Massachusetts, and Mr. Grimes, then a Senator from the State of Iowa. Notwithstanding the vigorous efforts of Mr. Ames and others interested with him, great difficulty was experienced in securing the required capital.

"In the Spring of 1867, the Crédit Mobilier Company voted to add 50 per cent to their capital stock, which was then $2,500,000, and to cause it to be readily taken, each subscriber to it was entitled to receive as a bonus an equal amount of first mortgage bonds of the Union Pacific Company. The old stockholders were entitled to take this increase, but even the favorable terms offered did not induce all the old stockholders to take it, and the stock of the Crédit Mobilier Company was never considered worth its par value until after the execution of the Oakes Ames contract hereinafter mentioned. On the 16th day of August, 1867, a contract was executed between the Union Pacific Railroad and Oakes Ames, by which Mr. Ames contracted to build 667 miles of the Union Pacific Road at prices ranging from $42,000 to $96,000 per mile, amounting in the aggregate to $47,000,000. Before the contract was entered into, it was understood that Mr. Ames was to transfer it to seven trustees who were to execute it, and the profits of the contract were to be divided among the stockholders in the Crédit Mobilier Company, who should comply with certain conditions set out in the instrument transferring the contract to the trustees. Subsequently, all the stockholders of the Crédit Mobilier Company complied with the conditions named in the transfer, and thus became entitled to share in any profits said trustees might make in executing the contract. All the large stockholders in the Union Pacific were also stockholders in the Crédit Mobilier, and the Ames contract and its transfer to trustees were ratified by the Union Pacific and received the assent of the great body of stockholders, but not of all. After the Ames contract had been executed, it was expected by those interested that, by reason of the enormous prices agreed to be paid for the work, very large profits would be derived from building the road, and very soon the stock of the Crédit Mobilier was understood to be worth much more than its par value. The stock was not in the market, and had no fixed market value, but the holders of it, in December, 1867, considered it worth at least double the par value, and in January or February, 1868, three or four times the par value; but it does not appear that these facts were generally or publicly known, or that the holders of the stock desired they should be."

As will be seen from the above statement, the stockholders of the Crédit Mobilier were also stockholders in the Union Pacific Company.

Like all great corporations of the present day, the Union Pacific Road was largely dependent upon the aid furnished by the Government for its success. The managers of the company, being shrewd men, succeeded in placing all the burdens and risks of the enterprise upon the General Government, while they secured to themselves all the profits to be derived from the undertaking. "The Railroad Company was endowed by Act of Congress with 20 alternate sections of land per mile, and had Government loans of $16,000 per mile for about 200 miles; thence $32,000 per mile through the Alkali Desert, about 600 miles, and thence in the Rocky Mountains $48,000 per mile. The Railroad Company issued stock to the extent of about $10,000,000. This stock was received by stockholders on their payment of five per cent of its face. When the Crédit Mobilier came on the scene, all the assets of the Union Pacific were turned over to the new company in consideration of full paid shares of the new company's stock and its agreement to build the road. The Government, meanwhile, had allowed its claim for its loan of bonds to become a second instead of a first mortgage, and permitted the Union Pacific Road to issue first mortgage bonds, which took precedence as a lien on the road. The Government lien thus became almost worthless, as the new mortgage which took precedence amounted to all the value of the road. The proceeds of this extraordinary transaction went to swell the profits of the Crédit Mobilier, which had nothing to pay out except for the mere cost of construction. This also explains why some of the dividends of the latter company were paid in Union Pacific bonds. As a result of these processes, the bonded debts of the railroad exceeded its cost by at least $40,000,000."

Mr. Ames was deeply interested in the scheme, being, indeed, one of its principal managers. Being a Member of Congress, he was peculiarly prepared to appreciate the value of Congressional assistance in behalf of the Crédit Mobilier. It would seem that the object of the Crédit Mobilier was to drain money from the Pacific Road, and consequently from the Government, as long as possible. Any legislation on the part of Congress designed to protect the interests of the Government, would, as a matter of course, be unfavorable to the Crédit Mobilier, and it was the aim of that Corporation to prevent all such legislation. The price agreed upon for building the road was so exorbitant, and afforded such an iniquitous profit to the Crédit Mobilier, that it was very certain that some honest friend of the people would demand that Congress should protect the Treasury against such spoliation. It was accordingly determined to interest in the scheme enough Members of Congress to prevent any protection of the National Treasury at the expense of the unlawful gains of the Crédit Mobilier. Mr. Oakes Ames, being in Congress, undertook to secure the desired hold upon his associates. The plan was simply to secure them by bribing them, and for this purpose, a certain portion of the Crédit Mobilier stock was placed in the hands of Mr. Ames, as trustee, to be used by him as he thought best for the interests of the company.

Provided with this stock, Mr. Ames went to Washington in December, 1867, at the opening of the session of Congress. "During that month," say the Poland Committee in their report, "Mr. Ames entered into contracts with a considerable number of members of Congress, both Senators and Representatives, to let them have shares of stock in the Crédit Mobilier Company at par, with interest thereon from the first day of the previous July. It does not appear that in any instance he asked any of these persons to pay a higher price than the par value and interest, nor that Mr. Ames used any special effort or urgency to get these persons to take it. In all these negotiations Mr. Ames did not enter into any details as to the value of the stock, or the amount of dividend that might be expected upon it, but stated generally that it would be good stock, and in several instances said he would guarantee that they should get at least 10 per cent. on their money. Some of these gentlemen, in their conversations with Mr. Ames, raised the question whether becoming holders of this stock would bring them into any embarrassment as Members of Congress in their legislative action; Mr. Ames quieted such suggestions by saying it could not, for the Union Pacific had received from Congress all the grants and legislation it wanted, and they should ask for nothing more. In some instances those members who contracted for stock paid to Mr. Ames the money for the price of the stock, par and interest; in others where they had not the money Mr. Ames agreed to 'carry' the stock for them until they could get the money, or it should be met by the dividends. Mr. Ames was at this time a large stockholder in the Crédit Mobilier, but he did not intend any of those transactions to be sales of his own stock, but intended to fulfil all these contracts from stock belonging to the company."

"It is very easy," says the New York *Tribune*, "to see that under these circumstances the stock of the

Crédit Mobilier was a very handsome investment, provided it could be purchased at par. Here was wherein Oakes Ames was such a profitable friend to Congressmen and Senators. He let them in, as he phrases it, on the ground floor. They got their stock at par, and the dividends which were ready to be paid were more than enough to pay for the stock. This is what is called in Wall Street parlance making one hand wash the other. The actual value of the stock thus sold at $100 a share would have been to anybody out of the circle of Oakes Ames's friends not purchasable for less than $300 or $400. But there was a film of decency thrown over the transaction by Mr. Ames, in charging several months' interest upon the stock at the time it was sold to the Members of Congress. This interest had accrued while he was holding it to see where it could be placed to the best advantage."

The motive of Mr. Ames in thus "placing," as he termed it, this immensely profitable stock among the Members of Congress, is thus stated by the Poland Committee:

"In relation to the purpose and motive of Mr. Ames in contracting to let Members of Congress have Crédit Mobilier stock at par, which he and all other owners of it considered worth at least double that sum, the Committee, upon the evidence taken by them and submitted to the House, cannot entertain a doubt. When he said he did not suppose the Union Pacific Company would ask or need further legislation, he stated what he believed to be true, but he feared the interests of the road might suffer by adverse legislation, and what he desired to accomplish was to enlist strength and friends in Congress who would resist any encroachment upon or interference with the rights and privileges already secured, and to that end wished to create in them an interest identical with his own. This purpose is clearly avowed in his letters to McComb, copied in the evidence, where he says he intends to place the stock 'where it will do the most good to us;' and again, 'We want more friends in this Congress.' In his letter to McComb, and also in his statement prepared by counsel, he gives the philosophy of his action, to wit: That he has found there is no difficulty in getting men to look after their own property. The Committee are also satisfied that Mr. Ames entertained a fear that when the true relations between the Crédit Mobilier Company and the Union Pacific became generally known, and the means by which the great profits expected to be made were fully understood, there was danger that Congressional investigation and action would be invoked. The Members of Congress with whom he dealt were generally those who had been friendly and favorable to a Pacific Railroad, and Mr. Ames did not fear or expect to find them favorable to movements hostile to it, but he desired to stimulate their activity and watchfulness in opposition to any unfavorable action, by giving them a personal interest in the success of the enterprise, especially so far as it affected the interest of the Crédit Mobilier Company.

"On the 9th day of December, 1867, Mr. C. C. Washburn, of Wisconsin, introduced in the House a bill to regulate by law the rates of transportation over the Pacific Railroads. Mr. Ames, as well as others interested in the Union Pacific Road, were opposed to this, and desired to defeat it. Other measures apparently hostile to that company were subsequently introduced into the House by Mr. Washburn, of Wisconsin, and Mr. Washburn, of Illinois. The Committee believe that Mr. Ames, in his distribution of the stock, had specially in mind the hostile efforts of the Messrs. Washburn, and desired to gain strength to secure their defeat. The reference, in one of his letters, to Washburn's move makes this quite apparent."

"The more recent legislation," says the New York *Tribune*, "which Ames's transactions with Members of Congress had reference to, may be stated in a few words. Secretary Boutwell insisted that half the earnings of the road in carrying mails and troops for the Government should be applied to the payment of interest on the loans that the Government had made to the road. The legislation obtained overruled the Secretary and enabled the road to postpone payment of interest until the bonds fell due—some thirty years hence. To sum up, it may be briefly stated that the Union Pacific and Crédit Mobilier together got the proceeds of liberal United States land grants, of donations of communities near the road, and the entire subsidy of Government bonds, as a clear profit. The proceeds of the mortgage bonds which displaced the Government lien, were sufficient to have built the road. To the original stockholders in the Union Pacific, the profit was something almost incredible. A share bought for $5 subscription became $100 Crédit Mobilier, which paid, as we have seen in the evidence concerning the Legislators who received it, dividends that amounted to at least treble its nominal value. It is of course evident that all legislation which favored the Union Pacific Railroad swelled the profits of the Legislators who became stockholders in the Crédit Mobilier. The awkwardness of this position was vastly increased by the thin disguise of purchase being torn away, under which the profit-bearing stock had been really the gift of Oakes Ames. The denial of the facts converted the transaction into a criminal act."

Reduced to plain English, the story of the Crédit Mobilier is simply this: The men entrusted with the management of the Pacific Road made a bargain with themselves to build the road for a sum equal to about twice its actual cost, and pocketed the profits, which have been estimated at about THIRTY MILLIONS OF DOLLARS—this immense sum coming out of the pockets of the tax payers of the United States. This contract was made in October, 1867.

"On June 17, 1868, the stockholders of the Crédit Mobilier received 60 per cent. in cash, and 40 per cent. in stock of the Union Pacific Railroad; on the 2nd of July, 1868, 80 per cent. first mortgage bonds of the Union Pacific Railroad, and 100 per cent. stock; July 3, 1868, 75 per cent. stock, and 75 per cent. first mortgage bonds; September 3, 1868, 100 per cent. stock, and 75 per cent. first mortgage bonds; December 19 1868, 200 per cent. stock; while, before this contract was made, the stockholders had received, on the 26th of April 1866, a dividend of 100 per cent. in stock of the Union Pacific Railroad; on the 1st of April, 1867, 50 per cent. of first mortgage bonds were distributed; on the 1st of July, 1867, 100 per cent. in stock again."

After offering this statement, it is hardly necessary to add that the vast property of the Pacific Road, which should have been used to meet its engagements, was soon swallowed up by the Crédit Mobilier.

This is the story of the Crédit Mobilier, as far as the facts have been permitted to become known. We shall now see how it came to make such a noise in the world.

Mr. Ames was not the only member of the company engaged in "placing" the stock where it would benefit the corporation. Dr. Durant, the President of the Pacific Railway, was engaged in securing his friends in the same way, and he received a portion of the stock to be used in this manner. Mr. Henry S. McComb, of Delaware, who was also interested in the scheme, now put in his claim for a part of the stock, which was being used as a corruption fund, "for his friends." His claim involved him in a quarrel with Oakes Ames, and Col. McComb had the mortification of seeing the stock he claimed assigned to Mr. Ames, for the use of *his* friends.

In the summer of 1872, in the midst of the Presidential Campaign, the quarrel between Ames and McComb reached such a point, that it was impossible to keep it quiet. McComb made public the facts in the case, and published a list of the Congressmen with whom Ames had said he had "placed" the stock, naming the number of shares sold to each. These were: Schuyler Colfax, Vice-President of the United States; Henry Wilson, Senator from Massachusetts; Jas. W. Patterson, Senator from New Hampshire; John A. Logan, Senator from Illinois; James G. Blaine, Member of Congress from Maine, and Speaker of the House of Representatives; W. D. Kelley, of Pennsylvania; James A. Garfield, of Ohio; James Brooks, of New York; John A. Bingham, of Ohio; Henry L. Dawes, of Massachusetts; Glenni W. Scofield, of Pennsylvania, and one or two others, who were not at the time of the exposure Members of Congress.

As may be supposed, the publication of the charges, and the list of names, created a storm of excitement throughout the country. The members implicated, as a rule, indignantly denied the charge of having purchased or owned Crédit Mobilier Stock. Not content with this, they declared themselves incapable of holding such stock, as it would have been, they said, a high crime against morality and decency to be connected in any way with the Crédit Mobilier. These denials were generally accepted. The persons making them had always borne high characters for veracity and integrity. Partisan orators and newspapers made the most of the charges, and made them so odious that the persons implicated repeated their denials with more bitterness.

Here was the fatal error of the Congressmen implicated in the affair. They deliberately denied all connection with Crédit Mobilier stock, and the position they assumed caused the country to believe that they had had no connection with it, because of their knowledge at the time that it was "too dirty a business for a Member of Congress to be concerned in." Had they frankly acknowledged the purchase of the stock, had they asserted that they thought the purchase legitimate, and that they relinquished their stock as soon as they discovered its true character, they would have saved their reputations with the public, which, while it might have thought them very foolish, would have acquitted them of criminal intentions; but they deliberately denied the whole business, and placed themselves in a position to be convicted of falsehood, if Ames's charges should be proved. Mr. Ames, on his part, repeated his charges, and declared his ability to prove them.

When Congress assembled, in December, 1872, Mr. Blaine, the Speaker of the House, wishing to vindicate his character, which he declared had been unjustly assailed, asked the House of Representatives to appoint a Committee to inquire into the charges of Ames and McComb, and to report the result of their investigations. The Committee was appointed, with Mr. Poland, of Vermont, as its Chairman. An effort was made to conduct the investigation in secret; but the indignant public demanded and obtained an open trial. On the 18th of February, 1873, the Committee reported to the House the result of its investigation.

The reader will remember that the Members of Congress had denied that they had owned Crédit Mobilier stock, and had indignantly repudiated the assertion that they had been bribed with it. The investigation was to determine whether they had owned the stock in question, as well as whether they had been bribed with it. They had warranted, by their course, the public inference that the mere ownership of the stock placed the Congressional holder of it in a terribly suspicious light. The stock was extremely valuable, it paid seven or eight hundred per cent. in a few months. Oakes Ames had asserted that he had sold this valuable stock to Congressmen for less than half the value set upon it by the Crédit Mobilier; and that, where the purchasers had not the ready money to pay for it, he had "carried" it for them, and had allowed them to pay for it out of the enormous dividends declared upon it, charging them a slight commission for this service. The investigation was to either triumphantly sustain the denials of the Congressmen in question, or prove them liars, by fastening upon them the ownership of the stock, which they had disclaimed.

The Committee, in their Report to the House, concerned themselves only with the members of that body. Their report failed to sustain the denials of the members as to the ownership of the stock, although it acquitted all but one of them of the charge of having been bribed. It fastened the ownership of the stock upon all but Mr. Blaine, and presented them, with this one exception, to the House and to the country as men convicted of falsehood. "The report admits," says the New York *Herald*, "that these Congressmen at first denied the receipt of money from Ames, and that, in some instances, their denials were met by the production of checks and receipts. The evidence of falsehood is conclusive against all, or nearly all of them."

THE CASE OF MR. BLAINE.

Mr. Blaine, the Speaker of the House, met the charge against him with a prompt denial when it was first made. The Committee fully sustained his denial, and reported that the evidence before them did not show any ownership of the stock by him at any time.

THE CASE OF MR. DAWES.

Mr. Henry L. Dawes, of Massachusetts, met the charge of ownership of the stock with a denial at the time it was made. He pronounced the charge a libel. Concerning him, the Committee reported as follows:

" Mr. Dawes had, prior to December, 1867, made some small investments in railroad bonds through Mr. Ames. In December, 1867, Mr. Dawes applied to Mr. Ames to purchase a $1000 bond of the Cedar Rapids Road, in Iowa. Mr. Ames informed him that he had sold them all, but that he would let him have for his $1000 ten shares of Crédit Mobilier stock, which he thought was better than the railroad bonds. In answer to inquiry by Mr. Dawes, Mr. Ames said the Crédit Mobilier Company had the contract to build the Union Pacific Road, and thought they would make money out of it, and that it would be a good thing; that he would guarantee that he should get ten per cent. on his money, and that if at any time Mr. Dawes did not want the stock, he would pay back his money, with ten per cent. interest. Mr.

Dawes made some further inquiry in relation to the stock of Mr. John B. Alley, who said he thought it was good stock, but not as good as Mr. Ames thought; but that Mr. Ames's guarantee would make it a perfectly safe investment. Mr. Dawes thereupon concluded to purchase the ten shares, and on the 11th of January he paid Mr. Ames $800, and in a few days thereafter the balance of the price of the stock at par, and interest from the July previous. In June, 1868, Mr. Ames received a dividend of sixty per cent. in money on his stock, and of it paid to Mr. Dawes $400, and applied the balance of $200 upon accounts between them. This $400 was all that was paid over to Mr. Dawes as a dividend upon this stock. At some time prior to December, 1868, Mr. Dawes was informed that a suit had been commenced in the courts of Pennsylvania by the former owners of the charter of the Crédit Mobilier, claiming that those then claiming and using it had no right to do so. Mr. Dawes thereupon informed Mr. Ames that as there was a litigation about the matter, he did not desire to keep the stock. On the 9th of December, 1868, Mr. Ames and Mr. Dawes had a settlement of these matters, in which Mr. Dawes was allowed for the money he paid for the stock, with ten per cent. interest upon it, and accounted to Mr. Ames for the $400 he had received as a dividend. Mr. Dawes received no other benefit under the contract than to get ten per cent. upon his money, and after the settlement had no further interest in the stock."

The Committee thus fail to sustain Mr. Dawes in his denial. They show that he received his shares in

December, 1867, and his first dividend on the 3d of January, 1868. This dividend was in Union Pacific bonds and stocks. The Committee state that it was an eighty per cent. dividend. The official report published in the New York *Herald* of December 21st, 1872, stated that it was a dividend of one hundred and twenty per cent.—sixty per cent. in first mortgage bonds and sixty in stock. The Committee also state that Mr. Dawes kept the stock nearly a year and surrendered it because "there was a litigation about the matter." Yet the Committee, in the face of these facts, declare that Mr. Dawes was ignorant of the true character of the stock which paid him such a tremendous dividend. Mr. Dawes is the Chairman of the great financial Committee of the House, that of Ways and Means, and is accustomed to dealing with financial questions.

The Case of Mr. Scofield.

Glenni W. Scofield, of Pennsylvania, was another of the Congressmen to whom Ames sold stock. Say the Committee:

"In 1866, Mr. Scofield purchased some Cedar Rapids bonds of Mr. Ames, and in that year they had conversation about Mr. Scofield taking stock in the Crédit Mobilier Company, but no contract was consummated. In December, 1867, Mr. Scofield applied to Mr. Ames to purchase more Cedar Rapids bonds, when Mr. Ames suggested that he should purchase some Crédit Mobilier stock, and explained generally that it was a contracting company to build the Union Pacific Road; that, as it was a Pennsylvania corporation, he would like to have some Pennsylvanian in it; that he would sell it to him at par and interest, and that he would guarantee he should get eight per cent. if Mr. Scofield would give him half the dividends above that. Mr. Scofield said he thought he would take $1000 of the stock, but before anything further was done Mr. Scofield was called home by sickness in his family. On his return, in the latter part of January, 1868, he spoke to Mr. Ames about the stock, when Mr. Ames said he thought it was all sold, but he would take his money and give him a receipt and get the stock for him if he could. Mr. Scofield therefore paid Mr. Ames $1041, and took his receipt therefor. Not long after Mr. Ames informed Mr. Scofield he could have the stock, but could not give him a certificate for it until he could get a larger certificate dividend. Mr. Scofield received the bond dividend of eighty per cent., which was payable January 3, 1868, taking a bond for $1000, and paying Mr. Ames the difference. Mr. Ames received the sixty per cent. cash dividend on the stock in June, 1868, and paid over to Mr. Scofield $600, the amount of it. Before the close of that session of Congress, which was toward the end of July, Mr. Scofield became, for some reason, disinclined to take the stock, and a settlement was made between them, by which Mr. Ames was to retain the Crédit Mobilier stock and Mr. Scofield took $1000 Union Pacific stock. The precise basis of the settlement does not appear, neither Mr. Ames nor Mr. Scofield having any full data in reference to it. Mr. Scofield thinks that he only received back his money and interest upon it. While Mr. Ames states that he thinks Mr. Scofield had ten shares of Union Pacific stock in addition. The Committee do not deem it specially important to settle this difference of recollection. Since that settlement Mr. Scofield has had no interest in the Crédit Mobilier stock, and derived no benefit therefrom."

Mr. Scofield held the stock about five months, and appears to have made a profit of about seventeen hundred dollars on the transaction.

The Case of Mr. Bingham.

The Committee say that:

" In December, 1867, Mr. Ames advised Mr. Bingham to invest in the stock of the Crédit Mobilier, assuring him that it would return him his money with profitable dividends. Mr. Bingham agreed to take twenty shares, and about the 1st of January, 1868, paid to Mr. Ames the par value of the stock, for which Mr. Ames executed to him some receipt or agreement. Mr. Ames received all the dividends on the stock or money. Some were delivered to Mr. Bingham, and some retained by Mr. Ames. The matter was not finally adjusted between them until February, 1872, when it was settled by Mr. Ames retaining the thirty shares of Crédit Mobilier stock, and accounting to Mr. Bingham for such dividends upon it as Mr. Bingham had not already received. Mr. Bingham was treated as the real owner of the stock from the time of the agreement to take it in December, 1867, to the settlement in February, 1872, and had the benefit of all the dividends upon it. Neither Mr. Ames nor Mr. Bingham had such records of their dealing as to be able to give the precise amount of these dividends."

Mr. Bingham appears from this, to have bought the stock in January, 1868, at par, at which time it was worth to any one else but "a friend of Mr. Ames" just four times its par value. He held the stock until February, 1872, receiving all the dividends in the meantime. "Taking the official list published in the *Herald* last December," says the New York *Herald* of February 19th, 1873, "we find that the dividends on twenty shares amounted to $10,900." Mr. Bingham was the only member who held this stock that did not deny it and try to make his innocence appear. He acknowledged the ownership, denied that he had been corruptly influenced by it, and maintained that he had a right to buy and hold the stock. Consequently Mr. Bingham is not one of those whom the Report convicts of falsehood.

THE CASE OF MR. KELLEY.

Mr. William D. Kelley, of Pennsylvania, was one of those who denied his connection with the Crédit Mobilier. Concerning him the Committee say

"They can find from the evidence that in the early part of the second session of the Fortieth Congress, and probably in December, 1867, Mr. Ames agreed with Mr. Kelley to sell him ten shares of Crédit Mobilier stock at par and interest from July 1, 1867. Mr. Kelley was not then prepared to pay for the stock, and Mr. Ames agreed to carry the stock for him until he could pay for it. On the 3d day of January, 1868, there was a dividend of eighty per cent. on Crédit Mobilier stock in Union Pacific bonds. Mr. Ames received the bonds, as the stock stood in his name, and sold them for ninety-seven per cent. of their face. In June, 1868, there was a cash dividend of sixty per cent., which Mr. Ames also received. The proceeds of the bonds sold and the cash dividends received by Mr. Ames amounted to $1376. The par value of the stock and interest thereon from the previous July amounted to $1047, so that after paying for the stock there was a balance of dividends due Mr. Kelley of $329. On the 23d day of June, 1868, Mr. Ames gave Mr. Kelley a check for that sum on the Sergeant-at-Arms of the House of Representatives, and Mr. Kelley received the money thereon. The Committee find that Mr. Kelley understood that the money he thus received was a balance of dividends due him after paying for the stock. All the subsequent dividends upon the stock were either in Union Pacific stock or bonds, and they were all received from Mr. Ames. In September, 1868, Mr. Kelley received from Mr. Ames $750, the money which was understood between them to be an advance to be paid out of dividends. There has never been any adjustment of the matter between them, and there is now an entire variance in the testimony of the two men as to what the transaction between them was, but the Committee are unanimous in finding the facts above stated. The evidence reported to the House gives some subsequent conversations and negotiations between Mr. Kelley and Mr. Ames on the subject. The Committee do not deem it material to refer to it in their report."

So Mr. Kelley, counted one of the most astute financiers of the House, got his stock without paying cash for it. He took ten shares in December, 1867, and in June, 1868, about six months later, received two dividends amounting to $1376, which paid the $1000 due on his stock (he getting it at par, when it was worth much more) and a profit of $329, after deducting the interest due Oakes Ames for carrying the stock. After that Mr. Kelley received all the dividends

The Case of Mr. Garfield.

Mr. James A. Garfield's case has not been helped by the Committee. They say of this gentleman, who is a Representative from Ohio:

"The facts in regard to Mr. Garfield, as found by the Committee, are identical with the case of Mr. Kelley to the point of reception of the check for $329. He agreed with Mr. Ames to take ten shares of Crédit Mobilier stock, but did not pay for the same. Mr. Ames received the eighty per cent. dividend in bonds, and sold them for ninety-seven per cent., and also received the sixty per cent. cash dividend, which, together with the price of the stock and interest, left a balance of $329. This sum was paid over to Mr. Garfield by a check on the Sergeant-at-Arms. Mr. Ames received all the subsequent dividends, and the Committee do not find that since the payment of the $329 there has been any communication between Mr. Ames and Mr. Garfield on the subject, until this investigation began. Some correspondence between Mr. Garfield and Mr. Ames, and some conversation between them during this investigation, wil' be found in the reported testimony."

Mr. Garfield must share with Mr. Kelley in the "sympathy" of the country. The Committee have not made him blameless in the public estimation.

THE CASE OF MR. BROOKS.

Concerning Mr. James Brooks, of New York, the Committee say:

"The case of Mr. Brooks stands upon a different state of facts from any of those already given. The Committee find from the evidence as follows:

"Mr. Brooks had been a warm advocate of a Pacific railroad, both in Congress and the public press. After persons interested in the Union Pacific Road had obtained control of the Crédit Mobilier charter, and organized under it for the purpose of making it a construction company to build the road, Dr. Durant, who was then the leading man in the enterprise, made great efforts to get the stock of the Crédit Mobilier taken. Mr. Brooks was a friend of Dr. Durant, and he made some effort to aid Dr. Durant in getting subscriptions for the stock. He introduced the matter to some capitalists in New York, but his efforts were not crowned with success. During this period, Mr. Brooks had talked with Dr. Durant about taking some of the stock for himself, and had spoken of taking $15,000 or $20,000 of it, but no definite contract was made between them, and Mr. Brooks was under no legal obligation to take the stock, or Durant to give it to him. In October, 1867, Mr. Brooks was appointed by the President one of the Government directors of the Union Pacific Road. In December, 1867, after the stock of the Crédit Mobilier was understood by those familiar with the affairs between the Union Pacific and the Crédit Mobilier to be worth very much more than par, Mr. Brooks applied to Dr. Durant, and claimed that he should have 200 shares of Crédit Mobilier stock. It does not appear that Mr. Brooks claimed he had any legal contract for the stock that he could enforce, or that Durant considered himself in any way legally bound to let him have any; but still, on account of what had been said, and the efforts of Mr. Brooks to aid him, he considered himself under obligation to satisfy Mr. Brooks in the matter.

"The stock had been so far taken up, and was then in such demand that Durant could not well comply with Mr. Brooks' demand for 200 shares. After considerable negotiation, it was finally adjusted between them by Durant agreeing to let Brooks have 100 shares of Crédit Mobilier stock, and giving him with it $5000 of Union Pacific bonds, and $20,000 of Union Pacific stock. Dr. Durant testified that he then considered Crédit Mobilier stock worth double the par value, and that the bonds and stock he was to give Mr. Brooks worth $9000, so that he saved about $1000 by not giving Brooks the additional 100 shares he claimed. After the negotiation had been concluded between Mr. Brooks and Dr. Durant, Mr. Brooks said, that as he was a Government director of the Union Pacific Road, and as the law provided such directors should not be stockholders in the company, he would not hold this stock, and directed Dr. Durant to transfer it to his son-in-law, Chas. H. Neilson. The whole negotiation with Durant was conducted by Mr. Brooks himself, and Neilson had nothing to do with the transaction, except to receive the transfer. The $10,000 to pay for the 100 shares was paid by Mr. Brooks, and he received the $5000 of Pacific bonds which came with the stock. The certificate of transfer of the 100 shares from Durant to Neilson is dated Dec. 26, 1867. On the 3d of July, 1868, there was a dividend of eighty per cent. Union Pacific bonds paid on the Crédit Mobilier stock. The bonds were received by Neilson, but passed over at once to Mr. Brooks. It is claimed, both by Mr. Brooks and Neilson, that the $10,000 paid by Mr. Brooks was a loan of that sum by him to Neilson, and that the bonds received from Durant, and those received from the dividend, were delivered and held by him as collateral security for the loan. No note or obligation was given for the money by Neilson, nor, so far as we can learn from either Brooks or Neilson, was any account or memorandum of the transaction kept by either of them. At the time of the agreement or settlement above spoken of between Brooks and Durant, there was nothing said about Mr. Brooks being entitled to have fifty per cent. more stock by virtue of his ownership of the 100 shares.

"Neither Mr. Brooks nor Durant thought of any such thing. Some time after the transfer of the shares to Neilson, Mr. Brooks called on Sidney Dillon, then the President of the Crédit Mobilier, and claimed that he or Neilson was entitled to fifty additional shares of the stock by virtue of the purchase of the 100 shares of Durant. This was claimed by Mr. Brooks as his right, by virtue of the fifty per cent. increase of the stock hereinbefore described. Mr. Dillon said he did not know how that was, but he would consult the leading stockholders, and be governed by them. Mr. Dillon, in order to justify himself in the transaction, got up a paper authorizing the issue of fifty shares of the stock to Mr. Brooks, and procured it to be signed by most of the principal shareholders. After this had been done, an entry of fifty shares was made on the stock ledger to some person other than Neilson. The name in two places on the book had been erased, and the name of Neilson inserted. The Committee are satisfied that the stock was first entered on the books in Mr. Brooks' name. Mr. Neilson soon after called for the certificate for the fifty shares, and on the 29th of February, 1868, the certificate was issued to him, and the entry on the stock-book was changed to Neilson. Mr. Neilson procured Mr. Dillon to advance the money to pay for the stock, and at the same time delivered to Dillon $1000 Union Pacific bonds, and fifty shares of Union Pacific stock as collateral security. These bonds and stock were a portion of dividends received at the time, as he was allowed to receive the same per cents. of dividends on these fifty shares that had previously been paid on the 100. This matter has never been adjusted between Neilson and Dillon. Messrs. Brooks and Neilson both testify they never paid Dillon, and Dillon thinks he has received his pay, as he has not now the collaterals in his possession. If he has been paid, it is probable it was from the collaterals in some form. The subject has never been named between Dillon and Neilson since Dillon advanced the money, and no one connected with the transaction seems able to give any further light upon it.

"The whole business by which these fifty shares were procured was done by Mr. Brooks. Neilson knew nothing of any right to have them, and only went for the certificate when told to do so by Mr. Brooks. The Committee find that no such right to fifty shares additional stock passed by the transfer of the one hundred, and from Mr. Brooks' familiarity with the affairs of the company, the Committee believe he must have known his claim to them was unfounded. The question naturally arises, how was he able to procure them. The stock at this time, by the stockholders, was considered worth three or four times its par value. Neilson sustained no relation to any of these people that commanded any favor, and if he could have used any influence he did not attempt it. If he had this right he was unaware of it till told by Mr. Brooks, and left the whole matter in his hands. It is clear that the shares were procured by the sole efforts of Mr. Brooks, and, as the stockholders who consented to it supposed, for the benefit of Mr. Brooks. What power had Mr. Brooks to enforce an unfounded claim to have for $5000 stock worth $15,000 or $20,000? Mr. McComb swears that he had heard a conversation between Mr. Brooks and Mr. John B. Alley, a large stockholder and one of the Executive Committee, in which Mr. Brooks urged that he should have the additional fifty shares because he was, or would procure himself to be, made a Government director, and also that, being a Member of Congress he would take care of the Democratic side of the House. Mr. Brooks and Mr. Alley both deny having had any such conversation, or that Mr. Brooks ever made such a statement to Mr. Alley. If, therefore, this matter rested wholly upon the testimony of Mr. McComb, the Committee would not feel justified in finding that Mr. Brooks procured the stock by such use of his position; but all the circumstances seem to point exactly in that direction, and we can find no other satisfactory solution of the above question propounded. Whatever claim Mr. Brooks had to the stock, either legal or moral, had been adjusted and satisfied by Dr. Durant. Whether he was getting for himself or to give to his son-in-law, we believe from the circumstances attending the whole transaction that he obtained it knowing that it was yielded to his official position and influence, and with the intent to secure his favor and influence in such positions.

"Mr. Brooks claims that he has no interest in this stock whatever; that the benefit and advantages of his right to have it he gave to Mr. Neilson, his son-in-law, and that he had had all the dividends upon it. The Committee are unable to find this to be the case, for in their judgment all the facts and circumstances show Mr. Brooks to be the real and substantial owner, and that Neilson's ownership is merely nominal and colorable. In June, 1868, there was a cash dividend of $9000 upon this 150 shares of stock. Neilson received it, of course, as the stock was in his name, but on the same day it was paid over to Mr. Brooks (as

Neilson says) to pay so much of the $10,000 advanced by Mr. Brooks to pay for the stock. This then repaid all but the $1000 of the loan, but Mr. Brooks continued to hold $11,000 of the Union Pacific bonds, which Neilson says he gave him as collateral security, and to draw the interest upon all but $5000. The interest upon the others, Neilson says, he was permitted to draw and retain. But at one time in his testimony he spoke of the amount he was allowed as being Christmas and New-Year's presents. Mr. Neilson says that during the last summer he borrowed $14,000 of Mr. Brooks, and now he owes Mr. Brooks nearly as much as the collaterals; but according to his testimony Mr. Brooks for four years held $16,000 in bonds as security for $1000, and received the interest on $11,000 of the collaterals. No accounts appear to have been kept between Mr. Brooks and Mr. Neilson; and doubtless what sums he has received from Mr. Brooks out of the dividends were intended as presents rather than the delivering of money belonging to him. Mr. Brooks' efforts procured the stock and his money paid for it. All the cash dividend he has received, and he holds all the bonds except those Dillon received, which seem to have been applied toward paying for the fifty shares. Without further comment upon the evidence, the Committee find that the 150 shares of the stock appearing on the books of the Crédit Mobilier in the name of Neilson, were really the stock of Mr. Brooks, and subject to his control, and that it was understood by both parties.

"Mr. Brooks had taken such an interest in the Crédit Mobilier Company, and was so connected with

Dr. Durant, that he must be regarded as having full knowledge of the relation between that company and the Railroad Company, and of the contracts between them. He must have known the cause of the sudden increase in value of the Crédit Mobilier stock, and how the large expected profits were to be made. We have already expressed our view of the propriety of a Member of Congress becoming the owner of stock possessing the knowledge. But Mr. Brooks was not only a Member of Congress, but he was a Government director in the Union Pacific Company. As such it was his duty to guard and watch over the interests of the Government in the road, and to see that they were protected and preserved. To insure such faithfulness on the part of Government directors, Congress very wisely provided that they should not be stockholders in the road. Mr. Brooks readily saw that though becoming a stockholder in the Crédit Mobilier was not forbidden by the letter of the law, yet it was a violation of the spirit and essence, and therefore had the stock placed in the name of his son-in-law. The transfer of the Oakes Ames contract to the trustees to the building of the road under the contract, from which the enormous dividends were all derived, was all during Mr. Brooks' official life as a Government director, must have been within his knowledge, and yet passed without the slightest opposition from him. The Committee believe this could not have been done without an entire disregard of his official obligations and duty, and that while appointed to guard the public interests in the road, he joined himself with the promoters of a scheme whereby the Government was to be defrauded, and shared in the spoil. In the conclusions of fact upon the evidence the Committee are entirely agreed.

"In considering what action we ought to recommend to the House, upon these facts, the Committee encounter a question which has been much debated: Has this House power and jurisdiction to inquire concerning offences committed by its members prior to their election and to punish them by censure or expulsion? The Committee are unanimous upon the right of jurisdiction of this House over the cases of Mr. Ames and Mr. Brooks upon the facts found in regard to them."

Thus we have the main facts in the case. Certain Congressmen who were charged with holding Crédit Mobilier stock, and who denied it, are shown by the Committee to have held this stock, and are thus convicted of falsehood.

Of all the men implicated, the Committee find that only James Brooks and Oakes Ames were influenced by corrupt motives, and they recommend the expulsion of these members. This verdict has been accepted by the public at large, as regards these two members, but the people are not disposed to accept the verdict of acquittal pronounced by the Committee in favor of the other members concerned. With regard to these, in spite of the facts stated in the report, the Committee declare that, "The only criticism the Committee feel competent to make on the action of these members in taking this stock is, that they were not sufficiently careful in ascertaining what they were getting, and that, in their judgment, the assurance of a good investment was all the assurance they needed. We commend to them, and to all men, the letter of the venerable Senator Bayard in response to an offer of some of this stock, found on page 74 of the testimony. The Committee find nothing in the conduct of either of these members in taking this stock that calls for any recommendation by the Committee."

In other words, the Committee, after deliberately showing the denials of the implicated Congressmen to be false, declare that these gentlemen were innocent victims of Mr. Oakes Ames. They declare that a number of the shrewdest, most acute, and business-like men in the House, men in whose hands the solution of the great financial problems of the day are lodged, engaged in an investment of which they did not know the nature. Truly Mr. Poland and his associates must entertain a very poor opinion of the intelligence of the people of this great country, when they ask them to be satisfied with this pitiful evasion. The members concerned in the transaction may be innocent, but the report of the Poland Committee has not caused the public to regard them in that light. The people are at a loss, also, to comprehend the mental status of a Committee which can recommend the expulsion of Mr. Ames for bribing Members of Congress, and yet solemnly declare that they have no evidence that any one has been bribed.

The New York *Herald* thus forcibly and clearly states the opinion of the country at large respecting this report:

"The report acquits Messrs. Dawes, Scofield, Bingham, Kelley, and Garfield of any corrupt motive or improper act on the following grounds :—First, because there is no evidence to show that they were aware of the great value of the stock they received from Oakes Ames; second, because they did not appear to know that the dividends would be paid in Union Pacific stock, and as the Crédit Mobilier was a State corporation they had a right to invest in it; third, because it is not proved that any corrupt consideration was asked of them by Ames, that they were only seeking legitimate investments, and that it does not seem that they voted for any measures favorable to the Crédit Mobilier while they held the stock. It is true that the Committee believe the favored Congressmen must have felt 'there was something so out of the ordinary course of business in the extraordinary dividends they were receiving as to render the investment itself suspicious,' and that they attribute to this feeling the anxiety of some of the purchasers to get rid of the stock; but the report declares that it can find no evidence of corrupt intention on the part of any of these members. The Committee argue that if the whitewashed Congressmen had known of the large dividends they were to receive, or if they had been aware that the dividends would be paid in Union Pacific bonds and stock and thus have given them an interest in a corporation depending upon Congress for legislation, they would then have been guilty of corrupt and illegal conduct in accepting the shares.

"A single fact sweeps away in an instant this whole

mass of false reasoning and fraudulent pleading. The stock was taken by some of the members in December, 1867, and by others in January and February, 1868. In some instances at the very moment of purchase, and in all cases within two or three weeks after purchase, these whitewashed Congressmen received eighty per cent. dividend on their shares in the first mortgage bonds and stock of the Union Pacific Railroad! If they did not know that they were bribed at the instant they completed the transaction, the guilty knowledge must have come to them very soon afterwards. Judge Poland and his associates stultify themselves when they argue that the knowledge of the amount and character of the dividends would be proof of guilt, and yet justify the men who held the stock and received the dividends in some cases for months and in others for years. They stultify themselves also when they pronounce Oakes Ames guilty of bribery, and find that he has bribed no person! Bribery is the giving or receiving a reward for a violation of official duty. Could Oakes Ames have committed this offence unless he gave this stock or sold it at a quarter of its value to these Congressmen, for the purpose of inducing them to violate their official duty? And if he did do this, can the men he bribed—the men who received his valuable gifts—be innocent? As well might Judge Poland and his Committee tell us that their report is fearlessly and impartially made in the cause of truth and justice alone. The Committee stultify themselves further when they suppress the evidence against Vice-President Colfax and shrink from the responsibility of making an allusion to his case. Their excuse is that Mr. Colfax is the presiding officer of the Senate, and as such is beyond their jurisdiction. Yet the keen and subtly-reasoning lawyers of the Committee must be familiar with the Constitution of the United States; they must know that the Vice-President can be impeached and removed from office on conviction of treason, 'bribery,' or other high crimes and misdemeanors, and that in the House of Representatives rests the 'sole power of impeachment.'"

It is a miserable business. The country expected of Mr. Poland and his associates a manly and straightforward investigation, and not a miserable effort to hunt up a couple of scape goats to bear the sins of those who were to be saved from expulsion. The people of the United States feel deeply the shame and humiliation of the whole affair, and they, let us thank Heaven, have not learned to consider party claims when the national honor is at stake. They had a right to expect of the Committee either a clear vindication of the accused parties, or an impartial and rigid meting out of justice to them. The result is appearing. They see their trusted public servants convicted of falsehood, stained with the ownership of the most questionable property of the present day, and they are gravely asked by a Committee of Congress to believe that the men whom they have trusted and honored, and whom they know to be keen, shrewd, practical business men, are a parcel of ignorant fools, unable to manage a simple investment in stocks with the prudence or care of the most ordinary man of business.

The Report of the Poland Committee did not touch the cases of the Senators, into which it inquired. It is customary in such cases to send the evidence to the Senate, when taken by a House Committee, and *vice versa*. This has been done in the present case, and it now remains for the Senate to deal with its own members. The Senate for a long time took no notice of the matter, but a Committee of investigation was at length appointed, which is still in session at the present writing. We shall notice the cases of Senators Wilson, Patterson, and Colfax, as developed before the Poland Committee.

The Case of Senator Wilson.

When the Presidential Campaign was at its height, Senator Wilson was charged with having bought Crédit Mobilier stock from Oakes Ames. His friend, General Hawley, of Connecticut, at once denied that Mr. Wilson had had any connection with the business, and this denial made, as it was commonly believed, with Mr. Wilson's knowledge and consent, had the effect of inducing the public to believe that Mr. Wilson had no knowledge of the speculation. Upon the examination before the Poland Committee it was made apparent from Mr. Wilson's own statement that he had bought this stock from Ames, on the terms upon which the others purchased it, with this difference, however, that he had bought it in his wife's name. Upon discovering that the Crédit Mobilier had become involved in a lawsuit, he became frightened, and returned the stock to Ames, receiving back the amount of his investment and ten per cent. interest. He claims to have lost money by the transaction.

THE CASE OF SENATOR LOGAN.

Senator Logan paid no attention to the charge against him during the campaign, neither denying nor admitting his ownership of the stock, and consequently, next to Mr. Blaine, was the most fortunate man connected with the investigation. He stated to the Committee that he had agreed to take ten shares of Mr. Ames, in February, 1868. The first two dividends paid for it, and gave him a balance of $329. He took Mr. Ames's check for this amount, and got it cashed. A few days after, he concluded to keep out of the affair, and repaid Mr. Ames the $329, with $2 interest. It seems that he had a friend who was a contractor on the Union Pacific Road, and who informed him concerning the operations of the Crédit Mobilier, and the letters of his friend made him think he would prefer not to keep the stock.

THE CASE OF SENATOR PATTERSON.

James W. Patterson, Senator from New Hampshire, was one of those charged with purchasing Crédit Mobilier stock. He denied the charge, and declared that he had had no connection with the stock at all. Mr. Ames, upon his examination by the Committee, made oath that he had sold Mr. Patterson thirty shares of the stock of the Crédit Mobilier. Mr. Patterson then stated that he had bought stock of Ames, but supposed that it was Union Pacific stock. He added, on the 21st of January, in a voluntary statement before the Committee: "I have never received any certificate of stock or other evidence of ownership on the Crédit Mobilier, and am not enough of a lawer to know how I could draw dividends on what I did not own." In support of his assertion, Mr. Patterson produced a letter writter to him by Ames during the late Senatorial contest in New Hampshire. Mr. E. H. Rollins had assailed Mr. Patterson in this contest for owning Crédit Mobiler stock, and Ames, at Patterson's request, wrote the latter a letter stating that the books of the Company did not show that he owned any stock.

Mr. Ames, who had listened patiently to Mr. Patterson's statement before the Committee, was then questioned by the Committee as to the accuracy of Patterson's statement. He at once produced his memoranda, and proceeded to read from it, amid a painful stillness, "a connected account of his transaction with Patterson. He invested $3000 for Patterson in Crédit Mobilier stock, in January, 1868; on February 14th he paid him $2223 in cash, which were the proceeds of the sale of the first bond dividend; $3000 in Union Pacific first mortgage bonds, less $105 retained for interest, and also thirty shares of Union Pacific stock. On June 19th, 1868, he paid him $1800 as a sixty per cent. cash divi dend. Some time in 1871 he settled the transaction and gave him about seventy shares Union Pacific stock. He supposed that Patterson knew he was buying Crédit Mobilier stock; he talked of nothing else with him. Ames explained his letter by saying that it was literally true although intended to give a wrong impression.

His good nature led him to write it at Patterson's importunity—to help him out of a fix. If Patterson had not got the certificate for the thirty shares, then it had been lost. He (Ames) had all the other certificates in his pocket except that. Patterson again denied any knowledge of the fact that Ames had invested his $3000 in Crédit Mobilier stock."

Mr. Patterson's testimony being so at variance with that of Mr. Ames, it was evident that one of them had misstated facts. Mr. Patterson had declared that he had never held Crédit Mobilier stock, and when Ames testified that he had sold him thirty shares, modified his statement by saying that he supposed that they were shares and bonds of the Union Pacific Company. Mr. Ames stated that Mr. Patterson was fully aware that he was buying Crédit Mobilier stock. In order to sustain this assertion, Mr. Ames, on the 26th of January, produced Senator Patterson's receipts. We quote from the report of the examination. The answers are those of Mr. Ames to the questions of the Committee:

" Q. I understand you to state that you had some other papers in reference to this transaction between you and Senator Patterson; will you be good enough to produce it? A. Senator Patterson testified that he never received any dividend from the stock, and that he had no money from me on account of it; here is a receipt which I present to this Committee. [The paper referred to was placed in evidence, and is as follows:]

" 'WASHINGTON, *June* 22, 1868.

" 'Received of Oakes Ames $1800, on account of

dividend received by him as trustee in stock held for my account. 'J. W. PATTERSON.'

"Q. Did you see him sign this paper? A. yes; he gave it to me at the time I wrote the receipt, and he signed it; the receipt is in my writing and the signature in his.

"Q. And made at the time of the date? A. Yes, Sir; I also hand to the Committee another paper. [Paper placed in evidence as follows :]

"'BOSTON, *May* 6, 1871.

"'Received of Oakes Ames 200 shares U. P. R. R. stock, seven hundred and fifty-seven dollars 24-100 in cash, on account of C. M. stock, and there is still due on the transaction thirty shares of stock in the C. M. of America, and 2000 in the Income bonds of the U. P. R. R. 'J. W. PATTERSON.'

"Q. Was that signed by him in your presence and given to you? A. Yes.

"Q. And at the date it bears? A. I presume so.

"Q. The paper itself is in your own handwriting? A. Yes, Sir.

"Q. This is the paper given at the time of the settlement made between you and him, of which you spoke in your testimony? A. Yes; that $1800 is the check I gave him on the Sergeant-at Arms, for which he gave me the receipt; that is the final settlement.

' Q. Have you still another paper? A. I have a letter Mr. Patterson wrote me in relation to this matter; he wrote me several, which I have destroyed; I found this last night in looking over my papers; it is a letter from Mr. Patterson.

"Q. You received it through the mail? A. I do not recollect how I received it; the letter is written here and I received it here; I received several others, which as I stated, I have torn up; this is all I have; this letter is written this winter, since the present investigation commenced.

"Q. Do you know whether it is in Mr. Patterson's own writing? A. I do not know that I can swear it is.

"Q. Have you had any conversation with him in reference to this letter? A. I have had several interviews with him since the letter was written.

"Q. In reference to the letter? A. Not in reference to the letter, but in reference to matters the letter alludes to.

"Q. In any of the conversations you have had with him has the fact that he had written such a letter been mentioned? A. I do not know that it has; I do not know whether it has or not; I think he asked me if I had got the letter he wrote me.

"Q. Is this the only one you have received from him this winter? A. No, Sir, I have received several and torn them up; I did not know that I had this until last evening.

"Q. Was there any envelope with it? A. I destroyed the envelope which I received it in; I received it when I got back from home—the 7th or 8th of January. [The letter referred to was placed in evidence, and is as follows:]

"'WASHINGTON, D. C., *Jan.* 4, 1873.

"'*The Hon.* OAKES AMES—*My Dear Sir:* The facts in respect to the Crédit Mobilier, so far as I had any connection with it, were as follows:

"'You came to me one day, knowing that a want of means was a chronic evil with me, and said, "Patterson, if you would like, I can let you have 30 shares of stock in the Crédit Mobilier, which I think will be a profitable investment, and will be a good thing for you." My reply, in substance, was that if you had anything which I could properly invest in, and out of which I could make some money, I should be glad to take it, but that I had not the money at that time, and must defer it until I could get it.

"'Your reply was that you presumed I could have it later when it might be convenient, and you regarded it a perfectly legitimate transaction. At that time you did not and could not anticipate you should ever ask for further legislation from Congress in respect to the road, and you never did, except when it was forced on you by the Secretary.

"'After this conversation with me you may have had the impression that I should take the stock some time, but for some reason or other, perhaps for a want of funds, I never took any of the stock. If I never had any stock in the company I could not, as I did not, have its dividends.

"'If *pressed* to know if I purchased at any time any bonds or stock of the road, you can say I did at the time they attempted to embarrass you when the value of the stock was depressed, and I paid you the full market value for it. I paid you $7000 in money for stock and bonds.

"'The stock I put into the hands of Mr. Morton immediately, to sell as soon as it should go up reasonably in the market, which he did.

"'I saw Mr. Morton on my way through, and he said he had never held any stock in the Crédit Mobilier for any one, but did not wish to have his name brought into the examination if it could be avoided. I am going to Ohio. I will see you on my return. *Don't fail to correct your original statement before the Committee. It must not be reported as it now stands.* Very truly, etc.,

"'J. W. PATTERSON.'"

The production of the receipts and of this remarkable letter, created a decided sensation both in the Committee and throughout the country. The issue was fairly and distinctly made. If the receipts were genuine and Mr. Ames had sworn to the truth, Mr. Patterson had perjured himself. It remained for Mr. Patterson to prove that the receipts were forgeries. It remained for him to show that the letter we have given was a forgery, and not an attempt on his part to induce Ames to swear to manufactured testimony.

On the 29th of January, Mr. Ames produced and exhibited to the Committee the check for $1800, for which the first receipt was given. The check bore Mr. Patterson's endorsement. He also submitted another receipt from Mr. Patterson, which was as follows:

"'WASHINGTON, Feb. 14, 1868.

"'Received of Oakes Ames three hundred and twenty-nine dollars for three bonds of U. P. R. R. Co. sold for me, being dividend of eighty per cent. in bonds or stock of Crédit Mobilier of America, held by him as trustee on my account.

"'J. W. PATTERSON.'"

To this was appended the following: "2400 bonds at 97, $2328; interest paid, 105; paid cash, $2223."

This is the condition of the matter at present. Mr. Patterson has not succeeded in upsetting Ames's testimony, and the receipts, the check, and letter are still to be explained, or proved forgeries.

THE CASE OF VICE-PRESIDENT COLFAX.

When the charge was made that Mr. Colfax had been a purchaser of Crédit Mobilier stock from Mr. Ames, that gentleman denied it, and in a speech at South Bend, Indiana, said: "Never having in my life a dollar of stocks of any kind that I did not pay for, I claim the right to purchase stock in the Crédit Mobilier, or Crédit Immobilier, if there is one; nor do I know of any law prohibiting it. Do I need to add that neither Oakes Ames, nor any other person, ever gave, or offered to give me one share, or twenty shares, or two hundred shares in the Crédit Mobilier, or any other railroad stock, and that unfortunately I have never seen or received to the value of a farthing out of the 270 per cent. dividends, or the 800 per cent. dividends, in cash stock, or bonds, you have read about for the past month, nor 100 per cent., nor the tenth of one per cent. I have said, that if twenty shares of it could be purchased at par, without buying into a perspective lawsuit, it would be a good investment, if as valuable a stock as represented; but never having been plaintiff nor defendant in a court of justice, I want no stock at any price with a lawsuit on top of it."

In short, Mr. Colfax's statement amounted to this: He had never purchased the stock from Mr. Ames, and had never received any dividends upon it.

This statement Mr. Colfax confirmed by a declaration under oath before the Poland Committee. The substance of this sworn statement may be thus stated in Mr. Colfax's own words:

"I state explicitly, that no one ever gave, or offered to give me any shares of stock in the Crédit Mobilier or the Union Pacific Railroad. I have never received, nor had tendered to me any dividends in cash, stock, or bonds accruing upon any stock, in either of said organizations."

Mr. Ames had from the first included Mr. Colfax in his list of the Congressmen who had purchased stock from him. Upon Mr. Colfax's denial of the charge, he declared his ability to prove his assertion.

On the 24th of January, Mr. Ames testified that he had purchased twenty shares of Crédit Mobilier stock for Mr. Colfax, in December, 1867, at the request of that gentleman. Mr. Colfax not having the money at the time, Mr. Ames advanced it. Soon after this, there was an eighty per cent. dividend declared in

Union Pacific bonds. Mr. Ames stated that he had sold these, and had applied the proceeds to paying for the stock bought for Mr. Colfax, after deducting the interest. Mr. Colfax then gave him a check on the Sergeant-at-Arms for $534.72, the balance of the purchase money. Mr. Ames further stated that in June there was a cash dividend on the Crédit Mobilier of $1200, which he gave to Mr. Colfax by a check payable to "S. C. or bearer," drawn on the Sergeant-at-Arms of the House.

Mr. Colfax emphatically denied Mr. Ames's statement, and declared that he had never received the $1200, or any of the stock or money to which Ames referred. The books of the Sergeant-at-Arms were produced, and exhibited to the Committee. It was found that in June, 1868, Mr. Ames had drawn a check on the Sergeant-at-Arms to "S. C. or bearer," and that this check had been paid to some one. This much of Mr. Ames's statement being sustained, Mr. Colfax found himself obliged to show that the check in question had not been paid to him. He utterly denied having received the money, and cross-questioned Ames rigidly, for the purpose of ascertaining if he (Ames) had drawn the money on this check. Ames declared that he had not, and intimated his belief that the money had been paid to Mr. Colfax. The Sergeant-at-Arms was then examined by Mr. Colfax. He stated that a check drawn by Oakes Ames to "S. C. or bearer," for $1200, had been paid at his office in June, 1868; but as he did not cash the check, he could not say to whom it was paid.

At the close of this day's session, the matter stood thus: Mr. Ames charged that he had paid Mr. Colfax a cash dividend of $1200 on Crédit Mobilier stock, the payment being made by a check for $1200, drawn on the Sergeant-at-Arms to "S. C. or bearer," and dated June 20th. Mr. Colfax, on his part, made oath that he had never seen this check, or received any of the money upon it. The statement of Mr. Ames as regarded the drawing of the check, and its payment to some one, on the 21st of June, being confirmed by the books of the Sergeant-at-Arms, the Committee decided to examine the accounts of the First National Bank of Washington City, where Mr. Colfax's accounts were kept. The books were produced before the Committee on the 28th of January, and Mr. Colfax's account examined. "There appeared a credit of $1968.63, dated June 22, 1868, two days after the date of Ames's check to 'S. C.,' on the Sergeant-at-Arms, and one day after that check was paid. This furnished only presumptive proof of the deposit of $1200, but all doubt was removed when the cashier produced a deposit ticket, bearing Mr. Colfax's signature, in which the $1968.63 was itemized, $1200 being cash, and the remainder drafts or checks."

The production of this account placed Mr. Colfax in a terrible position. Ames had sworn that Colfax had bought Crédit Mobilier stock of him; Colfax had denied it under oath. Ames had sworn that this stock had yielded in June, 1868, a dividend of $1200, which he had paid to Mr. Colfax by a check drawn to " S. C. or bearer" or the Sergeant-at-Arms. Mr. Colfax had denied all knowledge of this check, and had denied having received any money on it. The books of the Sergeant-at-Arms had shown that Ames had drawn a check to "S. C. or bearer" on the 20th of June, as he had stated, and that this check had been paid to some one on the 21st of June. Mr. Colfax's bank account had shown that, on the 22d of June, the very next day after the payment of the check, he had deposited in cash the exact amount of this check, namely $1200. The circumstantial evidence against him was appalling. His best friends stood aghast, and pitied him from their very souls.

Mr. Colfax repeated his denials respecting the stock, and declared that he would show that the $1200 deposited by him was received from another source. If he could succeed in doing this, his vindication would be complete. It seemed to the country at large very easy for Mr. Colfax to say where the $1200 came from, and to give the reason of its payment to him, and thus set the matter at rest. The bank account of Mr. Colfax was examined on the 28th of January, and it was not until the 11th of February that he offered any explanation of the source from which he had gotten the $1200. On the 11th of February, he appeared before the Committee, accompanied by Judge Hale, whom he had retained as his counsel, and made a statement under oath that the $1200, which he had deposited in cash in the First National Bank of Washington, on the 22d of June, 1868, was composed of two sums, of $1000 and $200 respectively. The $1000, he stated, he had received from a Mr. George F. Nesbitt, of New York, who had written him a letter congratulating him upon his nomination for the Vice-Presidency, and enclosing a $1000 bill to be used for political purposes during the campaign. The sender of the gift, Mr. Nesbitt, died a few years ago, and the letter in which the money was sent had, Mr. Colfax stated, been destroyed. Mr. Colfax submitted the evidence of several members of his family in proof of the reception of Nesbitt's letter. They swore to a recollection of it, and stated the incidents connected with its reception. The other $200 Mr. Colfax stated was received from his step-father, Mr. Mattnews, in payment of money borrowed from Mr. Colfax some time before. Mr. Colfax repeated his former denials concerning the stock and Ames's check.

This statement of Mr. Colfax was not accepted by the public as satisfactory. It amounted to this, in part: That a leading business man of New York had entrusted to the mail in a letter, a bill for $1000 dollars, without making any note of it, the man was dead, and the letter could not be found. Against this explanation was Oakes Ames's sworn statement, the proofs afforded by the books of the Sergeant-at-Arms, and the suspicious deposit of the exact amount of Ames's check. The New York *Evening Mail*, a candid and independent sheet, and very friendly to Mr. Colfax, in stating the popular judgment of the case as far as it had gone, said:

" Mr. Colfax's explanation of the $1200 deposit which was made to his credit at the time when Mr. Ames swears that he had given the former that amount, has been received with general disbelief, not unaccompanied by mockery and ridicule. It was certainly a remarkable co-incidence that Mr. Colfax should have received at that particular time $200 from his father-in-law and a $1000 note from an entire stranger, Mr. George F. Nesbitt, of this city—the latter, besides, congratulating Mr. Colfax on his nomination for Vice-President.

"The whole course of Mr. Colfax's explanations has been of such a character as to excite the apprehension that every one of them was an afterthought and a device more unworthy by far than the original offence. Therefore it has been generally assumed that the strange story of receiving a $1000 note from a man now dead and out of reach of inquiry was merely a desperate and despicable expedient."

This is the simple truth. Whether Mr. Colfax's statement be true or false, the public did receive it with incredulity, if not with open disbelief.

Mr. Colfax, in order to break down the statement of Ames as to the check, brought forward a Mr. Dillon, the bookkeeper of the Sergeant-at-Arms, who swore that he had an "impression" that he had paid the "S. C." check to Mr. Ames himself. He would not say more than that this was his impression. The New York *Tribune* of the 14th of January, 1873, contained this statement respecting the evidence of two of the witnesses brought forward by Mr. Colfax:

"Mr. Matthews, the Vice-President's stepfather, testified that he paid Mr. Colfax $200 about the middle of June, 1868, and said that he went to the office of the Clerk of the House and arranged for obtaining a part of his salary before the end of the month in order to pay this bill. Oakes Ames in examining the accounts in the Clerk's office finds that it does not appear that Mr. Matthews received any money on or about June 16, 1868, but that he was paid the full amount on the 28th of that month. The young man who pays money to members says that it is barely possible that Mr. Matthews got some money on the 16th on a memorandum, but there is no evidence in his office of it.

"Mr. Dillon, the bookkeeper of the Sergeant-at-Arms, said that he had a vague impression of having paid the $1200 on the S. C. check to Mr. Ames himself, and added in reply to a question that the amount was so large that he would be likely to remember it. Oakes Ames at the time called his attention to another payment, about the same time, of $1000. Mr. Dillon said that he remembered that, and that he paid the money to Mr. Ames in large bills. Mr. Ames turning to his memorandum book, replied that Mr. Dillon was mistaken, as that $1000 had been paid with a check to the order of S. M. Eldridge & Co., of Alexandria. Mr. Dillon denied that this could be possible, as if such had been the fact it would have been noted on the book. Today, Oakes Ames found the check drawn to the order of S. M. Eldridge & Co., showing Mr. Dillon to have been mistaken. Mr. Ames thinks that if Mr. Dillon was so much mistaken in a case where he was positive, and where he depended on his books to assist his memory, his vague impressions of what occurred at the time are not worth much."

In order to get at the facts of the case, for it was clear to all that either Oakes Ames or Schuyler Colfax was guilty of perjury, a member of the Poland Committee made an investigation of Mr. Colfax's deposits in the First National Bank of Washington. He found that two checks or drafts from Mr. Nesbitt to Mr. Colfax had been deposited by the latter in 1868, one in April, and the other on the 13th of July, of that year. Each of these drafts was for $1000. This discovery did not help Mr. Colfax much. It showed that Mr. Nesbitt had twice sent Mr. Colfax the sum of $1000, and had taken the precaution to insure the money against loss by sending each sum in the form of a draft payable to Mr. Colfax's order. This very precaution inclined people to doubt that Mr. Nesbitt would have been so reckless as to send Mr. Colfax a thousand dollar note in an unregistered letter, only a short while before he took the precaution to send a similar sum by a draft.

"Mr. Colfax," says the press dispatch from Washington of February 18th, "has no hesitation in saying that he did receive from Mr. Nesbitt, in each of the months of April, June, July, and October in that year, a remittance of $1000, making $4000 in all, the April and July remittances having been in checks. These remittances were made partly on personal and partly on political grounds. The letters accompanying two of them are in existence. Those covering the other two cannot now be found. Mr. Colfax, in his testimony, made no reference to any of the remittances except that of June, for the sole reason that that remittance only had any reference to or connection with the subject of the investigation before the Committee, and his counsel, with full knowledge of the facts, and to whom the whole responsibility in this regard belong, advised him that he could not properly open the subject of the remittance without bringing in extraneous and important matter before the Committee, and departing from the point of issue."

On the 19th of February, Mr. Colfax appeared before the Poland Committee, and produced Mr. Nesbitt's letters which accompanied the drafts received in April and July, but stated that he could not find the letter which accompanied the $1000 bill which he claimed to have received in June. He produced conclusive evidence as to the other three remittances, but could not produce evidence as satisfactory as to the June remittance.

There the case rests at present. Mr. Colfax has still before him the task of proving that he received $1000 from Nesbitt in June, and did not receive $1200 from Oakes Ames. He is still entangled in the terrible web of circumstantial evidence against him. That he may escape from it and vindicate himself is the wish of all good men. There is not a public man in America whose vindication would be more cordially hailed by the people. The people do not wish to believe him guilty; but they are appalled by the terrible mass of circumstantial evidence against him, and he must, in justice to himself, destroy this. It is the earnest wish of the writer, who has sought to present a simple statement of the facts of the case as far as they have been developed, that he may succeed.

CHAPTER IX.

THE DEPARTMENTS.

Organization and History of the State Department—The New Building—The Secretary of State—Duties of the various Bureaux of the Department—The Treasury of the United States—A noble Edifice—The Secretary of the Treasury—Detailed Statements of the various sub-divisions of the Treasury—Martin Renchan—The War Department—Its Organization—The United States Army—Army Headquarters—The Navy Department—Organization of the Bureaux—Department of the Interior—Its Organization—The Patent Bureau—The Patent-office Building—The Museum—An interesting Collection—The Washington Relics—The Declaration of Independence—The Model-room—Triumphs of American Ingenuity—The Post-office Department—The General Post-office Building—History and detailed Description of the Department—The Dead-letter office—The Bureau of Agriculture—Its Prospects and Promises.

The various Executive Departments of the Government are provided with handsome edifices for the accommodation of their chiefs and subordinate officials. These buildings are located with a view to placing them within easy access from both the Capitol and the Executive Mansion, and they constitute, together with the Capitol, the principal ornaments of the city. Each Department is presided over by a Secretary, who is by virtue of his office a member of the Cabinet of the President of the United States.

THE DEPARTMENT OF STATE

is usually regarded as the most important of the Executive branches of the Government, and its chief is considered the leading member of the Cabinet. This Department is at present occupying temporary quarters. A magnificent edifice is in course of erection, in the vicinity of the Treasury, which, when completed, will contain the offices of the State, War, and Navy Departments. It will require several years for its completion. It will be constructed of New England granite, and will be one of the most beautiful buildings in the city, as well as one of the largest.

In July, 1789, Congress organized a "Department of Foreign Affairs," and placed it in charge of a Secretary, who was called the "Secretary of the Department of Foreign Affairs." He was required to discharge his duties "conformably to the instructions of the President," but as his powers were derived from Congress, he was required to hold himself amenable to that body, to attend its sessions, and to "explain all matters pertaining to his province." In September, 1789, Congress changed the title of the Department to the "Department of State," and made a definite enumeration of the duties of the Secretary.

The head of the Department is the Secretary of State. His subordinates are an Assistant Secretary of State, a Chief Clerk, a Superintendent of Statistics, a Translator, a Librarian, and as many clerks as are needed. The Secretary receives a salary of $8000 per annum. He conducts all the intercourse of this Government with the Governments of foreign countries, and is frequently required to take a prominent part in the administration of domestic affairs. He countersigns all proclamations, and official documents issued by the President. If popular rumor be correct, the Secretaries of State have frequently written the messages, and inaugurals of the Presidents, and thus have kept those august officials from making laughing stocks of themselves. The duties of the office require the exercise of the highest ability, and the Secretaries of State have usually been among the first statesmen of our country. The first incumbent of the office was Thomas Jefferson. His successors have been, Edmund Randolph, of Virginia; Timothy Pickering, of Massachusetts; John Marshall, of Virginia; James Madison, of Virginia; Robert Smith, of Maryland; James Monroe, of Virginia; John Quincy Adams, of Massachusetts; Henry Clay, of Kentucky; Martin Van Buren, of New York; Edward Livingston, of Louisiana; Louis McLane, of Delaware; John Forsyth, of Georgia; Daniel Webster, of Massachusetts; Hugh S. Legare, of South Carolina; Abel P. Upshur, of Virginia; John Nelson, of Maryland; John C. Calhoun, of South Carolina; James Buchanan, of Pennsylvania; John M. Clayton, of Delaware; Edward Everett, of Massachusetts; William L. Marcy, of New York; Lewis Cass, of Michigan; Jeremiah S. Black, of Pennsylvania; William H. Seward, of New York; and Hamilton Fish, of New York, the present incumbent.

The *Diplomatic Bureau* is in charge of, and conducts all the official correspondence between the Department and the Ministers and other agents of the United States residing abroad, and the representatives of foreign powers accredited to this Government. It is in this Bureau that all instructions sent from the Department, and communications to commissioners under treaties of boundaries, etc., are prepared, copied, and recorded; all similar communications received by the Department are registered and filed in this Bureau, and their contents are entered in an analytical table or index.

The *Consular Bureau* has charge of all correspondence, and other business, between the Department and the Consuls and Commercial agents of the United States. Applications for such positions are received and attended to in this Bureau. A concise record of all its transactions is kept by the clerk in charge of it.

The *Disbursing Agent* has charge of all correspondence and other business relating to any and all expenditures of money with which the Department is charged.

The *Translator* is required to furnish translations of such documents as may be submitted to him by the proper officers of the Department. He also records the commissions of the Consuls and Vice-Consuls, when not in English, upon which exequaturs are based.

The *Clerk of Appointments and Commissions* makes out and keeps a record of all commissions, letters of appointment, and nominations to the Senate; makes out and keeps a record of all exequaturs, and when in English, the commissions on which they are issued.

He also has charge of the Library of the Department, which is large and valuable.

The *Clerk of the Rolls and Archives* has charge of the "rolls," by which are meant the enrolled acts and resolutions of Congress, as they are received by the Department from the President. When authenticated copies thereof are called for, he prepares them. He also prepares these acts and resolutions, and the various treaties negotiated, for publication in the newspapers and in book form, and superintends their passage through the press. He distributes through the United States the various publications of the Department, and receives and answers all letters relating thereto. He has charge of all treaties with the Indian tribes, and all business relating to them.

The *Clerk of Authentications* is in charge of the seals of the United States and of the Department, and prepares and attaches certificates to papers presented for authentication; receives and accounts for the fees; and records the correspondence of the Department, except the diplomatic and consular letters. He also has charge of all correspondence relating to territorial affairs.

The *Clerk of Pardons and Passports* prepares and records pardons and remissions of sentences by the President; and registers and files the papers and petitions upon which they are founded. He makes out and records passports; and keeps a daily register of the letters received, other than diplomatic and consular, and the disposition made of them. He also has charge of the correspondence relating to his business.

The *Superintendent of Statistics* prepares the "Annual Report of the Secretary of State and Foreign Commerce," as required by the Acts of 1842 and 1856.

THE TREASURY DEPARTMENT

was organized by an Act of Congress in 1789. This Act directed the appointment of a Secretary, Assistant Secretary, Comptroller, Treasurer, and Solicitor. The Department is located in a magnificent structure, situated on Pennsylvania Avenue, at the corner of Fifteeth Street West, fronting G Street. The old building was commenced in 1836, and was constructed of inferior brown sandstone, painted in imitation of granite. In 1855, the extension was begun. It is now nearly completed. This extension has more than doubled the size of the original edifice, and has made the whole building one of the handsomest and most imposing in the country. The old building extended along Fifteenth Street, and was ornamented with an unbroken Ionic colonnade, 342 feet long, which, though showy, was inconvenient, as it excluded the light from the rooms.

The plan of the extension flanks the old building at each end with massive granite masonry, and makes beautiful terminations of the north and south fronts, which serve to relieve the dreary monotony of the long colonnade, besides providing a large new building at each end. "There are two inner quadrangles formed by the old rear building, extending back from the eastern entrance. These courts are each 130 feet square. The walls of the extension are composed of pilasters, resting on a base which rises some twelve feet above the ground on the southern or lower side. Between the pilasters or antæ are belt courses, beautifully moulded, and the facings of the doors and windows are fine bold mouldings in keeping. In the centre of the southern, western, and northern fronts are magnificent porticoes. The west front has also the projecting pediments at the ends, corresponding with those on the east side, and each supported by square antæ at the angles, with two columns between. The whole building is of the Grecian or Ionic order, and is surmounted by a massive balustrade. The new structure is of the best and most beautiful granite in the world, brought from Dix Island, on the coast of Maine. The antæ and columns are monoliths. The large, solid antæ weigh nearly a hundred thousand pounds, and the columns some seventy-five thousand. The facility with which the immense masses are hewn out of the quarries, swung on board vessels, brought to the Capital, and raised to the positions which the architect in his studio designed them to occupy, conveys a high idea of American art and enterprise. The Treasury Building as extended, is 465 feet long, exclusive of the porticoes by 266 feet wide."

The courts are ornamented with handsome fountains. A very beautiful one adorns the space in front of the western portico at the entrance to the President's park, and another is now being constructed before the north front. The entrances are through massive gateways. The yard on the north and west sides is lower than the street, and broad flights of steps lead to it. A handsome granite balustrade extends along the north wall.

The interior arrangements are unusually fine. The architecture ranks next to that of the Capitol in its magnificence, and is peculiarly American in its details. Unlike most of the public buildings, the offices are large, airy, and handsome, presenting the appearance of splendid saloons, and affording a greater degree of comfort to the occupants than the narrow, cell-like apartments of the old Treasury.

Some of the apartments in the Treasury are noted for their beauty. The new Cash Room is one of the most magnificent halls in the world. The walls and ceiling are beautifully panelled with rare specimens of Italian marble, and all the interior arrangements and decorations are on a scale of magnificence consistent with the wealth of the nation.

The Secretary of the Treasury is a member of the President's Cabinet, and is chosen for his financial ability. He has the general charge of the finances and resources of the United States. He has very great discretionary powers, and is possessed of immense patronage. He recommends to Congress such measures as in his judgment are necessary, and shapes the financial policy of the Government. He superintends the execution of the laws respecting the revenue of the United States; also those relating to commerce and navigation, the survey of the coast, the light-house department, the marine hospitals of the United States, and the construction of certain public buildings for Custom Houses, Post-offices, and other purposes.

The first Secretary of the Treasury was Alexander Hamilton, of New York, and it is to him that the Department owes its admirable organization. There have been able men among his successors. The list of the Secretaries is as follows: Oliver Wolcott, of Connecticut; S. Dexter, of Massachusetts; Albert Gallatin, of Pennsylvania; George W. Campbell, of Tennessee; Alexander J. Dallas, of Pennsylvania; William H. Crawford, of Georgia; Richard Rush, of Pennsylvania; Samuel D. Ingham, of Pennsylvania; Louis McLane, of Delaware; William J. Duane, of Pennsylvania; Roger B. Taney, of Maryland; Levi Woodbury, of New Hampshire; Thomas Ewing, of Ohio; Walter Forward, of Pennsylvania; George M. Bibb, of Kentucky; Robert J. Walker, of Mississippi; William M. Meredith, of Pennsylvania; Thomas Corwin, of Ohio; James Guthrie, of Kentucky; Howell Cobb, of Georgia; Philip Francis Thomas, of Maryland; Salmon P. Chase, of Ohio; William Pitt Fessenden, of Maine; Hugh McCulloch, of Indiana; and George S. Boutwell, of Massachusetts.

The subordinate officers of the Department are two Assistant Secretaries, a Commissioner of the Revenue, a Superintendent of the Treasury Building, two Comptrollers, a Commissioner of Customs, six Auditors, a Treasurer, a Register, a Solicitor, a Chief of the Currency Bureau, a Commissioner of the Internal Revenue a Superintendent of the Coast Survey, and a Director of the Bureau of Statistics. There are over two thousand and fifty clerks in the Department, besides chiefs of division and higher officials, and employes of a lower grade.

The *First Comptroller* prescribes the mode of keeping and rendering accounts for the civil and diplomatic service, and the public lands, and revises and certifies the balances arising thereon.

The *Second Comptroller* keeps and renders the accounts of the Army and Navy and the Indian departments of the public service, and revises and certifies the balances arising thereon.

The *Commissioner of the Customs* prescribes the mode of keeping and rendering the accounts of the customs revenue and disbursements, and for the building and repairing of Custom Houses, etc., and revises and certifies the balances arising thereon.

The *First Auditor* examines and adjusts the accounts of the customs and revenue disbursements, appropriations and expenditures on account of the civil list and under private acts of Congress. The customs and revenue balances are reported by him to the Commissioner of the Customs, and the others to the First Comptroller, for their decisions thereon.

The *Second Auditor* examines and adjusts all accounts connected with the pay, clothing, and recruiting of the army; and for armories, arsenals, and ordnance; and those relating to the Indian Department. All balances are reported by him to the Second Comptroller, for his decision thereon.

The *Third Auditor* examines and adjusts all accounts for the subsistence of the army, for fortifications, the Military Academy, military roads, and the Quartermaster's Department, as well as for pensions, claims arising from military services previous to 1816, and for horses and other property lost in the military service. He reports his balances to the Second Comptroller for his decision thereon.

The *Fourth Auditor* examines and adjusts the accounts connected with the Navy Department, and reports his balances to the Second Comptroller for the final decision of that official.

The *Fifth Auditor* examines and adjusts all accounts for diplomatic and kindred services performed by order of the State Department. His balances are referred to the First Comptroller for decision.

The *Sixth Auditor* has charge of the accounts of the Post-office Department. He receives and audits all claims for services rendered the Post-office Department. His decisions are final, unless the claimant appeals within twelve months to the First Comptroller. He is charged with the collection of all debts due the Post-office Department, and all fines and forfeitures imposed upon the postmasters and mail contractors for neglect of duty; he oversees the prosecution of suits and legal proceedings, both civil and criminal, and sees that all lawful steps are taken to enforce the payment of moneys due the Department; sends out instructions to the marshals, attorneys and clerks of the United States in such cases; receives returns from each term of the United States Courts of the condition and progress of such suits and legal proceedings; has charge of all lands and other property assigned to the United States in payment of debts due the Post-office Department; and has power to sell and dispose of the same for the benefit of the United States.

In the office of the Sixth Auditor is a noted man in Washington, and one of the oldest public servants in the service of the country. He can be, when he choses, one of the most entertaining of companions, for his long experience has charged him brimful of anecdote and reminiscence. "Father Gobright," in his clever little work, thus speaks of him:

"Martin Renehan, an American citizen of Irish birth, well known for his wit, intelligence, and warm-heartedness, had served (at the White House) under Jackson and Van Buren's administrations as an usher, or man of all work. He was popular with everybody, and possessed a deservedly good character for integrity. He 'still lives,' and holds 'a little place' in the office of the Sixth Auditor of the Treasury.

"The lady of the White House, who did the honors, was a widow, the daughter-in-law of the President. She was an attractive young lady, and popular.

"President Harrison was very much of a gentleman, social and kind-hearted. During the first two weeks of his administration, an elderly man, very polite and patronizing, made frequent visits to the White House, in order to see the President, *privately*. Martin informed the new comer that he would gratify him, if he would come some morning at six o'clock. The visitor was punctual to the time. General Harrison was an early riser. Martin went up stairs gently, and tapped at the door; having received an invitation to enter, he did so. The General was sitting near the grate, in which were a few expiring coals. 'Is it possible,' Martin said, 'the weather being cold, that you have no more fire?' He replied:—

"'Martin, when at home I was accustomed to a wood fire; and if I had wood now, I'd replenish this fire myself, as I do not wish to call up my colored man' (the one he had brought with him from Ohio). Martin responded that he would supply the requisite fuel, and added, 'An elderly gentleman, sir, has been repeatedly calling here. He is of respectable appearance, and unassuming in his manners, and has elicited my sympathies. I, therefore, take the liberty of asking whether you will now give him a private audience?' 'Where is he?' 'In the green room,' replied Martin. 'Show him up,' said the President. Martin accordingly showed him up, and retired in order to give the stranger the full benefit of a strictly private interview. When the visitor had taken his departure, Martin returned to the President's room. 'Martin,' said the President, 'you have been kind to that man.' 'I have; I took him by the hand.' 'Are you aware,' asked the President, 'that he is looking for your place?' Martin replied, 'Your Excellency, I expected to go, as I am opposed to you in politics.' General Harrison said: 'John Quincy Adams told me all about you, and as long as I remain in the White House, *the Cabinet even can't remove you.*' Renehan responded, 'I am the last *Martin* in the nest, and I thought you were going to put me to flight.' 'Oh no,' the President replied, two *Martins* have already been banished from this house, (meaning Martin Van Buren and his son), and it would be bad luck to banish you, the only remaining Martin. So, you remain, and nestle in the battlements.' . . . .

"Mr. Tyler was, during his administration, the

recipient of a small wooden box. There was no accompanying note, giving an inventory of its contents, nor was there, at first, any one near by possessed of sufficient courage to open the box, after it had been whispered that it might be an infernal machine. The alarm of a little group, consisting of the President, Captain Waggaman, a relative of the President, and a negro servant, soon rose to a fearful height, when Martin Renehan was summoned in this great crisis. He came with quick breathing and hurried step, and soon learned the cause of the commotion.

"'Your Excellency,' he said, with an apparently serious look, and in his own vernacular, 'does well to be cautious in these high party times. The divil himself puts it into the heads of his children to manufacture infernal machines, and who knows but that powder and balls, and percussion dust, have been arranged with a view to blowing you up for vetoing the Bank bill!'

"'True, true,' remarked Mr. Tyler, receding a few steps from the box, and starting back as if it were on the eve of explosion; 'b-u-t I should like to see the contents, Martin.'

"'By the powers,' said the son of Erin, 'I'll chop it up in less than no time.' And away he ran down into the kitchen, and picking up a cleaver, hastily returned to execute his purpose.

"To this no objection was interposed. Martin placed the box on the table, turned up his cuffs, and prepared for the work.

"Captain Waggaman, who was in military costume,

retreated to a nook from which he could behold the operation without danger. The negro stood afar off, holding up his hands before him as a shield of defence, and Mr. Tyler took refuge behind a huge pillar. In peeping around it, his nose, which was by no means small, was alone perceptible to the brave Irishman.

"'Martin! Martin! ain't you afraid?' asked the President.

"'No, sir,' said Martin; 'it's better for me to die than that the President should be killed by such a divil of a machine. My death is nothing compared with your Excellency's.'

"But Martin went to work. Every cut of the cleaver caused a winking of the spectators' eyes, and a cold chill. At last, after much hacking, the inside of the box was exposed, and great was the joy of the alarmed company, when Martin put in *his hand, and took out the model of a stove!* Why, or by whom it was sent to the President, has never been ascertained. It is certain, however, that the timid group breathed 'freer and deeper' after this exposure.

"Mr. Tyler solemnly and emphatically counselled Martin not to talk about the matter. 'For,' said he, 'if you do, they'll have me caricatured.'

"Martin, while 'fixing things to rights' in the garret, found an old telescope, and laid it by for future use. One evening, the stars shining brightly, the sky unclouded, and while President Tyler was entertaining the Cabinet and foreign representatives at dinner, Martin, having nothing else to do, brought down his instrument and mounted it upon a table on the southern portico. But he could see through it no better than with his naked eyes. In vain, he tried to get the focus, and a long time elapsed before he discovered that 'the thing,' as he called it, with an emphatic adjective, had no glass in it! He talked to the telescope, and, in earnest words, to himself, in the true Irish accent, expressing his disappointment and displeasure.

"Mr. Webster meantime came from the dining room, to breathe the fresh air. Standing behind Martin, with his hands deep down in his own pockets, he was an attentive and pleased listener to Martin's imprecations on the telescope and his confusion in the effort to 'get the focus.'

"Martin, accidentally turning round, descried Mr. Webster, who said: 'Why, Martin, can't you see anything?' Martin was much embarrassed on discovering that his complaint and address to the telescope had been heard by Mr. Webster; but soon recovering his self-possession, he with his usual ready wit, said: 'Mr. Webster, I have been disappointed. I can't, as I wished, contemplate the heavenly bodies, but I am equally gratified in seeing an earthly luminary now before me.' Mr. Webster was so well pleased with what he had witnessed and heard, that he returned to the company and related accurately the whole story, to the delight of the entire dinner party."

The *Treasurer* receives, and keeps the public funds of the United States, in his own office and that of the depositories created by the Act of August 6th, 1846, and pays out the same upon warrants drawn by the

Secretary of the Treasury, countersigned by the First Comptroller, and upon warrants drawn by the Post-Master General, countersigned by the Sixth Auditor, and recorded by the Register. He also holds public moneys advanced by warrant to disbursing officers, and pays out the same upon their checks.

The *Register* keeps the accounts of the receipts and expenditures of the public funds; he receives the returns and makes out the official statement of commerce and navigation of the United States. He is the custodian of all the vouchers and accounts decided by the First Comptroller and the Commissioner of Customs, which are placed in his keeping by those officials.

The *Solicitor* is charged with the prosecution of all civil suits begun by the United States (with the exception of those originating in the Post-office Department), and issues instructions to the marshals, attorneys, and clerks of the United States, concerning them and their results. A report is made to him at each term from the United States Courts, showing the progress and condition of such suits. He is in charge of all lands and other property assigned to the United States in payment of debts (except those connected with the Post-office Department), and has power to sell and dispose of the same for the benefit of the United States.

The *Chief of the Currency Bureau* has charge of all the operations connected with the manufacture and distribution of the national and fractional currency authorized by Acts of Congress. His bureau has come to be one of the most important branches of the Treasury, and will be noticed more in detail farther on.

The *Commissioner of the Internal Revenue* prescribes the manner of collecting the various taxes imposed by the Government, for revenue. All returns are made to him by his subordinates. The moneys received from the people are paid to him by the collectors, and by him handed to the Treasurer of the United States.

The *Light House Board* is composed of officers of the Army and Navy, the Superintendent of the Coast Survey, and the Secretary of the Smithsonian Institution. The Secretary of the Treasury is *ex officio* President of this Board, and presides over its deliberations. The Board directs the building and repairing of lighthouses, light vessels, buoys and beacons, and contracts for the supplies necessary to maintain such establishments.

The War Department.

The War Department occupies a plain old-fashioned brick building situated on Pennsylvania Avenue, immediately west of the President's house. The present edifice is not adequate to the wants of the Department, and several of its branches are located in buildings in the vicinity of the Department and leased for the purpose. When the new building, now in course of erection, is completed, the Department will be transferred to it.

The War Department was organized by Act of Congress in August, 1789. It has been remodelled and reconstructed several times since then, and has now become one of the largest and most important establishments in the Government.

The Chief of the Department is the *Secretary of*

War, who is a member of the President's Cabinet. His subordinates are the General Commanding the Army, the Adjutant-General, the Quartermaster-General, the Paymaster-General, the Commissary-General, the Surgeon-General, the Chief of Engineers, and the Chief of Ordnance. The Secretary of War has the general supervision of the military affairs of the country, subject to the direction of the President. He has also a general superintendence of the whole Department, and all orders are issued in his name and by his authority. His orders and decisions can be revoked only by the President.

The first Secretary of War was Henry Knox, of Massachusetts, the gallant soldier of the Revolution. His successors have been, Timothy Pickering, of Massachusetts; James McHenry, of Maryland; S. Dexter, of Massachusetts; Roger Griswold, of Connecticut; Henry Dearborn, of Massachusetts; William Eustis, of Massachusetts; John Armstrong, of New York; James Monroe, of Virginia; William H. Crawford, of Georgia; Isaac Shelby, of Kentucky; John C. Calhoun, of South Carolina; James Barbour, of Virginia; Peter B. Porter, of New York; John H. Eaton, of Tennessee; Lewis Cass, of Ohio, Joel R. Poinsett, of South Carolina; John Bell, of Tennessee; John C. Spencer, of New York; William Wilkins, of Pennsylvania; William L. Marcy, of New York; George W. Crawford, of Georgia; Charles M. Conrad, of Louisiana; Jefferson Davis, of Mississippi; John B. Floyd, of Virginia; Joseph Holt, of Kentucky; Simon Cameron, of Pennsylvania; Edwin M. Stanton, of Ohio; Ulysses S.

Grant (acting), of Illinois; John M. Scofield, of Ohio; John A. Rawlins, of Illinois; William T. Sherman, of Ohio; and W. W. Belknap, of Iowa.

The *Adjutant-General* is the medium of communication to the Army of all general and special orders of the Secretary of War relating to matters of military detail. The rolls of the Army and the records of service are kept by him, and all commissions are made out in his office.

The *Quartermaster-General* is in charge of all matters pertaining to barracks and quarters for the troops, transportation, camp, and garrison equipage, clothing, fuel, forage, and the incidental expenses of the military service of the United States.

The *Commissary-General* has charge of all matters connected with the subsistence of the Army. The splendid manner in which our armies were fed during the four years of the rebellion affords brilliant testimony to the efficiency of this bureau.

The *Paymaster-General* has charge of the funds appropriated for the purpose of paying the officers and men of the army. He keeps the accounts of this branch of the service, and all the pay rolls, returns, and like documents are filed in his office.

The *Surgeon-General* is charged with the control of the medical service of the army. He prescribes rules for the government of the various hospitals, sick-camps, etc., and receives all returns, and issues all orders connected with the same.

The *Chief of Engineers* is the immediate head of the engineer establishment of the army. He has two bureaux under his control, his own, and that of the *Topographical Engineers.* His own bureau has charge of all matters relating to the construction of fortifications, and to the Military Academy. The Bureau of Topographical Engineers has charge of all matters relating to river and harbor improvements, and the survey of the lakes, the construction of military roads, and of military surveys in general.

The *Chief of Ordnance* has charge of all matters relating to the manufacture, purchase, storage, and issue of all ordnance, arms, and munitions of war. He also controls the management of the arsenals and armories of the United States.

The *Judge Advocate-General* is the law officer of the Department, and is in charge of the *Bureau of Military Justice.* He supervises all proceedings connected with courts-martial, courts of inquiry, and other military courts.

The *Headquarters of the Army* are located in a small red brick building on 17th Street West, south of Pennsylvania Avenue, and diagonally opposite the War Department. The building was originally a private residence, and has a very decidedly domestic and unmilitary appearance. Everything is plain and simple about it, and absolutely without show. It is the headquarters of General William T. Sherman, and strangers usually include it in their rounds, in the hope of getting a peep at the great soldier.

The Army of the United States is stationed principally on the frontier, only enough men and officers being retained in the older States to garrison the forts and occupy the various military stations in those sections. The President of the United States is the Constitutional Commander-in-Chief of the Army and Navy, but the immediate commander of the army is a General, whose headquartes are at Washington. The other higher officers are a Lieutenant-General, Five Major-Generals, Ten Brigadier-Generals. The Chief of Staff to the Commanding General, and the chiefs of the various Bureaux of the War Department are also Brigadier-Generals. The number of subordinate commissioned officers, and of enlisted men is regulated by the necessities of the service.

The Navy Department.

During the War of the Revolution the interests of the Navy were confided to a Bureau of the War Department. On the 13th of April, 1798, Congress enacted a law "to establish an Executive Department, to be denominated the Department of the Navy." It was not until after the close of the war of 1812-15, during which the Navy fought its way, against heavy obstacles, into favor with the public, that the Government began to bestow upon the service the fostering care it merited at its hands.

The building used by the Department is situated immediately in the rear of the War Department, and fronts on 17th Street West. It is a miserably rickety old building, and, together with the War Department forms the most unsightly object in the neighborhood. It contains many interesting trophies, such as colors taken from the enemy in battle, etc. The Department is to occupy a portion of the new State building, to which we have referred, when completed.

The Department is in charge of a Secretary of the Navy, who is a member of the President's Cabinet. His subordinates are an Assistant-Secretary, and the Chiefs of the Bureaux of Yards and Docks, Navigation, Construction and Repairs, Steam Engineering, Equipment and Recruiting, Ordnance, Provisions and Clothing, and Medicine and Surgery.

The head of the Department is the *Secretary of the Navy*, who is a member of the President's Cabinet. He is given the general charge of everything connected with the Navy, and the execution of all the laws relating thereto is confided to him. All instructions to officers in command of squadrons or vessels, all orders of officers, commissions of officers both in the Navy and in the Marine Corps, appointments of commissioned and warrant officers, and orders concerning the enlistment and discharge of seamen are issued by him. The orders and instructions from the different bureaux are issued by his authority, as are those of the Commandant of the Marine Corps.

The first Secretary of the Navy (who was also Secretary of War) was General Henry Knox. His successors have been: Timothy Pickering, of Massachusetts; James McHenry, of Maryland; George Cabot, of Massachusetts; Benjamin Stoddert, of Maryland; Robert Smith, of Maryland; Jacob Crowninshield, of Massachusetts; Paul Hamilton, of South Carolina; William Jones, of Pennsylvania; Benjamin W. Crowninshield, of Massachusetts; Smith Thompson, of New York; Samuel L. Southard, of New Jersey; John Branch, of North Carolina; Levi Woodbury, of New Hampshire; Mahlon Dickerson, of New Jersey; James K. Paulding, of New York; George E. Badger, of North Corolina; Abel P. Upshur, of Virginia; Thomas W. Gilmer, of Virginia; John Y. Mason, of Virginia; George Bancroft, of Massachusetts; William B. Preston, of Virginia; William A. Graham, of North Carolina; John P. Kennedy, of Maryland; James C. Dobbin, of North Carolina; Isaac Toncey, of Connecticut; Gideon Welles, of Connecticut; Adolph E. Borie, of Pennsylvania; and George M. Robeson, of New Jersey.

The *Bureau of Yards and Docks* has charge of all the navy yards, docks, wharves, buildings, machinery in navy yards, and everything connected with them, and the Naval Asylum. The Chief of the Bureau is usually an officer of the Navy, of the grade of Captain.

The *Bureau of Navigation* is in charge of all matters pertaining to the business of navigation. It oversees the preparation of charts and sailing directions, and issues them to the ships of the Government; and also provides chronometers, barometers, etc., and such books as are furnished by the Government to vessels of War. "The United States Naval Observatory and Hydrographical Office," at Georgetown, and the Naval Academy at Annapolis are under the general supervision of the Chief of this Bureau, who is usually a Captain in the Navy.

The *Bureau of Construction and Repairs* is also in charge of a Captain in the Navy, and is charged with the construction and repair of all vessels of war of the United States, and of the purchase of materials for such work. The plans for all new vessels are submitted to, and decided upon by this Bureau, under the authority of the Secretary.

The *Bureau of Steam Engineering* was formerly a part of that just mentioned, but since the almost universal employment of steam vessels, has become a separate branch of the Department. It is in charge of the Engineer-in-Chief of the Navy, to whom all plans for steam machinery are submitted for examination. He reports upon them to the Secretary, and decides upon them by authority of that individual.

The *Bureau of Equipment and Recruiting* was, also, until a few years ago, a part of the Bureau of Construction and Repairs. It is in charge of a Captain in the Navy, and superintends the enlistment of seamen and petty officers, the manning of vessels with efficient crews, the equipment of all ships put in commission, with sails, anchors, water tanks, and all other stores and supplies except provisions and ordnance stores.

The *Bureau of Ordnance* is in charge of a Captain in the Navy, and is one of the most important in the Department. It has charge of all ordnance and ordnance stores, the manufacture or the purchase of cannon, guns, powder, shot, shells, and like articles, and of the equipment of vessels of war with ordnance and ordnance stores of all kinds. All plans for improved arms or ammunition are submitted to, examined by, and decided upon by it, under the authority of the Secretary. The Chief of the Bureau is generally an officer of experience and ability.

The *Bureau of Provisions and Clothing* has charge of the collection and issuing of all the provisions and clothing for the use of the Navy, and of all contracts for furnishing such stores. Its duties are similar to those of the Commissary-General's and Quartermaster-General's Department in the Army.

The *Bureau of Medicine and Surgery* is in charge of the Chief Surgeon of the Navy. It has authority over everything relating to medicines and medical stores, the treatment of the sick and wounded, and the management of naval hospitals.

The *Marine Corps* is under the immediate direction of a Commandant, who has the rank of Brigadier-General. It consists of a force of picked soldiers, detachments of whom are assigned to vessels of war for the purpose of preserving order and doing guard duty, and assisting in action. They have their own officers, and while forming a part of the naval establishment, are yet distinct from it.

The Department of the Interior.

The Department of the Interior is one of the most important branches of the Government, but is comparatively new, having been organized in 1849. It is given the control of certain portions of the public service, which had been previously attached to the Treasury and State Departments. It at present occupies the building erected for the use of the Patent-office, and, although it has no legal claim to its quarters, has nearly crowded the Patent Bureau out of the building.

The Head of the Department is the *Secretary of the*

Interior, who is a member of the President's Cabinet His subordinates are the Commissioners of the Public Lands, Patents, Indian Affairs, and Pensions, and the Superintendent of the Census. The Secretary is charged with the general supervision of matters relating to the public lands, the pensions granted by the Government, the management of the Indian tribes, the granting of patents, the management of the Agricultural Bureau, of the lead and other mines of the United States, the affairs of the Penitentiary of the District of Columbia, the overland routes to the Pacific, including the great Pacific Railways, the taking of the Census, and the direction of the acts of the Commissioner of Public Buildings. The Insane Hospital for the District of Columbia and the Army and Navy is also under his control.

The first Secretary of the Interior was Thomas Ewing, of Ohio, appointed by President Taylor. His successors have been Alexander H. H. Stuart, of Virginia; Robert McClelland, of Michigan; Jacob Thompson, of Mississippi; J. P. Usher, and O. H. Browning, of Illinois; Jacob D. Cox, of Ohio; and Columbus Delano, of Ohio.

The *Commissioner of the General Land Office* has charge of the survey, management, and sale of the public lands of the United States. He issues the titles therefor, whether derived from confirmations of grants made by former Governments, by sales, donations of grants for schools, military bounties, and public improvements, and likewise the revision of Virginia military bounty-land claims, and the issuing of scrip in lieu thereof. The Land Office audits its own accounts. It is also charged with laying off the land grants made to the various railroad schemes by Congress, which is a heavy undertaking in itself. The mines belonging to the Government are also in charge of this office.

The *Commissioner of Pensions* examines and adjudicates all claims arising under the various and numerous laws passed by Congress, granting bounty lands or pensions for military and naval services rendered the United States at various times. The rebellion greatly increased the pension list.

The *Commissioner of Indian Affairs* has charge of all the matters relating to the Indian tribes on the frontier. The Government has at sundry times purchased the lands of various tribes residing east of the Mississippi River, and has settled the Indians upon reservations in the extreme West. For some of these lands a perpetual annuity was guaranteed the tribes, for others an annuity for a certain specified time, and for others still a temporary annuity, payable during the pleasure of the President or Congress. The total sum thus pledged these tribes, amounts to nearly twenty-one and a half millions. It is funded at five per cent., the interest alone being paid to the tribes. This interest amounts to over two hundred thousand dollars. It is paid in various ways—in money, in provisions, and in clothing. The Commissioner has charge of all these dealings with the savages.

The *Census Bureau* is now a permanent branch of the Department of the Interior. It is in charge of a

Superintendent, and is assigned the duty of compiling the statistics which constitute the Census of the Republic. This enumeration is made every ten years. Some idea of the magnitude of the task may be gained from the fact that the tabulation and publication of the Census of 1870 were not completed in January, 1873.

The *Bureau of Patents* is a part of the Department of the Interior; but is, in all its proportions and features, so vast and imposing that it is almost a separate Department, as, indeed, it will doubtless become ere long. It is in charge of a Commissioner of Patents, who is appointed by the President of the United States, by and with the advice and consent of the Senate. It is entrusted with the duty of granting letters patent, securing to the inventor the control of and the reward from articles beneficial to civilization. It was formerly a part of the Treasury Department, and is one of the best known branches of the Government. Patents are not, as some persons suppose, monopolies, but are protections granted to individuals as rewards for, and incentives to discoveries and inventions of all kinds pertaining to the useful arts. This Bureau is allowed to charge for these letters of protection only the cost of investigating and registering the invention. It is a self-supporting institution, its receipts being largely in excess of its expenditures, so that it is confidently expected that it will be able, before many years have elapsed, to pay for its splendid building entirely out of its own earnings. From July, 1836, to December, 1860, it issued 31,004 patents, a fact which attests its industry, and the fertility of the American inventive genius. During the rebellion many more patents were issued, so that the whole number cannot now be much less than forty thousand.

A large library of great value is attached to the Patent-office, containing many "volumes of the highest scientific value; under judicious arrangement, a collection already rich and ample is forming, of every work of interest to the inventors, and that new, increasing, important class of professional men—the attorneys in patent cases. Upon its shelves may be found a complete set of the reports of the British Patent Commissioners, of which there are only six copies in the United States. The reports of French patents are also complete, and those of various other countries are being obtained as rapidly as possible. A system of exchanges has been established, which employs three agents abroad; and, in addition to various and arduous duties, the librarian annually despatches several hundred copies of the reports."

Persons having business with the bureau will always do well to avail themselves of the services of some experienced and responsible attorney, of whom there are many in Washington and elsewhere. This will save endless trouble and annoyance, and much expense, for with all its excellences, the Patent-office is thoroughly under the dominion of red tape.

The building in which this Bureau and the Depart- of the Interior are located, is commonly known as *The Patent-office*. It occupies two whole squares or blocks of the city, and fronts south on F Street, north on G.

Street, east on 7th Street West, and west on 9th Street West. The length of the building, from Seventh to Ninth Streets, is 410 feet, and the width, from F Street to G Street, is 275 feet. It is built up along the four sides, with a large interior quadrangle about 265 by 135 feet in size. It is constructed in the plainest Doric style, of massive crystallized marble, and though devoid of exterior ornament is one of the most magnificent buildings in the city. It is grand in its simplicity, and its architectural details are pure and tasteful. It is ornamented with massive porticoes, one on each front, which add much to its appearance. The eastern portico is much admired. That on the south front is an exact copy of the portico of the Pantheon at Rome.

The interior is divided into three stories. The ground and second floors are arranged in offices for the accommodation of the business of the Interior Department, but the third floor is occupied by an immense saloon extending entirely around the quadrangle. This is used as the Model Room, but partakes, as far as the south hall is concerned, of the character of a museum. The models and other articles are arranged in glass cases on each side of the room, ample space being left in the centre for promenading. There are two rows of cases, one above the other—the upper row being placed in a handsome light gallery of iron, reached by tasteful iron stairways, and extending entirely around the east, north, and west halls. The halls themselves are paved with handsome tiles. The ceiling is supported by a double row of imposing pillars, which also act as supports to the galleries, and both the walls and ceiling are finished in marble panels and frescoes. A more beautiful saloon is not to be found in America.

You enter from the beautiful south portico, pass through the marble hall, and up the broad stairs to the door of the south hall. Entering it, you find a large register, with pens and ink, at the right of the door, in which you are expected to record your name and the date of your visit.

The first case on the right of the entrance contains Benjamin Franklin's press, at which he worked when a journeyman printer in London. It is old and worm-eaten, and is only held together by means of bolts and iron plates, and bears but little resemblance to the mighty machines by which the printing of to-day is done. But a greater mind than that which invented the steam-press, toiled at this clumsy old frame. It calls up the whole history of the philosopher, and quietly teaches a powerful and wise lesson, as it stands there in its glass case, safe from the defiling hands of relic-hunters.

The next case is devoted to models of water-closets, which though useful and instructive, are not calculated to deepen the patriotic impressions aroused by Franklin's press. Then come models of "fire-escapes," some of which are curiosities in their way, and well worth studying. The impression left by the majority, however, is that if they constitute one's only hope of escape in case of fire, an old-fashioned headlong leap from a window may just as well be attempted at once.

Near by are the models of those inventive geniuses

who have attempted to extinguish conflagrations by discharging a patent cartridge into the burning mass. The guns from which these cartridges are thrown are most remarkable in design.

Then follow tobacco-cutting machines of various kinds, all sorts of skates, billiard-table models, ice-cutters, billiard registers, improved fire-arms, and toys of different designs, among which is a most ingenious model of a walking horse.

Having reached the end of this row of cases, we cross over to the south side of the hall. The first cases contain models of cattle and sheep stalls, vermin and rat traps, and are followed by a handsome display of articles in gutta percha, manufactured by the Goodyear Company. They are well worth examining carefully.

In the bottom of one of these cases is an old mariner's compass of the year 1604, presented by Ex-Governor Wise, of Virginia, then U. S. Minister to Brazil, in the name of Lieutenant Sheppard, U. S. N. The ticket attached to the compass is written in the bold, running hand of the famous ex-rebel statesman. Near by is a razor which belonged to the celebrated navigator, Captain Cook. It was recovered from the natives of the island upon which he was murdered, and is hardly such an instrument as any of those who behold it would care to use. A piece of the first Atlantic cable lies just below it.

Several of the cases following contain the original treaties of the United States with Foreign Powers. They are written upon heavy sheets of vellum, in wretchedly bad hands, and have a worn and faded appearance. All, save the treaties with England and the Eastern nations, are written in French, and are all furnished with a multiplicity of red and green seals. The first is the treaty with Austria, and bears the weak, hesitating signature of Francis I. The signature of Alexander I., attached to the first Russian treaty, has more character in it. The treaty of peace with England in 1814, which ended our second war with that Power, bears the signature of George IV., which is so characteristic of the individual, that one almost seems to see the contemptible monarch's face on the parchment. The treaty of 1803, with the Republic of France, is signed "*Bonaparte*," in a nervous, hasty hand. There is no hesitation about the signature; it is not a clerkly hand, but it is vigorous and decisive. Bernadotte's smooth and flowing hand, treacherous and plausible in appearance, and a true index of his character, adorns the first treaty with Sweden. The original treaty with Turkey is a most curious document. It consists of a number of long slips of parchment, covered with columns of Turkish characters. Near by it hangs a bag, in which it was conveyed to this country. The bag is its legal covering or case, and is provided with a huge ball of red wax by way of a seal. Next to it is the first treaty of alliance with France—the famous treaty of 1778—which gave the aid of the French king to the cause of the suffering and struggling States of the New Republic. It is signed by the illfated Louis XVI. The "Louis" is written in a round, scholarly hand, but the lines are delicate, as if the pen did not press the paper with the firmness of a true king. The French treaty of 1822 bears the autograph of Louis XVIII., and that of 1831, the signature of Louis Philippe. Don Pedro I., Emperor of Brazil, has affixed his hand to the Brazilian treaty, and the name of Ferdinand (the last, and least) graces that with Spain. These old parchments are very interesting, and one may well spend an hour or two in examining them.

In the glass cases with the treaties are several handsome Oriental articles—a Persian carpet, and horse-cover, presented to President Van Buren by the Imam of Muscat, and two magnificent rifles, presented to President Jefferson by the Emperor of Morocco. These rifles are finished in the highest style of Eastern art, and are really very beautiful. In the same cases are collections of medals, some of European sovereigns, and others of American celebrities. Among them is a copy of the medal awarded by Congress to the captors of Major Andre. Near these are several splendid Eastern sabres, presented by the great Ali Pacha, the Bey of Egypt, to Captain Perry and the officers of the U. S. Ship of War Concord, at Alexandria (Egypt) in 1832.

The next cases at once absorb our attention, for they contain the Washington relics, which are amongst the greatest treasures of the nation. They consist of the camp-equipage, and other articles used by General Washington during the Revolution. They are just as he left them at the close of the war, and were given to the Government for safe keeping after his death. Here are the tents which constituted the headquarters in the field of the great soldier. They are wrapped tightly around the poles, just as they were tied when they were struck for the last time, when victory had crowned his country's arms, and the long war was over. Every cord, every button and tent-pin is in its place, for he was careful of little things. His blankets, and the bed-curtain worked for him by his wife, and his window-curtains, are all in an excellent state of preservation. His chairs are in perfect order, not a round being broken; and the little square mirror in his dressing-case is not even cracked. The washstand and table are also well kept. His knife-case is filled with plain horn-handle knives and forks, which were deemed "good enough for him;" and his mess-chest is a curiosity. It is a plain wooden trunk, covered with leather, with a common lock, the hasp of which is broken. It is divided by small partitions of thin wood, and the compartments are provided with bottles, still stained with the liquids they once held, tin plates, common knives and forks, and other articles pertaining to such an establishment. In these days of luxury, an ordinary sergeant would not be satisfied with so simple and plain an establishment; but our forefathers doubtless considered it well suited to their great commander. His cooking utensils, bellows, andirons, and iron money-chest, all of which went with him from Boston to Yorktown, are in the same case, from the top of which hangs the suit of clothes worn by him upon the occasion of the resignation of his commission as Commander-in-Chief at Annapolis, in 1783. A hall-lantern, and several articles from Mount Vernon, a "travelling secretary," Washington's sword and cane, and a surveyor's compass, presented by him to Captain Samuel Duvall, the surveyor of Frederick County, Maryland, are in the same case, as are also a number of articles taken from Arlington House, and belonging formerly to the Washington family.

A coat worn by Andrew Jackson at the battle of New Orleans, and the war-saddle of the Baron De Kalb, a bayonet used by one of Braddock's soldiers, and found on the fatal field upon which that commander met his death-wound, together with the panels from the State-coach of President Washington, complete the collection.

The original draft of *The Declaration of Independence*, with the signatures of the Continental Congress attached, is framed and placed near the Washington case. It is old and yellow, and the ink is fading from the paper. Looking at it, you can hardly realize that this was indeed the first bold proclamation of those great principles which changed the destiny of the world. Near it hangs Washington's Commission as Commander-in-Chief of the American Army, bearing the bold, massive signature of John Hancock, President of the Continental Congress.

In the same case is a plain model, roughly executed, representing the framework of the hull of a Western steamboat. Beneath the keel is a false bottom, provided with bellows and air-bags. The ticket upon it bears this memorandum: "*Model for Sinking and Raising boats by bellows below.* A. LINCOLN. *May* 30, 1849."

By means of this arrangement, Mr. Lincoln hoped to solve the difficulty of passing boats over sand-bars in the Western rivers. The success of his scheme would have made him independently wealthy; but it failed, and, twelve years later, he became President of the United States. During the interval, however, the model lay forgotten in the Patent-office; but, after his inauguration, Mr. Lincoln got one of the employés to find it for him. After his death, it was placed in the Washington case.

The opposite case contains another memento of him—the hat worn by him on the night of his assassination.

Passing by a couple of cases filled with machinery for making shoes, we see a number of handsome silk robes, and Japanese articles of various kinds, presented to Presidents Buchanan and Lincoln by the Tycoon of Japan.

The remainder of the hall is devoted to models of machines for making leather harness and trunks, models of gas and kerosene oil apparatuses, liquor distilleries, machines for making confectionery, and for trying out lard and fat. Also methods of curing fish and meat, and embalming the dead. A great medley. A splendid model of a steel revolving tower, for harbor defence, stands near the door, and is one of the most conspicuous ornaments of the room.

The other halls are devoted exclusively to models of patented machinery, and other inventions. The cases above and below are well filled; models of bridges span the spaces between the upper cases, and those of the larger machines are laid on the floor of the hall. Here is every thing the mind can think of. Models of improved arms, clocks, telegraphs, burglar and fire alarms, musical instruments, light-houses, street cars, lamps, stoves, ranges, furnaces, peat and fuel machines, brick and tile machines, sewing machines, power looms, paper-making machinery, knitting machines, machines for making cloth, hats, spool-cotton, for working up hemp, harbor cleaners, patent hooks and eyes, buttons, umbrella and cane handles, fluting machines, trusses, medical instruments of gutta percha, corsets, ambulances and other military establishments; arrangements for excluding the dust and smoke from railroad cars, railroad and steamboat machinery, agricultural and domestic machinery of all kinds, and hundreds of other inventions, line both sides of the three immense halls. One might spend a year in examining them, and learn something new every day. For every article one can think of, there are at least half a dozen models, and there are many inventions to be seen of which nine people out of ten have never dreamed before. The number increases every year. As the country grows greater, new wants are felt. They are sure to be supplied, and the model-room of the Patent-office keeps a faithful record of the history of our civilization.

The Post-office Department.

The building known as the General Post-office covers almost an entire block, and is located nearly opposite the Patent-office. It is bounded by E and F Streets north, and Seventh and Eighth Streets west. It is 300 feet long, from north to south, and 204 feet wide, from east to west. It is built of white marble, in the Corinthian style of architecture, and is the best specimen of the Italian palatial ever erected upon this continent. It is rectangular in form, with a spacious interior courtyard, 95 by 194 feet in size. On the Seventh Street side there is a vestibule, which constitutes the grand entrance to the building. The ceiling is composed of exquisitely ornamented marble panels, supported by four marble columns; and the walls, niches, and floor are of marble, the floor being richly tesselated. On Eighth Street there is an entrance for mail wagons, handsomely ornamented. The city Post-office is in the F Street side of the building, and is tastefully arranged.

The Postal service of the country is the oldest branch of the Government. As early as the year 1792, a proposition was introduced into the General Assembly of Virginia, to establish the office of "Post-Master-General of Virginia and other parts of America." The proposition became a law, but was never carried into effect. In 1710, during the reign of Queen Anne, the British Parliament established a General Post-office for all Her Majesty's dominions. By this act, the Post-Master-General was permitted to have "one chief letter office in New York, and other chief letter offices at some convenient place or places in each of Her Majesty's provinces or colonies in America." When the Colonies threw off their allegiance to the Crown, especial care was given to preserving as far as possible, the postal facilities of the country. When the Federal Constitution was adopted, the right was secured to Congress "to establish Post-offices and Post-roads." In 1789 Congress created the office of Post-Master-General, and defined his duties. Other laws have since been passed, regulating the increased powers and duties of the Department, which is now, next to the Treasury, the most extensive in the country.

The Post-Master-General, the head of the Department, is a member of the President's Cabinet, and is in charge of all the postal affairs of the United States. The business of the various branches of the Department is conducted in his name and by his authority. He has a general supervision of the whole Department, and issues all orders concerning the service rendered the Government through his subordinates.

During the first administrations of the Government, the Post-Master-General was not regarded as a Cabinet Minister, but simply as the head of a Bureau. In 1829, General Jackson invited Mr. Barry, the gentleman appointed by him to that office, to a seat in his Cabinet. Since that time the Post-Master-General has been recognized as *ex officio* a Cabinet Minister.

The first Postmaster-General was Samuel Osgood, of Massachusetts. His successors have been Timothy Pickering, of Massachusetts; Joseph Habershaw, of Georgia; Gideon Granger, of Connecticut; Return J. Meigs, of Ohio; John McLean, of Ohio; William T. Barry, of Kentucky; Amos Kendall, of Kentucky; John M. Niles, of Connecticut; Francis Granger, of New York; Charles A. Wickliffe, of Kentucky; Cave Johnson, of Tennessee; Jacob Collamer, of Vermont; Nathan K. Hall, of New York; Samuel D. Hubbard, of Connecticut; James Campbell, of Pennsylvania Aaron V. Brown, of Tennessee; Joseph Holt, of Kentucky; Montgomery Blair, of Maryland; William Dennison, of Ohio; Alexander W. Randall, of Wisconsin; and John A. J. Cresswell, of Maryland.

The subordinate officers of the Department are three Assistant Post-Master-Generals, and the Chief of the Inspection office.

The *Appointment Office* is in charge of the First Assistant Post-Master-General. " To this office are assigned all questions which relate to the establishment and discontinuance of post-offices, changes of sites and names, appointment and removal of post-masters and route and local agents, as, also, the giving of instructions to post-masters. Post-masters are furnished with marking and rating stamps and letter balances by this bureau, which is charged also with providing blanks and stationery for the use of the Department, and with the superintendence of the several agencies established for supplying post-masters with blanks. To this bureau is likewise assigned the supervision of the ocean mail steamship lines, and of the foreign and international postal arrangements."

The *Contract Office* is in charge of the Second Assistant Post-Master-General. " To this office is assigned the business of arranging the mail service of the United States, and placing the same under contract, embracing all correspondence and proceedings affecting the frequency of trips, mode of conveyance, and times of departures and arrivals on all the routes; the course of the mail between the different sections of the country, the points of mail distribution, and the regulations for the government of the domestic mail service of the United States. It prepares the advertisements for mail proposals, receives the bids, and takes charge of the annual and occasional mail lettings, and the adjustment and execution of the contracts. All applications for the establishment or alteration of mail arrangements, and the appointment of mail messengers, should be sent to this office. All claims should be submitted to it for transportation service not under contract, as the recognition of said service is first to be obtained through the Contract Office as a necessary authority for the proper credits at the Auditor's office. From this office all postmasters at the ends of routes receive the statement of mail arrangements prescribed for the respective routes. It reports weekly to the Auditor all contracts executed, and all orders affecting accounts for mail transportation; prepares the statistical exhibits of the mail service, and the reports of the mail lettings, giving a statement of each bid; also, of the contracts made, the new service originated, the curtailments ordered, and the additional allowances granted within the year."

The *Finance Office* is in charge of the Third Assistant Post-Master-General. " To this office is assigned the supervision and management of the financial business of the Department, not devolved by law upon the Auditor, embracing accounts with the draft offices and other depositories of the Department, the issuing of warrants and drafts in payment of balances, reported by the Auditor to be due to mail contractors and other persons, the supervision of the accounts of offices under orders to deposit their quarterly balances at designated points, and the superintendence of the rendition by postmasters of their quarterly returns of postages. It has charge of the dead-letter office, of the issuing of postage stamps and stamped envelopes for the prepayment of postage, and of the accounts connected therewith.

" To the Third Assistant Post-Master-General all postmasters should direct their quarterly returns of postage; those at draft offices their letters reporting quarterly the net proceeds of their offices; and those at depositing offices their certificates of deposit; to him should also be directed the weekly and monthly returns of the depositories of the Department, as well as applications and receipts for postage stamps and stamped envelopes, and for dead letters."

The *Inspection Office* is in charge of a Chief Clerk. " To this office is assigned the duty of receiving and examining the registers of the arrival and departures of the mails, certificates of the service of route agents, and reports of mail failures; noting the delinquencies of contractors, and preparing cases thereon for the action of the Post-Master-General; furnishing blanks for mail registers and reports of mail failures; providing and sending out mail bags and mail locks and keys, and doing all other things which may be necessary to secure a faithful and exact performance of all mail contracts.

" All cases of mail depredation, of violations of law by private expresses, or by the forging and illegal use of postage stamps, are under the supervision of this office, and should be reported to it.

" All communications respecting lost money letters,

mail depredations, or other violations of law, or mail locks and keys, should be directed to 'Chief Clerk, Post-office Department.'

"All registers of the arrivals and departures of the mails, certificates of the service of route agents, reports of mail failures, applications for blank registers, and all complaints against contractors for irregular or imperfect service, should be directed 'Inspection Office, Post-office Department.'"

The *Dead Letter Office* forms an important portion of the Department. To this office are sent all letters held for postage, or unclaimed by the parties to whom they are addressed. Letters sent to this office are carefully examined, and if they are of value to the writer, are returned to him. Letters with a request printed or written on the envelope, to return to the writer in a given number of days if not called for, are not advertised, but are sent to the Dead Letter Office, and immediately returned to the writer.

The business of the Dead Letter Office is very extensive. As many as from four to five millions of letters are sent to it in some of its busiest years. These are of all kinds, and from as many different sorts of people. They are carefully examined, and if they contain money, checks, or valuables, or information of value to the person addressed, a register is kept of them and their contents. Those which are worthless are destroyed, but valuable letters are returned to their writers, if practicable. Foreign letters are returned unopened to the countries whence they were sent. Some idea of the usefulness of the office may be formed from a perusal of the following statement of the Post-Master-General concerning its operations for a recent year:

"In the examination of domestic dead letters, for disposition, 1,736,867 were found to be either not susceptible of being returned or of no importance, circulars, etc., and were destroyed; about 333,000 more were destroyed after an effort to return them—making about 51 per cent. destroyed. The remainder were classified and returned to the owners as far as practicable. The whole number sent from the office was 2,258,199, of which about 84 per cent. were delivered to owners, and 16 per cent. were returned to the Department; 18,340 letters contained $95,169 52, in sums of $1 and upward, of which 16,061 letters, containing $86,638 66, were delivered to owners, and 2,124, containing $7,862 36, were filed or held for disposition; 14,082 contained $3,436 68 in sums of less than $1, of which 12,513, containing $3,120 70, were delivered to owners; 17,750 contained drafts, deeds, and other papers of value representing the value of $3,609,271 80, of these 16,809 were restored to the owners, and 821 were returned and filed; 13,964 contained books, jewelry, and other articles of property, of the estimated value of $8,500; of these 11,489 were forwarded for delivery and 9,911 were delivered to their owners; 125,221 contained photographs, postage stamps, and articles of small value, of which 114,666 were delivered to owners; 2,068,842 without inclosures. Thus, of the ordinary dead letters forwarded from this office, about 84 per cent. were delivered, and of the valuable dead letters (classed as money and minor) about 89 per cent. were delivered. The decrease of money letters received (about 3000) is probably owing to the growing use of money orders for the transmission of small sums."

The Bureau of Agriculture.

The Bureau of Agriculture was formerly a part of the Patent Office, but is now possessed of a separate and distinct existence. It forms a part of the Department of the Interior, but is in many respects a distinct department. It is in charge of the Commissioner of Agriculture, who already aspires to the dignity of a Secretaryship, and a seat in the Cabinet. Its quarters are among the handsomest and most enviable in Washington. It is located in an elegant building, erected within the grounds of the Smithsonian Institution. About twenty acres of this tract have been devoted to the uses of the bureau, and have been laid off with much taste, and at a considerable expense. The building is constructed of pressed brick, and has a pretty Mansard roof. It is one hundred and sixty-six feet, by sixty. The basement is well lighted, and contains, besides furnace and stove rooms, a laboratory and folding rooms. Upon the first floors are the offices, the library, and a second laboratory for the lighter work. The rooms of the Commissioner, three in number, are finished with the patent wood-paper, lately coming into use. The paper was cut for the purpose from the most beautiful woods the country affords, and the panels inlaid with rare varieties, are by far the richest, and more beautiful than any panel-work in the Capitol.

"The halls are laid with imported tiles, and the wall

and ceilings are tastefully preserved. Upon the second floor is the main hall, fitted up with massive walnut cases, made air tight, for the specimens which compose the museum. This will soon be the most complete, interesting, and valuable collection pertaining to agriculture to be found anywhere. Visitors will remember the great California plank, which stood in one of the underground halls of the Patent Office, and was partially discernible on a bright day. It has been manufactured into a large and elegant table, and stands in the museum. It is seven feet by twelve, and looks like a billiard table with the cloth and outer guard removed, and then highly polished. The legs and frame are made of a fine species of cedar, found in Florida. The top of the table, composed of this single plank, is without a knot or seam, and looks as rich as mahogany. Through communications with our consuls in all parts of the world, official arrangements have been entered into, to send appropriate specimens to this museum.

"On this same floor are rooms in which work connected with preparing specimens is done, and also the statistical Bureau of the Department. This bureau has regular correspondents in every school district of the country, and the whole subject of receiving and recording the conditions of the various crops is now so perfect that the monthly reports are in great demand in commercial circles, as affording the best attainable data from which to prejudge the character of our harvests. The seed rooms are fitted up in the most convenient manner for sorting, packing, and mailing the various kinds. The varieties used are selected with care from the catalogues of the best foreign and domestic dealers.

"The fourth floor, which is immediately under the roof, extends over the whole building, and resembles in all respects a great grain warehouse. An elevating platform connects it with the basement, and gives an easy method of raising the supplies of seed-grain, which are kept in this thoroughly dry and well ventilated space.

"A very large variety of flower seeds, seeds of shrubs and shade-trees, and such varieties of foreign fruits and vegetables as it is thought may be raised in some portions of the Union, will be kept on hand. The communications through the State Department with all our consuls, have, in most cases been answered, and active measures have been taken by most to contribute to the supplies named. A system of international exchanges has also been introduced, which promises most valuable returns. Through the Smithsonian Institute, the department has been put in communication with the leading foreign societies interested in agriculture, and many of them are now exchanging both reports and specimens with us. In many cases, the consuls of foreign nations are coöperating with our own.

"Particular attention is being given to the fibrous grasses which are widely used in the manufacture of lasting and beautiful cloths in China and some other sections. Specimens of such grass, and portions of the material made, in all stages of manufacture, are now on exhibition in the museum. A tract of several acres has been set apart, near the building, which is to be covered with such useful varieties of these fibrous grasses as can be obtained.

"The shade-trees of the whole country will be represented in these grounds, so far as it is possible to make them grow. There are one thousand four hundred native varieties already planted, and it is expected that nearly as many more will be added, besides a large number of foreign trees.

"The display of flowers in these grounds will soon exceed anything to be found in the country. They are massed together in sections according to the season in which they are most brilliant, either in leaves or flowers."

CHAPTER X.

THE PRESIDENT OF THE UNITED STATES.

Statement of the Duties and Privileges of the President—How he is chosen—The Inauguration—Reminiscences of the Inaugurations in Washington—An interregnum in the Government—Inauguration of Abraham Lincoln—What it costs the President to live—Economy in the White House—A poorly-paid Official—The President's Title—His Visitors—His Enemies—Difficulties of his Position—The Cabinet—The White House—Description of it—Internal Arrangements—The East Room—The State Apartments—The Private Apartments—The Etiquette of the White House—"Who's who" in Washington—Rules for social Intercourse among Officials—The President's Levees—The Scene in the East Room—The Comicalities of a Levee—The New Year Receptions—A brilliant Scene—The State Dinners—How they are conducted and what they cost—That "wonderful Steward"—Description of a State Dinner—The Sorrows of the White House—Who have died there —The daily Life of the President—How President Grant fills up the twenty-four Hours—A busy Life—General Grant at Home with his Family—Social Evenings at the White House—An independent President.

THE second coördinate branch of the General-Government is the Executive, the branch charged with the execution of the laws passed by the Legislative branch. The Constitution of the United States defines with great minuteness the rights and privileges of the Executive, and provides that "the Executive power shall be vested in a President of the United States of America. He shall hold his office during the term of four years, and, together with the Vice-President, chosen for the same term, be elected as follows:

"Each State shall appoint, in such manner as the Legislature thereof may direct, a number of electors, equal to the whole number of Senators and Representatives to which the State may be entitled in Congress; but no Senator, or Representative, or person holding an office of trust or profit under the United States, shall be appointed an elector. The electors shall meet in their respective States, and vote by ballot for President and Vice-President, one of whom, at least shall not be an inhabitant of the same State with themselves; they shall name in their ballots the person voted for as President, and in distinct ballots the person voted for as Vice-President; and they shall make distinct lists of all persons voted for as President, and all persons voted for as Vice-President, and of the number of votes for each, which lists they shall sign and certify, and transmit, sealed, to the seat of the Government of the United States, directed to the President of the Senate. The President of the Senate shall, in the presence of the Senate and House of Representatives, open all the certificates, and the votes shall then be counted; the person having the greatest number of votes for President shall be the President, if such number be a majority of the whole number of electors appointed; and if no person have such majority, then, from the persons having the highest numbers, not exceeding three, on the list of those voted for as President, the House of Representatives shall choose immediately, by ballot, the President. But in choosing the President, the votes shall be taken by States, the representation from each State having one vote; a quorum for this purpose, to consist of a member or members from two-thirds of the States, and a majority of all the States shall be necessary to a choice; and if the House of Representatives shall not choose a President, whenever the right of choice shall devolve upon them, before the fourth day of March next following, then the Vice-President, elected by the Senate shall act as President, as in the case of the death or other constitutional disability of the President. The person having the greatest number of votes as Vice-President shall be the Vice-President, if such number be a majority of the whole number of electors appointed; and if no person have a majority, then, from the two highest numbers on the list, the Senate shall choose the Vice-President; a quorum for the purpose shall consist of two-thirds of the whole number of Senators, and a majority of the whole number shall be necessary to a choice. But no person constitutionally ineligible to the office of President shall be eligible to that of Vice-President of the United States.

" The Congress may determine the time of choosing the electors, and the day on which they shall give their votes, which day shall be the same throughout the United States.

" No person except a natural-born citizen, or a citizen of the United States at the time of the adoption of this Constitution, shall be eligible to the office of President; neither shall any person be eligible to that office who shall not have attained to the age of thirty-five years, and been fourteen years a resident within the United States.

" In case of the removal of the President from office, or of his death, resignation, or inability to discharge the powers and duties of the said office, the same shall devolve on the Vice-President, and the Congress may by law provide for the case of removal, death, resignation, or inability, both of the President and Vice-President, declaring what officer shall then act as President, and such officer shall act accordingly, until the disability be removed, or a President shall be elected.

" The President shall at stated times receive for his services a compensation, which shall neither be increased nor diminished during the period for which he shall have been elected, and he shall not receive, within that period, any other emolument from the United States, or any of them.

" Before he enter on the execution of his office, he shall take the following Oath or Affirmation.

" 'I do solemnly swear (or affirm), that I will faithfully execute the office of President of the United States, and will, to the best of my ability, preserve, protect, and defend the Constitution of the United States.' "

The President is the Chief Magistrate of the Republic. He is also, by virtue of his office, the Commander-in-Chief of the Army and Navy of the United States, and of the Militia of the several States when in the actual service of the United States. He has the power to pardon and grant reprieves, except in cases of impeachment. He appoints all officials of the Government, and, constitutionally, has the power to remove them when he deems it his duty to do so. He negotiates treaties with foreign Powers, and conducts the official intercourse of this Government with them. He executes, or causes to be executed, the laws of Congress, and from time to time lays before that body such information as he deems proper, respecting the state of the country, and recommends such measures as he judges necessary and expedient.

The President is elected, as has been stated, in November, and enters upon the duties of his office on the 4th of March next following his election. The Constitution does not prescribe any ceremony for the inauguration of the President, neither does it oblige him to engage in any public ceremony upon that occasion. It simply requires him to take the oath of office, and this oath may, with perfect propriety, be administered at any place in the Union by any magistrate properly qualified to administer oaths. It is the custom, however, to make the inauguration an occasion of great public display and rejoicing. For days before the Fourth of March, crowds of strangers, military organizations and civic societies pour into the city, and on the appointed day, shortly before the hour of noon, a grand procession is formed, which, proceeding to the lodgings of the President-elect, escorts him down Pennsylvania Avenue to the Capitol, accompanied by the retiring President. These two upon reaching the Capitol, repair to the Senate Chamber, where the two Houses of Congress and the high officers of the Government await them. From the Senate Chamber, the assembled company proceed to the eastern portico of the Capitol, which is prepared for the occasion, and here, in the presence of the immense throng assembled in the grounds below, and the officials of the Government clustered about him, the new President takes the oath of office at the hands of the Chief Justice of the United States, and delivers an address in which he enunciates the leading principles by which he expects to be guided during his administration. The day is a holiday at the Capital, and the festivities end with a grand ball at night, given in honor of the new President.

Thomas Jefferson was the first President inaugurated in the City of Washington. This was on the 4th of March, 1801. Since then the city has witnessed seventeen inaugural ceremonies, no two of which were precisely alike. It has happened that the 4th of March has upon two occasions fallen on a Sunday, namely, in 1821, after the second election of Mr. Monroe, and in 1848, after the election of General Taylor. As no legal oath can be administered on Sunday, which, in the eyes of the law is "a dead day," the inauguration was in each case postponed until the 5th, and thus the Republic has been for two days without a President.

Perhaps the most remarkable inaugural ceremony ever witnessed in Washington, was that of Abraham Lincoln, on the 4th of March, 1861. Rumors of plots to assassinate him were so plentiful that it became advisable for him to pass through the State of Maryland with the utmost secresy. He was in Washington before any one but his most trusted friends was aware of his movements. Threats against his life were openly made after his arrival, and it seemed proper to the General Government to take the utmost precautions to protect him and to secure his peaceful inauguration. A force of regulars, under the personal command of General Scott, was stationed throughout the city, commanding the route of the procession, and every precaution was taken to make sure of a peaceful inauguration. Beyond a doubt, the threats that had been uttered were made by idle, irresponsible bullies who never meant to put them into execution, but they had the effect of causing the gravest apprehension on the part of the authorities. Mr. Lincoln was conducted to the Capitol with great display. He was received by the Senate, and escorted to the east portico, where he delivered his address, and took the oath before Chief Justice Taney. His second inauguration, March 4, 1865, was accompanied with one of the finest displays ever witnessed in Washington. The ceremonies took place in the east portico of the Capitol. The morning was dark and lowering, but as the President placed himself in front of the venerable Chief Justice to pronounce the solemn vow, the sun burst from behind the heavy clouds, and shone down upon him with all its brilliancy.

The President receives a salary of $25,000 per annum. At the commencement of each term the Executive Mansion is furnished anew by the General Government, the cost being defrayed by a Congressional appropriation, so that in addition to his salary, the President receives a furnished house. The kitchen and pantry are supplied to a considerable extent by the same body. Congress pays all the employés about the house, from the private secretary to the humblest bootblack; it provides fuel and lights; keeps up the stables; and furnishes a corps of gardeners and a garden to supply the Presidential board with fruits, flowers, and vegetables. Besides this, the President receives many presents from private parties.

It is proposed to increase the salary of the President to $50,000 per annum, and the proposition has caused considerable discussion throughout the country. Many arguments have been advanced for and against the proposed increase, and the matter has become almost a party question. The simple truth is that the present salary of the Executive is not sufficient to enable him to live in a style consistent with the dignity of his office. It was fixed by law at a time when the purchasing power of money was double what it is now. No private gentleman of means, with a large family, would consider this sum sufficient for his wants, and it is certainly a shame to expect the Chief Magistrate of the Republic to live on a sum which requires him to exercise a pinching economy which must of necessity verge upon niggardliness. The President of the United States is required by public opinion to maintain a style and mode of life consistent with the reputation of the great and powerful nation over which he presides, and with the dignity of his high position. This imposes upon him many expenses which as a private citizen he could avoid. The people do not like to see him trying to save expense, and they were quick enough to resent the economical efforts of Mr. Lincoln, or rather of Mrs. Lincoln. The President is constantly appealed to in behalf of charitable and benevolent enterprises, and he is expected to assist them. His gifts cannot be modest like those of a private individual. His donation must be munificent and worthy of a President. He is expected to entertain the various officers of the Government, the Members of Congress, the Foreign Ministers, and illustrious strangers visiting the Capital. All this requires a heavy outlay, and any one who has had the experience of trying to live up to the requirements of society can understand how great the outlay is. $25,000 are not enough to enable him to do this, and the consequence is that nearly all of the Presidents have had to support the dignity of the nation at their own private cost, and have left the White House very much poorer than when they entered it. $50,000 per annum would be barely enough to enable the President to meet the demands upon him, and $100,000 would not be too much. It is a shame that the Chief Magistrate of this enormously wealthy country should have to practise economy in anything. It is all very well to talk about "Republican simplicity," and "Spartan manners." This is neither a simple nor a Spartan age. The country is very rich, the wealthy and cultivated classes live in a style which requires a large outlay, and it is a shame for the First Citizen of the Republic to be obliged to be thrown in constant contact with these, and yet to be compelled to put up with an income which any of them would consider inadequate to the necessities of their social position.

The official title of the Chief Magistrate is "Mr. President." By courtesy he is also called "Your Excellency." The only Executive officer in the Union who has any legal claim to the title, of "Your Excellency" and "His Excellency," is the Governor of Massachusetts.

Access to the President is easy to those having business with him, or any legitimate excuse for calling upon him. The President's time is valuable, the labors of his office are not light, and he is not fond of receiving strangers who call merely to pay their respects to him. In order to gain admittance to the President strangers must make application to the Aide-de-Camp on duty, who has charge of the ante-room.

All sorts of people come to see the President, on all sorts of business. His immense patronage makes him the object of the efforts of many unprincipled men. His integrity is subjected to the severest trials, and if he come out of office poor, as happily all of our Presidents have done, he must indeed be an honest man. His position is not a bed of roses, for he cannot hope to please all parties. His friends exaggerate his good qualities, and often make him appear ridiculous, while his enemies magnify his faults and errors, and slander and persecute him in every imaginable way. Pitfalls are set for him along every step of his path, and he must be wary indeed, if he would not fall into them The late President Buchanan once said that there were at least two persons in the world who could not echo the wish experienced by each American mother, that her son might one day be President, and that they were the retiring and the incoming Presidents, the first of whom was worn and weary with the burden he was laying down, and the other for the first time fully alive to the magnitude of the task he had undertaken.

The Constitution provides the President with a Council of advisers. These are the Secretaries in charge of the various Executive Departments. They constitute the Cabinet of the President. They meet at regular times, at the summons of the Executive, in a chamber in the White House set apart for the purpose. This is located on the second floor of the mansion, and is plainly but comfortably furnished. The President is not obliged to be governed by the advice of his Cabinet, but he naturally gives great weight to the opinions of his advisers, and usually adopts their view, and suggestions as far as they concern their own Departments.

Visitors having business with the President, are admitted at any hour, if he be unengaged. It is his desire that all such calls be made in the morning.

The official residence of the President is the Executive Mansion, or, as it is more commonly known, the "White House." It is situated on Pennsylvania Avenue, near the western end of the city, and adjoining the Treasury, War, and Navy Departments. The grounds in front are handsomely ornamented, and in the rear a fine park stretches away to the river. The location is attractive, and commands a magnificent view of the Potomac, but it is not healthy. Ague and fever prevail in the Spring and Fall, and render it anything but a desirable place of residence. The building is constructed of freestone painted white—hence its most common name, the "White House." It was designed by James Hoban, and was modelled after the palace of the Duke of Leinster. The cornerstone was laid on the 13th of October, 1792, and the house was ready for occupancy in the summer of 1800. It was partially destroyed by the British in 1814. It has a front of 170 feet, and a depth of 86 feet. It contains two lofty stories of rooms, and the roof is surrounded with a handsome balustrade. The exterior walls are ornamented with fine Ionic pilasters. On the north front is a handsome portico, with four Ionic columns in front, and a projecting screen with three columns. The space between these two rows of pillars is a covered carriage way. The main entrance to the house is from this portico, through a massive doorway, which opens into the main hall. The front has a rusticated basement, which gives a third story to the house on this side, and by a semicircular projecting colonnade of six columns, with two flights of steps leading from the ground to the level of the principal story.

The front door opens into a handsome hall, divided midway by a row of imitation marble pillars, and ornamented with portraits of the former Presidents of the Republic. On the right of this hall, is a handsome apartment designed as a grand banqueting hall, which occupies the entire eastern side of the house. It is a beautiful apartment, and is handsomely furnished. It is used during the levees and upon great state occasions. The President sometimes receives here the congratulations of his fellow citizens, and has his hand squeezed to a jelly by his enthusiastic friends. The East Room is eighty-six feet long, forty feet wide, and twenty-eight feet high. Three splendid chandeliers hang from the ceiling, and shed a brilliant light through the apartment at night.

Adjoining the East Room are three others, smaller in size, the whole constituting one of the handsomest *suites* in the country. The first, adjoining the East Room, is the *Green Room*, the next the *Blue Room*, and the third the *Red Room*. Each is handsomely furnished, the prevailing color of the apartment giving the name.

The Red Room is elliptical in form, having a bow in rear, and is one of the handsomest in the house. It is used by the President as a general reception-room. He receives here the official visits of the dignitaries of the Republic, and of foreign ministers. Previous to the completion of the East Room, this apartment was used for all occasions of public ceremony.

The building contains thirty-one rooms of considerable size. West of the Red Room is the large dining-room used upon State occasions, and adjoining that is the small dining-room, ordinarily used by the President and his family. The stairs to the upper story are on the left of the main entrance, and are always in charge of the door-keeper and his assistants, whose business it is to see that no improper characters find access to the private portion of the house.

The north front has six rooms, which are used as chambers by the family of the President, and the south front has seven rooms—the ante-chamber, audience-room cabinet-room, private office of the President, the ladies' parlor, and two others, used for various purposes. The ladies' parlor is immediately over the Red Room, and is of the same size and shape.

There are eleven rooms in the basement, which are used as kitchens, pantries, butler's room, etc. The house is built in the old style, and has an air of elegance and comfort extremely pleasing to the eye. The furniture is, as a general rule, costly, but a little more taste might have been exhibited in its selection and arrangement.

The upper floors of the mansion are occupied with the business and living apartments of the President and his family. "The room which during the administrations of Mr. Lincoln and Mr. Johnson was a public waiting-room, is now the reception room of General Dent, where Robert M. Douglass, President Grant's private secretary, and Mr. Crook also have desks. This is a large, airy apartment, warmly carpeted, with mahogany furniture (which has set there since Martin Van Buren's time), freshly upholstered with green morocco; and with green curtains, twenty-five years old, draping the windows. Next, on the same side of the corridor, is the room formerly used by General Badeau, a very pleasant one. Captain Morrow, one of Mr. Johnson's most accomplished secretaries, worked and slept there. On the opposite side of the corridor from this room is the clerks' room; adjoining that, and opposite General Dent's reception room, is the room occupied by the President's military secretaries, Generals Babcock and Porter. Between the secretaries' room and the library is the Cabinet Room—President Grant's business office and reception room—the same used by Mr. Johnson. It is a large oblong apartment, carpeted with crimson and white. An extensive black-walnut table stands in the centre, sentinelled by chairs. On the east side stands a massive black-walnut desk; on the south side, to the right of the door, opening from the corridor, a lounge or sofa; in the south-west corner, to the left of the door, a stand with a silver ice-pitcher; and at the centre of the west side is the fireplace. On the mantel is a clock, indicating the time of the day and the day of the month, with a thermometer and barometer attached; to the right and left of the clock sit two black metal ornaments. Several heavy chairs, like those near the table, are disposed near the walls, and one or two small desks or tables sustain a weight of orderly books and papers. The walls and high ceiling are frescoed on a yellow ground tint. Tapestry and lace curtains are drawn aside from the windows, whence the view across the lawn below and beyond through the foliage to the river is distant, serene, and beautiful.

"The neighboring library is the stateliest apartment on the upper floor. Much of the furniture, save the mahogany book-cases next the walls, is of solid oak, with maroon-colored upholstery, ornamented with brass-headed nails. Here, as well as in the Cabinet-room, the President receives officially; and here, occasionally in the evenings, both the President and Mrs. Grant entertain somewhat informally their guests.

"The eight remaining rooms of the fourteen on the second floor are devoted to the private use of the President and family. There is first a private parlor, fitted up especially for the use of Mrs. Grant, to which only intimate acquaintances of the family are invited. The furniture is ebony, covered with blue satin; the hangings of blue satin and lace. The pictures and other adornments give this room a sumptuous look. Adjoining it on one side is a spare room, with black-walnut furniture and light-red trimmings. Adjoining it on the other side—at the extremity of the west end of the mansion—with windows looking south and west, is Nellie Grant's room. This is a blue boudoir fit for a princess, with a soft blue carpet strewn with rose-buds, and large clear mirrors reflecting the tints and decorations of the walls. Items: a low mattrass bed, mahogany frame with high head-board, six chairs, a large marble-topped centre-table, a marble wash-stand, a graceful "what-not" in the corner, loaded with knick-knacks; a picture of playing kittens over the mantel, and a coal fire. Directly opposite his sister's room, across the corridor, sleeps Jesse Grant. His bed-room is nicely furnished—much like the other, save that the trimmings are red, and omitting a few mirrors and fancy articles.

"The state bedchamber is a magnificent apartment, furnished with rosewood and crimson satin, and papered with purple and gold. The bedstead, massive and high, is richly carved, and conopied with damask curtains, pendant from a gilded hoop near the ceiling. On the other side of the bed are laid soft cushions for the feet. Two costly wardrobes, with full-length mirrors set in their doors, stand against the walls. Two arm-chairs, deeply cushioned, and several other chairs, are diposed over the thick velvet carpet. Mrs. Grant's writing desk stands near a window. One of the curiosities of the chamber is a cigar-case from China, inlaid with pearls and various kinds of wood, presented to General Grant by Captain Ammon, of the United States Navy. The wash-stand and its furniture are stained with purple devices—national historical scenes, perched over by the American eagle, etc., etc. The ceiling of the chamber is profusely frescoed, and an ample coal fire burns under the marble mantel, casting its bright rays upon the polished furniture, and touching with tints of bronze the central chandelier. A dressing-room adjoins the state bedchamber, and opens into the chamber occupied by Mr. Dent. The latter is furnished comfortably in old-fashioned style. The adjacent spare room was formerly used as a bed-chamber by President Johnson."

The social observances of the White House are prescribed with great exactness, and constitute the Court Etiquette of the Republic. At the very outset of the Republic the social question became one of great magnitude, and in order to adjust it upon a proper basis, Washington caused a definite *Code* to be drawn up; but the rules were too arbitrary and exacting to give satisfaction, and society was not disposed to acknowledge so genuine an equality as the code required amongst its members. Frequent and bitter quarrels arose in consequence of the clashing of social claims, and at last a code was agreed upon, which may be stated as follows: The President and his family are recognized as the head and front of the social structure. The President, as such, must not be invited to dinner by any one, and accepts no such invitations, and pays no calls or visits of ceremony. He may visit in his private capacity, however, at pleasure.

An invitation to dine at the White House takes precedence of all others, and a previous engagement must not be pleaded as an excuse for declining it. Such an invitation must be promptly accepted in writing.

During the winter season, a public reception, or levee, is held once a week, at which guests are expected to appear in full dress. They are presented by the Usher on such occasions, and have the honor of shaking hands with the President. These receptions last from eight until ten o'clock.

On the 1st of January and the 4th of July, the President holds public receptions, at which the Foreign Ministers present in the city appear in full court dress, and the officers of the Army and Navy in full uniform. The Heads of Departments, Governors of States, and Members of Congress are received first, then the Diplomatic Corps, then officers of the Army and Navy, and then the doors are thrown open to the public generally for the space of two hours.

The *Vice-President* is expected to pay a formal visit to the President on the meeting of Congress, but he is entitled to the first visit from all other persons, which he may return by card, or in person.

The Judges of the Supreme Court call upon the President and Vice-President on the annual meeting of the Court in December, and on New Year's Day. They are entitled to the first call from all other persons.

Members of the Cabinet call upon the President on the 1st of January and the 4th of July. They are required to pay the first calls, either in person or by card, to the Vice-President, Judges of the Supreme Court, Senators, and the Speaker of the House of Representatives on the meeting of Congress. They are entitled to the first call from all other persons.

Senators call in person upon the President and Vice-President on the meeting of Congress, New Year's Day, and the 4th of July; if Congress is in session at the last named time. They also call first upon the Judges of the Supreme Court, and upon the Speaker of the House of Representatives, on the meeting of Congress. They are entitled to the first call from all other persons.

The Speaker of the House of Representatives calls upon the President on the meeting of Congress, on New Year's Day, and on the 4th of July, if Congress is in session. The first call is due *from* him to the Vice-President, and to the Judges of the Supreme Court, but *to* him from all others.

Members of the House of Representatives call in person upon the President on the meeting of Congress and on New Year's Day, and by card or in person on the 4th of July, if Congress is in session. They call first, by card or in person, upon the Vice-President, Judges of the Supreme Court, Speaker of the House, Senators, Cabinet officers, and Foreign Ministers, soon after the opening of the session.

Foreign Ministers call upon the President on the 1st of January. They call first, in person or by card, upon the Vice-President, Cabinet officers, Judges of the Supreme

Court, and the Speaker of the House, on the first opportunity after presenting their credentials to the President. They also make an annual call of ceremony, by card or in person, on the above mentioned officials soon after the meeting of Congress. They are entitled to first calls from all other persons.

The Judges of the Court of Claims call in person upon the President on New Year's Day and the 4th of July. They pay first calls to Cabinet officers and Members of the Diplomatic Corps, and call annually, by card or in person, upon the Vice-President, Judges of the Supreme Court, Senators, Speaker and Members of the House, soon after the meeting of Congress.

The intercourse of the other officers of the Government is regulated by superiority of rank in the public service.

The intercourse of the families of officials is regulated by the rules which govern the officials themselves.

The levees, or public receptions of the President, are held weekly during the session of Congress. The East Room and the whole suite of State apartments are used upon this occasion.

The President takes his position in one of the smaller apartments, generally in the Red or Blue Room. He is attended by his Cabinet, and the most distinguished men in the land. Near him stands his wife, daughter, or some relative, representing the mistress of the mansion. Visitors enter by the main hall, and are presented to the President by the Usher, who first asks their names, residences, and avocations. The President shakes each one by the hand cordially, utters a few pleasant words in reply to the greetings of his guest, and the visitor is then passed on to be presented to the lady of the White House, to whom he pays his respects. Then he passes on into another room, to make way for the crowd behind him. This regular routine is kept up for the space of two hours, and then the President and his family "go off duty," devoutly thanking heaven for the respite thus accorded them.

The levees are fine things for strangers, but they are downright hard work for the President and his wife. The former is obliged, by an absurd custom, to shake hands with every man presented to him, and he often has his hand bruised and made sore by the vigorous squeezing it is subjected to. Imagine, good reader, what it must be to go through this once a week during each session of Congress.

The levees are very popular, and they bring a strange conglomeration of people into the parlors of the White House. The President is the property of the nation, and every citizen has a right to assert his ownership by attending on these occasions. "There is a crowd at the entrance door before it is opened, and as soon as it is, there ensues an invasion *en masse* and occupation of the entire lower portion of the house. The liveliest scenes take place in the dressing-room and in the hall leading from it, where gentlemen make prodigious efforts to join their ladies. In the dressing-room, there is sometimes the greatest confusion. It has been known to be so crowded, that lifting the arms to unfasten a cloak was a work of time, and to drop a glove was to lose it irrevocably. If successful in being relieved of wrappings, the next thing a lady must try to do is to join her escort, but to do that she must first reach the dressing-room door. If in this struggle, her fresh illusion dress, covered with puffs and ruchings, is so used as to make it fit only for the rag-bag, she must not on that account return. 'Press on' is the motto, 'and spoil your neighbor's dress' the inference. Reaching the door, one reaches bedlam. Gentlemen are struggling with each other and with the police, who vainly endeavor to keep order, and ladies are frantically calling husbands by their Christian names, and receiving replies from half a dozen 'Charlies,' who are not their own. 'Madam,' says a policeman, 'who do you want?' 'My husband,' replies the matron. '*What* did you say was his name?' 'Mr. Tompkins.' And forthwith 'Mr. Tompkins' is bawled aloud, and five gentlemen respond from various quarters. 'What's his other name?' demands the policeman. 'Charlie,' is the answer; and to Charlie Tompkins not a few answer. Some ladies in despair glide with the current, or rather are guided by it, and find their escorts when and where they can. The same order of march is pursued as at the receptions—through the Red Room to the Blue, and afterwards wherever possible. The Blue Room is seen at its best by gaslight, and presents a brilliant appearance. The row of ladies in the evening is not so long, and consequently less stiff, and all have little groups in front of them. Gentlemen are numerous enough in the evening. Almost all the members of the Cabinet attend whenever a levee is held. They are announced by their titles. 'The Secretary of

State and Mrs. Fish,' 'The Secretary of War and Mrs. Belknap,' and so on. Then are seen the Congressmen, some of whom have previously dined out and seem disposed to embrace each other without regard to politics. General Butler enters with his daughter and her cousin, Miss Florence Hildreth. The foreigners come in—'The Russian Minister,' 'The British Minister,' 'The Peruvian Minister,' and so on through the list.

"In the East Room at levees, the scene would be grand, but that the objection the countryman made with regard to being unable to see the town for the houses applies, and one is unable to see the people for the people. It is often the case that for an hour, perhaps, you see none but those who are wedged next to you. If any of these happen to be persons of note in elegant attire, you are fortunate, and can pass your time agreeably in investigating the mysteries of a complicated overskirt, or in admiring pointlace and diamonds; but it is as likely as not that your neighbors are of the kind who do not object to wearing bonnets and cloaks to full dress entertainments, and in that case your inspection need not be prolonged.

"If, however, it were possible to be perched somewhere, and to look down on the crowd, the sight would be something worth remembering. Three enormous and magnificent chandeliers, with their numberless burners, give the room the brightness of noonday. The ladies are dressed in ball attire, satins glisten, diamonds flash, velvets and softening laces give effect to beautiful wearers. The uniforms of officers glitter in the crowd. Eight mirrors, placed at intervals in the room, reflect the splendor of the present. Eight Presidents, seven of whom are dead, look down from their portraits on the walls, and represent the glory of the past. Meanwhile, the Marine Band is playing without, and promenaders pass beneath the crimson curtains draping the entrance to the wide hall, and find in walking there some relief from the pressure of the crowd.

"In spite of discomforts, those who know what to expect will attend the levees winter after winter, and it seems as if the house, so full of historical associations with its beautiful rooms, brilliant lights and throng of notabilities, must be acknowledged to possess superior attractions."

Besides these public levees, the ladies of the White House hold receptions at stated periods, to which invitations are regularly issued. The President sometimes appears upon these occasions, but is under no obligation to do so.

It has long been the custom for the President to give a series of State dinners during the session of Congress, to which the various members of that body, the higher Government officials, and the Diplomatic Corps are successively invited. In order to show attention to all, and offend none, it is necessary to give quite a number of these entertainments during the session. During Mr. Lincoln's administration the custom was "more honored in the breach than the observance," but it was revived by President Johnson, and under General Grant has become one of the prominent features of the life at the White House.

"The 'State Dining-room' at the White House is a handsome apartment. A long table, rounded at the ends, extends through the middle of it, at which thirty-six can be comfortably seated. There is plenty of room besides, for the servants to perform their duties admirably. New mirrors and chandeliers have been added since the administration of President Grant, but the carpets, upholstering, and papering have descended from the Johnson *régime*. The exquisite taste of Martha Patterson is seen on the daintily tinted walls, the figures of the carpet so nicely adjusted to the size of the room, the dark green satin damask at the windows, and the quaint chairs, under her supervision arranged to match. A clock, as ancient as the days of Madison, adorns one of the marble mantels, whilst a pair of hydra-headed candlesticks, grim with age, descended from nobody knows whose brief reign, graces the other. With the exception of a pair of modern mahogany side-boards, the furniture seems to have belonged to the era of Washington or Jefferson, it is so solid and sombre. The White House was modelled after the palace of the Duke of Leinster, and the State Dining-room, more than any other part of the building, is suggestive of a baronial hall. But if there is one thing more than another from which the State Dining-room suffers it is from a dearth of silver.

"'Steward Melah,' the silver-voiced Italian whom Government employs to look after this part of its business, actually wrings his hands with terror and dismay when he 'sets' the table for State occasions. 'Why, madam,' says Melah, 'there isn't enough silver in the White House to set a respectable free-lunch table.' Now, the incomparable Melah has been steward in the Everett House, Boston, the Astor, New York, the Stetson, at Long Branch, the St. Charles, New Orleans, and having served in these first-class capacities it may be possible that his ideas are too exalted for the same kind of work in the White House. It must be remembered that all these state dinners are paid for out of the President's private purse. The President, however, has put this delicate matter into Steward Melah's hands, and the Italian 'gets up' a dinner according to the quality of the guests. These dinners cost from three to fifteen hundred dollars, though the average cost is about seven hundred. The state dinner of which Prince Arthur had the honor of partaking was composed of twenty-nine courses, and cost fifteen hundred dollars; but it is only when royalty is to be entertained that these feasts assume such costly proportions. This modest sum does not include the wine and other beverages, for these come under a separate 'item.' In no other Administration has the Government appointed a man to spend the President's money. Heretofore the 'ladies of the White House' have looked after this part of the official business, and it will at once be seen what frugality is necessary in order to make both ends of the Presidential year meet; but no man during the existence of the Republic has ever been the recipient of so many costly gifts as the present Executive, and he reflects honor in return by his unexampled and reciprocal generosity.

"A rare work of art adorns the centre of the long table in the State Dining-room. It is several feet long, and, perhaps, two feet wide, and is composed of gilt and looking-glass. The foundation is a long mirror, and this is beached by a perpendicular shore, three inches in height, but of no appreciable thickness. Little fernlike upheavings may be seen rising out of the tawdry gilt at equal distances apart, and these are used as receptacles for natural flowers. But, lest the guests should look into this mirror, and see each other facetiously reflected at moments, too, when the human mouth assumes anything but poetic proportions, large vases of flowers are strewn on the glassy surface, and the mischief of the mirror is nipped in the bud. The ornament is not merely ornamental; it is useful. It answers the very purpose to help out a social ambuscade, for it can be so arranged as to hide the President from any guest from whose presence he is suffering, whether said person comes under the head of enemy or friend.

"Conversation at a state dinner cannot be general. Each guest must depend upon his own neighborhood. The quality of the conversation depends entirely upon the kind of people who manufacture it. Mike Walsh terrified Mrs. Franklin Pierce at a state dinner, by talking about his going 'a fishing on Sunday.' A modern Congressman filled up the official time between each mouthful, by telling his next lady neighbor the exact things which his palate craved. He didn't 'like 'French dishes,' but he was 'fond of pork and beans, as well as ice cream and canned peaches.' No doubt the word 'Jenkins' will be flung at the writer for these social criticisms; but *gentleman* is the highest term which can be applied to a politician, and the people have just as much right to a description of an official dinner as any other public event, especially when the Government employs a public functionary in the person of Steward Melah to see the dignity of the nation carried to the perfection point.

"Once upon a time, an accomplished young American woman had the honor to dine with the Czar of all the Russias. During the royal entertainment, a plate of delicious grapes was passed around. It is true, the young lady saw the golden knife which rested on the side of the basket, but as the fruit came to her first she had no way of learning its use; so she did just as she would have done in America—she reached out her dainty fingers, and lifted from the dish a whole stem of grapes. What was her consternation to see the next person, as well as all the other guests, take the golden knife and sever a single grape each, and transfer it to their plates. Had a young Russian lady in this country helped herself to a whole chicken, the error would have been precisely the same. It is true, the young woman committed no crime, but her feelings and those of her friends would have been spared, had she learned the etiquette of royal tables before she became an Emperor's guest.

"A man who will go to a state dinner, eat with his knife, and remain ignorant of the use of his finger bowl, should be expelled from Congress, and ever afterwards be prohibited from holding any place of honor or trust under the Government. Who does not long for the good old 'courtly' days of Hamilton and Jefferson? The writer of this paper has once during the winter had the supreme honor of seeing a gentleman of the old school hand a lady to her carriage. Oh! that an artist had been on the spot to photograph this noble picture. The old man stood with hat uplifted; his right hand touched the tips of the lady's fingers; the wind played with the scanty locks of his uncovered head, and there was a dignity and purity about his movements that reminded one of the out-door service when the preacher says 'ashes to ashes.' The superb manners of the old gentleman could only be felt; they cannot be described.

"It is the evening of the President's state dinner. The guests are not only invited, but expected to be punctually in their places at seven o'clock, P. M. President and Mrs. Grant are already in the Red Room, awaiting the company. The ladies have disrobed themselves of outer wrappings, and, like graceful swans, they sail slowly into the presence. Mrs. Grant is in full evening dress—jewels, laces, and all the et ceteras to match. Her lady guests are attired as handsomely as herself, and the gentlemen are expected to wear black swallow-tail coats and white neck-ties.

"President Grant leads the way, with the wife of the oldest Senator present on his arm—not the oldest Senator in years, but the one who has enjoyed the longest term of office. The President is followed by the other guests, while Mrs. Grant, assisted by the husband of the woman who honors the President by her exclusive attention, brings up the rear, and after a slight confusion, the guests are most comfortably seated. When no minister is present, the Divine blessing is omitted, unless it be the Quaker thankfulness—the silence of the heart. In the beginning of the feast, fruits, flowers, and sweetmeats grace the table, whilst bread and butter only give a Spartan simplicity to the 'first course,' which is composed of a French vegetable soup, and according to the description by those who have tasted it, no soup, foreign or domestic, has ever been known to equal it. It is said to be a little smoother than peacock's brains, but not quite so exquisitely flavored as a dish of nightingales' tongues, and yet 'Professor Melah' is the only man in the nation who holds in his hands the receipt for this aristocratic stew.

"The ambrosial soup is followed by a French croquet of meat. Four admirably trained servants remove the plates between each course, and their motions are as perfect as clock-work. These servants are clad in garments of faultless cut, which serve to heighten to the last degree their sable complexions. White kid gloves add the finishing touch to this part of the entertainment. The 'third course' of the dinner is composed of a filet of beef, flanked on each side by potatoes the size of a walnut, with plenty of mushrooms to keep them company. The next course is dainty in the extreme. It is made up entirely of the luscious legs of partridges, and baptized by a French name entirely beyond my comprehension. It will readily be seen that a full description of the twenty-nine courses would be altogether too much to give in this book, so we pass to the dessert, not omitting to say that the meridian or noon of the feast is marked by the guests being served bountifully with frozen punch. As a general rule, wine is served about every third course. Six wine glasses of different sizes, and a small bouquet of flowers are placed before each guest at the beginning.

"The dessert is inaugurated by the destruction of a rice pudding, but not the kind which prompted the little boy to run away to the North Pole because his mother 'would have rice pudding for dinner.' It is not the same dish which our Chinese brethren swallow with the aid of chopsticks, but it is such a pudding as would make our great grandmothers clap their hands in joy. Charles Lamb has made roast pig classic; Professor Melah's rice pudding is worthy to be embalmed in romance or story, or at least to be illustrated in *Harper's Weekly*. This Presidential dish cannot be described except by the pen of genius, therefore it can only be added that no plebeian pies or pastry are allowed to keep it company. After the rice pudding, canned peaches, pears, and quinces are served. Then follow confectionery, nuts, ice-cream, coffee, and chocolate, and with these warm, soothing drinks the Presidential entertainment comes to an end, the host and his guests repair to the Red Room, and after fifteen minutes spent in conversation the actors in a state dinner rapidly disappear."

The White House is not altogether identified with gayety. It has had its sorrows as well. Presidents

Harrison and Taylor both died in the Executive Mansion. Willie Lincoln, the favorite child of President Lincoln, also died here, and only three years afterwards the lifeless body of the murdered President was laid in sorrowful state in the East Room, amidst the agonized mourning of a great people. In almost the same spot where he had stood to look his last upon the face of his dear boy, all that was mortal of the Martyr lay, all unconscious of the wild storm of grief that was raging over the land for him. Around him gathered the magnates of the Republic, men rich in honors, wisdom, and experience, all terrified, dumb with dismay. The firm hand was gone from the helm, and, for a while, the ship of State drifted helplessly upon the dark waters which encompassed it. Then, with standards draped and drooping, bells tolling, and cannon booming a mournful dirge, the body was borne away from the great hall, through the crowded cities of the land, each of which showered its highest and proudest honors upon it, while the whole nation mourned as it had never mourned before since Washington died, and laid in the tomb in that great Western land, with which his fame is so inseparably connected.

The present occupants of the White House are President Grant and his family. A pleasant writer has thus sketched the life and habits of this family:

"The family at the White House rise early—at 7 or 7.30. Our republican lord and master tolerates no valet, but draws on his pantaloons and buttons his suspenders with unassisted hands. Haply he repairs to the convenient bath-room to meet his barber, where the morning newspapers—the *Chronicle* and the *Republican* —are brought to him for ante-prandial perusal. Breakfast is served from 8 to 8.30 in the private dining-room on the main floor; west of the ante-room, which is just west of the vestibule. The meal is substantial and good—for example, a steak, potatoes, home-made biscuit, muffins, and waffles, or 'grits.' The President likes best the plainest food, and all are light eaters. The entire family drink coffee, including Mr. Dent, who is now in his 85th year. The President stickles for promptitude at the breakfast table, and, when any of the family are late, wears a grave and reproachful countenance. He is seldom bothered in this way by any one but Jesse, of which sedate, long-headed, but mischievous youngster he is very fond. When Jesse comes in belated, and beholds his father's face, his own is overcome with a cloud of mortification. 'Jesse,' solemnly observes his mother, 'don't you know you ought to be in to breakfast in time? I think papa is looking a little angry.' To which the child, lugubrious, has naught to say till the President laughs (as he invariably does), an assurance that he needn't fear a further scolding.

"At the breakfast table old Mr. Dent occupies the first seat. The President sits at his left, Mrs. Grant at his right, Nellie Grant at the side of the President, and Jesse beside his mother. The ascendancy of the Dent above the Grant family, not only in the White House, but elsewhere under the ægis of the administration has been remarked as singular, inasmuch as the favored Dents are kindred of the President's wife, while the neglected Grants are the President's own blood-relations. One explanation is not very complimentary to the abilities or manners of the Grant family at large. But perhaps the best explanation lies in the influence exercised by Mrs. Grant over her husband, and in the fortunate tact with which her kin have retained his favor. Mrs. Grant's father has the reputation of a kind-hearted and worthy old gentleman. The slurs and supercilious smiles of Washington politicians and women have not in the least disturbed the respect and deference with which he is uniformly treated at the Executive Mansion.

"The family sit at breakfast about three-quarters of an hour. Politics are never discussed at the table; though the President, who carries his newspapers there and lingers over them, occasionally utters a remark betraying his sensitiveness to criticism. To be sure he never finds anything to complain of in the daily newspapers published in the Capital—they are all his devoted, humble servants; but such is not invariably the case in the columns of journals from New York and other cities—even those printed in the Republican dialect. From these annoyances he takes refuge in jokes with Jesse and in pleasant, often lively, converse with Mrs. Grant. Her he addresses as 'Mrs. Grant,' who calls him familiarly 'Ulyss,' or with playful formality, 'Mr. Grant.'

"After breakfast, between 9 and 10 o'clock, the President lights his cigar and takes a short walk. As he emerges from the front portico of the White House, where an orderly or two stand in waiting, he returns salute mechanically with the old military habit, and passes down the steps. He wears a closely-buttoned black frock overcoat, a silk tile, and rather soiled kid gloves; and walks slowly, with head bent forward after the manner of Napoleon I., one hand behind him and the other holding his cigar. He seldom looks up, and does not like to be accosted or accompanied on this early promenade.

"Returning, the President goes to his office at 10 A. M., and there begins to receive callers and transact the business of the day. Members of the Cabinet have the precedence, of course, over all others. On days when the Cabinet meets few other visitors are admitted. Senators and Representatives are, as a rule, received after members of the Cabinet; though a previous engagement by some one else with the President may keep them airing their heels in the corridor. Most visitors who are not well known at the White House— no matter what may be the pressing nature of their wish —are at the mercy of General Dent, who manages an interview for them or not, as he pleases. Probably a good many who have failed to get an audience would be more likely to thank than to curse the doorkeeper, if they could comprehend the mortification they were saved from. To a person of acute sensibilities no ordeal could be less agreeable than that of an official call (being a stranger) upon President Grant. A conscious lack of tact, and a morbid distrust of most of the politicians and strangers with whom he is brought in contact, have confirmed the President in an oysterlike habit of demeanor in their presence, and in the use of forms of speech so monosyllabic that they sound to the startled listener like the crack of the shutting himself up by that bivalve in his shell. This method of self-defence is not brilliant, nor very intellectual in any respect. But it is non-committal and secure. Very few politicians or schemers (there *are* exceptions) 'get the start' of this listening, quiet man. Very few citizens, who press their 'views' upon him, or solicit his influence in the most apparently innocent matter, get a square answer out of him. He hears, ponders, and inwardly digests, that he may find, next day or fortnight, no weak word of acquiescence to abide by or regret.

"While the President is thus immersed in official duties (with his secretaries, clerks, and other *attachés* of the official household), the family life in the daytime deserves a little sketch. Mrs. Grant does not often leave home before 11 o'clock. Some days she drives out on a calling or shopping expedition, which lasts till near lunch time—1.30 o'clock. An elaborate lunch is served, chiefly because there are usually guests to partake of it. On Tuesday the ladies who assist Mrs. Grant at her receptions are present. Old Mrs. Dent and General Dent almost invariably lunch at the White House. The President does not lunch more than once or twice in a fortnight.

"Mrs. Grant's reception day is also 'Cabinet day.' After the adjournment of the Cabinet it is customary for the President and the Cabinet ministers to descend and pay their respects to the lady of the mansion. The President frequently remains at the side of his wife till the close of the ceremony.

"The children, Nellie and Jesse, 'go to school at home.' That is to say, their teachers come to them and set up a miniature school at the White House. Both children have the same teacher of English—a lady who comes daily and is with them from 9 till 12.30. A French and a German teacher come on alternate days, and a music teacher for Nellie Grant twice a week. This young lady is not accounted so proficient in her studies or as a pianist as she proved herself not long ago to be as a plucker of flowers for a prince, and the juvenile Jesse has won more laurels as a dry joker and odd little genius, generally, than have fallen on him in reward for scholarship.

"At 3 P. M. 'office hours' are over; when, with the President, business comes to a full stop. There is now an interval of two hours before dinner, which is spent in various ways. Disenthralled from work and lighting a cigar, Mr. Grant strolls through the house in search of his children, whom he generally finds frolicking with playmates. Taking Jesse by the hand, he easily entices him away to the stables, where the grooms and horses expect this visit from their master every afternoon.

"The stables stand in the southwest part of the grounds, near the Navy Department. They are built of brick, and divided into four compartments. The carriages fill one compartment. There are five vehicles —an open English hunting carriage, used by the family; a Landower, used by the family; a top buggy and a light road wagon, used by the President for fast driving; a basket phaeton for the children; and a two-horse wagon for rough ordinary use. The carriages bear the monogram 'U. S. G.' on the panels. The harness suspended in the carriage room is strong and serviceable, without much ornamentation. About half a dozen saddles are displayed, one of which, a Mexican saddle, is heavily mounted with silver. The stable proper has three compartments, which accommodate a stud of twelve horses. In one compartment stands General Grant's war horse, Cincinnati, still used under the saddle and occasionally for carriage driving. He is a big dark bay, thirteen years old, and has lost none of his old 'style' and majesty of movement. Next to him are stalled St. Louis and Egypt, two fine carriage horses, and a filly named Julie. In the opposite compartment are Jessie's two Shetland ponies, Billy Button and Reb —the latter the sire of Billy Button. These ponies are driven with the basket phaeton. Here, too, are Mary and a black saddle-pony called Jeff. Davis, a natural pacer, and very fast, which the President sometimes mounts and skurries away with into the suburbs. The third compartment contains two Hambletonian fillies, Rebecca and Loretta, foaled last spring. A handsome two-year-old Hambletonian colt, a bright sorrel, occupies a large stall by himself. The President expects great things from him. Jennie, a blooded brood mare, is kept in a building near the house. The stables are well lighted, airy and clean. They are presided over by a black coachman and two darkey grooms, one of whom acts as footman. Their livery consists of coats of olive brown, garnished with enormous silver buttons, plain pantaloons, top boots, black stovepipe hats, with broad bands and massive silver buckles, and white gloves. They grin cavernously when the President comes, and descant upon the condition and prospects of the equine fold. To them the Sphinx, unbending, responds with polysyllabic effluence, talking horse with happy unreserve. All the animals know him for a friend. Particularly old Cincinnati pricks his ears, and nods and blinks welcome with a look that says as plainly as words, 'My dear old master, how are you? You and I know a thing or two. Come, pat me on the neck. I'm glad to see you looking so well, and glad that you haven't forgotten, any more than I have, the art (or the necessity) of holding your tongue! But when, my dear master'—with a brighter gleam on the eye and quivering red nostrils—'when are you going to get up another war?' The President, holding his cigar aside, approaches the steed and caresses him. These two, the Man and the Horse, knitted together on many a battle-field into one Centaur—is the time gone by for them to appear again at the head of armies, with tramping hoofs and a desolating sword?

"Meantime Mrs. Grant and her guests, or that matron with her daughter Nellie, are strolling through the conservatory and green-houses. The conservatory, built out from the west wing of the White House, is one of the largest in the country. It is filled with a magnificent collection of exotics. An aquarium stands at one end. A flight of steps and a short path from the conservatory lead down to a green-house, also filled with flowers. Behind this green-house is the grapery, where several varieties of foreign grapes are grown. A good deal of choice fruit is cultivated here. The other three green-houses are set at intervals in the grounds west of the mansion. In summer the open-air gardens yield plenteously flowers and vegetables. Here the family walk on summer afternoons, as the locality is always secluded. Since the grounds south of the mansion have been rendered less liable to public intrusion, the walks and views there will probably be availed of in the same way. Mrs. Grant is enthusiastic as a schoolgirl over fine scenery, and quietly fond of flowers. I have at this moment in mind a little story which was told to me not long ago, illustrating the influence of natural scenery upon her really gushing temperament, and illustrating likewise the naïve and tender quality of her affection for her husband. It was in 1868, on their northern trip, that the President and Mrs. Grant, with a small party of friends, were seated on the cabin deck near the stern of a river steamboat, chatting and whiling the sunny hours away. A brief cessation of talk left every one free to contemplate the unusual loveliness of the view from the bosom of a broad embayment of the stream. The President, smoking, fixed his emotionless gaze on the passing ripples. Mrs. Grant sat as if rapt. Turning suddenly, unconscious or regardless of everything save the delightful influence of the moment, she poured into her husband's ears a flood of charming pet words. Without moving a muscle, but galvanized it seemed by the shock of the situation, the President simply blushed a great red blush, that surged up, inundating his ears and threatening to turn his hair and beard to crimson. At which hot signal, endearments were superseded by a burst of merry laughter.

"The remaining hour before dinner is with Mr. Grant an hour of exercise—if exercise can be said to consist in a sluggish walk. Sometimes he turns to the right, past the Treasury, down F Street, or down even to the populous Avenue. But this is when he is less harassed than common, and is not averse to meeting and conversing with acquaintances. His sense of relief from the day's official worry manifests itself then in interested glances at the street scenes and the people. Like a babe roused from stupor, he 'notices things,' and does not fail in politeness, especially to ladies. He has a bow and an uncovered head for all pretty women and damsels, though his mouth hardly bends into a smile responsive to the most coquettish provocation. On other afternoons he walks up the Avenue to Twenty-first Street, thence out to the northern suburbs, making a long detour, and returning by the way of Fourteenth Street and New York Avenue, with a fair but tobacco-chastened appetite for the 5 o'clock meal.

"Dinner and those who sit down to it are required to be punctual. Like the other meals served, it is devised by the steward, who has the easy task of ministering to simple tastes and very moderate hunger. Roast beef is the favorite viand. Not more than three kinds of vegetables make up the body of the feast. Hominy is a welcome dish, and bread is one of the chief props of the Presidential stomach. A wholesome dessert is brought on duly and swallowed with deliberation. By this time the august family are in high humor, and no one who had the unhappy fortune to meet the President amid the bustle of the day would recognize him in his present unrestrained, good-natured self. He does not flash forth wit-lightning—the urchin Jesse is the humorist of the circle. But, if it has happened to be a reception day, he joins in talk about the guests, and is even said to be a fair judge of ladies' toilettes. At the table he is quite 'at home;' there his children find him tender; and there, it is rumored, he receives with edifying patience whatever blunt remonstrance his Democratic father-in-law may take it into his head to make against his course in regard to the 'niggers' of the land. Subsequent to coffee leaps a cigar from his side pocket, and again, for the fourteenth or fifteenth time, he smokes. A walk long enough to reduce the cigar to ashes brings him home again. Now the New York papers are brought in. Happily the levees, which, once a week at the height of the season, used to demand his presence and Mrs. Grant's in the Blue Room from nine till midnight, are over.

"Though Mrs. Grant keeps a thrifty eye on the housekeeping arrangements at the White House, the steward relieves her of much responsibility and care. So her evenings, like the President's, are quite her own.

"To those who remember the literally ceaseless anxiety and toil that fell to Mr. Lincoln and Mr. Johnson, the leisure of Mr. Grant and the diversions he devotes it to, seem to render his lot as President very enviable. The number of his secretaries and clerks in this piping time of peace exceeds the number employed by his predecessors in time of war and in the busiest period of reconstruction. These assistants, chiefly tried staff officers who were accustomed to relieve General Grant from a still heavier load when he was commander of the army, form a cabinet within a cabinet around him, so well disciplined as to dispose of all the routine, and capable enough to shoulder most of the minor responsibilities, of his administration.

"During the winter he often attended, with Mrs. Grant, the receptions of the Cabinet Ministers, and accepted invitations to private dinner and dancing-parties. At these his quiet demeanor was conspicuously noticeable. The rare instances when he unbent himself won him forgiveness for many an oversight and for whole half-hours of aggravating reticence. He seems to like society, or rather to be grimly amused by the glitter, noise, and palaver of a well-dressed and distinguished throng. But it takes a friend who is on very familiar terms with him, or a woman of superior and pertinacious tact, to 'draw him out' to the extent of more than a few short sentences in such assemblies. Though I encountered the President on some of these occasions, I never saw him appear so much at his ease as he did at the annual gathering (of males exclusively) at Colonel John W. Forney's one night last January. Our friend Forney had then collected in his house on Capitol Hill the most unwonted conglomeration of human beings ever brought together in Washington. Black spirits and white, blue spirits and gray, of politics, were incorporated in skins of as many hues. Members of the Cabinet; Foreign Ministers and Secretaries; Senators and members of both parties; newspaper correspondents of the Radical, the 'Conservative Republican,' the Democratic, and the 'Ku-Klux' press; clerks of the two Houses of Congress; local politicians; lobbyists; mulattoes and negroes—all were assembled in a grand stag party, free to scramble on the table for supper, and under it for sherry and champagne. The Sphinx arrived unnoticed, and was soon hobnobbing with his host and a number of other gentlemen. With a cigar in one hand and a glass of wine in the other (he did but sip the wine), he was protected from hand-shaking; and it was really quite good to see him loosen his lips and threaten with abnormal fluency to solve himself. Yet at the close of that evening he remained as great a Riddle as before.

"The other night he attended a 'literary reunion' at the house of a distinguished resident of the District. Given the place of honor at the entertainment, which was also attended by the Vice-President, General Sherman, and a large additional company of ladies and gentlemen, he displayed, I am told, from first to last the sullen infestivity which makes him in refined society so hard a guest to get along with. Many complimentary pleasantries were introduced, which he was expected to recognize by some sign or other. His gloomy countenance gave no token, in the midst of all the hilarity, that he was in the slightest degree entertained.

"The President's evenings at home are passed, with few exceptions, in the society of his wife and children. Nothing but the most important business can induce him to give an official audience at night. If visitors are admitted they are received, according to their station or the grade of their intimacy at the White

House, in the Red Room below stairs, or in the library, or in the private parlor on the second floor. Old Mr. Dent is not seldom present, and receives from the family, and from those who call and quickly discern the proprieties and customs of the family circle, the most scrupulous consideration. At these evening gatherings at home the President is said to display a genial frankness and a conversational facility which are nowhere else disclosed, and therefore nowhere else appreciated. The children are sent to bed between nine and ten. Mrs. Grant retires later; when the President resumes, for an hour or so, his newspapers and cigars. Queer visitors sometimes apply late at night to see him. About three months ago the night police arrested a man who insisted on seeing the President. He had a long piece of iron, with a telegraph glass-cap at the end of it, concealed in his sleeve—an ugly tool, which might have put a bloody and regretable period to the life of one of the most amiable, stubborn, incomprehensible of men."

NOTE.—Since this Chapter was written the Salary of the President has been increased to Fifty Thousand dollars per annum.

CHAPTER XI.

THE SMITHSONIAN INSTITUTION.

History of the Bequest of James Smithson—The Plan for diffusing Knowledge among Men—Organization of the Smithsonian Institution—The Building—The Museum—Description of the Collection.

In the year 1828 there died in England a gentleman possessed of a large fortune. His name was James Smithson, and he was a member of one of the best families in the kingdom. By the terms of his will he left as a legacy to the United States of America, the sum of $515,169, "to found at Washington, under the name of the Smithsonian Institution, an establishment FOR THE INCREASE AND DIFFUSION OF KNOWLEDGE AMONG MEN." The General Government accepted the trust thus confided to it, and, in 1846, an Act was passed by Congress establishing the Smithsonian Institution. In May, 1847, President Polk laid the corner stone of the edifice with Masonic ceremonies.

The Board of Regents, in whose hands the control of the Institution is vested, drew up the following general plan, upon which the operations of the Institution have been conducted, this plan being, in their judgment, best calculated to carry into effect the wishes of the founder:

"*To Increase Knowledge.* It is proposed: 1. To

stimulate men of talent to make original researches, by offering suitable rewards for memoirs containing new truths; and, 2. To appropriate annually a portion of the income for particular researches, under the direction of suitable persons.

"*To Diffuse Knowledge.* It is proposed: 1. To publish a series of periodical reports on the progress of the different branches of knowledge; and, 2. To publish, occasionally, separate treatises on subjects of general interest.

"*Details of Plan to Increase Knowledge.* I. By stimulating researches. 1. Facilities to be afforded for the production of original memoirs on all branches of knowledge. 2. The memoirs thus obtained to be published in a series of volumes, in a quarto form, and entitled Smithsonian Contributions to Knowledge. 3. No memoir, on subjects of physical science, to be accepted for publication, which does not furnish a positive addition to human knowledge, resting on original research; and all unverified speculations to be rejected. 4. Each memoir presented to the Institution to be submitted for examination to a commission of persons of reputation for learning in the branch to which the memoir pertains, and to be accepted for publication only in case the report of this commission is favorable. 5. The commission to be chosen by the officers of the Institution, and the name of the author, as far as practicable, concealed, unless a favorable decision be made. 6. The volumes of the memoirs to be changed for the transactions of literary and scientific societies, and copies to be given to all the colleges, and principal libraries, in this country. One part of the remaining copies may be offered for sale; and the other carefully preserved, to form complete sets of the work, to supply the demand for new institutions. 7. An abstract, or popular account, of the contents of these memoirs to be given to the public through the annual report of the Regents to Congress. II. By appropriating a part of the income, annually, to special objects of research, under the direction of suitable persons. 1. The objects, and the amount appropriated, to be recommended by counsellors of the Institution. 2. Appropriations in different years to different objects; so that in course of time each branch of knowledge may receive a share. 3. The results obtained from these appropriations to be published, with the memoirs before mentioned, in the volumes of the Smithsonian Contributions to Knowledge. 4. Examples of objects for which appropriations may be made: (1.) System of extended meteorological observations for solving the problem of American storms. (2.) Explorations in descriptive natural history, and geological, magnetical, and topographical surveys, to collect materials for the formation of a Physical Atlas of the United States. (3.) Solution of experiment problems, such as a new determination of the weight of the earth, of the velocity of electricity and of light; chemical analyses of soils and plants; collection and publication of scientific facts, accumulated in the offices of Government. (4.) Institution of statistical inquiries with reference to physical, moral, and political subjects. (5.) Historical researches, and accurate surveys of places celebrated in American history.

(6.) Ethnological researches, particularly with reference to the different races of men in North America; also, explorations and accurate surveys of the mounds and other remains of the ancient people of our country.

"*Details of the Plan for Diffusing Knowledge.* I. By the publication of a series of reports, giving an account of the new discoveries in science, and of the changes made from year to year in all branches of knowledge not strictly professional. 1. These reports will diffuse a kind of knowledge generally interesting, but which, at present, is inaccessible to the public. Some reports may be published annually, others at longer intervals, as the income of the Institution or the changes in the branches of knowledge may indicate. 2. The reports are to be prepared by colaborators eminent in the different branches of knowledge. 3. Each colaborator to be furnished with the journals and publications, domestic and foreign, necessary to the compilation of his report; to be paid a certain sum for his labors, and to be named on the title-page of the report. 4. The reports to be published in separate parts, so that persons interested in a particular branch can procure the parts relating to it without purchasing the whole. 5. These reports may be presented to Congress for partial distribution, the remaining copies to be given to literary and scientific institutions, and sold to individuals for a moderate price. II. By the publication of separate treatises on subjects of general interest. 1. These treatises may occasionally consist of valuable memoirs translated from foreign languages, or of articles prepared under the direction of the Insti-

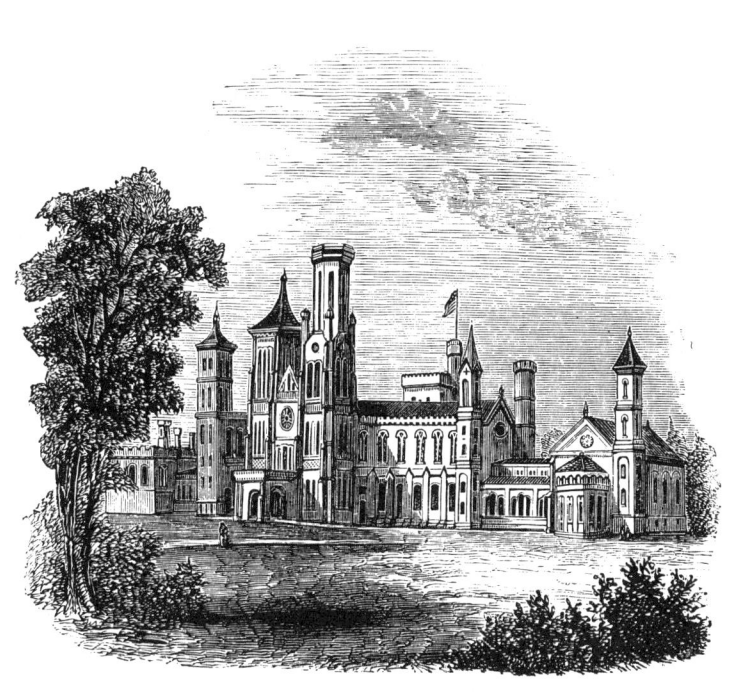

SMITHSONIAN INSTITUTE.

tution, or procured by offering premiums for the best exposition of a given subject. 2. The treatises should, in all cases, be submitted to a commission of competent judges, previous to their publication.

"The only changes made in the policy above indicated have been the passage of resolutions, by the Regents, repealing the equal division of the income between the active operations and the museum and library, and further providing that the annual appropriations are to be apportioned specifically among the different objects and operations of the Institution, in such manner as may, in the judgment of the Regents, be necessary and proper for each, according to its intrinsic importance, and a compliance in good faith with the law."

The Act of Congress, organizing the Institution, makes the President and Vice-President of the United States, the Cabinet Ministers, the Chief Justice of the United States, and the Mayor of Washington, members *ex officio* of the Institution. The Board of Regents, charged with the control of the Institution, consists of the President of the United States, the Mayor of Washington, three Senators of the United States, three members of the House of Representatives, who are *ex officio* Regents, six persons not members of Congress, two of whom must be citizens of Washington, and members of the National Institute of that city, and the other four citizens of any of the States of the Union, no two of whom are to be chosen from the same State. The Board of Regents make annual reports of their conduct of the Institution to Congress.

The real "power behind the throne" is the Secretary of the Institution, who is its Executive officer. He has charge of the edifice, its contents, and the grounds, and is given as many assistants as are necessary to enable him to conduct the varied operations of the Institution. The property of the Institution is placed under the protection of the laws for the preservation and safe keeping of the public buildings and grounds of the City of Washington.

Upon the organization of the Institution, Congress set apart for its use a portion of the public grounds lying to the westward of the Capitol, and between it and the Potomac River. Fifty-two acres comprised the grant, which was known as the "Smithsonian Reservation." They were laid out under the supervision of the gifted landscape gardener and horticulturalist, Andrew Jackson Downing. He died while engaged in this pleasant task, and his memory is perpetuated by a memorial erected in the grounds in 1852, by the American Pomological Society, and consisting of a massive vase resting on a handsome pedestal, with appropriate inscriptions, the whole being of the finest Italian marble.

The building is situated near the centre of the grounds as they originally existed, the centre of the edifice being immediately opposite Tenth Street West. It is constructed of a fine quality of lilac gray freestone, found in the new red sandstone formation, where it crosses the Potomac, near the mouth of Seneca Creek, one of the tributaries of that river, and about twenty-three miles above Washington. It is an admirable and beautiful building material, and is seen to excellent advantage in this edifice. The stone is very soft at first, and is quarried with comparative ease. In its fresh state, it can be worked with the chisel and hammer; but it hardens rapidly upon exposure to the air and weather, and will withstand, after a time, the severest usage.

The structure is in the style of architecture belonging to the last half of the twelfth century, the latest variety of rounded style, as it is found immediately anterior to its merging into the early Gothic, and is known as the Norman, the Lombard, or Romanesque. The semi-circular arch, stilted, is employed throughout —in doors, windows, and other openings.

The main building is 205 feet long by 57 feet wide, and, to the top of the corbel course, 58 feet high. The east wing is 82 by 52 feet, and, to the top of its battlement, 42½ feet high. The west wing, including its projecting apsis, is 84 by 40 feet, and 38 feet high. Each of the wings is connected with the main building by a range, which, including its cloisters, is 60 feet long by 49 feet wide. This makes the length of the entire building, from east to west, 447 feet. Its greatest breadth is 160 feet.

The north front of the main building is ornamented with two central towers, the loftiest of which is 150 feet high. It has also a handsome covered carriage way, upon which opens the main entrance to the building. The south central tower is 37 feet square, 91 feet high, and massively constructed. A double campanile tower, 17 feet square, and 117 feet high, rises from the northeast corner of the main building; and the southwest corner has a lofty octagonal tower, in which is a spiral stairway, leading to the summit. There are four other smaller towers of lesser heights, making nine in all, the effect of which is very beautiful, and which once caused a wit to remark that it seemed to him as if a "collection of church steeples had gotten lost, and were consulting together as to the best means of getting home to their respective churches."

The building was seriously damaged by fire in January, 1865. The flames destroyed the upper part of the main building and the towers. Although the lower story was saved, the valuable official, scientific, and miscellaneous correspondence, record books, and manuscripts in the Secretary's office, the large collection of scientific apparatus, the personal effects of James Smithson, Stanley's fine collection of Indian portraits, and much other valuable property, were destroyed. Fortunately, the Library, Museum, and Laboratory were uninjured. The fire made no interruption in the practical workings of the Institution, and, soon after, the burned portions were restored.

The Museum occupies the ground floor, and is the principal attraction to the majority of visitors. It is a beautiful hall containing two tiers of cases, in which are placed the specimens on exhibition. Access to the upper tier of cases is had by means of a light iron gallery, which is reached by stairways of the same material. The Official Guide to the Institution, which may be purchased in the hall, thus describes the Museum:

"Under these provisions, the Institution has received

and taken charge of such Government collections in mineralogy, geology, and natural history as have been made since its organization. The amount of these has been very great, as all the United States Geological, Boundary, and Railroad Surveys, with the various topographical, military, and naval explorations, have been, to a greater or less extent, ordered to make such collections as would illustrate the physical and natural history features of the regions traversed.

"Of the collections made by thirty Government expeditions, those of twenty-five are now deposited with the Smithsonian Institution, embracing more than five-sixths of the whole amount of materials collected. The principal expeditions thus furnishing collections are the United States Geological Surveys of Doctors Owen, Jackson, and Evans, and of Messrs. Foster and Whitney; the United States and Mexican Boundary Survey; the Pacific Railroad Survey; the Exploration of the Yellow Stone, by Lieutenant Warren; the Survey of Lieutenant Bryan; the United States Naval Astronomical Expedition; the North Pacific Behring Straits Expedition; the Japan Expedition, and the Paraguay Expedition.

"The Institution has also received, from other sources, collections of greater or less extent, from various portions of North America, tending to complete the Government series.

"The collections thus made, taken as a whole, constitute the largest and best series of the minerals, fossils, rocks, animals, and plants of the entire continent of North America, in the world. Many tons of geological and mineralogical specimens, illustrating the surveys throughout the West, are embraced therein. There is also a very large collection of minerals of the mining regions of Northern Mexico, and of New Mexico, made by a practical Mexican geologist, during a period of twenty-five years, and furnishing indications of many rich mining localities within our own borders, yet unknown to the American people.

"It includes, also, with scarcely an exception, all the vertebrate animals of North America, among them many specimens each of the Grizzly, Cinnamon, and Black Bears; the Panther, Jaguar, Ocelot, and several species of Lynx or Wildcat; the Elk, the Mexican, Virginian, White-tailed, Black-tailed, and Mule Deer; the Antelope, Rocky Mountain Goat and Sheep; several species of Wolves and Foxes, the Badger, Beaver, Porcupine, Prairie Dog, Gopher, and also about seven hundred species of American Birds, four hundred of Reptiles, and eight hundred of Fishes, embracing Salmon, Trout, Pike, Pickerel, White Fish, Muskalonge, Bass, Redfish, etc.

"The greater part of the Mammalia have been arranged in walnut drawers, made proof against dust and insects. The birds have been similarly treated, while the reptiles and fish have been classified, as, to some extent, have also been the shells, minerals, fossils, and plants.

"The Museum hall is quite large enough to contain all the collections hitherto made, as well as such others as may be assigned to it. No single room in the country is, perhaps, equal to it in capacity or adaptation to its purposes, as, by the arrangements now being perfected, and denoted in the illustration, it is capable of receiving twice as large a surface of cases as the old Patent-office Hall, and three times that of the Academy of Sciences of Philadelphia.

CHAPTER XII.

THE UNITED STATES OBSERVATORY.

Location of the Observatory—The Work performed here—The Chronometer Room—The Equatorial—The Transit Instrument—The great Astronomical Clock—A Scientific Curiosity.

The United States Observatory is situated upon an elevated site, southwest of the President's House. It is near the Georgetown line, and commands a fine view of the city, the Potomac River, as far down as Fort Washington and Mount Vernon. It is in charge of a corps of Naval officers, being a part of the property of the Navy Department. The officers in charge are selected for their scientific knowledge and skill, the duties required of them here being of the highest order. The establishment holds a high rank among the Observatories of the world, and it is said that only one—that of Russia—excels it in excellence and thoroughness.

Besides performing the usual astronomical duties of such an establishment, the officers of the Observatory are the keepers of all the nautical books, maps, charts, and instruments belonging to the Navy.

Principal among these, are the Chronometers belonging to the Government, which are kept in a room set apart for that purpose. These instruments are purchased by the Navy Department with the understanding that they are to be tested in the Observatory for one year. They are placed in the chronometer room, and carefully wound and regulated. They are examined daily, and compared with the Great Astronomical Clock of the Observatory, and an accurate record of the movements of each one is kept in a book prepared for that purpose. The temperature of the room is also examined daily, and recorded. These minute records enable the officers of the Observatory to point out the exact fault of each imperfect chronometer. Thanks to this, the maker is enabled to remedy the defect, and the instrument is made perfect. At the end of the year, the instruments found to be unsatisfactory are returned to their makers, and those which pass the test are paid for. The returned instruments are usually overhauled by the makers, and the defects remedied. They are then sent back for a trial of another year, at the end of which time they rarely fail to pass.

There are usually from 60 to 100 chronometers on trial at the Observatory, and the apartment in which they are kept is one of the most interesting in the establishment.

The researches connected with the famous "Wind and Current Charts," begun and prosecuted so successfully by Lieutenant Matthew F. Maury, whose services were unfortunately lost to the country by his participation in the Rebellion, are conducted here, and also those connected with "The Habits of the Whale," and other ocean phenomena.

The Equatorial, which is the largest telescope in the Observatory, is mounted in the revolving dome which rises above the main building. It has a fourteen-feet refractor, and an object-glass nine inches in diameter. Its movements are most ingenious, being regulated by machinery and clock-work. Its powers are so great, that it renders stars visible at mid-day; and, if directed to a given star in the morning, its machinery will work so accurately that it will follow with perfect exactness the path of the star, which will be visible through it as long as the star is above the horizon.

The Meridian and Mural Circles are in one of the rooms below.

The Transit Instrument is placed in the west wing of the building, under a slit twenty inches wide, extending across the roof, and down the wall of the apartment on each side, to within four or five feet of the floor. It was made by Ertel & Son, of Munich, and is a seven-foot achromatic, with a clear aperture of 5.3 inches. "The mounting consists of two granite piers, seven feet high, each formed of a solid block of that stone, let down below the floor and imbedded in a stone foundation eight feet deep, and completely isolated from the building. Midway between the piers, and running north and south, is the artificial horizon, composed of a slab of granite ten feet long, nineteen inches deep, and thirteen inches broad; it rests on the foundation, and is isolated from the floor, with the level of which the top of it is even, with a space all around it of half an inch; in the middle of this slab, and in the nadir of the telescope, there is a mortise, nine inches square and ten inches deep, in which the artificial horizon is placed to protect it from the wind during the adjustment for collimation, or the determination of the error of collimation of level, and the adjustment for stellar focus, verticality of wires, and the other uses of the collimating eye-piece."

The great Astronomical Clock, or "Electro-Chronograph," is placed in the same room with the Transit Instrument, and used in connection with it to denote sidereal time. It was invented by Professor John Locke, of Cincinnati, and is one of the most remarkable instruments in the world. By means of an electrical battery in the building, the movements of this clock can be repeated by telegraph in any city or town in the land to which the wires extend. With the wires connected with it, its ticks may be heard in any part of the country, and it will record the time so accurately, that an astronomer in Portland or New Orleans can tell with exactness the time of day by this clock.

It also regulates the time for the city. There is a flag-staff on top of the dome, upon which a large black ball is hoisted at ten minutes before noon every day. This is to warn persons desiring to know the exact time to examine their watches and clocks. Just as the clock records the hour of twelve, the ball drops, and thus informs the city that it is high noon.

To the average visitor the Observatory will not offer many attractions. Yet it is well worth visiting. It is one of the few places in the Capital into which the taint of political corruption has not crept, and in which a lover of his country can feel proud of everything and ashamed of nothing. For this reason, if no other, it merits a visit. It is open to strangers each day between the hours of 9 A. M. and 3 P. M., and an accomplished and genial officer will always be found ready to explain the mysteries of the establishment to those who desire to know them.

CHAPTER XIII.

MAKING MONEY.

The Currency of old Times—How paper Money came to be used—The art of Engraving—How the Treasury Notes are prepared—Precautions against Counterfeiting—The Bureau of Engraving and Printing—Description of the Processes of making and issuing Treasury Notes—Precautions against the improper use of the Plates—Description of the Paper used—Printing the Notes—The Work of the Bureau—A "System of Checks and Balances."

In "the good old days before the War" a very small amount of money was sufficient for the wants of the business community, and the circulating medium consisted only of gold, silver, and copper coins issued by the General Government. Besides these, the banks of the various States issued large quantities of notes, redeemable on demand in the legal currency of the Republic. These notes were generally worth their full value in the States in which the banks issuing them were located, but in other States they were received only at a discount, the rate of which varied according to circumstances.

In those days, the metal currency of the country was sufficient for the wants of the country, as has been said. At the beginning of the war, however, the gold and sil er began to disappear from circulation, as is common at such periods, and those who held the precious coins began to horde them as a safeguard against the evils which all dreaded. This created a stringency in the money market, which was severely felt by all classes of the community. The trouble was made greater by the fact that the Government was demanding heavy supplies of all kinds, to be delivered almost immediately, and that there was not ready money enough in the country to carry on the work required. In order to remedy this, the issue of paper money by the Government was resolved upon. The necessary acts were passed by Congress, and approved by the President, and the notes were issued by the Treasury Department. At first the "Demand Notes," or *Greenbacks*, as they are most commonly called, were issued. Then followed the Postal Currency, then the National Currency, or notes of the National Banks, and lastly the Fractional Currency. The volume of paper money in circulation increased steadily after the first issue. At present it is the main dependence of the country, gold and silver having passed almost entirely out of circulation, and become articles of commerce.

It will be interesting to examine the successive stages by which the notes of the Government are prepared.

The first step in making paper money is to determine upon an appropriate design for the note or bond. This is usually selected by the Secretary of the Treasury The designs for the fractional notes are drawn up in the Treasury; but the Greenbacks, the National Bank notes and the bonds, were designed by the *American Bank Note Company*, and the *National Bank Note Com-*

pany, of New York. The former designed the Treasury notes or Greenbacks, and the latter the National currency.

The design being selected, the plate is prepared by one of the companies mentioned, in its own establishment. Every care is taken to prevent an improper use being made of any part of the work or of the materials used. The great end is to make a note which shall defy the skill of counterfeiters.

The drawing selected for the new note is much larger in size than the note, and is prepared with the greatest care by the best artists. It is photographed upon a steel plate of the exact size required for the note, by which process its proportions are uniformly reduced. The outlines are then faintly cut in the steel, and the plate is sent to the engraver to fill up. This is a very slow process. A part of it is done by hand, but the delicate and intricate tracery work, which will defy any but the very best counterfeiters to imitate, is done by machinery, the machine, of course, being directed by a skilled workman. The greatest care is taken by the engravers to have their work as perfect as possible. Every line is cut separately, and frequently half a dozen different persons are employed upon a single plate. One man excels in landscape, another in portraits, another in animal figures, and to each one is assigned the part he can perform best. From two to four months' constant and careful work is spent on one of these plates before it is ready for use.

The plate which comes thus from the hands of the engraver is not used to print from, but is retained by the company as a mould from which others are made. It is called a "die," and the process by which copies are taken from it is termed transferring.

The original "die" is engraved on soft steel, and after being completed is placed in a crucible filled with animal carbon, and hermetically sealed. The crucible is then placed in a furnace, and subjected to an intense but regulated heat, which volatilizes the carbon and causes it to combine with the steel, thus rendering that metal as hard as it can be made. The "die" is then taken to the transfer press, which is a powerful machine, capable of exerting a pressure of thirty-five tons, by the mere exertion of the workman's foot. The "die" is placed on the press, and a roller of soft steel passed over it, the powerful press forcing the soft metal into each line of the hardened "die." This process is repeated as often as necessary, the press working with mathematical exactness. A raised impression of the original die is thus made upon the roller, which in its turn is subjected to the action of volatilized carbon and hardened. These rollers, or secondary "dies" are carefully preserved in the vaults of the company, and guarded with every possible precaution. When a note plate for printing is wanted, they are passed by the press over a plate of soft steel, and a sunken impression is made. This last plate is then hardened in its turn and used for printing.

In the Treasury notes and National Currency notes, two plates are used, whenever either side of the note is printed in two colors. In the Treasury notes, the face is printed in black and green, and the back in green. In the National Bank notes the face is printed in black, and the back in green and black, the picture in the centre being in black, and the border in green. A separate impression by a separate plate is necessary for each of these colors. This adds greatly to the cost of the notes, but is a cheap process in the end, as it is a sure protection against counterfeits.

It is acknowledged that a perfect fac-simile of the notes of the Government cannot be made by hand. An exact copy of every line, every shade, every letter, can, however, be obtained by photography, which science a few years ago seemed to break down every protection against spurious money. The old bank notes, printed in plain black and white, were imitated so successfully that the banks were obliged to resort to the use of colored notes. A photograph does not reproduce colors, its effects being simply in black and white, and for a while the counterfeiters were puzzled. Their ingenuity triumphed, however. They found a process by which the colored inks used could be removed without disturbing the black ink of the note, and they removed these colored inks, photographed the rest of the note, and reprinted the colored parts in imitation of the originals.

The American Bank Note Company, of New York, in order to prevent this practice, purchased the patent of a new chemical green ink, which had just been invented. This ink has almost put a stop to counterfeiting. It is of such a nature that it cannot be removed from the paper without the paper being destroyed by the means used, or the black ink combined with it on the same note being removed at the same time. The ink has been tested by the most eminent chemists in the land, who have been unable to discover any means of overcoming the obstacles presented by it to the arts of the counterfeiters. There are some few counterfeits in circulation, but unless prepared in a manner to be hereafter described, they may be easily detected.

The paper for the notes and bonds is selected with great care, its quality and finish being important features in a genuine note or bond. It is kept in a place of security, and is, or ought to be, issued with certain restrictions which insure its being used only for legitimate purposes. In the establishments of the Bank Note Companies of New York, not a sheet can leave the paper wareroom without being accounted for, but the Treasury officials are said to be more careless.

The greater part of a Treasury note is printed from the steel plate, but a portion of the colored work is done like ordinary printing, with a hand-press. The plate is kept warm by means of a brazier containing fire, in order to keep the ink in a proper state. The ink is passed all over the plate with a roller, and is then wiped off with a cloth, which leaves it only in the lines or diagram cut in the plate. It is then laid under a winch press, and an impression taken. The presses are required to be of the most accurate description, as the least difference in the position of the plates when two or more colors are used, would ruin the note. The numbers are printed by an ingenious little machine, and the signatures of the Treasurer and Register of the Treasury are engraved on the plate. The National Bank officials sign their notes by hand.

Thus, the reader will see that the best materials, the best skill, and the greatest care are employed in the preparation of the notes and bonds of the Government. The great object is to prevent counterfeiting.

The National Bank Notes are printed by the American and National Bank Note Companies, but the Treasury Notes, the Government Bonds and the Fractional Notes are now printed by the Bureau of Engraving and Printing in the Treasury, which is one of the most interesting and systematic portions of the great Department. A pleasant writer in the New York *World*, gives the following excellent and accurate account of the operations of this bureau:

"The operations of the Printing Bureau develop a degree of skill, ability, and scientific knowledge, as well as of integrity, diligence, and watchfulness, upon the part of its officers and employés that challenges the respectful consideration of the country; the more so that it has existed and increased in spite of an organized effort and determination on the part of moneyed monopolies, who have spared no endeavor to break up the system of printing money by the Government altogether, both in securing legislation, curtailing its operations and in creating prejudice against the officers having charge of it.

"The 'beautiful money,' as I once heard a little child characterize a new greenback, fresh from the Treasury, possesses an added attraction, independent of its intrinsic value, after going through this bureau, and watching its system of operation. I never look at one of these bills since my visit there, that I do not see again the engravers with their fine instruments, carefully tracing the lines which cost so strict precision lest a mistake shall render the whole worthless; the man who attentively superintends and manages the geometrical lathe machine; the strong, keen faces of the printers, blackened with the adjuncts of their toil, each with a girl to attend his press; the women who count the money after it is printed; the superintendents of the drying and counting rooms; and the young ladies, dressed in the most bewitching styles, plainly and neatly, but in exceeding good taste, who act as book-keepers and copyists. All these flash instantly before me, and I feel a personal interest in the work which they so successfully achieve.

"There are fourteen divisions in the bureau, including the machine and store-room. Under Mr. McCartee's management, Henry C. Jewell has organized a system of expense accounts, by which can be known the actual cost of every piece of work done in the bureau, and the aggregate expenses of the bureau by the day, week, or month. This is an ingenious piece of accounting skill, and a great help in making up the records and arriving at the actual affairs of the bureau. The want of such a system of accounts was felt to be a great fault with the old management, and much credit is due to those who have so successfully bridged over the defect.

"The completed plates, as well as the dies and rolls in process of preparation, are all kept locked in the plate vault, to which there are three keys, in the hands of three different custodians, one of whom is appointed by the Treasurer another by the Comptroller of the Currency, and the third by the Chief of the Bureau of Engraving and Printing. To add to the security the watchman, with whom there must needs be collusion in any attempt at fraud, is constantly changed, so that no one of these guardians knows at any time what is to be his post of duty the following night. No roll, plate, or die can be taken from the vault except upon requisition from the Superintendent of Printing, made to and receipted for, by the three custodians. The plates being prepared and locked up, we will now look after the paper used in the manufacture of our securities.

"The material upon which our money is printed has been the subject of discussion and examination ever since the making of the same became one of the recognized institutions of the country.

"How to obtain for this purpose a distinctive paper, difficult to counterfeit, was for a long time the study of experts and detectives connected with the Department. Spencer M. Clark, the originator, and for seven years the controlling genius of this bureau, said, in a letter to the Secretary of the Treasury, in July, 1867 : 'All attempts to place absolute checks on blank paper are futile so long as the paper is an article of commerce. . . . You may surround such paper with triple rows of bars and guard it by a regiment of watchmen uselessly. The paper thus guarded may be secure from theft, but an evil-disposed person can, for a few shillings, procure precisely the same paper, on which money can be printed, without disturbing your guards. Until a peculiar and distinctive paper is alone used, which is manufactured under efficient Treasury control, and of a character which can nowhere else be obtained than in the Treasury, all attempts to protect blank paper in the wareroom will be found puerile and worse than useless, because it will increase cost without increasing security.' The desirable attainment appreciated and looked forward to by Mr. Clark has been accomplished under the management of Mr. McCartee. The paper now used is manufactured by Wilcox & Co., at Glen Mills, near Philadelphia. The Treasury Department has at these mills a Government Superintendent, who is under the control of the Secretary, but directed by Mr. McCartee.

"This Superintendent, Mr. Bemis, takes account of all the paper manufactured, and receipts to the manufacturers for it. Each sheet is registered as it comes from the machine, and the keys of these registers are kept by the Government Superintendent. So complete is this system of registration that not one sheet can, by any carelessness or inattention, fail to be registered. This paper is made with a peculiar fibre running through it, which is produced by the use of jute, a coarse fibrous plant, a native of the East Indies, but lately introduced and grown in the Southern States. Silk has also been used for fibre, but not so successfully as jute. The paper thus manufactured is peculiar and distinctive, and has never been counterfeited except by producing the fibrous appearance in the process of printing, which is easily detected.

"The Government Superintendent has a corps of counters and examiners under his direction, and the paper is carefully counted and examined as received from the makers, and packed away for shipment. The account is sent to the Department, and paid each day by the Secretary. This paper is supplied to the bank-note companies upon requisition from the bureau. Mr. Bemis makes his report to the Printing Bureau of all the paper delivered to him; also, to the Secretary of the Treasury. Every bill received is entered on an invoice book, after being correctly certified to by the proper officer, and then paid by the disbursing clerk of the Treasury Department. When the sheets of paper are ready for use they are first given to the bank-note companies, where the backs and tints are printed. They are then sent to the Treasury Department, where they are carefully counted and examined, the imperfect ones, if there are any, delivered to the Secretary, under whose direction a commission is appointed to destroy them. The perfect backs are held for finishing and printing by the counting division. It is necessary to keep a large number of these on hand, for the reason that the tint has to be thoroughly seasoned, or it will become disfigured or blurred in printing—mashed, as the printers phrase it. These backs are furnished to the printers upon requisition by the superintendent of that particular division. Before going to the printer they are received in the wetting room, counted and wet down preparatory to printing, and are delivered to the printers each morning, every man receipting to the superintendent of the wetting division for the number of sheets drawn each day. The wetting room is a separate division with its corps of counters. At the same time the paper held by it is under the control of the Superintendent of the Printing Division. After a hundred sheets are printed they are delivered to and counted by the counters of the examining division. They are then distributed on the drying racks and run into the drying-room, where they are subjected to a high degree of heat over night. They are then taken off the racks, examined, counted, and delivered to the counting division of the bureau, to be held there for sealing. The process of seal printing is the same as the first, and the sheets have to go through the entire operation a second time to receive the seal, after which they are sent to the hydraulic press-room, where they are subjected to a great pressure, which gives the surface its smooth and beautiful finish, driving the ink into the paper, and causing the figures to stand out in clear relief.

"They are then ready for the numbering-room, where they receive the last touch of printing from machines attended by women and girls. These machines are so adjusted as to change the numbers for a whole series. The two red numbers on each bill are put on by these machines. Great care is necessary in this work that no mistakes are made, and the bills are critically examined to see if they are correct. If mistakes are made they must be altered at once, as the red ink soon hardens and becomes indelible, while at first it is easily removed. The mistakes, if not discovered in time to rectify, are charged to the one who makes them, as this has been found to be the only method possible to establish adequate care on the part of the numberers. The numbering finishes the printing of the money, and the sheets are then carried to the superintendent of the separating division, under whose charge they are trimmed and separated. This process is one of great interest and a vast improvement upon the past manner of doing the work. The separation was formerly accomplished by girls with scissors, and required great care and long time for its tedious fulfilment. Machinery has now occupied the place of all this pains-taking labor. The sheets are put through the separating machines, and come out as carefully cut apart as the most dexterous fingers could have done it.

"They are then needled, which process also requires great care in placing the sheets so accurately together that when they are put through the cutting machines, hundreds of them together, the glittering edge of the blade falls on the right line, never deviating a hair's breadth—a process reaching the perfection of precision. After being cut apart the notes are packed in boxes for delivery to the Treasurer the next morning, and ready to be issued by Uncle Sam, in the multifarious ways opened for their use.

"It is the uniform rule of the bureau that no sheet of paper pass from the custody of one superintendent to his operatives, or to another superintendent without a verified count and a written receipt, which is made a permanent record in a book especially provided for that purpose. At the conclusion of each day's labor, the operatives in every room report to the superintendent, before they leave the building, how much paper they have received, and how much they have finished, returning the balance, and thus completing their account with the Department. The superintendent of each room makes a report on a printed form at the close of each day, which shows first, the amount of paper received by him up to that morning; second, the amount delivered by him up to that morning; third, the amount received during that day; fourth, the amount delivered that day; fifth, the amount on hand that evening. This report is delivered to the Chief of the Bureau of Engraving and Printing, and a duplicate sent to the Secretary. From these reports, the Secretary compiles a report of the operations of the bureau, which must correspond with the one made by the Chief of the Bureau.

"When any given issue of notes or bonds is completed, a report is made to the Secretary of the Treasury, showing when the work was begun, the several dates at which the blank paper was delivered to the several sub-divisions; the amount delivered at each date; the denominations of notes printed; the number of the denomination; the number of perfect and imperfect sheets of each kind, when the manufacture is completed; the several dates at which the finished currency of that issue was delivered to the Treasurer, and the amount delivered at each date, thus making a complete history of the issue.

"As a test of the thoroughness of the system: if a note printed in the Department at any time since its organization be returned to the Superintendent, his books will show the date at which the blank paper was delivered to the Superintendent of Printing; when and by whom the note was printed, sealed, numbered, separated, and delivered to the Treasurer of the United States.

"All the notes for the National Banks are engraved and printed by the bank-note companies in New York; forwarded to the Comptroller of the Currency; delivered to the Chief of the Bureau of Printing and Engraving, where they are numbered, sealed, trimmed, and separated; again returned to the Comptroller of the Currency, and by him delivered to the different National Banks, where they are perfected by receiving the signatures of the President and cashier. The red seal affixed to all the different forms of securities is imprinted in the Treasury Department.

"So complete is the system of checks adopted in the Bureau of Printing and Engraving, that it is difficult to see how it is possible for loss to occur to the Government, either by over-issue or abstraction. The paper is first registered at the mills, and every sheet manufactured has to be accounted for, from the time it is made until it is delivered to the Treasurer, finished, both by the Bureau of Printing and Engraving, and the bank-note companies. To accomplish a fraudulent issue, it would be necessary for a general collusion to exist between the superintendents of the different divisions, and also between the operatives in each division, and between the superintendents and the operatives. The fact that several prominent officers of the printing bureau are appointed by the Secretary, and are in no way indebted to the Chief of the Bureau of Printing and Engraving for their positions, establishes a strong probability against danger. Of the notes and securities partially printed in New York, and finished in the Treasury, a fraudulent issue is clearly impossible without criminal collusion between the companies and the Treasury Department.

"The establishment of this bureau by the Government, has been met from the first by the active opposition of large moneyed monopolies, who have left nothing undone to prevent and retard its operations. Under the supervision of Spencer M. Clark this was particularly the case. By persistent misrepresentations the bureau became notoriously of bad repute, which culminated in a call for an examination by James Garfield, which was conducted by a Congressional committee of which he was made chairman. This committee gave the charges circulated against the bureau and its superintendent a thorough and searching examination, and the majority report reviewed and undermined those charges in an exhaustive manner. Not only the allegations in regard to irregularities in the business concerns of the bureau, but also those concerning the immorality of the superintendent, were carefully investigated by this committee, and a full vindication of both given in the majority report. It was through this effort to displace Mr. Clark that the slanderous stories were first set afloat in regard to the ladies employed in the Treasury Department; and it has taken years to undo the wrong then done. Notwithstanding the fact that this bureau is and always has been considered an entirely separate division of the Department proper, and hence had the reports been true in regard to it, they could not have affected the entire Department; that distinction did not appear to the general public, and in consequence the whole has suffered from the imputation.

"The policy of having our money and securities printed at a point distant from the seat of Government has often been a subject of deprecation. It is at least a matter of questionable propriety—this allowing plates and dies of such great value to remain in the hands of parties only commercially connected with the Government. The exclusive privileges which these companies are able to exercise enable them to control prices and dictate terms to it.

"The following figures from Mr. Garfield's report show the conclusions to which the Committee arrived on this subject: 'Fractional currency produced in the Treasury building costs per 1000 impressions $20.37½. Fractional currency furnished by the bank-note companies costs per 1000 impressions $58.77. Postal currency amounting to $20,192,556, furnished by the bank-note companies, costs the Government $393,548.99; if issued in the Treasury Department the cost would be about $158,571.89. A series of bonds printed in the Treasury costs $10,460.10; the same furnished by the bank-note companies costs $48,370.60. The cost of paper, printing, and numbering United States notes by contract with the bank-note companies is $104 per 1000 impressions; the same work in the Treasury costs $34 per 1000 impressions.' After giving these figures the report says: 'It will thus be seen that a very large amount might be saved to the Government by transferring the work from the bank-note companies to the Treasury Department.'

"Notwithstanding the companies do not register, and the sealing, numbering, trimming, and cutting is not done by them, the part of the work done by the bureau is done at less cost than is that of the companies, although the latter pay the girls employed from 70 to 85 cents a day, while the Government pays from $1.50 to $4.50 per day.

"A great part of the work done in this bureau is done by women and girls. The superintendents spoken of through this article are all women; the counters are women; the books are all kept by ladies; each printer has a girl or woman to attend his press, and pays her himself, although the pay is guaranteed by the bureau; he is obliged to pay her whether he makes a good day's work or not; the price is also regulated by the bureau."

CHAPTER XIV.

JUSTICE.

The Judiciary Branch of the Government—The Supreme Court of the United States—Who comprise it—Its Jurisdiction and Powers—The "Old Senate Chamber"—Description of it—The "most Interesting Room in the Capitol"—Reminiscences of the old Days of the Senate—The Supreme Court in Session—The Opening of the Court—The Chief Justice of the United States—An enviable Position—A Roll of great Men—The former Chief Justices—Chief Justice Chase—Reputation of Judge Chase—Well won and worthily worn Honors—The Attorney General of the United States.

WASHINGTON CITY is popularly regarded as the fountain head of Justice as well as of Law. The Supreme Court of the United States holds its sessions here.

The Supreme Court of the United States is the highest and most august legal tribunal in the land. It is composed of the Chief Justice of the United States, and eight Associate Justices, all of whom are appointed by the President of the United States, by and with the advice and consent of the Senate, and hold office during good behavior. Five of the Justices constitute a quorum for the transaction of business. The Court holds one session annually, commencing on the first Monday in December, and sits daily during the term, Sundays excepted, from 11 A. M., until 3 P. M. The Justices, besides sitting annually in Washington, are each judges of the Circuit Courts. Their circuits embrace the various States of the Union, which are fairly divided amongst them, and after the adjournment of the Supreme Court, they begin to hold their Circuit Courts.

The officers of the Supreme Court are the Attorney-General, a clerk, deputy clerk, reporter, marshal, and crier. The attorneys and counsellors practising in this Court are few in number, and are men of high character and the greatest legal ability. They must have had three years' practice in the Supreme Court of the State in which they reside, and must be men of good standing in their profession, and of good moral character.

The Supreme Court has exclusive jurisdiction over all civil controversies in which a State is a party, except in those between a State and its own citizens. In cases between a State and citizens of another State, or aliens, its jurisdiction is original, but not exclusive. The trials of issues in fact are by jury, but the most of the cases brought before it are decided by the Court. It has appellate jurisdiction from the State and Circuit Courts, in cases which are provided for by law.

The sessions of the Court are held in the main or central building of the Capitol, in the hall formerly used by the Senate of the United States, and known as "the Old Senate Chamber." It is a beautiful apartment, and is regarded by many persons as the most perfect chamber in the Capitol. It is semi-circular in form, is seventy-five feet long, forty-five feet high, and forty-five feet wide in the centre, which is its widest part. A row of handsome green pillars of Potomac marble extends across the eastern, or rear side of the hall, and the wall which sweeps around the western side, is ornamented with pilasters of the same material. The ceiling is in the form of a dome, is very beautiful, and is ornamented with square caissons of stucco. A large sky-light, in the centre of the room lights the chamber.

A handsome white marble clock is placed over the main door, which is on the western side. Opposite, from the eastern wall, a large gilded eagle spreads his wings above a raised platform, railed in, and tastefully draped, along which are arranged the comfortable arm-chairs of the Chief Justice and his associates, the former being in the centre. Above them is still the old "eastern gallery of the Senate," so famous in the history of the country. The desks and seats of the lawyers are ranged in front of the Court, and enclosed by a tasteful railing. The floor is covered with soft, heavy carpets; cushioned benches for spectators are placed along the semicircular wall, and busts of John Jay, John Rutledge, Oliver Ellsworth, and John Marshall, former Chief Justices, adorn the hall.

"The room is furnished in soft, yet sombre colors, and the wood-work is of mahogany so old and dark as to deserve its original name of Madeira-wood, for its rich wine-stains; there is nowhere anything glaring or dissonant, and nothing can exceed the pleasure of the place when on a chilly day the great chimneys, at either end of the loggia behind the Justices, send out the cheerful crackle and flitting illumination of their broad wood-fires. It is perhaps a dull and stupid case which makes the air soporific, the place is vacant save for those who necessarily have to do with it, and if one or more of the reverend seigniors be not asleep they simulate admirably; or it is perhaps a great field-day, there is a full bench of gray, sagacious heads, beautiful women fill their appointed places and rustle all the time after they are in them, civilians throng upon the other side, some orator, erect and stately as a field-marshal, deploys the battalions of his words, the forces of his arguments, and every name of political or legal note, clustering around him on the floor, listens in eager silence. There is Reverdy Johnson with his head of the Cæsars; Black, restless as fire; the venerable Thomas Ewing, who looks as if he had just stepped out of Plutarch; Cushing, in some intense but icy reverie; Evarts, polished and keen as the blade of a rapier."

The hall is very much as the Senate left it, having been only slightly altered to suit the convenience of the Court. It is full of the most interesting memories. Here were gathered the men whom the nation will always delight to call great. It is a woful thing to contrast the Senators who sit in the gaudy hall in the new North Wing with the immortals who once tenanted this Chamber. On the 4th of January, 1859, as the Senate took its leave of the little Chamber for its new hall, Senator Crittenden, of Kentucky, recalled some of the memories of the place in an eloquent address. "This Chamber," he exclaimed, "has been the scene of great events. Here questions relating to

American Constitutional law have been debated, and questions of peace and war decided. Questions of empire, too, have occupied the attention of those assembled in times past. This was the grand theatre upon which these things have been enacted. Great men have been actors here. The illustrious dead that have distinguished this body in times past naturally rise to our view on this interesting occasion. I speak only of what I have seen, and but partially of that, when I say that here, within these walls, I have seen men whose fame is not surpassed, and whose power, ability, and patriotism, are not eclipsed by anything of Grecian or Roman name. I have seen Clay, Webster, and Calhoun, and Benton, and Leigh, and Wright, and Clayton (last though not least), mingle together in this body at one time, and unite their counsels for the benefit of their country. It seems that they have left their impressions on these very walls, and this majestic dome seems almost to echo with the voice of their eloquence. There are hosts of others I might mention, but it would take too long. Their names are in no danger of being forgotten, nor their services unthought of or unhonored."

"The Senate," said Vice-President Breckenridge, on the same occasion, "has assembled for the last time in this Chamber. Henceforth it will be converted to other uses. Yet it must remain forever consecrated with great events, and sacred to the memories of departed orators and statesmen, who here engaged in high debates, and shaped the policy of their country. There sat Calhoun, *the* Senator, inflammable, austere, but not overwhelmed by his deep sense of the importance of his public functions, seeking the truth, and then fearlessly following it. There was Webster's seat, he, too, every inch a Senator. Conscious of his own vast power, he reposed with confidence on himself, and, scorning the contrivances of smaller men, he stood among his peers all the greater for the simple dignity of his Senatorial demeanor. On the outer circle sat Henry Clay, whose imperious and ardent nature, untamed by age, exhibited in the Senate the same vehement patriotism and appreciated eloquence that of yore electrified the House of Representatives and the country. All the States may point with gratified pride to the services in the Senate of their patriotic sons, among whom are the names of Adams, Hayne, Wright, Mason, Otis, Pinckney, and the rest—I cannot number them—who, in the record of their acts and utterances, appeal to their successors to give the Union a destiny not unworthy of the past."

The hall has also its unpleasant memories, for it was here that the famous encounter between Senators Benton, of Missouri, and Foote, of Mississippi, occurred on the 17th of April, 1850, in which Mr. Foote drew a revolver and cocked it, and the matter came near resulting in bloodshed on the floor of the Senate. It was a disgraceful scene, and sent a thrill of indignation throughout the whole country. Here, also, on the 22nd of May, 1856, Preston S. Brooks, a Representative from South Carolina, attacked and barbarously beat Senator Sumner, of Massachusetts, inflicting upon him injuries from which the Senator has never recovered.

The "Old Senate Chamber" is decidedly one of the pleasantest places in the city, and will well repay a visit. A stranger should endeavor to be present at the opening of the Court. Precisely at eleven o'clock in the morning, the door just back of the Judges' platform is thrown open, and the Marshal of the Court enters, walking backward, with his gaze fastened upon the door. Upon reaching the centre of the chamber, he pauses, and cries in a loud voice:

"The Honorable, the Judges of the Supreme Court of the United States."

All present in the chamber immediately rise to their feet, and remain standing respectfully. Then, through the open door, headed by the Chief Justice, enter the members of the Court, one by one, in their large, flowing robes of black silk. There is something very attractive about these old men, nearly all of whom have passed into the closing years of life. They ascend their platform, range themselves in front of their seats, and the Chief Justice makes a sign to the "Crier," who immediately makes the following proclamation:

"O yea! O yea! O yea! All persons having business before the Honorable, the Judges of the Supreme Court of the United States, are admonished to draw near and give their attendance, for the Court is now in Session. God save the United States, and this Honorable Court!"

The Judges and other persons take their seats, and the business of the day begins.

The Chief Justice of the United States is the highest legal officer of the Republic. His position is one of the proudest in the world, and he is looked upon by the people with more confidence and respect than any other member of the Government. It has rarely been the case that the maddest of politicians have ventured to question the integrity of the Court, and the Chief Justice has almost always been safe from political persecution.

The office has been filled from the first by men of high character and great ability. The first Chief Justice was John Jay, of New York, appointed September 26, 1789. In 1794, Chief Justice Jay resigned his position to accept the post of Envoy Extraordinary to England.

President Washington then appointed John Rutledge, of South Carolina, in 1795, during a recess of the Senate. Mr. Rutledge presided at the August term of the Court in 1795, but in the following December, the Senate refused to confirm his nomination. William Cushing, of Massachusetts, at that time one of the Associate Justices, was then appointed and confirmed by the Senate, in January, 1796, but he declined to serve.

Oliver Ellsworth, of Connecticut, was then appointed. He was confirmed by the Senate March 4, 1796. At the close of the August term, 1799, he resigned his position, in order to accept the appointment of Minister Plenipotentiary and Envoy Extraordinary to France. In 1800, John Jay, of New York, was again appointed by the President, and confirmed by the Senate; but he declined to serve.

John Marshall, of Virginia, was appointed by President John Adams, in January, 1801, and confirmed by the Senate. At the time of his appointment he was Secretary of State. He continued to act in both capacities until the close of Mr. Adams's term in March, 1801. He held the office of Chief Justice until his death in 1835. He was justly regarded as one of the purest and most learned judges that ever sat on the bench. He was also noted for his plainness of person and address, and his childlike simplicity and freshness of character.

Judge Marshall was succeeded by Roger Brooke Taney, of Maryland, who was nominated by President Jackson, and confirmed by the Senate in March, 1836 He died in Washington on the 12th of October, 1864 He was a man of pure character, vast learning and great legal ability, and in every way a fitting successor to John Marshall. His decision in the Dred Scott Fugitive Slave case, made him very unpopular with the anti-slavery party, and he was unjustly and cruelly assailed for it. He was too honest not to decide according to his convictions of duty, and too fearless to care for the opposition raised against him.

Upon the death of Judge Taney, President Lincoln was overwhelmed with solicitations from the friends of various public men, each one urging that the vacancy should be filled by the appointment of his favorite. After a careful consideration of all the claims presented to him, Mr. Lincoln adhered to his original idea, and on the 6th of December, 1864, nominated Salmon P. Chase, of Ohio, to be Chief Justice, which nomination was unanimously confirmed by the Senate, and Mr.

Chase was sworn into his office on the 15th of December, 1864. "Notwithstanding his apparent hesitation in the appointment of a successor," says Mr. Carpenter, "it is well known to his most intimate friends, that 'there had never been a time during his Presidency, when, in the event of the death of Judge Taney, he had not fully intended and expected to nominate Salmon P. Chase for Chief Justice.' These were his very words uttered in connection with this subject."

Judge Chase had been Mr. Lincoln's Secretary of the Treasury during his first term, and had conducted the finances of the nation with a genius and vigor which had secured the confidence of the capitalists and people of the country for the bonds of the Government, even when the military situation seemed hopeless. During the political campaign of 1864, he was brought forward prominently as the candidate for the Presidency of the extreme Radical wing of the Republican party, who were dissatisfied with Mr. Lincoln, and this came near occasioning a serious rupture between Lincoln and Chase, a consummation for which certain parties labored most diligently. Fortunately for the country, their labors were in vain. Mr. Carpenter, in his interesting narrative of "Six Months in the White House," says: "The Honorable Mr. Frank, of New York, told me that just after the nomination of Mr. Chase as Chief Justice, a deeply interesting conversation upon this subject took place one evening between himself and the President, in Mrs. Lincoln's private sitting-room. Mr. Lincoln reviewed Mr. Chase's political course and aspirations, at some length, alluding to what he had felt to be an estrangement from him personally, and to various sarcastic and bitter expressions reported to him as having been indulged in by the ex-Secretary, both before and after his resignation. The Congressman replied that such reports were always exaggerated, and spoke warmly of Mr. Chase's great services in the hour of the country's extremity, his patriotism, and integrity to principle. The tears instantly sprang into Mr. Lincoln's eyes. 'Yes,' said he, 'that is true. We have stood together in the time of trial, and I should despise myself if I allowed personal differences to affect my judgment of his fitness for the office of Chief Justice.'"

Judge Chase is a native of New Hampshire, and a member of the famous New England family of that name. He is a nephew of the great Bishop Chase, of Ohio, and was partly reared by him. He is sixty-five years old, and is splendidly preserved. Personally he is one of the most imposing men in the country. His head is grand and massive, and his features are striking and intellectual. The likeness on the Treasury notes is admirable, and will give the reader an excellent idea of the man. In point of ability Judge Chase has few equals, and no superiors in the land. He fills his exalted position with a grace and dignity peculiarly gratifying to his countrymen, who, without respect of party, are justly proud of his fame.

The salary of the Chief Justice is $6500, that of each Associate Justice $6000, and that of the Attorney-General, $8000. The officers of the Court receive salaries proportionate to their positions and services.

The Attorney-General is the Legal Adviser of the

President, and the counsel for the Government in all suits in the Supreme Court, in which the United States are concerned. It is his duty, when required by the President or requested by the heads of departments, to give his opinion, which is generally submitted in writing, upon any matter concerning their departments. He is required to be learned in the law, and to take an oath to discharge faithfully the duties of his office. He is a member of the President's Cabinet, and is allowed an assistant, three clerks, and a messenger.

CHAPTER XV.

THE NAVY YARD.

History and Description of the Navy Yard—A Model Establishment—The Grounds—The Officers' Quarters—The Machine Shops—Excellence of the Work done here—The Iron-Foundry—The Ordnance Department and its Work—The Pyrotechnical Laboratory—The Ship Houses.

THE Navy Yard is situated on the Eastern Branch of the Potomac, at the southern termination of Eighth Street East. A line of horse cars connects it with the Capitol and the upper portions of the city. In the year 1800 several large ships of war were ordered to be built at Washington, and the formation of a Navy Yard at the Capital was begun under the supervision of Commodore Tingey. The present site was chosen and the vessels ordered were constructed as rapidly as possible. This duty performed, Commodore Tingey proceeded to arrange the new Navy Yard with a view to furnishing increased accommodation for the future construction and equipment of large vessels of war. It was at one time hoped that this would become the principal yard of construction belonging to the Government, but the lack of water in the Potomac near Washington has prevented this hope from ever being realized. Still the yard is one of the most important in other respects in the Union.

The Navy Yard covers an area of twenty acres, and is enclosed with a high brick wall. The main entrance is at the foot of Eighth Street East, and consists of a handsome gateway designed by the late Benjamin H. Latrobe, Esq. Just within the entrance are several large residences set apart for the use of the officers (and their families) on duty at the yard. Extensive quarters for the Marines and other enlisted men are close by.

The grounds are handsomely and tastefully laid off, are well shaded, and are kept in excellent condition. Quantities of marine artillery, shot, and shell, are arranged about the grounds both for safe keeping and for ornament. The effect of them in many cases is very fine. Among them are many trophies won by our Navy during the earlier wars of the Republic and during the Rebellion. The beautiful column erected to the memory of the heroic officers and men who fell at the siege of Tripoli, occupies a conspicuous place.

The Machine Shops are extensive, and most interesting. They are kept busy at all times, for this is one of the principal establishments of the Government for constructing the equipments of vessels. The articles turned out here have stood the severest tests, and are acknowledged to be among the best in the service. The anchors and cables made here are particularly good.

Two heavy "Nasmyth," or Steam Hammers, weighing 3600, and 2240 pounds, are used for forging anchors. The forges attached to them are worked by a fan blower, which is turned by the steam engine in the machinist's department. A "Kirk," or Direct Steam Hammer, in connection with a blast forge, is used for working up the scrap iron of the various Navy Yards and war vessels into bolts and blooms.

The massive chain cables turned out from this yard, are made in another shop, which is provided with a Hydrostatic press for testing their strength. Nearly one hundred men are employed in forging these cables.

A separate department is provided for the manufacture of galleys, cabooses, copper powder-tanks, and the various articles of brass-work needed in a ship of war.

The large iron-foundry is kept constantly at work, casting heavy articles of iron used for machinery. Steam cylinders, shafts, and such articles, are made here.

The ordnance department manufactures light brass ordnance, boat howitzers, shot, shells, percussion caps, musket and pistol balls, and improved projectiles of various kinds. The percussion-cap and bullet-making machines are very interesting, as are many of the others in use.

In the boiler-making department, the immense boilers used in the largest class ships of war are made in the most skilful manner. The boilers made here are of the very best description, and are thoroughly and severely tested before being received into the service.

The "machine shop" is fitted up with every description of apparatus used in making marine steam engines and machinery of other kinds. It is one of the most complete establishments in the yard.

The "rolling mill" is provided with a two hundred horse-power engine, and a full equipment of machinery. Here are manufactured all the bolts, sheathing, braziers' and boiler copper used in the Navy, and here the scrap-iron is worked into bolts and bars.

The pyrotechnical laboratory is on the western side of the yard. It employs a large force of operatives. Ammunition of all kinds, rockets, torpedoes, etc., are prepared here.

There are two large ship-houses for building ships, at the edge of the water, one on each side of the yard. One of these is provided with a marine railway for hauling up vessels for repairs.

CHAPTER XVI.

COUNTERFEITING.

Efforts to Prevent Counterfeiting—How the work of Counterfeiting is carried on—Description of the Process—Making Counterfeit Money—Who are the Counterfeiters—The Treasury Plates in the hands of Counterfeiters—Where the Work is done—How the Counterfeit Bills are circulated—Who are the Customers for Counterfeit Money—An infamous Business—The Profits of the Business—Its Dangers—How Counterfeiters are Detected and Captured—The Penalty for Counterfeiting.

THE Government officials honestly and energetically exert themselves to prevent, and to detect the issuing and circulation of counterfeit money; but in spite of all their efforts the notes of the Treasury and the National Banks have been imitated successfully, and each day brings to light some attempt at similar imitations.

Strange as it may appear, the very complicated character of the workmanship of our Treasury and National Bank Notes, offers the counterfeiter his best chance of success, since they enable him to produce an imitation, which like the original depends, with most persons, and even with some good judges, upon its general character for its success. The simpler the note, the harder it is to counterfeit it, for where the lines are few and strongly characteristic, a glance will serve to detect the imitation.

It is for this reason that the notes of the Bank of England cannot be successfully counterfeited.

Counterfeiting requires skill, since the plates from which the bogus notes are printed must be prepared by a process exactly similar to that by which the genuine plates are made, and the workman to be successful, must be a skilled engraver. The majority of the counterfeiters in this country are said to be foreigners, who, having learned and practised their trade in Europe, come to this country for the especial purpose of engaging in this disreputable and dangerous undertaking. Englishmen, Germans, and Italians are principally engaged in it. Sometimes an engraver who has been discharged from one of the Bank Note printing establishments for some fault, or who has fallen into habits of dissipation, becomes a counterfeiter. There was an instance a few years ago, of a singular nature. An engraver, employed in the Treasury Department, was detected in the act of engraving facsimiles of the genuine plates for some outside persons. Fortunately the bogus plates were secured by the Department.

The heaviest operations are carried on in the fractional notes, bills of a larger denomination being generally examined with more care by persons receiving them. Next to the fractional notes, the bills of the National Banks are the most popular with the counterfeiter. They are difficult to imitate, but some very successful counterfeits of this class have been made. Their circulation is so general in all parts of the country that few persons examine them closely, or look to see the character of the picture on the back, which is distinctive in each denomination. The fives of this issue can, without very much trouble, be altered to fifties, which is often done. Indeed, the operations of the counterfeiters with this class of notes are exerted chiefly to alter their denominations. There are few counterfeits, if any, of the whole note now in circulation, and the altered note may be detected by examining the picture on the back, and seeing if it is that which properly belongs on a bill of that denomination.

The *Greenbacks* or *Legal Tenders* are the most difficult of all to imitate. Counterfeits of this class, however, have been issued. The genuine notes being novel in character, and having many distinctive features, are easily recognized, and it is almost impossible to alter the denomination. The green ink cannot be removed without injuring the note, and thus prevents them from being photographed.

Still as we have said, there have been counterfeits of this kind. The fifty and one hundred dollar notes have been imitated successfully. A one hundred dollar counterfeit was executed in St. Louis a few years ago, and with such skill that ten thousand dollars worth of the bogus bills were put in circulation before the counterfeiter was caught and the plate secured.

Notes and bonds are not unfrequently presented at the Treasury for examination, and are found to have been printed from the original plates, but without the authority of the Department.

The question arises how did these plates pass into the hands of these parties? The Government detectives have captured from the counterfeiters fac-simile impressions taken from the plates used in the Treasury. A few years ago such discoveries were common: of late they have been less frequent. Another question of importance is, how do the counterfeiters procure the genuine paper on which their spurious bills are printed, and without which these bills would be worthless?

Very little, if any, of the work of counterfeiting is carried on in Washington. The locality is too dangerous. The manufacturers seek the concealment which a large city affords them, and their principal headquarters are in New York. All sorts of devices are resorted to to disguise and screen the business.

"The dealers in counterfeit money are the most mischievous, and the most difficult to reach, of all who are connected with counterfeiting. They have their agents, confederates, and customers in every city in the country. The circulation of the fractional currency is universal, and as soon as a successful counterfeit is made, large quantities are sent to all points in the country; the mails and the expresses are made the medium of its transportation; the counterfeits are put in circulation simultaneously in different sections, and, if they are good imitations, they are 'shoved' in enormous quantities before they are detected.

"The West is the great market for these spurious issues. There is not a city, scarcely a town, without its agent, and he knows his customers, coolly calculates the question of supply and demand, and does a lively business. Estimating the counterfeits at one-third the whole amount of fractional currency in circulation, the West has its full share of that third—indeed, it is a common remark out West, that the counterfeits, for all ordinary purposes, are quite as good as the genuine notes.

"There, as at the East, the customers may be classed as follows: The small corner grocers, who buy the counterfeits for the very convenient purpose of making change to their customers; the bar-keepers, who can easily work off more or less of this sort of change upon their more or less inebriated patrons, who are not particular what they 'take' from the counter, or from behind it; stage drivers, canal men, butchers, drovers, pedlars, and other itinerants can use this stuff to a considerable amount; and some of it is worked off at the doors of country shows, when people pressing in are more eager to secure a front seat than careful to note the quality of their change. Of course we are speaking only of certain persons in these kinds of business.

"The counterfeiter estimates among his profits the simplicity and cheapness of his tools, if he only intends to make a plate or two; the facility with which the notes can be circulated; the extent and universality of the circulation of the genuine notes, inducing a general carelessness as to their character; the chances of avoiding detection in his business; the chances of escape or non-conviction; and the direct profit derived from the work itself. To the manufacturer it is not, on the whole, a paying business. Those who have been arrested present no indication of unusual prosperity, and they say they have barely made a living. They make the plate or plates and the dealers make the money, paying the engraver about the same sum, or a little less, than he could have earned in an honest manner.

"Before the counterfeits are put in circulation they go through so many hands, and there are so many partners in the scheme, that the individual profits are quite small. The dealers get from thirty to forty-five dollars on the hundred, and of course the small users, who receive or expect to get the full represented value of the note, pay proportionately larger prices. As there is no redemption, beyond the actual cost of the plate and materials employed in the manufacture, it is all profit, as the bills pass from hand to hand. But considering the risks, the detectives have not yet caught the counterfeiter who would, or could, under the circumstances, admit that he had done a paying business.

"The most successful counterfeiter was the notorious Jerry Cowsden, who executed a counterfeit of the fifty cent note so skilfully that it could not be distinguished from the genuine. He was arrested some time since, but before his arrest he had succeeded in putting into circulation upwards of $5000 of the bogus notes. So excellent were the counterfeits that the notes will probably pass the same as the genuine, and even be redeemed eventually.

"The Treasury officials make untiring exertions to arrest and bring the counterfeiters to justice. Experienced detectives are employed, and the assistance of the police authorities of the great cities is judiciously retained. The game is a difficult one, however.

Of the numerous communications sent to the authorities advising them to watch certain men, not one in ten ever amounts to anything. They are frequently prompted by malice and the desire to annoy some one by police espionage or an unjust arrest. Of all the counterfeit cases that have been brought to the notice of the police in the last four years, only five or six have been brought to a satisfactory conclusion. It took several months to work up two of the most important cases, and in every instance the capture was complete, comprising the plates, tools, machinery and criminals.

"The men detailed go prepared for any emergency or resistance, and have full authority to do all that may be necessary in the 'premises,' to the extent of breaking in and searching thoroughly in all suspected spots. The marshal lends valuable assistance, takes care of the counterfeiters when caught, keeps all the plates, 'traps' and tools till the trial is over, and the prisoner, if convicted, is sent to Sing Sing, while the plates are sent to the Treasury Department at Washington."

CHAPTER XVII.

THE PUBLIC SERVANTS.

Number of Office-Holders in the United States—Immense patronage of the Government—The Number of Officials in Washington—How Offices are given—Who procure them—The rush for Office—Mr. Lincoln's Opinion of Office-Seekers—Offices given as a Reward for Political Services—The Government Employés in Washington—Their Life and Peculiarities—How Offices are taken away—Demoralizing Tendencies of Official Life—An Independent Official and an Indignant Cabinet-Minister—A Roland for an Oliver—Daily Life at the Departments—A Tread-Mill Existence—Facts about Salaries— Blackmailing the Government Clerks—How Political Contributions are made—An infamous System—The Penalty of a Refusal—A Satisfied Ambition—Advice to Office-Seekers—Anecdote of Judge Chase—The Female Clerks—Account of the Women employed in the Departments—Who they are—Their Lives and their Duties—Injustice to them by the Government.

It is generally known in a vague way that the patronage exercised by the General Government is enormous, but few persons have any idea of the actual proportions which it has assumed. We cannot better express them than by stating that there are within the gift of the Government nearly sixty thousand offices, drawing salaries of various sizes from the Treasury of the United States. This vast army of officials is scattered over the entire country, but each individual office-holder is attached to Washington City by the ties that connect him with the Department of the public service to which he belongs. Of this army, about one-tenth, or six thousand, are on duty in Washington. This estimate includes every Government employé whose name is on the rolls of the various branches of the Governmental service, from the grade of Assistant Secretary of a Department down to the humblest laborers employed in the public offices and workshops. They are of all ages and conditions, of both sexes, and hail from all parts of the country. They are generally strangers to the city, and hold their offices by so uncertain a tenure that they rarely acquire the character of citizens of Washington. They are merely sojourners at the Capital.

At the beginning of each new Administration, if there is a change of politics as well as of rulers, the civil service of the Government is overhauled. "To the victors belong the spoils," is the maxim of each conquering party, and the holders of office under the old Administration are summarily turned out of their positions to make way for the friends of the party into whose hands the Government has fallen. Over fifty thousand positions of various kinds are to be filled, and it is safe to say that for each position there are at least twenty applicants. Each Member of Congress, or Secretary, each prominent supporter of the Administration in the various States, has his hands full of gifts; for it is the local politicians, after all, that regulate and decide the filling of offices within their respective States. The only trouble is to decide upon the proper person. There are so many things to be considered, and, as only one man can be appointed to each office, there are so many to be offended. The Members of Congress, and other politicians certainly have their annoyances at this period, but the persons most to be pitied are the President and the Heads of the Departments. They are terribly bothered by the claims of the politicians, and the demands made upon them by office-seekers of all kinds. Mr. Lincoln had a holy horror of office-seekers, and he had reason to be, for they caused the poor man some of the unhappiest moments of his life. He tried hard to be just; and, as a matter of course, pleased the successful ones, but was bitterly assailed by those whom he was compelled to disappoint. "As the day of his reinauguration approached, he said to Senator Clark, of New Hampshire, 'Can't you and others start a public sentiment in favor of making no changes except for good and sufficient cause? It seems as if the bare thought of going through again what I did the first year here, would *crush* me. . . . To remove a man is very easy, but when I go to fill his place, there are twenty applicants, and of these I must make nineteen enemies.'" Again, he said: " Sitting here, where all the avenues to public patronage seem to come together in a knot, it does seem to me that our people are fast approaching the point where it can be said that seven-eighths of them are trying to find how to live at the expense of the other eighth."

Fitness for the position is the last quality demanded of an aspirant to a public office. Men are appointed for political reasons. They serve a political party with fidelity, and contribute actively to its success, and as a reward they are given positions in the service of the Government, to which they are utterly unsuited. Consequently, the public service is often badly performed, and the country at large is the sufferer. No corporation or mercantile house of any standing would think of employing the men upon whom the Government is forced to depend. There is, however, some hope that a change will be inaugurated ere long. We have a law, passed within the last few years, for the reformation of the Civil Service, by which incompetent officials may be driven out of office, and properly qualified persons put in their places. But the law is yet unexecuted, and the need of Reform is growing greater every day.

It is astonishing to see the amount of ingenuity, energy, and patience exerted by persons to secure offices to which they are utterly unsuited, and in which they can earn but a meagre support. The same qualities exhibited in any other pursuit would secure independence, if not wealth, but thousands every year prefer depending upon the Government. These Government employés are made up of all sorts of people. Poets, preachers, lawyers, doctors, artists, authors, merchants, mechanics, and loafers are represented in the various Departments. You may know them as a general rule, by their affectation of superiority to the townspeople, their general seedy appearance, and their imitations of the airs and style of "the first men in the Government." They form a "colony" distinct in themselves from the Washingtonians proper, with whom they rarely deign to associate unless they are invited to partake of their hospitality, when it is amazing to see how quick they are to accept the invitations. The majority of them are unmarried, or persons whose families are at their own homes. Living is high in Washington, and few of the salaries given are sufficient for the support of a family. The majority of the clerks live at private boarding houses, or in private families, where the " home comforts" exist only in the imagination of the landlady. Board is high and absorbs a large part of the official's salary. After paying for clothing, washing, and other necessaries, there is very little money left, so that the average Government official has no chance of saving money, while enjoying an abundant need of economy.

The appointments to positions in the various Departments and their branches are nominally made by the President, but in reality the choice is made by the officers immediately in charge of the Departments, their recommendations being usually acted upon by the President. Changes are constantly made, and the struggle for place goes on from year's end to year's end. As appointments are not made upon the merits of the applicants, their capacity forms no ground for retaining them in office. Each one holds his place, it would seem, by the favor of the head of his bureau, and as a means of retaining that place, he exerts himself to secure the favor of his chief. The higher officials take good care to show their subordinates that they hold their official lives in their hands. Consequently, there is a feeling of uncertainty on all sides, from the Secretary down, as no one knows at what moment he may lose his place. Men fawn upon their superiors in the most sickening manner. They exert themselves, not to discharge their official duties well and faithfully, but to please their superiors by flattering them and by pandering to their whims and caprices. All things considered, it must be confessed that the holding of a Government clerkship is not calculated to develop the manhood of the incumbent. One so rarely sees true manliness and independence in the Departments, that when these qualities are encountered, you feel like hugging the owner of them. The writer calls to mind a Federal official, far removed from the corrupting influences of the Capital, whose independence and fearlessness of official displeasure were so absolutely without a parallel that they deserve to be perpetuated. The official in question was a resident and a citizen of the sovereign State of Alabama, and it may be, had never seen the glories of Washington, and, having never laid eyes on his official chief, may have regarded him as a mere man, like unto himself. He was postmaster of his village, and, what was greater in his eyes, proprietor of the only store in the town. To him, the Post-Master-General of the United States, wishing to obtain certain information respecting the geography of the State of Alabama, addressed this note:

"DEAR SIR: You will please inform this Department at your earliest convenience how far the Tombigbee River runs up.
"Your obedient servant,
"AMOS KENDALL, Post-Master-General."

The unterrified holder of a Government office at once replied as follows:

"Hon. AMOS KENDALL, Post Master-General,

"SIR: I have the honor to acknowledge the receipt of yours of the —— inst., and to report, in accordance with your instructions, that the Tombigbee River doesn't run up at all.

"Your obedient servant,
"JOHN THOMPSON, P. M."

The reply was apt, but the august head of the Post-office Department couldn't see the joke, and his dignity was fearfully ruffled. Determined to make an example of the daring Alabama P. M., which should strike terror to the soul of every official in the Department, he sent the following communication to the offender:

"SIR: You will, upon receipt of this, close the office of which you are in charge, and forward your accounts to this Department, as the Post-office at —— is discontinued from this day.

"Your obedient servant,
"AMOS KENDALL."

In due time the Post-Master-General received the following reply to his order:

"Hon. AMOS KENDALL, Post-Master-General,

"SIR: Yours of —— received. In accordance with your instructions, I forward to you the accounts of this office, which has been closed by your order. They are as follows:

John Thompson, in Account with the United States,
    Dr.
To Cash received for postage $0.75
    Cr.
By paper and string used in tying up letters
        sent by mail $1.50
    Balance due John Thompson $0.75
            " Your obedient servant,
                        "JOHN THOMPSON."

The business of the Departments commences at nine in the morning, and closes at three in the afternoon. The balance of the twenty-four hours the clerks are at liberty to employ as they please. Some are men of family, others have nothing to occupy their time. Some spend their leisure in lounging about the city or the hotels, or in visiting their friends, and others are employed as newspaper correspondents for the journals in the States. Their spare moments hang horribly upon them, and they are eager for any means of driving off the "blues," a disease peculiar to Washington.

Their duties are very monotonous, consisting of the same set routine every day, and the holidays are few and far between.

The salaries paid by the Government to its employés are small. A Secretary at the head of a Department receives $8000. Assistant-Secretaries, $3500. The Chief Clerks of the Departments receive $2200; the heads of the Bureaus from $3500 to $2000; and the salaries of the other clerks range from $1800 to $600.

Small as these salaries are, the recipient is not allowed to enjoy the whole amount. The "Party" by whom the official was put in power claims a share of it for political uses, and clerks and other officials must pay the black-mail thus levied upon them, or lose their positions. Whenever money is needed for political purposes, the leaders of the party in power, whatever be its name, levy an assessment upon each Federal office holder, the sum being regulated by the size of his salary. The clerks and the humbler officials are bled the worst, the great officers of the Government being too powerful to be fleeced in this way. A circular is sent to each, informing him that he is expected to contribute a certain specified sum for the purpose of defraying the campaign or contingent expenses of the Party. He is requested to send it to a designated person by a given time. This polite request is the most peremptory of orders, and is understood as such. No clerk dares disregard it; his official head would answer for his disobedience. It matters not how much he may need the sum, which is always a heavy burden to him; he must pay it or give up his place to some one who will be more liberal. His family may be ill, or in want of comforts of the most necessary kind, his wife may need the money for the household expenses, but no matter, it must go to the Party. True, he has earned it, but it is not his. It is the Party's, and if his wife or child were dying for want of the comforts that money would bring them, he would have to pay it to the bloodhounds demanding it of him, or lose his place under the Government. Of course, the reason that would be assigned for his discharge would not be his refusal to pay this money. Oh, no! the political black-mailers understand their work better than this. They would accuse him of incompetency, neglect of duty, or something of the kind, or the Chief of his bureau would, without assigning any reason, politely tell him that his services were no longer required, and set him adrift. And not once a year only do these black-mailers make their demands. The poor clerks are liable to them at any moment, whenever the Party needs money, and out of a salary of one thousand dollars, may be forced to "*give*" the Party one hundred dollars.

The worst feature of all is, that it is said that much of the money thus extorted goes into the pockets of private individuals. It is well known that all of it, if really used by the party demanding it, is expended for the purpose of perpetuating those systems of bribery and corruption which have disgraced our land in the eyes of the civilized world.

It is astonishing to see what a rage for office possesses some people. They seem incapable of doing anything but hang around the Departments, hoping to obtain employment. Some years ago, a politician applied to the President for "a thousand dollar Consulship." The President informed him that the Consulships were all disposed of. He then said he would take "a clerkship in the Treasury office." He was equally unsuccessful in this attempt. He did not give up, however. He kept on trying, and at last succeeded. He became "*deputy door keeper to the Senate coal cellar.*"

To the thousands of persons who display such eagerness to secure appointments under the Government, we would say, "Turn your attention to some honest pursuit, and let Government clerkships alone." To nine men out of ten such offices are utterly unprofitable. The salaries are small, the tenure by which they are held is uncertain, and they are generally more vexatious than profitable. A Government clerk has at least twenty rivals constantly working against him, each one hoping to have him discharged and be appointed in his stead. All sorts of stories are told to his prejudice, many of which are devoid of truth, and he is haunted with a fear of being discharged, which poisons all his pleasures. He has no independence while in office, no true manhood. If his opinions differ from those of the Chief of his bureau or department, he dare not express them, for his Chief tolerates no such liberty on the part of his subordinates. He must openly avow his implicit faith in all his superiors, on pain of dismissal, and must cringe and fawn upon them, even when they rob him—in the name of their Party—of his earnings. And, at last, at the end of four years, if not sooner, he must give way to some new man, and seek some other mode of employment. His clerkship has, by this time, unfitted him for business pursuits, or mechanical labor. It has engendered ideas and habits which are so many obstacles to his success in other employments. To young men of ambition a Government clerkship of any kind is a positive curse, and is generally the ruination of a promising career.

It is related of Chief Justice Chase that, after graduating, he "found himself dependent on his own exertions to procure his support in his law studies. He went to Washington intending to open a private school. He waited in vain for scholars till his money was gone, and then, feeling discouraged, asked his uncle, the Senator, to get him an office under the Government. The old gentleman promptly refused: 'I'll give you half a dollar to buy you a spade to begin with,' he said, 'for then you might come to something at last, but once settle a young man down in a Government office, he never does anything more—it's the last you hear of him. I've ruined one or two young men in that way, and I'm not going to ruin you.'"

About 600 of the Government employés in Washington are females. They are employed in several of the Departments, principally in the Treasury. The highest salary paid them is about $900, the lowest $600.

"General Spinner's account of the beginning of the present system of female employment in the Treasury is that female employés were smuggled in. When Treasury notes were first issued, four of them were engraved on a sheet, and it was necessary that they should be separated with shears before sending them out of the Treasury. 'I went to Mr. Chase,' says General Spinner, 'and said to him, a woman can use scissors better than a man, and she will do it cheaper. I want to employ women to cut these notes.' Mr. Chase assented heartily, the more so that the attention of every one in Washington was then very specially called to the number of women once in comfortable and in many cases in affluant circumstances, who were suffering absolute want. In the city, many well known residents were reduced to privation almost immediately after the war broke out, and from desolated Virginia, families came by hundreds, demanding food for themselves and their little ones. Women came who had lived handsomely in the neighborhood of Washington, whose homes were destroyed and who actually had not the means to procure a shelter. To these, whenever possible, places were given as 'clippers,' and so the first foothold was gained. Those who needed work received it, and political influence was never brought into the question. But this was no light employment, easy as 'cutting paper' may sound. Incessant use of the shears made warts and blisters on many delicate hands; the number of hours' service required was regulated by the pressure of business, and often these ladies were kept until dark at their work and obliged sometimes to return to the Department after night. These appointments were made informally, and had no official existence. Females were not mentioned in appropriation bills until a year or so later. Those first employed during 1862 were paid out of the fund for temporary or additional clerks, at the rate of $600 per annum.

"When it was noised abroad that employment was given in Washington to women, crowds of them from almost all parts of the country began to flock here, and then appeals were made to Members of Congress and other influential men to obtain positions for the new-comers. Some of these—most of them, perhaps, I should say—were cases of absolute necessity; others left good employment, to come for the sake of variety and seeing life at the national Capital, or because $600 sounded very large in the country. Many were the disappointments in consequence; for board was found to eat up the greater portion of the salary, and the new life demanded a different style in dress from the ordinary garb of a village school mistress, or farmer's daughter, accustomed to act as 'help.' Naturally, in the wholesale making of appointments which followed the successful experiment made of allowing women to perform other duties than the mechanical one of clipping notes, care was not always used in making selections. Many were appointed during the war, who had no business inside the department, who earned nothing, and who brought discredit on all their companions. Some of these were young, thoughtless girls, who, pleased with the new life, passed much of their time in flirting and chattering and laughing boisterously in the halls of the building and on the staircases. These are all gone now, or else grown wise enough to know better. Those who pass through the halls of the Treasury to-day see nothing of the kind—at least I do not, nor do I know of any one who does, and I write with authority and not as one of the scribes.

"In view, then, of the means of securing a clerkship being through political influence alone, whatever may be the merits of the case, it is surprising that so many who are really deserving—so many who, from culture and past associations, ought to rank, and do rank among the highest and best in the land—are to be found in all the departments. Women hold clerkships in the Treasury, War, Interior, and Post-office Departments. During two or three months in the year, the Agricultural Department furnishes employment for some, and the year round two have positions there. The temporary employment in the Department last named is the putting up of seeds for distribution, and occasionally copying is given out. Of those mentioned as being permanently connected with the Department, one is a taxidermist, and the other assists Professor Glover in taking charge of the museum. The latter is the widow of a Western editor, and at one time had entire control of the paper, an agricultural one, herself. She is a woman of much intelligence, and has made a study of botany and natural history, which enables her to fill her present position with credit to herself. The taxidermist who prepares the birds and insects for the museum, is spoken of by the officials of the Department as being a proficient in her profession. She is a German, and has been connected with the Department two or three years. She has a private room in the building.

"It may be mentioned here that the Commissioner of Agriculture, while he favors the employment of women, has discouraged the establishment of clerkships for them in his Department, simply because of the manner in which appointments are made. He says that for the three positions as copyists, which a bill now before Congress proposes to give to females in that Department, he has already received a hundred applications, backed by the strongest political influence. If, he says, he could himself select women from among those he knows who need the places, and who are women of high standing, intellectually and morally, he would gladly furnish them with work, but under the present system, he dreads the battle before him.

"In the Quartermaster-General's Office, the only bureau of the War Department where there are female clerks, provision is made by law for thirty, and the number is always full, but never exceeded. Most of these are widows of army or navy officers, or children or sisters of those who have been killed or injured in the war. Others among them have no war claims, but have other reasons quite as good for needing the positions. Many belong by birth and education to the highest class of society; others, while lacking the superior advantages of the first, have equal reason to be honored and respected. The work done in this office is copying and recording, and sometimes the registering of letters, which last is entering in a book an abstract of their contents, with the names and addresses of the writers. Three comfortable rooms are given up to these ladies, and they are furnished with all the usual office conveniences. The rooms are not so handsome as those in the Treasury, but are much less public. No male clerks are in these rooms. The work is under the sole charge of a lady, who is, herself, one of the best representatives of female clerks of the higher class. She is the widow of a naval officer who died in the service, and is a lineal descendant of Benjamin Franklin. At all times, as now, she has occupied a high social position. She has children dependent on her. Although her duties are attended with greater responsibilities than are incident to those placed under her charge, she receives the same salary, $900 per year. Some of the clerks in this bureau have been in other days wealthy, and accustomed to every luxury. The same is, however, true of every bureau where women are employed. It may be stated as a fact that, whereas a man by his vote or his electioneering services may secure employment under Government, a woman must attain it through her dire necessities and her bereavements. In the bureau under discussion, I am told by one of the officers connected with the Quartermaster-General's office, this is specially true. He assured me that great care has been used in the appointments made, and party pressure has secured the admission of very few.

"In the Patent Office, fifty-two female clerks are allowed by law, who have rooms given up to their use in the building. One of their number superintends the work done by them, which is chiefly copying. This superintendent is said to be a woman of remarkable business capacity. One of the clerks in this office was mentioned to me as the daughter of a major in the late war, who died a year or two ago, and left this young lady, who is highly educated, dependent on her own exertions for her support. Another is the widow of a surgeon who was killed during the war. Some ten or twelve women have work given them from the Patent Office, to be done at their homes. This is usually the drawing of models. Those who have fixed salaries receive for their drawings $1000 per annum. Others are paid by the piece, and make as much as those who give the work out will allow. Such work is rarely distributed justly. I have heard great complaints that some who are favorites are allowed to do more than their share, while others have barely enough work given them to make it worth doing.

"A few female clerks are employed in copying pension rolls in the Pension Office, who have a room provided for them in the Patent Office building.

"In consequence of the number of letters failing to reach their destination, passing to and from the army, the work in the Dead Letter Office increased rapidly during the war. When it was found necessary to increase the number of clerks, women were appointed, many of whom still hold their positions. There are forty-seven female clerks, who address 'return letters' —that is, letters which have miscarried, and which are to be returned, if the signature or anything in the body of the letter gives any clue to the writer of it. There are ten women who fold the 'dead letters,' and there are three who translate foreign letters. All dead letters are opened by the male clerks, who occupy an extremely imposing-looking room, large and well ventilated, on the second floor in the Post-office building. Around the upper portion of this room runs a gallery, in which the female clerks are at work. They are thus placed directly under the roof, where there is no attempt made at ventilation. This gallery is the receptacle of all the foul air from the room below, and it is believed that the sudden death of one of the female clerks, some two or three months ago, was in consequence of constantly breathing this poisoned atmosphere. Among those who are employed in this office, is one old lady sixty-seven years of age, who has been there for three years, and who does the same quantity of work required of the younger ones—the re-directing of 200 letters every day. This lady has a remarkable history. She is the widow of a clergyman; when the war broke out, her only son became hopelessly insane, and, to use her own words, 'As he could not go to the war, I went myself.' As an assistant manager of the United States Sanitary Commission for a certain State, she raised $10,000 in money, and collected and distributed 90,000 hospital articles. She was in the field, in the hospital, and travelling between certain large cities until the close of the war. Just as she finished her great work, she had the misfortune to fall and break one of her limbs. This confined her to her room for six months. Her daughter's husband died about this time, leaving her with three children, and little or no income. Not long afterwards the mother was defrauded of some property, and thus the whole family found themselves dependent on their own exertions for their support. After an unsuccessful attempt at taking boarders, the mother and daughter determined to come to Washington and apply for clerkships in the departments. 'Friends tried to dissuade us,' says the old lady; 'they said we must not come here to mingle with such people as they thought were in the departments, but I said if it were true such persons were here, we might see them, but never *mingle* with them. But we have *not* seen them. I have been three years in the Post-office Department, and my daughter is in the Treasury, and we have met none but respectable women.'

"In speaking of the Treasury Department, in relation to the employment of women as clerks, great care is necessary. It is so difficult to give a fair idea of the condition of any class which has been made the subject of such persistent attacks. Let me say, in the first place, that if intimate personal knowledge of a subject can give any one a right to express a strong opinion upon it, I have the right to give one on this subject, and yet it is not opinions, but facts, which I wish to use. I know not one woman, but many in that Department, and I have known some of them for six or seven years. I have yet to have the first one pointed out to me concerning whom wrong was known. I have heard of some such, but I do not believe they could be found in the building now. And in view of writing justly I have made inquiries and have received from heads of bureaus and from clerks alike the same reply. 'Take the same number of women from any class of society and you will scarcely find as many of refinement, cultivation, and perfect propriety of demeanor as you will find here.' Such targets for newspaper and Congressional abuse have these clerks been made, that each seems to feel herself responsible for the honor of the whole. A year ago the question agitating all was, 'Will we be given a man's pay where we do man's work?' But now it seems preferable to bear with the glaring injustice than, by endeavoring to be righted, endure the humiliation of another debate in Congress. In relation to the injustice mentioned, it should be known that the salaries of women clerks are fixed by law, and if they work so well that more difficult tasks and more responsible duties are given them, they are promoted to desks similar to those filled by men with a salary of $1800 per annum, and are paid the same as the newest and most ignorant appointment, $900. In some of the bureaus, it must be admitted that there are women who do not earn half the last sum, who are retained because some prominent man urges it. One was pointed out to me, a relative of a certain minister to a European court, who is unable to do the simplest counting correctly. I know of others who habitually shirk work and let the burden fall on their more willing companions, but these are the exceptions which any one who writes from personal knowledge can well afford to mention. Then, too, it cannot be said that *all* are ladies by right of birth or education. Some have been chambermaids, some cooks, some nurses. Two or three years ago every dissatisfied servant wanted to get into the Treasury. A very few of these have made good clerks, and, so far as I know, all have acted as becomes respectable women. It is truer nowhere than it is in the Departments, that every one finds her own level. The fact of being in the Treasury proves nothing for or against a woman socially. What she has been before she will remain if she chooses. To the ladies *par excellence* the best society of Washington is at all times open. The true state of affairs is too well known here for clerical work *per se* to make or mar a woman's social status. Having noticed these facts let it be understood that there is a great mixture in the Treasury, while at the same time it is to be understood as well, that about seven hundred women hold positions there, and it could not be expected that all should be taken from the higher classes.

"The Internal Revenue Bureau is one which deserves very special mention, not only because of the number of women who are employed in it, but equally for the kind of work they do. Copying, and beautiful copying, is the least of their clerical attainments. The writing of one of these copyists in particular looks like copperplate, it is so firm and regular, and such varieties of style are used. The husband of this lady died on Christmas day, and an appointment has been given her in the bureau in which he was a clerk, as a support for herself and her child.

"The lady in charge of one of the divisions in this bureau, where copying, recording, and filing of letters is the principal work, has held her present position for seven years. She is highly spoken of by all who have business dealings with her, as possessing every qualification necessary to the discharge of her duties. Her salary is the same as that of the most ordinary clerk, $900 per annum. Every man who entered the office at the same time as herself has been gradually promoted to the highest salaries, or found better employment outside, while she remains, and must remain, unless Congress should amend the law, unrewarded, no matter how diligent are her labors. A man who has charge of a division usually receives at least $1800, and some receive as much as $2500, per annum. There are forty-five female clerks in this division. Of them there is but one who has no one but herself to support, and she is a woman of fifty, with white hair, not a giddy young girl.

"Another is a widow with a daughter, also a widow, and her two little ones to provide for. The outside life of women like these can well be imagined. The six hours passed in the office are probably the least fatiguing of the day. Inevitable sewing must be done, and, where so many are to be cared for, it often happens that it is necessary for meals to be cooked at home. Many of the women clerks live in attics or in shabbily furnished rooms in remote corners of the city, and prepare their food, of the plainest description, by means of a gas stove.

"Many of the women clerks in the Internal Revenue are employed on 'head work,' as it is called in contradistinction to mechanical copying. Some of these sort papers to be filed, and, as returns of 150 different kinds are received at the office, it is necessary to know the nature of each document before any assortment can be made, and to be well acquainted with the routine work of the bureau. Others are employed to some extent in examining, approving and recording reports of surveys of distilleries and other important papers, and so highly is the business capacity of these esteemed that their opinions are received without question. This is probably one of the most incessantly busy offices in the Department, and its general superintendent says the women clerks are the most attentive to their duties, and that he wonders at it, since they have no incentive to work, well knowing that no reward of better pay is in store for them.

"In almost every bureau of the Treasury women are employed, and it being impossible to mention all, the three which are allowed female clerks by law, and do not have them, under the head of temporary clerks, are selected. One of these has been noticed already, the other two are the offices of the Comptroller of the Currency and the Treasurer.

"In the former, besides copyists and correspondents, there are those who count money to be sent to the national banks, and others who count the mutilated or defaced money returned by the banks for redemption. Among the last is one who is considered very remarkable as a detector of counterfeits. She has detected spurious notes in many instances which have passed through the hands of skilful bank officers and been considered genuine.

"One young lady in this office has charge of the correspondence with the national banks and engraving companies; the letters are written for the most part from memoranda prepared by the chief of the division. There is a complicated routine connected with this work I have no space to describe, but the desk is a most important one, and was formerly occupied by a male clerk receiving $1400. The desk was taken from him because he was 200 letters behind hand. The work is now always up to date, and has been during the four or five years this lady has had it under her charge.

"Another important desk is that of the young lady who prepares an abstract of the circulation issued to and returned by national banks, by means of which an immediate answer can be given when information is asked as to the outstanding circulation of any particular bank. Another laborious work, requiring great care and exactness, is preparing an abstract of the number of notes of each denomination returned by each bank.

"Many of those employed in this office are women of superior attainments and known social position. One there is, who was among the first appointed in the office, who is a native of the District. She resigned some three or four years ago to be married, and after the short interval of two years returned a widow with a child to support. Her husband, a physician, died very suddenly. He had been an assistant surgeon in the army.

"In the Treasurer's office women are employed as copyists; as counters of money, old and new, and of coupons; to compare drafts and pay-warrants; as accountants; and to discount torn notes and prepare burnt and partially destroyed money for redemption."

CHAPTER XVIII.

THE ARMY MEDICAL MUSEUM.

Ford's Theatre—Scene of the Assassination of President Lincoln—The Medical Museum of the U. S. Army—Value of the Museum—The Officers in Charge—Objects of the Institution—The Collection—The Library—Curious Objects to be seen here—The Craniological Cabinet—The Japanese Manikin—The Microscopic Department—Wilkes Booth's Skull—General Sickles's Leg—The "Treasures of the Nation."

On 10th Street West, between E and F Streets North, there is a plain stuccoed building, which a few years ago was suddenly thrown into painful prominence in the history of the country. At the time of its erection it was hoped that it would become the best and most popular theatre in the city, but no one dreamed that it would ever be the scene of such a terrible tragedy as that which occurred within its walls. It was built and conducted by John T. Ford, Esq., a well known and popular manager, from whom it derived its name.

On the night of the 14th of April, 1865, President Lincoln was assassinated by John Wilkes Booth, while witnessing a performance in this theatre. He was conveyed from the box in which he was shot, to a dwelling-house on the opposite side of the street, where he died at twenty-two minutes past seven o'clock the next morning.

The theatre was immediately closed by the Government, as it was felt that the place was henceforth too sacred to be put to its former uses. The action of the Government was endorsed by the entire country, and, in accordance with the national wishes, Congress purchased the building from Mr. Ford, and remodelled it for the use of the Government. It has been rendered fire-proof, and the interior has been thrown into a large square hall, with a gallery running around the upper part. It was formerly used as a receptacle for the captured archives of the Southern Government, but it is now used to contain the collection of the Medical Museum of the Army of the United States.

"Scientific men regard the Army Medical Museum as one of the most important adjuncts of the Government. In a war like the war of the rebellion, when the medical department was brought into contact with every species of wound and every sort of disease, a vast deal of knowledge, necessarily of benefit to suffering humanity, must be acquired. It is the object of the Medical Museum to illustrate the wounds and diseases treated during the war, while the medical and surgical histories of the war now in preparation will give the process of treatment and its results.

"Dr. J. J. Woodward, formerly of Philadelphia, has been the inspiring genius of the Museum. He has been most ably assisted by Dr. Otis, also of Pennsylvania. Dr. Woodward has charge of the medical and Dr. Otis of the surgical department. The former has in preparation the medical, the latter the surgical history of the late war. The first volumes of both histories are now ready, and 5000 copies of each will be issued by this Congress. In the first of the medical volumes the bulk of the space is taken up with tabular statements of the diseases which prevailed and the numbers dying of each during the entire period of the war. The succeeding volumes will treat of these diseases, the treatment pursued, and give photographs of the organs affected in each disease.

"In the past two or three years a medical and surgical library has been collected in connection with the Museum. This library now contains about 19,000 volumes, conveniently arranged in the fire-proof building of the Museum, and open to the public under essentially the same regulations as those of the Library of Congress. Many rare books belong to this library. One of these was among the first of printed books. The very first books printed after the art of printing was discovered were religious and medical works. The one to which I refer was published in Venice in 1480, and is the work of Petrus de Argelatu. It is illuminated and bound in vellum. Another rare work is a copy of Galen, which belonged to the Dutch anatomist Vierodt, and has been annotated by him. These books and others as valuable have been purchased by the agents of the Museum abroad, who are instructed to be constantly on the lookout for valuable works to be sold. Generally they are bought for a nominal price. Since the scope and character of the library have become known physicians throughout the country have become interested, and many valuable contributions have been received.

"The Museum preserves specimens of the organs affected by diseases treated in army hospitals. Specimens of all peculiar cases are preserved. Also, there are specimens of bones fractured by missiles of all kinds, and wherever possible specimens of the soft parts of the body wounded have been preserved. The various missiles are shown, and the form taken by them on striking the body. It will easily be seen how much material for the study of pathology is thus afforded. Besides such specimens as those just indicated there are numerous skeletons of animals of all kinds, birds, fishes, and reptiles, to be used in the study of comparative anatomy, among others, skeletons of the horse, the buffalo, the grizzly bear, the elk, the walrus, and the ray. One of these last, caught in the James River, has been presented to the Museum. Those who have read the early history of Virginia compiled in the old time may remember that it chronicles the fact that once, when Captain John Smith of wonderful memory was one day bathing in the James River, he received a sudden shock, and many days elapsed before he recovered from it. It was supposed that he was struck by the 'stingaree.' Now the 'stingaree' is a corruption of the stinging ray, and such a specimen is shown in the Museum. The ray is a fish of the cartilaginous species, not having the vertebrated form. It has wings, each measuring about fourteen inches across the widest part; and it has a very long tail, in which is implanted a sting which resembles in its effects a shock of electricity, and produces temporary paralysis. The ray darts in among a shoal of fish, electrifies them, and then proceeds to devour them.

"An especial source of pride in the Museum is the large and valuable craniological cabinet. It contains nearly 1000 specimens, including a large number of crania of existing tribes of Indians, a series of skulls from tumuli, and many rare specimens of artificial deformation of the cranium. It is the most complete cabinet of the kind in the country. Among the specimens of artificial deformation of the skull are those of Flathead Indians. These skulls are a great blow to phrenology. They are perfectly flat on top, forming almost a right angle with the forehead. This singular deformity is esteemed a beauty among the Indians of this tribe, and the children of the chiefs must, because of their rank, have the flattest heads of all. Boards are tightly bound to infants' heads from the time they are born until their heads cease to grow, and thus the desired effect is produced. It would naturally be supposed that the brain would be injured and probably reduced in size, but such is not the case, hence the contradiction to phrenological dogmas. By measurement the brain capacity is found to be very great—greater than that of certain other tribes of Indians, neighbors to the Flatheads, who use no such devices to alter the skulls given them by nature. Phrenologists used to maintain that by using artificial means for developing certain bumps on the skull and depressing others certain desirable characteristics would be developed and undesirable ones suppressed; but it appears that the inner surface of the cranium by no means corresponds in elevations and depressions to the outer surface. The method used for measuring the brain capacity of a skull is singular to those outside the medical profession. Small shot are poured in through a hole in the top of the skull, and these run into all the little nooks and corners until the cavities are all filled. Then the shot are poured out and measured.

"Some Indian arrows were shown which had been extracted from soldiers stationed on the plains who had fallen victims to Indian vengeance. The arrow-heads are made of barrel-hoops, and are so sharp that they easily cleave a skull. One arrow was shown me sticking through a portion of the shoulder-blade of a buffalo. The point of the arrow was on the outside of the bone, showing that the arrow-head had passed into the body of the buffalo on one side, through it, entering the bone on the opposite side.

"The collection of Dr. Gibson, late of the Pennsylvania University, is now included in the Army Medical Museum. It was purchased at the sale of the effects of Dr. Gibson's son, himself a prominent physician in Richmond, Va., up to the time of his death. In this collection are several pictures of patients afflicted with cancer, some of them painted by Dr. Gibson himself, but these are of small value. The most valuable portion of the collection is the number of specimens showing how bones knit after being fractured.

"One of the curiosities of the Museum is a Japanese manikin, which, by the way, is not a man, but a woman. The Japanese idea of the internal structure of the human form divine is, to say the least, peculiar. It is hard to say on what it can possibly have been founded. The heart is represented as a red apple and the liver as a yellow one, and the stomach bears a strong resemblance to a pomegranate. The lungs are five green leaves of the oak-leaf pattern grouped together. These organs are piled inside the body after a promiscuous fashion, the lungs being below all the others.

"Models of the most approved plans for hospitals used during our war are shown in the Museum; also models of the various styles of ambulances.

"The microscopic department of the Museum is by far the most interesting, but to give any idea of it would require a more extensive knowledge of the scientific use of the microscope than I possess. Dr. Woodward has made many and valuable discoveries by its means and many improvements in its use. During almost every session of Congress some of the Representatives and Senators are invited to the Museum. Dr. Woodward gives an exhibition of the wonders made visible by the microscope and demonstrates the means by which it is made of benefit in the science of medicine and surgery. When the Medical Convention meets in Washington these exhibitions are given the assembled doctors, and invariably call forth unbounded admiration. Indeed the members of the medical profession throughout the country who have any knowledge of the Army Medical Museum and its several departments are enthusiastic in its praise, and as the extent of the collection becomes better known its usefulness is widely increased, not only by affording opportunities of study to the professional man, but also in promoting the ends of justice in supplying evidence for comparison in criminal trials.

"Among the specimens preserved are the bones of the amputated legs of General Sickles and General T. W. Sherman, and that portion of J. Wilkes Booth's skull which was fractured by the fatal ball. It is a singular fact, and strikingly illustrative of poetical justice, that the fatal wounds of Wilkes Booth and his victim were strikingly alike—that is to say, the balls entered the skull of each victim at nearly the same spot, but the trifling difference made an immeasurable difference in the sufferings of the two. Mr. Lincoln was unconscious of all pain, while his assassin suffered as exquisite agony as if he had been broken on the wheel."

CHAPTER XIX.

THE LIBRARY OF CONGRESS.

The new Halls of the Library of Congress—A model library—Description of the Arrangements for storing the Books—History of the Library—The first Purchases—Vandalism of the British—Mr. Jefferson's Library—Growth of the Collection—The great Fire—Destruction of a Part of the Library—The new Collection—Mr. Spofford appointed Librarian—What he has done for the Library — The Collection increased — Purchase of Peter Force's Library—The new Copyright Law—Rules of the Library—Description of the Collection—An Object of National Pride—The Law Library—The most complete Collection in the World—Description of the Law Library.

The three halls which contain the magnificent National collection known as the Library of Congress, occupy the whole of the western projection of the main building of the Capitol, above the basement. The entrance is from the Rotunda, through a narrow passage way which leads directly into the central hall of the Library. The halls are among the most beautiful and elegantly constructed in the Capitol. They are fire-proof, and are admirably adapted to their purposes. The material used for the fitting up of the room, shelving, etc., is cast-iron.

The main hall is 91 feet long, 34 feet wide, and 34 feet high, with three stories of iron book-cases on either side. "On the lower story are alcoves 9 feet wide, 9 feet 6 inches high, and 8 feet 6 inches deep, with seven shelves on each side and at the back. On the second story are similar alcoves, excepting that their projection is but 5 feet, which leaves a gallery resting on the fronts of the alcoves beneath 3 feet 6 inches in width. A similar platform is constructed on the alcoves of the second story, forming a gallery to approach the upper book-cases, thus making three stories, receding as they ascend. These galleries, which are continued across the ends of the hall, are protected by pedestals and railings, and are approached by semi-circular stair-cases, also of cast-iron, recessed in the end walls. The ceiling is wholly composed of iron and glass, and is embellished with ornate panels and foliated pendants. The pilasters which divide the alcoves are tastefully ornamented, and the whole is painted a delicate cream color, relieved by gilding.

This beautiful hall opens upon the western portico of the Capitol, from which a fine view of the city, the river, and the Virginia shore opposite is obtained.

Two large halls, constructed more recently, extend from the main hall eastward, one at the north and the other at the south end of that hall. They are each 95 feet long, 29 feet 6 inches broad, and 38 feet high. They are constructed of iron and are finished like the main hall, the principal difference being that they have each a fourth tier of book-shelves. The total cost of the halls has been nearly $300,000

The history of the Library is an interesting one. It grew from a very small beginning, and very slowly. On the 24th of April, 1800, Congress, at the suggestion of Mr. Jefferson, appropriated the sum of $5000, to be expended by the Clerks of the two Houses, under the direction of a Joint Committee, for books for the use of those bodies, and the various officers of the Government. In 1802, regulations were adopted for the government of the Library, and a Librarian was appointed. When the British burned the Capitol in 1814, the entire collection, numbering 300 volumes, was destroyed, the British soldiers and sailors using the books as materials for firing the North Wing.

Mr. Jefferson, with a view to remedying the loss, and relieving himself of the financial difficulties in which he had become involved, offered his own library to Congress. His collection was large and valuable, numbering about 7500 books. His proposition was accepted by Congress in January, 1815, and he was paid the sum of $23,950 for his library, which was transferred to Washington, and placed in the Post-office building, where Congress was sitting. In 1818, it was removed to the Capitol, and temporarily placed in a room near the Chamber of the Supreme Court. In 1825, it was placed in the hall it now occupies. It was the nucleus of the present Library. Some of Mr. Jefferson's political enemies had labored hard to prevent the purchase of his library by Congress, and Mr. King, of Massachusetts, endeavored to cause the insertion of a clause into the bill authorizing the purchase, requiring that all books of an atheistical, irreligious, and immoral tendency found in the collection, should be rejected, thus attempting to revive an old slander upon the great Statesman. To the surprise of Mr. Jefferson's enemies, the collection was found unobjectionable on the grounds indicated by Mr. King, and particularly rich in Bibles and theological and philosophical works.

In December, 1851, the Library numbered 55,000 volumes. On the 24th of December, a defective flue set fire to that portion of the building, and the hall and 35,000 volumes were destroyed. Twenty thousand volumes, among which was fortunately the greater part of Mr. Jefferson's collection, were saved, in consequence of being in an adjoining apartment.

The Library was removed to another room, and appropriations were made by Congress for the rebuilding of the hall and the purchase of new books. These appropriations were liberal, but the misfortune of the Library was that it had not a director competent to the task of making it really useful to the public. The real life and growth of the Library date from the appointment of the present Librarian, Mr. Ainsworth R. Spofford, of Cincinnati, in December, 1864. Mr. Spofford brought to his new position a practical acquaintance with books, and with the wants of the reading public. He at once set to work to reorganize the Library, and soon had it arranged upon the plan which has since proved so useful and convenient to the readers using the collection. "The Jeffersonian system of classification was abandoned as unsuited to the necessities of readers consulting a large library, and a new catalogue of the books, arranged alphabetically under the head of authors, was issued, followed by another catalogue, arranged according to subjects. Congressmen, now finding that the Library was of practical use to them, voted liberal appropriations for its enlargement, and (in 1866) the books which had been collected by the Smithsonian Institution—numbering some 40,000 volumes in all—found a resting place on its shelves, relieving the Regents from the expense of caring for them. The Library of Peter Force, purchased of him for $100,000, was a more valuable acquisition, embracing some 45,000 separate titles, among which were many valuable works on early American history, with maps, newspapers, pamphlets, and manuscripts, illustrating the colonial and revolutionary epochs."

By the terms of the Act of 1870, relating to Copyrights, the Librarian of Congress is placed in charge of the entire copyright system of the country. All entries and records relating to copyrights are made and kept in his office. The law also requires that two copies of the best edition of each copyrighted book shall be deposited with the Librarian of Congress, within thirty days after the publication of the same.

There are now about 200,000 volumes in the Library, and the number is being daily enlarged by the operations of the copyright law, and by judicious purchases. An excellently arranged catalogue has been printed, and can be consulted at any time while the Library is open. The whole system is in charge of a Joint Committee of the two Houses of Congress, but the regulations for its government are prescribed by the President of the Senate and the Speaker of the House. The Library is kept open every day except Sunday, during the Session of Congress, from 9 A. M. until 3 P. M., and for the same time on Tuesdays, Thursdays, and Saturdays during the recess. Any one may consult the books in the hall, under certain prescribed regulations, but only the following persons are privileged to take them away: the President of the United States, the Vice-President, the Members of the two Houses of Congress, Judges of the Supreme Court, Cabinet Ministers, the Diplomatic Corps, the Secretary of the Senate, the Clerk of the House, and the Agent of the Joint Committee on the Library.

The following rules are required to be observed by all visitors to the Library:—"1. Visitors are requested to remove their hats. 2. No loud talking is permitted. 3. No readers under sixteen years of age are admitted. 4. No book can be taken from the Library. 5. Readers are required to present tickets for all books wanted, and to return their books and take back their tickets before leaving the Library. 6. No reader is allowed to enter the alcoves."

The Library is one of the pleasantest places in the Capitol, and one of the most interesting. "In the South Wing are the treasures of the Force collection, now being catalogued and classified, and partly piled up in stacks. There are nearly 1000 volumes of American newspapers, including 245 printed prior to 1800: a large collection of the journals and laws of the colonial Assemblies, showing the legislative policy which culminated in their independence; the highly prized publications of the presses of the Bradfords, Benjamin Franklin, and Isaiah Thomas; forty-one different works of Increase and Cotton Mather, printed at Cambridge and Boston, from 1671 to 1735; a perfect copy of that rarest of American books, Eliot's Indian Bible; and a large and valuable collection of 'incunabula,' illustrating the progress of the art of printing from its infancy. The manuscripts are even more valuable than the printed books, including two autograph journals of George Washington—one dated 1775, during Braddock's expedition, and one in 1787, at Mount Vernon; two volumes of an original military journal of Major-General Greene, 1781–82; twelve folio volumes of the papers of Paul Jones while commanding American cruisers in 1776–78; a private journal left by Arthur Lee while minister to France in 1776–77; thirty or forty orderly books of the Revolution; forty-eight volumes of historical autographs of great rarity and interest; and an immense mass of manuscript materials for the 'American Archives'—a documentary history of America, the publication of which was commenced by order of Congress. The only cause for regret connected with this wing of the Library, where the literary treasures collected by Peter Force are enshrined, is that his life could not have been spared long enough to have seen his beloved collection so well cared for by the Republic.

"In the North Wing are the illustrated works and collections of engravings, which always attract visitors, who can sit at the tables there provided for their accommodation and enjoy the reproductions of the choicest art treasures of the Old World. In the upper gallery of this wing are bound copies of the periodicals of all nations, embracing complete series of the leading magazines of Great Britain and of the United States. An adjacent attic hall is devoted to the collection of newspapers—those repositories of general information which had been ignored prior to the administration of Mr. Spofford, but to which he has paid especial attention. Among the unbroken files are those of the New York *Evening Post* from the issue of its first number in 1801, the London *Gazette* from 1665, the French *Moniteur* (royal, imperial, and republican) from 1789, the London *Times*, and the London *Illustrated News*. The prominent daily journals of New York are now regularly filed, and bound at the close of each year, and there is a complete set of all the newspapers which have been published in the District of Columbia, including over one hundred which no longer live.

"A rigid enforcement of that provision of the copyright law which makes it obligatory to deposit in the Library a copy of every work 'entered according to act of Congress,' secures a complete collection of American publications, which could not be otherwise obtained. These copyright books are of increasing importance, extent, and value, and will constitute a curious record of the growth and style of our national literature. There is, of course, a complete collection of all the varied publications of the Federal Government, and by law fifty additional copies of each work are printed for the Library of Congress, to be used in a well-regulated system of international exchanges, which brings in return the valuable public documents of other nations. Liberal appropriations are annually made by Congress for the purchase of books and newspapers, while the large amount of binding required is executed at the government printing-office without taxing the funds of the Library. The annual appropriations—after provision has been made for the foreign and domestic serials, and for the most important issues of the press abroad in jurisprudence, political economy, history, and allied topics—are distributed in the purchase of books in all departments of literature and science, no general topic being neglected, although as yet none can be assumed as being complete. To that end auction lists and trade catalogues are assiduously read and profited by, and especial attention is paid to the collections of dealers in second-hand books—those purveyors for good libraries.

"The Library of Congress is thus beginning to assume national proportions, and is rapidly gaining on the Government libraries at Paris and at London, while it is made more practically useful than any other great library in the world by the annual issue of a printed catalogue of its accessions. With this catalogue—arranged alphabetically by authors and again by subjects—it is an easy task for the frequenters of the Library to obtain books on any subject desired, especially when they can obtain the further aid of the accomplished librarian and his willing assistants. The practical result is shown by the register of books taken from the Library by those enjoying that privilege. Fifteen years ago not more than three out of five Congressmen used the Library; now nine out of ten take out books, some having over a hundred volumes during a session Nor can any one visit the Library at any time when its doors are open without finding from ten to fifty citizens seated at the reading-tables, where all can peruse such books as they may request to have brought to them from the shelves. The Library is thus thrown open to any one and every one, without any formality of admission or any restriction, except that slight barriers exclude the visitors from the book-shelves, and prevent them from taking down the books without the knowledge of the attendants.

"Bibliophilists find on the shelves of the Library of Congress much that they regard as precious, although the profane call it trash, in the shape of formidable folios exquisitely printed by the Elzevirs, or the small Aldus editions of classical authors, easily carried in the capacious pockets of students of the old school. Many of these antique books, like the dowagers and the spinsters who grace the wall-seats of a ball-room, will gratefully repay a little attention from the student, and will convince him that in literature, as in agriculture, 'the new grain cometh up from the old fields.' The ashes of Wycliffe were scattered to the winds, but despotic bigotry could not destroy Wycliffe's Bible. Homer's birth-place and his burial-place are unknown, but numerous editions of his Iliad delight and interest our heroes and our lovers. Our legislators ponder over the patriotic sentiments of Sidney, our poets read Tasso and Dante, our scholars revel in the writings of Molière and Cervantes, and our statesmen, in studying the noble diction of Bacon, draw 'from the well of pure English undefiled.' Indeed, the Library of Congress with its two hundred thousand volumes, may well be compared to the island of Delos, where the ancient Greeks and their neighbors used to meet in peace, forget foreign and domestic strife, and harmoniously join in festivities—for it is the neutral ground of the national metropolis, where learning is domesticated, and where studious men and women can meet, undisturbed by the noisy clamor of mercenary politicians."[*]

The Law Library occupies the room in the basement of the main building formerly occupied by the Supreme Court of the United States. The apartment is semi-circular in form. The massive, groined arched ceiling rests upon short Doric columns. The wall is adorned with a sculptured group representing Fame crowned with the rising sun, and pointing to the Constitution, while Justice holds her scales.

The collection numbers upwards of 25,000 volumes, and forms the most complete law library in the world. The book cases project from the semicircular wall, and form alcoves. "Lincoln's Inn Library contains a large number of books, but two-thirds of them are works on miscellaneous subjects; and although the library of Halle, in Germany, and the Advocates' Library at Edinburgh are rich in ancient law, neither of them has been kept up: indeed, the latter was recently offered for sale. In the Law Library of Congress are every volume of English, Irish, and Scotch reports as well as the American; a copious collection of case law; and a complete collection of the statutes of all civilized governments, including those of Russia since 1649, which

---

[*] Col. T. B. Thorpe.

fill about one hundred quarto volumes. There are also many curious law-books, including the first edition of Blackstone's Commentaries, and an original edition of the report of the trial of Cagliostro, Rohan, and La Motte for the theft of Marie Antoinette's diamond necklace. All the books are bound in calf or sheep, of that 'underdone pie-crust color' in which Charles Dickens described a lawyer's library as dressed, and they are much used by the eminent legal gentlemen who come to Washington to practise in the Supreme Court."

CHAPTER XX

WASHINGTON NIGHT LIFE.

Monotony of Washington Life—The Search for Excitement—Gambling in Washington—The "Hells"—Dangers of such Places to Strangers—The First Class Houses—The "Congressional Faro Bank"—Description of the Establishment—Precautions against Intruders—A magnificent Establishment—A Palace of Vice—The Proprietor—The Suppers—The Game—How it is Played—Who are the Players—A Distinguished Company—The great Men of the Land—Where the People's Money goes—Picture of the Group around the Table—Food for patriotic Reflections—The Theatres—Their Business and Frequenters—The Canterburies.

TIME hangs heavy upon the hands of the large floating population of Washington. There is a terrible monotony about life at the Capital, and after the shades of night come down over the city, the men who pass through so much excitement in the day bethink themselves of some way in which to pass with pleasure the hours of the evening. Dinners, balls, parties, the theatre, and other amusements less innocent, fill up the time of some, but those who have no invitations out, or who do not care to accept them, seem to gravitate by a common impulse towards the gaming hells which abound in the city. During the war about one hundred gambling houses flourished in Washington. One of these establishments during the years 1863, 1864, and 1865, cleared over half a million dollars annually. In 1866 it was closed by its proprietors because the times were too dull to warrant its continuance, and in that year its profits were over $50,000. In 1865 it was estimated by the Chief of Police that there were about 550 professional gamblers in the city, or about one gambler to every 218 inhabitants. Since the war the number has steadily decreased, and it is estimated that there are now about seventeen gambling houses left in the city, and about eighty professional gamblers. Of this number only some four or five establishments are what a professional player would term "respectable houses."

The majority of these houses fully merit the name of "hells," which is commonly applied to them. They are managed and frequented by the most infamous of the gambling class, and every advantage is taken of a visitor. He is made drunk, forced to play, and swindled out of his money. The frequenters of these places are desperate men, and think nothing of taking human life. Visitors are expected to play, and are apt to be insulted or assaulted if they refuse to do so. The amount of villainy practised in these places increases as one descends the scale of their so-called respectability.

You never see in these places the men who frequent the first-class houses. The visitors are men who cannot get into better establishments, and strangers to the city. The proprietors keep their decoys about the hotels and the Capitol. They are well-dressed, rather flashy in fact, have an abundance of time on their hands, and are the most obliging men in Washington. They will introduce themselves to strangers, take any amount of trouble to show them the sights of the city, and end by taking them to the "hell" to which they are attached, where the poor victims are made drunk and fleeced of their last dollar. They rarely make a mistake in accosting strangers, for they are keen judges of human nature. They know a lobby-agent or an office-seeker at a glance, and as their time would be wasted upon such persons, pass them by and ply their arts upon those who are strangers and sight-seers. They are paid a commission upon the winnings from their victims, on which they live very handsomely.

Persons visiting Washington would do well to avoid these over-civil "gentlemen." Honest men are not apt to take up sudden fancies for strangers, and such demonstrations afford good presumptive evidence that your new acquaintance is plotting your ruin. Give him a wide berth. Decline his proffered civilities, and beware how and where you drink with him.

The better class houses cluster in the neighborhood of Pennsylvania Avenue and Thirteenth and Fourteenth Streets. They generally occupy the floor or floors above the street of some house, the lower part of which is used for business purposes, and a stranger, passing by, would never suspect their true character. One of these, the most elegant of all, is known throughout the city as "the Congressional faro bank," and is located not far from Willard's Hotel. The visitors to the better class houses are men of note, whose names are well known to the world, and who are such as can be depended on by the proprietor. It is not easy for a stranger to obtain admission to these places. He must be properly introduced, that is, brought to the establishment and vouched for by some one known to the proprietor. Once admitted, he has "the run of the house." The lower class houses are patronized by Government clerks and employés, and by the ordinary visitors to the city.

We shall introduce the reader to the establishment known as "the Congressional faro bank," which is a fair sample of the four "first class houses" of the city. It occupies the two upper stories of a handsome brick building, the street floor of which is used as a drug store. You enter from the street, pass through a brilliantly lighted vestibule, and up a flight of handsomely carpeted stairs. Near the top of the stairway is a latticed door, which is closed. By pulling a silver bell knob at one side, you ring a gong bell within, and the negro on duty opens the door, having first identified you through the lattice work. Passing through the door which closes behind you, you ascend three more steps, and turning to the left, find yourself in a magnificent and brilliantly lighted apartment. The room opens into another back of it, and the two occupy the entire floor of the building. The apartment is magnificently furnished. The walls are hung with fine paintings, the floor is covered with an exquisite carpet, and the furniture is of the richest and costliest description, the windows are draped with heavy curtains which, besides heightening the air of splendor which pervades the apartment, prevent the light from being seen without, and give to the upper part of the house, as viewed from the street, a deserted appearance. Several tables are scattered through the room, at which men are always seated at play. Go when you will, some one is engaged in the fascinating and demoralizing business of the place. The back room is used as a dining-room, and here an elegantly spread table provides the visitor with refreshments. The table and wines are free to all, and no one is urged to play as a means of paying for the repast; but the shrewd proprietor understands that few of his guests will have the assurance to partake of his elegant hospitality without risking something at the tables in the front room.

The proprietor is, as men of his class go, a gentleman. That is, he is a man of dignified bearing, courtly manners, and, according to his lights, an honest man. He would scorn to commit what he considered a mean or dishonest act. He will treat you fairly, entertain you elegantly, win your money by legitimate means, and send you away with the impression that he is the cleverest fellow in Washington, and you heave a sigh of pity as you think of his calling.

The servants attached to the establishment are negroes of the better class. They are well trained, many of them having been brought up as the *valets*, or butlers of the Southern gentry, and answer better for such places than whites, inasmuch as they are quiet, uncommunicative, attentive and respectful. One of these men is always in charge of the front door, and visitors are admitted with caution.

The playing in this establishment is fair. It is carried on in the front room, and the principal game is faro. Towards ten or eleven o'clock it begins in earnest. "The table upon which faro is played is not unlike an ordinary dining-table with rounded corners. At the middle of one side, the place generally occupied by the head of a family, the dealer sits in a space of about three square feet, which has been fashioned in from the table. The surface is covered with tightly drawn green ladies' cloth. The thirteen suit cards of a whist pack are inlaid upon the surface in two rows, with the odd card placed as at the round of the letter U. The dealer has a full pack, which he shuffles, then inserts in a silver box with an open face. This box is laid upon the table directly to his front.

"The cards are confined within it by a stiff spring, and the top card is visible to all, save a narrow strip running about its edge, which is necessarily covered by the rim of the box to hold it securely in position.

"The game now begins. The dealer pushes out the top card, and the second card acted upon by the spring rises and fills its place. The second card is pushed off likewise laterally through the narrow slit constructed for the exit of all the cards. This pair thus drawn out constitutes a 'turn,' the first one being the winning and the second the losing card; so that the first, third, fifth, and in the same progression throughout the fifty-two are winning cards, and the second, fourth, and sixth, etc., are the losing cards. The betting is done this way: The player buys ivory checks and never uses money openly. The checks are white, red, blue, and purple. The white checks are one dollar each, the red five dollars, the blue twenty-five and the purple one hundred dollars.

SCENE IN A FIRST-CLASS GAMBLING HOUSE DURING THE SESSION.

"Having provided himself with the number of checks (which in size resemble an old-fashioned cent), he lays down any amount to suit his fancy on any one card upon the table—one of the thirteen described. Suppose the deal is about to begin. He puts one hundred dollars in checks on the ace. The dealer throws off the cards till finally an ace appears. If it be the third, fifth, seventh, etc., card the player wins, and the dealer pays him one hundred dollars in checks—the 'bank's' loss. If, however, it were the second, fourth, sixth, etc., card the dealer takes the checks and the bank is one hundred dollars winner. Should a player desire to bet on a card to lose, he expresses this intention by putting a 'copper' in his checks, and then if the card is thrown off from the pack by the dealer as a losing card the player wins. This is practically all there is in faro.

"It should be remembered that the losing cards fall on one pile and the winning cards on another. When only four cards remain in the box there is generally lively betting as to how the three under cards will come out in precise order, the top one being visible. In this instance alone the player can treble his stake if fortunate in his prediction. This evolution is a 'call.'

"A tally board is kept, showing what cards remain in the box after each turn. This provision is to guard the player. Of course four of each kind are thrown from the box—four aces, etc.

"Some one will inquire how does the bank make it pay while taking such even chances? In this way.

If two of a kind should come out in one 'turn,' as, for instance, two aces, half of the money bet on the ace, either to win or lose, goes to the bank. This is known as a 'split.' They are very frequent, and large sums pass to the dealer through this channel. That is where the bank makes the money."

So much for the game. As for the players, they are thoroughly "respectable." They are chiefly men past the first flush of youth, and who play deliberately. Here you may see the "great" men of the country, as they are called, men high in position and authority in the land, men charged with the handling of the funds of the Nation. Governors, Congressmen, officers of the Army and Navy, who are not ashamed to sport their country's "blue and gold" in such a place, men whose names are as familiar to the public as the newspapers which herald them. The proprietor counts the magnates of the land among his intimate friends, and many of the "leading" men of the land have been his debtors for loans and advances of money. It is a well known fact in Washington, that during a certain memorable session of Congress, the proprietor of a noted gambling house received from the Sergeant-at-Arms nearly all the salaries of a large portion of the members of the Lower House, upon presenting orders made payable to him by said members. It makes you feel nervous to see paymasters and financial agents of the Government clustering around the tables of this place, and you are not surprised when you hear that a certain individual whom you have noticed here, has become a defaulter. Sad as is the assertion, it is nevertheless true, that the greatest men this country has ever produced, have been frequenters of these fashionable "hells." This has been so for fully half a century, and it seems hardly probable that the practice will be discontinued. The proprietor of the house we are discussing could tell you rare stories of our great men, living and dead, in and out of power, but he never talks of these things except in the society of his confidential friends.

The Washington Correspondent of the New York *World* is responsible for the truth of the following picture of a scene characteristic of this establishment, the truthfulness of which will not be denied by any one well informed as to matters at this place: "A single glance at the group around the faro-table when a game is going on will reveal the character and, in many cases, the identity of the persons playing. It is a well-dressed group, and well worth a sketch. Here, standing shoulder to shoulder with an ex-General in the Union army, whose long straight hair, dark mustache, and somewhat flashy dress mark his identity, is a Senator of the United States, bearded and tall, with a face corrugated with wrinkles—the result of intense study of knotty financial problems. No man is better known than he. He holds in his hand a stack of blue chips, worth twenty-five dollars apiece. He wins well and loses better, and is warmly welcomed at the gaming-table. Vis-à-vis, watching a huge pile of red chips, valued at five dollars apiece, stands another United States Senator. He hails from the far West, and this is a favorite resort of his after the evening dinner party or caucus. He does not exhibit the same stoicism as his friend, but flushes and pales alternately through his gray beard as his money is doubled or swept away by the turn of the cards. One of the richest mining States on the Pacific coast also has a representative from the Senate, who is a desperate better, and who always plays to win. His bald head fairly glistens with satisfaction when he has a 'run.' Another far Western and another Pacific State watch the cards through Senatorial spectacles, but the bets they make are few and far between.

"The 'other end of the Capitol' is represented none the less fully. Two sons of Illinois are to be seen here— the one tall, with a full, flowing beard, the other short and thick-set, with hair and mustache black as the raven's wing. New York, Pennsylvania, Indiana, Ohio, Missouri, and Minnesota seldom fail of having one or more representatives around the faro-table. Some one has called this establishment the 'Congressional faro bank.' If the fact that a dozen or more Senators or Congressmen visit it every night for gambling purposes be taken into consideration, the name may not be misapplied. There are some, however, who rarely show in these lower rooms, but use the upper stories, which are nicely fitted up, and where there is no danger of detection or intrusion. On these occasions the game is generally whist, euchre, or poker, and sometimes keno. There is a waiter constantly in attendance to bring up wines, cigars, etc., and also to give notice of the approach of any one who does not belong to the party.

"There are, however, other visitors to this place, who occupy equally prominent positions with the Congressmen in public life. The Indian Bureau sends a heavily built man, with a swarthy complexion and black, restless, glittering eyes. This man smokes as he plays, and, when unusually excited, gives vent to exclamations that at once show his Indian blood. People from almost every department of the Government, and business men known in Washington as well and familiarly as almost any of the public officials, nightly crowd this place. Bank clerks, bookkeepers, and society men, may be seen late at night crowding around the fatal board, whose countenances, incapable of repressing emotion, form a picture which the beholder never forgets."

The theatres play a prominent part in the night life of Washington. There are two of these, of which the best and most frequented is a handsome new establishment conducted by Mr. John T. Ford. Performances are given during the winter only, and the establishments are managed on the "Star" system. Generally a very fair business is done during the season, for the city is full of strangers and others with plenty of spare time, who gladly avail themselves of the amusement thus offered them.

The acting is scarcely above the average, except when some travelling company visits the city. The "Star," of course, is not included in this criticism. Actors who could not earn a decent living in our larger cities, flourish in Washington, and furnish food for the dramatic criticisms of the "grave and reverend seigniors" of the Government.

Once or twice during the winter a brief opera season is inaugurated, and is well supported. The Washingtonians are dear lovers of good music, and profess to be keen critics of such performances. Certain it is, that they come out in goodly numbers to hear singers seeking their patronage, but we have heard them applaud lustily and even *encore* performances which a really cultivated audience would receive with a forbearing silence, to say the least.

Besides the theatres, there are one or two fine halls in the city, used for concerts, lectures, and exhibitions, which are well patronized during the winter season, the majority of the audiences being made up of strangers.

Canterburies and concert halls abound also. They are as low and disgusting as such places in our large cities usually are, and are quite as well patronized. They are great favorites with the Department Clerks, who constitute the "great men" of such places, and, alas that it should be so, you may generally see high officials in these polluted halls. The performances are simply disgusting, oftentimes brutal. The company is flashy, and largely made up of thieves and street walkers. The police have several times made descents upon these places, and arrested both proprietors and guests, but the evil continues.

CHAPTER XXI.

OLD PROBABILITIES

The Signal Service of the United States Army—"Old Probabilities" on Duty—The Signal Service in War—The Peace Establishment— How Candidates are admitted—The School at Fort Whipple—Practical Instruction—The Duties of the Service—Organization and practical Workings—The Signal Stations—Watching the Weather—Sending in Reports—Work of the Washington Office—Making up the Synopsis —The Probabilities—Excellence of the System—Tracking a Storm.

ONE of the best, though one of the most recent sections of the Government is that branch of the War Department known as the Signal Bureau. The Chief of this bureau has been humorously termed "Old Probabilities," in consequence of his daily prognostications as to the state of the weather for the next twenty-four hours. "Old Probabilities" is General Albert J. Meyer, one of the most accomplished and thoroughly competent officers on duty at Washington. The operations of the bureau are conducted under his immediate and constant supervision. He is assisted by a corps of trained and well qualified assistants, and has brought the service to a condition of efficiency and usefulness of which he may well be proud.

The Signal Service is charged with a double duty. In time of war its members accompany the army, and transmit messages from point to point by means of a system of flag-telegraphing. In peace their duties consist in observing and transmitting to Washington accurate reports as to the condition of the weather. The Signal Corps is composed of a commanding officer, with the rank of Brigadier-General, several commissioned officers, and a certain number of sergeants and enlisted men. The sergeants are required to be proficient in spelling, the ground rules of arithmetic, including decimal fractions, and the geography of the United States, and are required to write a legible hand. They are examined in these branches before being admitted into the service. They are also subjected to a medical examination, and only men of sound physical condition are accepted. They are regularly enlisted into the military service of the United States, and are subject to the regulations for the government of the army.

Immediately upon admission to the corps, each sergeant is sent to Fort Whipple, in Virginia, opposite Washington, where he is taught the duties of his profession, which are "chiefly those pertaining to the observation, record and proper publication and report, at such times as may be required, of the state of the barometer, thermometer, hygrometer, and rain-gauge, or other instruments, and the report by telegraph or signal, at such times as indicated, and to such places as may be designated by the chief signal officer, of the observations as made, or such other information as may be required." The text books used in the school at Fort Whipple are Loomis's "Text Book of Meteorology," Buchan's "Hand Book of Meteorology," Pope's "Practical Telegraphy," and the "Manual of Signals for the

United States Army." Instruction in the use of the instruments is also given, and the sergeant is taught to operate the telegraph. He is required to make daily recitations, and when he is considered prepared, by his instructor, he is ordered before an examining board, and is subjected to a rigid examination. If he is found properly qualified, he is assigned to a signal station in some part of the country, and is allowed an enlisted man to assist him in his duties.

There are between forty-five and fifty signal stations, located in various parts of the Union, from the Atlantic to the Pacific, and from British America to the Gulf of Mexico. Each of these is supplied with a full set of the instruments necessary for ascertaining the condition of the weather, etc., and is in charge of an observer sergeant, who is required to make observations three times a day, by means of his instruments, which are adjusted to a standard at Washington. These observations are made at 8 A.M., at 4 P. M., and at midnight. Each post of observation is furnished with a clock which is regulated by the standard of Washington time, so that the observations are taken precisely at the same moment all over the United States. The result of each observation is immediately telegraphed to the Signal office at Washington, the Government having made arrangements with the telegraph companies to secure the instant transmission of these messages. The reports are limited to a fixed number of words, and the time of their transmission to a fixed number of seconds. The signal stations, as at present located throughout the country, " have been chosen or located at points from which reports of observations will be most useful as indicating the general barometric pressure, or the approach and force of storms, and from which storm warnings, as the atmospheric indications arise, may be forwarded with greatest dispatch to imperilled ports."

The work of the observers at the stations is simple. It is limited to a reading of their instruments at stated times, the transmission to Washington of the results of these observations, and of information of any meteorological facts existing at the station when their tri-daily report is telegraphed to Washington. The work of the officers on duty at the Signal office in Washington is of a higher character, and demands of them the highest skill and perfect accuracy. The reports from the various stations are read and recorded as they come in, and from them the officer charged with this duty prepares a statement of the condition of the weather during the past twenty-four hours, and indicates the changes most likely to occur within the next twenty-four hours. These statements are prepared shortly after midnight, and are at once telegraphed to the various cities and important ports of the Union, in time for their publication in the newspapers the next morning.

Professor Maury, of the Signal office, thus sums up the workings of the service: "Each observer at the station writes his report on manifold paper. One copy he preserves, another he gives to the telegraph operator, who telegraphs the contents to Washington. The preserved copy is a voucher for the report actually sent by the observer; and if the operator is careless and makes a mistake, he cannot lay the blame on the observer, who has a copy of his report, which must be a fac-simile of the one he has handed to the operator. The preserved copy is afterward forwarded by the observer-sergeant to the office in Washington, where it is filed, and finally bound up in a volume for future reference.

"When all the reports from the various stations have been received they are tabulated and handed to the officer (Professor Abbé) whose duty it is to write out the synopses and deduce the 'probabilities,' which in a few minutes are to be telegraphed to the press all over the country. This is a work of thirty minutes. The bulletin of 'probabilities,' which at present is all that is undertaken, is made out thrice daily, in the forenoon, afternoon, and after the midnight reports have been received, inspected, and studied out by the accomplished gentleman and able meteorologist who is at the head of this work. The 'probabilities' of the weather for the ensuing day, so soon as written out by the professor, are immediately telegraphed to all newspapers in the country which are willing to publish them for the benefit of their readers.

"Copies of the telegrams of 'probabilities' are also instantly sent to all boards of trade, chambers of commerce, merchants' exchanges, scientific societies, etc., and to conspicuous places, especially sea-ports, all over the country.

"While the professor is preparing his bulletins from the reports just furnished him by telegraph, the sergeants are preparing maps which shall show by arrows and numbers exactly what was the meteorologic condition of the whole country when the last reports were sent in. These maps are printed in quantities, and give all the signal stations. A dozen copies are laid on the table with sheets of *carbon* paper between them, and arrow stamps strike in them (by the mainfold process) the direction of the wind at each station. The other observations as to temperature, barometric pressure, etc., etc., are also in the same way put on them. These maps are displayed at various conspicuous points in Washington—*e. g.*, at the War Department, Capitol, Observatory, Smithsonian Institution, and the office of the chief signal officer. They serve also as perfect records of the weather for the day and hour indicated on them, and are bound up in a book for future use.

" Every report and paper that reaches the Signal office is carefully preserved on a file, so that at the end of each year the office possesses a complete history of the meteorology of every day in the year, or nearly 50,000 observations, besides the countless and continuous records from all of its self-registering instruments.

" When important storms are moving, observers send extra telegrams, which are dispatched, received, acted upon, filed, etc., precisely as are the tri-daily reports. One invaluable feature of the system as now organized by General Myer is that the phenomena of any particular storm are not studied some days or weeks after the occurrence, but while the subject is fresh in mind To the study of every such storm, and of all the 'probabilities' issued from the office, the chief signal officer gives his personal and unremitting attention. As the observations are made at so many stations, and forwarded every eight hours, or oftener, by special telegram from all quarters of the country, the movements and behavior of every decided storm can be precisely noted; and the terrible meteor can be tracked and 'raced down' in a few hours or minutes. A beautiful instance of this occurred on the 22d of February, 1871, just after the great storm which had fallen upon San Francisco. While it was still revolving around that city, its probable arrival at Corinne, Utah, was telegraphed there, and also at Cheyenne. Thousands of miles from its roar, the officers at the Signal office in Washington indicated its track, velocity, and force. In twenty-four hours, as they had forewarned Cheyenne and Omaha, it reached those cities. Chicago was warned twenty hours or more before it came. Its arrival there was with great violence, unroofing houses and causing much destruction. Its course was telegraphed to Cleveland and Buffalo, which a day afterward it duly visited. The president of the Pacific Railroad has not more perfectly under his eye and control the train that left San Francisco to-day than General Myer had the storm just described.

"While the observers now in the field are perfecting themselves in their work, the chief signal officer is training other sergeants at the camp of instruction (Fort Whipple, Virginia), who will go forth hereafter as valued auxiliaries. It has been fully demonstrated by the signal officer that the army of the United States is the best medium through which to conduct most efficiently and economically the operations of the Storm Signal Service. Through the army organization the vast system of telegraphy for meteorological purposes can be, and is now being, most successfully handled. 'Whatever else General Myer has not done,' says the New York *World*, 'he has demonstrated that there can be, and now is, a perfect net-work of telegraphic communication extending over the whole country, working in perfect order, by the signal-men, and capable of furnishing almost instantaneous messages from every point to the central office at Washington.

"At present the signal officer aims only to give a synopsis of each day's weather, and a statement of what weather may be expected or *will probably occur*. The 'probabilities' so far have been most beautifully verified and confirmed. It is not thought wise to undertake more than can be securely accomplished. The synopses and 'probabilities' are all that intelligent shippers and careful seamen require. Shippers will not send their vessels to sea if the weather synopsis indicates threatening or alarming weather. Travellers can consult the 'probabilities' before leaving home; and any severe storm that menaces any city or port is now specially telegraphed thither, and the announcement is made by bulletins posted in the most public places.

THE END.

POLITICS AND PEOPLE
The Ordeal of Self-Government in America

An Arno Press Collection

Allen, Robert S., editor. **Our Fair City.** 1947

Belmont, Perry. **Return to Secret Party Funds:** Value of Reed Committee. 1927

Berge, George W. **The Free Pass Bribery System:** Showing How the Railroads, Through the Free Pass Bribery System, Procure the Government Away from the People. 1905

Billington, Ray Allen. **The Origins of Nativism in the United States, 1800-1844.** 1933

Black, Henry Campbell. **The Relation of the Executive Power to Legislation.** 1919

Boothe, Viva Belle. **The Political Party as a Social Process.** 1923

Breen, Matthew P. **Thirty Years of New York Politics, Up-to-Date.** 1899

Brooks, Robert C. **Corruption in American Politics and Life.** 1910

Brown, George Rothwell. **The Leadership of Congress.** 1922

Bryan, William Jennings. **A Tale of Two Conventions:** Being an Account of the Republican and Democratic National Conventions of June, 1912. 1912

The Caucus System in American Politics. 1974

Childs, Harwood Lawrence. **Labor and Capital in National Politics.** 1930

Clapper, Raymond. **Racketeering in Washington.** 1933

Crawford, Kenneth G. **The Pressure Boys:** The Inside Story of Lobbying in America. 1939

Dallinger, Frederick W. **Nominations for Elective Office in the United States.** 1897

Dunn, Arthur Wallace. **Gridiron Nights:** Humorous and Satirical Views of Politics and Statesmen as Presented by the Famous Dining Club. 1915

POLITICS AND PEOPLE

Ervin, Spencer. **Henry Ford vs. Truman H. Newberry:** The Famous Senate Election Contest. A Study in American Politics, Legislation and Justice. 1935

Ewing, Cortez A.M. and Royden J. Dangerfield. **Documentary Source Book in American Government and Politics.** 1931

Ford, Henry Jones. **The Cost of Our National Government:** A Study in Political Pathology. 1910

Foulke, William Dudley. **Fighting the Spoilsmen:** Reminiscences of the Civil Service Reform Movement. 1919

Fuller, Hubert Bruce. **The Speakers of the House.** 1909

Griffith, Elmer C. **The Rise and Development of the Gerrymander.** 1907

Hadley, Arthur Twining. **The Relations Between Freedom and Responsibility in the Evolution of Democratic Government.** 1903

Hart, Albert Bushnell. **Practical Essays on American Government.** 1893

Holcombe, Arthur N. **The Political Parties of To-Day:** A Study in Republican and Democratic Politics. 1924

Hughes, Charles Evans. **Conditions of Progress in Democratic Government.** 1910

Kales, Albert M. **Unpopular Government in the United States.** 1914

Kent, Frank R. **The Great Game of Politics.** 1930

Lynch, Denis Tilden. **"Boss" Tweed:** The Story of a Grim Generation. 1927

McCabe, James D., Jr. (Edward Winslow Martin, pseud.) **Behind the Scenes in Washington.** 1873

Macy, Jesse. **Party Organization and Machinery.** 1912

Macy, Jesse. **Political Parties in the United States, 1846-1861.** 1900

Moley, Raymond. **Politics and Criminal Prosecution.** 1929

Munro, William Bennett. **The Invisible Government** and **Personality in Politics:** A Study of Three Types in American Public Life. 1928/1934 Two volumes in one.

Myers, Gustavus. **History of Public Franchises in New York City,** Boroughs of Manhattan and the Bronx. (Reprinted from **Municipal Affairs,** March 1900) 1900

Odegard, Peter H. and E. Allen Helms. **American Politics:** A Study in Political Dynamics. 1938

Orth, Samuel P. **Five American Politicians:** A Study in the Evolution of American Politics. 1906

Ostrogorski, M[oisei I.] **Democracy and the Party System in the United States:** A Study in Extra-Constitutional Government. 1910

Overacker, Louise. **Money in Elections.** 1932

Overacker, Louise. **The Presidential Primary.** 1926

The Party Battle. 1974

Peel, Roy V. and Thomas C. Donnelly. **The 1928 Campaign:** An Analysis. 1931

Pepper, George Wharton. **In the Senate** and **Family Quarrels:** The President, The Senate, The House. 1930/1931. Two volumes in one

Platt, Thomas Collier. **The Autobiography of Thomas Collier Platt.** Compiled and edited by Louis J. Lang. 1910

Roosevelt, Theodore. **Social Justice and Popular Rule:** Essays, Addresses, and Public Statements Relating to the Progressive Movement, 1910-1916 (*The Works of Theodore Roosevelt,* Memorial Edition, Volume XIX) 1925

Root, Elihu. **The Citizen's Part in Government** and **Experiments in Government and the Essentials of the Constitution.** 1907/1913. Two volumes in one

Rosten, Leo C. **The Washington Correspondents.** 1937

Salter, J[ohn] T[homas]. **Boss Rule:** Portraits in City Politics. 1935

Schattschneider, E[lmer] E[ric]. **Politics, Pressures and the Tariff:** A Study of Free Private Enterprise in Pressure Politics, as Shown in the 1929-1930 Revision of the Tariff. 1935

Smith, T[homas] V. and Robert A. Taft. **Foundations of Democracy:** A Series of Debates. 1939

The Spoils System in New York. 1974

Stead, W[illiam] T. **Satan's Invisible World Displayed,** Or, Despairing Democracy. A Study of Greater New York (The Review of Reviews Annual) 1898

Van Devander, Charles W. **The Big Bosses.** 1944

Wallis, J[ames] H. **The Politician:** His Habits, Outcries and Protective Coloring. 1935

Werner, M[orris] R. **Privileged Characters.** 1935

White, William Allen. **Politics:** The Citizen's Business. 1924

Wooddy, Carroll Hill. **The Case of Frank L. Smith:** A Study in Representative Government. 1931

Wooddy, Carroll Hill. **The Chicago Primary of 1926:** A Study in Election Methods. 1926